China Engages Global Governance

This book focuses on China's increasing involvement in global governance as a result of the phenomenal rise of its economy and global power. It examines whether and in what ways China is capable of participating in multilateral interactions; if it is willing and able to provide global public goods to address a wide array of global problems; and what impact this would have on both global governance and order. The book provides a comprehensive assessment of China's increasing influence over how world affairs are being managed; how far China, with increasing clout, interacts with other major powers in global governance, and what the consequences and implications are for the evolving global system and world order. This book is the first to explore China's engagement with global governance in traditional and new securities.

Gerald Chan is Professor and Head of the Department of Political Studies at the University of Auckland, New Zealand. His publications include *China and International Organisations*; *Chinese Perspectives on International Relations*; and *China's Compliance in Global Affairs*.

Pak K. Lee is Lecturer in Chinese Politics and International Relations/International Political Economy at the University of Kent, UK.

Lai-Ha Chan is Chancellor's Postdoctoral Research Fellow of the UTS China Research Centre at the University of Technology, Sydney, Australia. She is the author of *China Engages Global Health Governance: Responsible Stakeholder or System-Transformer?* and co-editor of *China at 60: Global–Local Interactions*.

China policy series
Series Editor: Zheng Yongnian
China Policy Institute, University of Nottingham, UK

1 **China and the New International Order**
   Edited by Wang Gungwu and Zheng Yongnian

2 **China's Opening Society**
   The non-state sector and governance
   Edited by Zheng Yongnian and Joseph Fewsmith

3 **Zhao Ziyang and China's Political Future**
   Edited by Guoguang Wu and Helen Lansdowne

4 **Hainan – State, Society, and Business in a Chinese Province**
   Kjeld Erik Brodsgaard

5 **Non-Governmental Organizations in China**
   The rise of dependent autonomy
   Yiyi Lu

6 **Power and Sustainability of the Chinese State**
   Edited by Keun Lee, Joon-Han Kim and Wing Thye Woo

7 **China's Information and Communications Technology Revolution**
   Social changes and state responses
   Edited by Xiaoling Zhang and Yongnian Zheng

8 **Socialist China, Capitalist China**
   Social tension and political adaptation under economic globalisation
   Edited by Guoguang Wu and Helen Lansdowne

9 **Environmental Activism in China**
   Lei Xei

10 **China's Rise in the World ICT Industry**
    Industrial strategies and the catch-up development model
    Lutao Ning

11 **China's Local Administration**
　 Traditions and changes in the sub-national hierarchy
　 Edited by Jae-Ho Chung and Tao-chiu Lam

12 **The Chinese Communist Party as Organizational Emperor**
　 Culture, reproduction and transformation
　 Zheng Yongian

13 **China's Trade Unions – How Autonomous Are They?**
　 Masaharu Hishida, Kazuko Kojima, Tomoaki Ishii and Jian Qiao

14 **Legitimating the Chinese Communist Party since Tiananmen**
　 A critical analysis of the stability discourse
　 Peter Sandby-Thomas

15 **China and International Relations**
　 The Chinese view and the contribution of Wang Gungwu
　 Zheng Yongnian

16 **The Challenge of Labour in China**
　 Strikes and the changing labour regime in global factories
　 Chris King-chi Chan

17 **The Impact of China's 1989 Tiananmen Massacre**
　 Edited by Jean-Philippe Béja

18 **The Institutional Dynamics of China's Great Transformation**
　 Edited by Xiaoming Huang

19 **Higher Education in Contemporary China**
　 Beyond expansion
　 Edited by W. John Morgan and Bin Wu

20 **China's Crisis Management**
　 Edited by Jae Ho Chung

21 **China Engages Global Governance**
　 A new world order in the making?
　 Gerald Chan, Pak K. Lee and Lai-Ha Chan

China Engages Global Governance

A new world order in the making?

Gerald Chan, Pak K. Lee and Lai-Ha Chan

LONDON AND NEW YORK

First published 2012
by Routledge
711 Third Avenue, New York, NY 10017

Simultaneously published in the UK
by Routledge
2 Park Square, Milton Park, Abingdon, Oxon OX14 4RN

Routledge is an imprint of the Taylor & Francis Group, an informa business

First issued in paperback 2013

© 2012 Gerald Chan, Pak K. Lee and Lai-Ha Chan

The right of Gerald Chan, Pak K. Lee and Lai-Ha Chan to be identified as authors of this work has been asserted by them in accordance with sections 77 and 78 of the Copyright, Designs and Patents Act 1988.

All rights reserved. No part of this book may be reprinted or reproduced or utilized in any form or by any electronic, mechanical, or other means, now known or hereafter invented, including photocopying and recording, or in any information storage or retrieval system, without permission in writing from the publishers.

Trademark notice: Product or corporate names may be trademarks or registered trademarks, and are used only for identification and explanation without intent to infringe.

British Library Cataloguing in Publication Data
A catalogue record for this book is available from the British Library

Library of Congress Cataloging-in-Publication Data
Chan, Gerald.
  China engages global governance: a new world order in the making?/
Gerald Chan, Pak K. Lee and Lai-Ha Chan.
  p. cm. – (China policy series; 21)
  Includes bibliographical references and index.
  1. China–Foreign relations–21st century. 2. International organization.
3. International cooperation. 4. International relations. I. Lee, Pak K.
II. Chan, Lai-Ha. III. Title. IV. Series: China policy series; 21.
  JZ1734.C48 2011
  327.51–dc22
                                                                    2011015564

ISBN: 978-0-415-55713-9 (hbk)
ISBN: 978-0-415-72590-3 (pbk)
ISBN: 978-0-203-69833-4 (ebk)

Typeset in Times
by Wearset Ltd, Boldon, Tyne and Wear

For our Beloved Ones

Contents

List of figures	xi
List of tables	xii
About the authors	xiii
Preface and acknowledgements	xiv
List of abbreviations	xvii
Introduction	1
1 Global governance: the building blocks	8
2 Chinese perspectives on global governance	23
3 Peace and security	40
4 Finance and trade	59
5 Human rights and humanitarian intervention	79
6 Environmental protection	92
7 Public health	110
8 Food safety	125
9 Energy security	141
10 Transnational organized crime	158

Conclusion 174

Appendices 185

Notes 188
Index 262

Figures

2.1	Number of Chinese journal articles on global governance, 1979–2009	24
4.1	China's growing power in the World Bank	63
4.2	Projected quota shares in the IMF after the reform agreed in 2010	66
4.3	The appreciation of the yuan	76
8.1	China's foodstuff exports and imports, 1980–2008	125
8.2	Top ten destinations of China's food exports, 2005 and 2006	126
8.3	The number of recalls by the US Consumer Product Safety Commission	137
9.1	Crude oil consumption in China, India and the US	142
9.2	China's production and consumption of crude oil	142
10.1	Incidence of piracy and armed robbery against ships, 1994–2009	167

Tables

1.1	The growth of IGOs and INGOs, 1909–2008	14
3.1	The assessment rates (%) of the permanent five for the UN regular budget	42
3.2	China's personnel contribution to the UNPKO (as of November 2010)	43
4.1	Selected indicators of China's economic growth, 1978–2008	60
4.2	US trade with China ($ million)	71
4.3	Current account balances of selected countries (percentage of GDP)	72
5.1	Status of China's participation in major human rights instruments	82
7.1	Top ten Patent Cooperation Treaty applications by country of origin, 2005–2009	120
7.2	China and G8 contributions to the World Health Organization in 2008–2009	123
8.1	The MRL of the chlorpyrifos standard in vegetables and the MRL of the oxytetracycline standard in fish and aquatic products	135
9.1	China's top five crude oil supplying countries, 1995, 2001 and 2007 (share of the total imports as measured by volume)	147
10.1	Total number of Somali pirate attacks, 2005–2009	167
C.1	China's involvement in various issue areas in comparison with other emerging powers	180–2

About the authors

Gerald Chan is Professor and Head of the Department of Political Studies at the University of Auckland, New Zealand.

Pak K. Lee is Lecturer in Chinese Politics and International Relations/International Political Economy in the School of Politics and International Relations at the University of Kent, United Kingdom.

Lai-Ha Chan is Chancellor's Postdoctoral Research Fellow of the UTS China Research Centre at the University of Technology, Sydney, Australia. All three spent their formative years in Hong Kong.

All three received their PhDs from Australian universities (Griffith, New South Wales, Griffith respectively). They have jointly published a number of articles that have appeared in *Review of International Studies* (2011), *Global Public Health* (2009), *China Security* (2009), *Third World Quarterly* (2008) and *Contemporary Politics* (2008). Most recently, Lai-Ha Chan has published *China Engages Global Health Governance: Responsible Stakeholder or System-Transformer?* (New York: Palgrave Macmillan, 2011). They also have contributed to an edited volume entitled *China at 60: Global–Local Interactions* (Singapore: World Scientific; London: Imperial College Press, 2011).

Preface and acknowledgements

This book has been a long time in the making. It started to germinate when the three of us were associated with home institutions different from our present ones. In September 2005 Pak came from Hong Kong to Wellington, New Zealand, on a family visit. He and Gerald had an enjoyable lunch one day at the Skyline Restaurant at the top of Wellington's cable car station near Victoria University of Wellington. Gerald returned to Victoria University in mid-2005 after a couple of years working as a senior fellow heading a China project at the Centre of International Studies at Cambridge, in collaboration with the Royal Institute of International Affairs at Chatham House in London. He had just finished his book manuscript on China's compliance in global affairs and was looking around for an interesting and worthwhile topic to do research on. Pak suggested something along the lines of China's participation in global governance, given that there existed at that time quite a large amount of literature on global governance. Gerald took on the idea, kept it somewhere at the back of his mind, and thought about it on and off. One day towards the end of September 2005, for more reasons than one, it struck Gerald that this was the topic he should do, and so the idea began to grow slowly but steadily. It clicked partly because it seemed a progressive step to move from global compliance to engagement with global governance.

Important events intervened. In September 2006 Gerald moved across half the world to take up the first chair of East Asian Politics and the directorship of the Centre for Contemporary China Studies at Durham University, UK. And towards the end of the year, Pak travelled from Hong Kong to take up his lectureship in Chinese Politics and International Relations/International Political Economy at the University of Kent, UK. Since both of them were physically closer to each other than before, they had more opportunities to meet up, most often in the café of Foyle's Bookshop in London. Since they shared common academic interests, in the core area of Chinese international relations, they decided to join forces for this book project.

As time went by, the scope of the project turned out to be too big for them to handle. Luckily, in 2008, Lai-Ha was about to receive a doctorate in Chinese International Relations from Griffith University, Brisbane, Australia, with a focus on China's engagement with global public health. She then obtained a postdoctoral research fellowship at the China Research Centre of the University of Technology, Sydney. Being a friend and a colleague of Gerald and Pak from our Hong Kong days, Lai-Ha's enthusiasm to join the project provided a huge impetus.

In early 2009 Gerald returned from the UK to New Zealand to take up a chair and headship of the Department of Political Studies at Auckland University. The three of us continued to collaborate intermittently across the seas and to meet occasionally in twos or threes in Auckland, Cambridge, Canterbury, London and Sydney, facilitated by a regular flow of e-mails and drafts, which became a daily activity, seven days a week, towards the final writing stage. Because of the time zone differences between New Zealand, Australia and the United Kingdom, we continued each other's work around the clock – a contemporary version of the phrase, 'the sun never sets on the enterprise.'

We have jointly published a number of journal articles during the course of the project that appeared in *Global Public Health*, *Third World Quarterly*, *China Security*, *Contemporary Politics* and *Review of International Studies*. In addition, we have been heavily involved in the publication of an edited volume entitled *China at 60: Global–Local Interactions* (Singapore: World Scientific; London: Imperial College Press, 2011). We would like to thank the following publishers: Taylor & Francis Journals for permission to reprint extracts from 'China's environmental governance: the domestic-international nexus', *Third World Quarterly*, Vol. 29, No. 2 (2008), pp. 291–314, and 'Rethinking global governance: a China model in the making?', *Contemporary Politics*, Vol. 14, No. 1 (2009): pp. 3–19 and Cambridge University Press for permission to reprint extracts from the article 'China in Darfur: Humanitarian Rule-Maker or Rule-Taker?', *Review of International Studies*, 2011.

We acknowledge the funding contributions from the University of Technology, Sydney, in supporting Lai-Ha's fieldwork in Geneva in November 2010, and from the Faculty of Arts, University of Auckland, in supporting Gerald's research and writing. Thanks go to Steven Su for his excellent research assistance. Gerald is grateful to the University of Auckland and its Department of Political Studies for giving him a new lease of life back in New Zealand. Pak would like to acknowledge the generous support of the School of Politics and International Relations at Kent for granting him a study leave in September–December 2010, enabling him to speed up the writing process. The School also provides an intellectually stimulating environment for him to explore International Relations beyond China Studies, strengthening his determination to situate China Studies in the discipline of Political Science. This affirms the age-old Chinese saying, *ren wai you ren, tian wai you tian* (literally translated as 'beyond people, there are people; beyond sky, there is more sky'). He is also grateful to Charlotte Betteridge, Jody-Lan Castle and Eileen Tsang for their 'indirect' research support. Warm thanks are due in particular to Marie Lamy (now at the National University of Singapore) and Tanja Woerdehoff (now studying for an LLM at Kent and renamed Mrs Tanja Rogers in June 2011), and to Pak's former undergraduate students at Kent, for their helpful comments and research assistance on parts of the book manuscript. It always gives him great pressure to observe the intellectual development of his former students, including without doubt Lai-Ha.

We would like to dedicate this book to our beloved ones, for their understanding and endurance of our fixation on this project, which has taken away time that we would otherwise spend with them.

Gerald Chan, Pak K. Lee, Lai-Ha Chan
Auckland, Canterbury, Sydney

Abbreviations

ABM	Anti-Ballistic Missile
AG	Australia Group
AIDS	acquired immune deficiency syndrome
AML	anti-money laundering
APG	Asia/Pacific Group on Money Laundering
AQSIQ	Administration of Quality Supervision, Inspection and Quarantine
ARF	ASEAN Regional Forum
ARVs	anti-retrovirals
ASAT	anti-satellite
ASEAN	Association of Southeast Asian Nations
AU	African Union
BASIC	Brazil, South Africa, India and China
BDA	Banco Delta Asia
BRIC	Brazil, Russia, India and China
BTWC	Biological and Toxin Weapons Convention
CADFund	China–Africa Development Fund
CAIT	*Climate Analysis Indicators Tool*
CCP	Chinese Communist Party
CD	Committee on Disarmament
CDOs	collateralized debt obligations
CEDAW	Convention on the Elimination of All Forms of Discrimination against Women
CGPCS	Contact Group on Piracy off the Coast of Somalia
CMF	Combined Maritime Forces
CMS	cooperative medical scheme
CNEIC	China Nuclear Energy Industry Corporation
CNOOC	China National Offshore Oil Corporation
CNPC	China National Petroleum Corporation
CRC	Convention on the Rights of the Child
CTBT	Comprehensive Nuclear-Test-Ban Treaty
CTF-151	Combined Task Force 151
CWC	Chemical Weapons Convention

DPRK	Democratic People's Republic of Korea
DRC	Democratic Republic of Congo
ECOSOC	UN Economic and Social Council
EEZ	exclusive economic zone
EiS	Eyes in the Sky
EKC	environmental Kuznets curve
ESPO	East Siberia–Pacific Ocean
EU	European Union
FAO	Food and Agriculture Organization
FATF	Financial Action Task Force on Money Laundering
FDA	Food and Drug Administration
FDI	Foreign Direct Investment
FIU	Financial Intelligence Unit
FMCT	Fissile Material Cut-off Treaty
FOCAC	Forum on China–Africa Cooperation
FTA	Free Trade Agreement
G7	Group of Seven industrialized countries
G8	Group of Eight
GAVI	Global Alliance for Vaccines and Immunization
GDP	gross domestic product
GEF	Global Environment Facility
GNPOC	Greater Nile Petroleum Operating Company
GONGO	government-organized NGO
H5N1	avian influenza
HCOC	Hague Code of Conduct against Ballistic Missile Proliferation
HDR	Human Development Report
IAEA	International Atomic Energy Agency
ICCPR	International Covenant on Civil and Political Rights
ICERD	International Convention on the Elimination of All Forms of Racial Discrimination
ICESCR	International Covenant on Economic, Social and Cultural Rights
ICISS	International Commission on Intervention and State Sovereignty
ICSPCA	International Covenant on the Suppression and Punishment of the Crime of Apartheid
IEA	International Energy Agency
IGOs	intergovernmental organizations
IHR	International Health Regulations
IMB	International Maritime Bureau
IMF	International Monetary Fund
IMO	International Maritime Organization
INFOSAN	International Food Safety Authorities Network
INGOs	international nongovernmental organizations
IOCs	international oil companies
IPE	Internation Petroleum Exchange
IRTC	Internationally Recommended Transit Corridor

ISC	Information Sharing Centre
ISR	International Sanitary Regulations
JODI	Joint Oil Data Initiative
KMG	KazMunaiGas
LMG	Like-Minded Group
MALSINDO	MALaysia–Singapore–INDOnesia
MDGs	Millennium Development Goals
MoH	Ministry of Health
MoU	memorandum of understanding
MRL	maximum residual limit
MSPA	Maritime Security Patrol Area
MSSI	Malacca Strait Security Initiative
MTCR	Missile Technology Control Regime
NATO	North Atlantic Treaty Organization
NCCTs	Non-Cooperative Countries and Territories
NGOs	non-governmental organizations
NIEO	new international economic order
NINJA	no income, no job or assets
NOCs	national oil companies
NPC	National People's Congress
NPT	Treaty on the Non-Proliferation of Nuclear Weapons
NSG	Nuclear Suppliers Group
ODA	official development aid
ODI	overseas direct investment
OECD	Organization for Economic Cooperation and Development
OHCHR	Office of the High Commissione for Human Rights
OPEC	Organization of Petroleum Exporting Countries
PAROS	Prevention of an Arms Race in Outer Space
PBC	People's Bank of China
PCT	Patent Cooperation Treaty
PEAC	Pesticide Eco-Alternatives Centre
PHEIC	public health emergencies of international concern
PRC	People's Republic of China
PSI	Proliferation Security Initiative
R2P	Responsibility to Protect
RASFF	Rapid Alert System for Food and Feed
ReCAAP	Regional Cooperation Agreement on Combating Piracy and Armed Robbery
RMSI	Regional Maritime Security Initiative
ROC	Republic of China
SAIC	State Administration for Industry and Commerce
SALW	small arms and light weapons
SARS	severe acute respiratory syndrome
SDA	State Drug Administration
SDRs	special drawing rights

SEPA	State Environmental Protection Administration
SFDA	State Food and Drug Administration
SHADE	Shared Awareness and Deconfliction
Sinopec	China Petroleum and Chemical Corporation
SPA	State Pharmaceutical Administration
SPRs	strategic petroleum reserves
SPS	Sanitary and Phytosanitary Measures
SUA	Suppression of Unlawful Acts (against the Safety of Maritime Navigation)
TFG	Transitional Federal Government
TOC	transnational organized crime
TRIPS	Trade-Related Aspects of Intellectual Property Rights
UDHR	Universal Declaration of Human Rights
UK	United Kingdom
UN	United Nations
UNCAC	United Nations Convention against Corruption
UNCHR	UN Commission on Human Rights
UNCLOS	UN Convention on the Law of the Sea
UNCTAD	UN Conference on Trade and Development
UNDP	UN Development Programme
UNEP	UN Environment Programme
UNHRC	UN Human Rights Council
UNICEF	UN Children's Fund
UNPKO	UN peacekeeping operations
UNROCA	UN Register of Conventional Arms
UNSAS	UN Standby Arrangements System
UNSC	UN Security Council
UNTOC	UN Convention against Transnational Organized Crime
UPR	universal periodic review
US/USA	United States of America
USSR	Union of Soviet Socialist Republics
WHO	World Health Organization
WIPO	World Intellectual Property Organization
WMD	weapons of mass destruction
WTO	World Trade Organization

Introduction

Much has been said in the mass media and in academic and policy-making circles about the rise of China and its impact on the world.[1] Witnessing the growing influence of China, leaders of major powers, including the United States and the United Kingdom, have frequently called on the Chinese to use their leverage to put pressure on recalcitrant rulers and resolve the nuclear weapons crisis in North Korea and internal conflicts in Myanmar and Sudan. China is no longer an Asian power only; it is now widely assumed to be a global power, and no global problems can be successfully handled without China's involvement. Evidence abounds. In July 2008 a new grouping of seven core members of the World Trade Organization (WTO) – Australia, Brazil, China, the European Union, India, Japan and the US – was formed by Pascal Lamy, the director-general of the organization, with the aim of pushing forward the Doha round of global trade negotiations.[2] China was invited by the US to join the Group of Eight industrialized countries and other emerging economic powers at the G20 summit, held in Washington, DC, in mid-November 2008, to discuss ways to deal with the looming global financial crisis.[3] The economic downturn has tarnished the Anglo-American model of capitalism, giving China an opportunity to expand its influence abroad, particularly in developing nations.[4]

For its part, China endeavours to make its voice heard in global institutions. With full endorsement of her candidacy by the Chinese government, Margaret Chan, a Hong Kong Chinese, was elected director-general of the World Health Organization in November 2006. Sha Zukang, a Chinese diplomat, became the United Nations Under-Secretary-General for Economic and Social Affairs in July 2007, heading the global organization's Department of Economic and Social Affairs. In July 2008 China broke its long-standing silence at the Doha round of global trade negotiations. Along with India, it blocked a compromise trade deal brokered by Pascal Lamy.[5] It is now beyond dispute that China's proactive participation is a *sine qua non* for tackling a host of global issues.

Two questions

While it is now publicly acknowledged that China is emerging rapidly as a great power, particularly since the 1990s, these are questions as to (1) how we can comprehend the extent of China's growing power; and (2) what kind of world order would likely emerge in the wake of a rising China. China watchers and economists often cite China's aggregate economic size in terms of gross domestic product (GDP) and annual growth rates, which will be discussed in Chapter 4, as indicators of the rise of China. However, owing to the country's large population of more than 1.3 billion people, its per capita income is as low as that of Angola, Albania or El Salvador. Why do we not regard these three countries as emerging great powers? Among the countries of the G20 grouping, China's per capita GDP ranks seventeenth, just above Indonesia and India.[6] Why does China attract more attention than other emerging economies in the grouping in discussions on peace and security, global trade and finance, environmental protection, energy security, and so on? Why are there calls for a condominium between the US and China, forming a G2, in the twenty-first century rather than between the US and Russia, the latter being more influential in Europe and the Middle East due to its geographical location, its having more nuclear weapons than China, and its enviable oil and gas resources?[7] A narrow focus on China's growing material preponderance will distract our attention from the more important political issues that have far-reaching implications and significance. One needs to note that great power status implies not only more power and rights in agenda-setting and policy-making, but also more responsibility for the stability of the global order. Is China in competition with the US for global leadership or hegemonic position? Is China willing to take on additional responsibility for the world? If this is not the case, how can we categorize China? Should we be careful not to exaggerate China's prowess or potential for stabilizing the world? A closely related question is why China rejects the notion of a G2 which would give it elevated status in the world, a status it would value.[8] Last but not least, do other states, including both established powers and secondary ones, defer to China and accept its authority?[9] Answers to these questions will in part be contingent on whether China can articulate and project its own norms and values and whether these norms and values can take root in and shape the interests and preferences of other countries.

While the term 'hegemony' is understood and used pejoratively by the Chinese as *baquan* ('coercive dominance'),[10] in the Western social science literature it refers to 'the way in which the dominant social groups achieve rulership or leadership on the basis of attaining social cohesion and consensus'.[11] John Ikenberry and Charles Kupchan argue that a hegemon can exert dominance over secondary states in two ways: by the manipulation of material incentives – threats of sanctions or promises of reward; and by socializing the elites of other states into its own norms and beliefs. Even when a hegemon's material power is in decline, the hegemonic order it has created may still be durable and influential.[12] From this perspective, it is one thing to say that the relative material power of the US is now on the wane, but it might be another thing to conclude that China will replace the US as the new hegemon.[13]

To gain a better understanding of China's power, we have to conceptualize it as a social and relational phenomenon.[14] We propose to gauge and comprehend the 'powerfulness' of China by examining its involvement in global governance. We hypothesize that China is accorded great power status because it is involved more than many other emerging countries in various areas of global concern, its normative influence varying across issues. The extent and limits of China's powerfulness are to be determined by its interactions with other state and non-state actors in global governance. China scholars do not seem to have made use of the substantial and rapidly growing literature to study the role of China in global governance, while China has not been on the radar screen of many students of International Relations. The divide between the two worlds of China Studies and International Relations is far from being bridged. In studying China's engagement with global governance, we intend to go beyond the two prime focuses of the prevailing study of China's external relations in order to seek insights into China's power and behaviour.[15]

The first focus is on compliance and cooperation, as previously studied by Ann Kent and one of us (Gerald Chan).[16] In his book on China's compliance behaviour in global affairs, Chan looks into the country's compliance with international norms and rules in the areas of world trade, arms control and disarmament, environmental protection and human rights. In that book, China's compliance is used as a measure to gauge the country's responsibility in world affairs. That and previous studies have already illustrated that in its early stages of participation in global governance, China has tended to consciously comply with the explicit rules of international organizations, enabling it to tap into their resources, earn the goodwill of international society, restore its shattered reputation, and preserve an international environment favourable to its economic growth. As a latecomer on the international scene, China has not fully mastered the skills and resources to reset the agenda of global institutions. With increasing power and knowledge about their modus operandi, however, China may be convinced that it could afford to re-examine the means and ends of those international organizations of which it is a member and then make an effort to reinterpret and modify them in ways which would better serve its own interests as well as those of the developing world.

In China's increasing involvement in multilateralism and integration into the international economy, its leaders and scholars have openly opposed American hegemony, the inequality between the developed and the developing worlds, and the exploitation of the developing world by the industrialized West. They claim that the norms, principles and rules of the institutions of global governance primarily serve the interests of the more powerful, advanced capitalist countries. They therefore call for a reform of the institutions of global governance in order to build a global order that is more propitious to the development of the Third World. Coincidentally some Western literature also argues that present-day liberal global governance is 'distorted' insofar as it disproportionately reinforces and promotes the interests and agenda of the dominant states and global capital. Could the growing power of China, the most populous developing country in the world, be manifested in facilitating progressively greater global social justice and human welfare in the evolving architecture of global governance?

4   *Introduction*

With increasing hard and soft power at its disposal, China may start to embark on a process of reshaping or reconceptualizing the practices, rules, regulations and goals of the organizations, so that it would no longer be at the receiving end of international socialization or social learning. Rather, it would become a source of global norms and rules, rivalling in some ways those espoused by the West, by claiming that the China 'model' would better serve global development and peace. This book moves from a focus on China's compliance with international rules and norms and cooperation with international institutions to an examination of China's growing demand for a greater say in managing global affairs and the subsequent impact on the resultant global governance. Attention will be paid to what global order China would like to fashion, and whether the country's rapid rise will put it on a collision course with major world powers or lead it to closer collaboration among them due to mutual adaptation and mutual accommodation to each other's primary interests.

In relation to the second focus, Chan's book mentioned above covers in some depth the four areas of trade, arms control, environmental protection and human rights, of which some are regarded as 'traditional' or 'conventional' securities. This book, *China Engages Global Governance*, goes further, to cover public health, energy security, transnational crime and food safety ('non-traditional' or 'new' securities). In addition, it shifts the focus to the struggle among big powers to manage global governance, taking into account China's changing position and status in the world, shaped by its new demands and aspirations. It goes beyond the traditional ambit of inter-state relations, especially China–US relations, to cover a wider and more complex network of relationships involving other actors such as international regimes, international institutions, civil society organizations and business organizations. This widening scope of issues and actors reflects the increasing complexity of global governance today, a complexity we hope to unravel from the perspective of China's engagement with it.

As to the question of whether China would be a benign and responsible great power, as the Chinese government claims, there is no lack of dissenting views. A recent study of the relationship between powerful states and global governance argues that a concert of great powers – referring to the United States and the European Union – is both a necessary and a sufficient condition for effective global governance. The study *suspects* that an inclusion of new powers, such as China, into the club of great powers would undermine the effectiveness of global governance because of preference divergence.[17] Another thesis, known as 'autocratic revival', contends that China's increased presence in the international arena would lead to growing rivalries with existing democratic powers and undermine international cooperation.[18] Benita Ferrero-Waldner, then EU Commissioner for External Relations and European Neighbourhood Policy, questioned in July 2005 the compatibility between the worldviews of China and Europe. She pointed out subtly that while some in China have advocated building a 'multipolar world', for the EU, 'it is not the number of poles which counts, but rather the basis on which they operate'. Instead, the EU's 'vision is a world governed by rules created and monitored by multilateral institutions … for putting the world in good, multilateral order'.[19] Given that multilateralism is at the heart of global governance, Ferrero-Waldner's remarks remind us that we should be careful not to take China's multilateral engagement with global governance for granted and that its foray into institutions of global governance may bring it into conflict with the established powers over what and how the norms and rules are to be made. Yet, despite continuing speculation, little detailed study has been done about how global governance would be changed as a result of China's increasing involvement. This book tries to fill this gap and aims to make an assessment of China's increasing influence over how the world is being governed, how other major powers react to this challenge, and what will be the likely shape of the international order as a consequence.

To help shed light on the two puzzles – how powerful China is in terms of providing viable solutions to various global issues; and what the resultant world order would be in the wake of China's rise – this book addresses three clusters of questions. In the first cluster are: What is global governance? How has it changed over time? How can we understand global governance? What are the major issues in global governance? The study of this first cluster of questions gives a context in which to assess the rise of China and its impact on global governance.

In the second cluster, we ask: In what way does China increase its say and sway in global governance? What approaches does it employ? Is there a China global policy? Is China prepared to lead the world or does it tend to free-ride on others' efforts and contributions? What are the problems facing China in its aspiration to become a rich and powerful nation, with a louder voice in world affairs and a greater sense and share of global responsibility? What are the prospects of such a trend of development for China and for the rest of the world?

The policies of reform and opening to the outside world, started in the late 1970s, have led China to achieve phenomenal economic growth and to strengthen its international engagement. China's development has become an integral part of global development. In some ways edging closer to the situation of the now sole superpower, the United States, what this rising power, China, does or does not do increasingly affects us all. As China increases its involvement in global affairs, it would be natural for it to demand a greater say in how global affairs are run so as to protect and promote its interests. This is not unlike the behaviour of many rising powers before it. This rising power, however, is huge in many respects; it has the longest surviving civilization; and it comes from the East (Asia). In what way and to what extent other big powers may accommodate or frustrate China's rise is likely to define conflict and cooperation, and hence the prospects for war and peace, in the world.

What then are China's wants and demands? It is difficult to say for sure, partly because the Chinese authorities do not seem to have spelt them out clearly, and partly because these wants and demands change according to circumstances and they can be perceived as different things by different people at different times. In general terms, China proclaims that it wants peace and development and friendly relations with others. More specifically, gauging from its development experience and its foreign policy statements in the recent past, the country:

- aspires to become strong and wealthy;[20]
- wants to be seen as a responsible member of the international community;[21]
- cares about its international image;[22]
- demands international respect;[23]
- is trying to regain its rightful place in the world;[24] and
- argues for the democratization of international relations to thwart American 'hegemony'.[25]

More importantly, we will address in the third cluster: What are the consequences of China's rise? What is the linkage between China's rise and its global responsibility, and between the pursuit of its national interest and the shouldering of its global responsibility? To what extent do its rise and development affect its desire and capability to involve itself in the management of global affairs? In what way does its increasing involvement in global affairs alter the influence and interest of other states? Is there any widespread consensus on the 'right' of China to lead? Does China's increasing involvement in the management of world affairs bring greater peace, stability and prosperity to the world, or is it more likely to bring about the opposite effect: conflict, instability and 'leadership deficit'?

Globalization provides the context against which we try to look for answers to some or all of the above questions. We may place more emphasis on some questions than on others. The study of globalization has become a cottage industry, like the rise of China. The abundance of books introducing this topic has overwhelmed beginners and to some extent specialists in the field. The study of global governance is following suit, and beginning to take a fair share of the book market as well as the attention of members of the academic community. However, much is still focused on what global governance is, what the pros and cons of globalization are, and the approaches to the study of both. Relatively few studies, however, attempt to ask how global governance works and fewer still attempt to answer why global governance works the way it does. In other words, few seem to question seriously the assumptions under which global governance has worked since the end of the Second World War, treating the status quo as something given. Although it is increasingly apparent that China has now acquired a global big power status, there is as yet little or no book-length treatment of the impacts of China's engagement with global governance on global order.[26] This book intends to fill that void.

The plan

This study, the first of its kind on China's engagement with global governance made in a focused yet comprehensive manner little matched before, begins by setting out the context – the basis of global governance; and Chinese perspectives on it (chapters 1 and 2) – in which to posit China's involvement in various issue areas in global politics. As will be elaborated in Chapter 1, the theoretical thread that runs through the chapters is global public goods and the associated concepts of collective action and free-riding.

The book's subtitle, *A new world order in the making?*, carries two senses. One is that of a new world in which the referent is moving gradually from a state-centric focus to one that also emphasizes the needs and wants of individuals and groups of individuals; that is, from traditional national security to human security. The second sense is that a rising China poses serious challenges to the status quo powers, which have to make changes and adjustments in order to accommodate this newcomer.

Chapter 2 discusses Chinese perspectives on global governance, particularly its understanding of the proper role of the state in the rule-making and steering process. Together, chapters 1 and 2 form the theoretical part of this book. Chapters 3 to 5 are about China's activities in 'traditional' securities: peace and security, world trade and finance, human rights and humanitarian intervention. Chapters 6–10 analyse Chinese practices in 'new' securities, namely environmental protection, public health, food safety, energy security and transnational organized crime. In the Conclusion, we summarize our findings and explore how the evolving global order will likely take shape as a result of China's increasing involvement in it.

1 Global governance
The building blocks

> The demand for governance in world affairs has never been greater.
> Oran R. Young, 1999[1]

> There is no universally accepted and agreed definition of 'governance'.
> Anne Mette Kjær, 2004[2]

Global governance has become a catchphrase in the study of world affairs since the late 1980s. The core questions of this book having been presented in the Introduction, this chapter aims to elucidate the concept of global governance and to provide the context in which Chinese perspectives on global governance and participation in various issue areas of global governance will be examined in the following chapters. It begins by explaining what global governance is, and then traces the origins and development of the concept, before turning to a discussion of the focus of governance studies in this book. In so doing, we will discuss not only global governance, but also related concepts such as governance itself, globalization and global public goods. This chapter proceeds as follows. The first section looks at global governance from two major perspectives: the perspectives of international institutions; and those of Political Science/International Relations scholars. The aim is to highlight the essence of global governance in the contemporary literature. The second section explores why we study global governance in the age of globalization and discusses the historical transformation of global governance institutions in the light of the changing narrative of international relations. The third section examines the contested nature of global public goods and queries how their provision can address trans-sovereign challenges.

What is global governance?

Global governance concerns the issue of how the world is governed; that is, how global problems are handled and how global order and stability can be ensured, in the absence of an overarching central authority or world government to regulate. To understand global governance, the following questions need to be asked:

What is global? What is governance? In what ways does governance differ from the conventional notions of politics and government? Why do we study global governance today? How have global governance institutions been transformed in the course of globalization? How does global governance relate to collective action and the provision of global public goods?

Views of international institutions

What is global? The word global usually refers to a situation that goes beyond the international or the inter-state system. Its use evokes a wide array of actors in world affairs, ranging from individuals and social groups to international organizations and others, apart from states, as a major set of actors. What is governance? Perhaps the most authoritative definition of governance comes from a report compiled by the Commission on Global Governance, consisting of twenty-six prominent members from around the world, chaired by Ingvar Carlsson, a former Swedish prime minister, and Shridath Ramphal, a former secretary-general of the British Commonwealth. The report, entitled *Our Global Neighbourhood*, published in 1995,[3] defines governance in a global context as

> The sum of the many ways individuals and institutions, public and private, manage their common affairs. It is a continuing process through which conflicting or diverse interests may be accommodated and co-operative action may be taken. It includes formal institutions and regimes empowered to enforce compliance, as well as informal arrangements that people and institutions either have agreed to or perceive to be in their interest.[4]

The report carries on to say that 'states and governments remain primary public institutions for constructive responses to issues affecting peoples and the global community as a whole.'[5] It stresses, however, that global governance does not mean global government, nor does it imply world federalism.[6] In a way, the definition is carefully crafted to avoid suggesting any infringements on state sovereignty.

To the United Nations Development Programme (UNDP), governance is

> the exercise of economic, political and administrative authority to manage a country's affairs at all levels. It comprises mechanisms, processes and institutions through which citizens and groups articulate their interests, exercise their legal rights, meet their obligations and mediate their differences.'[7]

Apparently this definition takes states as the basis to look at governance at both the sub-national level and the global level.

In short, global governance is seen by these international institutions as the activities and decisions of states, international organizations and individuals to manage a wide variety of traditional security issues as well as new security threats. Traditional security refers to military-oriented national security threats (i.e. mostly 'high politics'), while new securities are concerned with such issues as environmental degradation, the spread of infectious diseases, transnational crime, and the scramble for national resources (i.e. 'low politics'). This kind of distinction between high and low politics, between traditional and new security threats, is sometimes difficult to make, as the boundaries between the two categories are often blurred. There are cases in which such categorization may become controversial, cases such as economic and trade issues and even terrorism. The distinction, however, may serve some heuristic and analytical purposes.

Some academic perspectives

The main reason why Anne Mette Kjær suggests that there is no universally accepted and agreed definition of governance is probably that while the term 'governance' has become part of day-to-day vocabulary, different scholars have different ideas about what the term denotes and there are very many of these ideas. The concept of governance can be traced back to the Greek verb *kybernân* ('to pilot' or 'steer').[8] It was used by Plato in his effort to design a system of rule. This Greek term gave rise to the medieval Latin word *gubernare*, which carried the same connotation of piloting, rule-making or steering. The term has been used as synonymous with government, the exercise of power by political leaders. In political science it refers to the attempts of an actor, e.g. the state, to steer other actors, domestically or internationally, in the pursuit of collective goals and ends.[9] The concept of governance was not widely used until the 1980s when it re-emerged with a new and much broader meaning to include not only the function of the central authority, but also a wide array of non-state actors and a broad range of social, economic and political issues.

John Gerard Ruggie provides a contemporary working definition of governance: 'the workings of the system of authoritative rules, norms, institutions, and practices by means of which any collectivity manages its common affairs'. The key difference between governance and politics, according to Ruggie, is that governance is about 'producing public goods' whereas politics is about 'competition in the pursuit of particular interests'.[10] James Rosenau points out the similarities and divergences between governance and government. Both governance and government consist of 'rule systems, of steering mechanisms through which authority is exercised in order to enable systems to preserve their coherence and move towards desired goals'. Effective steering mechanisms are those that have capacities to evoke compliance by those towards whom their directives are issued. While governments generate compliance through legal prerogatives, governance derives its effectiveness from 'traditional norms and habits, informal agreements, shared premises and a host of other practices that lead people to comply with their directives'.[11] Rules and regimes are thus viewed as key ingredients of governance.

As further elaborated below, key to an understanding of the post-Westphalian system of global governance is the need to incorporate new issues and actors.

A wide array of non-traditional security threats (such as financial instability, environmental degradation, human rights abuse, spread of contagious diseases, transnational crime and energy shortages) and non-state actors have occupied legitimate places on the agenda of global governance.[12] With these in mind, Thomas Weiss and Ramesh Thakur offer a goal-oriented definition of the concept. For them, global governance is the sum of rules, norms, institutions and practices by means of which states, citizens and intergovernmental and non-governmental organizations combine to address and manage a host of life- or wealth-threatening transnational problems at the global level, based on a growing recognition that the problems go beyond the capacity of individual states to tackle. Global governance aims to bolster order, stability and predictability in international transactions and cross-border activities in the absence of an overarching central authority (i.e. a world government).[13] In a similar vein, Raimo Väyrynen identifies global governance as 'collective actions to establish international institutions and norms to cope with the causes and consequences of adverse supranational, transnational, or national problems'.[14] According to Margaret Karns and Karen Mingst, the pieces of global governance, a phrase they often use in their popular textbook, fall into six broad categories: (1) intergovernmental organizations (IGOs) and non-governmental organizations (NGOs); (2) international rules and laws, which include more than 3,600 multilateral agreements, apart from numerous legal practices and opinions; (3) international norms or 'soft law' in the areas of human rights and environmental protection; (4) international regimes, that is, principles, norms, rules and decision-making structures, in specific issue areas; (5) ad hoc arrangements and groupings that do not have any legal basis, such as the G7/8 and G20, and global conferences or world summits; and (6) private governance, of which the most typical example is credit-rating agencies, such as Moody's Investors Service.[15] Robert Keohane and Joseph Nye argue that to properly understand global governance in the twenty-first century, it is not enough to study only multilateral cooperation among states. To them, it is crucial to understand how a variety of actors, operating in networks, interact in the context of norms that are widely accepted among the actors.[16]

One can conclude from a brief review of the academic literature that governance – the sum of rules, norms, institutions and practices – is produced by the collective activity of state and non-state actors, and governance is linked with the search for order. Governance is created to foster a global order that can enhance stability and predictability, and meet the demand for effective responsiveness to growing insecurities and uncertainties and peaceful transformation.[17] As will be discussed in detail below, we argue in this book that the rules, norms, institutions and practices are about the supply of global public goods. In other words, focus is on how various actors, in particular China for the purpose of this book, establish rules, norms, institutions and practices to provide global public goods to buttress collective action to solve problems shared by humanity.

Obviously, in contrast to the definitions offered by international institutions, scholarly discussions of governance and global governance give greater weight to the roles played by a multiplicity of actors as well as norms and rules and their making and implementation in governing globalization and managing global problems in an orderly fashion. While 'governance without government' suggests an absence of central authority, the effectiveness of global governance hinges on the willingness of actors to comply with certain norms and rules, the ability of the norms and rules to constrain the behaviour of actors, and equally on the capacity of international institutions to create order by forging a consensus on the content and substance of norms and rules and to enforce them when actors fail to automatically comply with them. As James Rosenau has noted, 'governance is a system of rule that works only if it is accepted by the majority (or, at least, by the most powerful of those it affects).'[18] Therefore, underpinning the prevailing multilateral arrangements and activities that constitute effective global governance are values, norms and rules and compliance with them by major actors. This perspective signifies a new approach to the study of global politics, a break with the tradition that prevailed in the Cold War era in which inter-state relations and great power politics formed the core of international politics.

Why global governance?

Like the concepts of interdependence, international regime and globalization shortly before it, global governance has come into popular use since the 1980s. A key issue in the study of global governance is how and why global politics is now shaped not only by the state but also by a multitude of other non-state actors such as NGOs, transnational corporations and international organizations. According to Michael Barnett and Kathryn Sikkink, 'the overarching narrative of [international relations] has changed from one of anarchy in a system of states to governance within a global society', and the 'emerging field of global politics is increasingly focused on the study of global governance'.[19] Why has the study of international relations gone beyond the study of relations between sovereign states under conditions of anarchy? We may address this by examining the ineffectiveness of the state in tackling the most pressing global challenges.

From government to governance

The fall of the Bretton Woods system of fixed exchange rates in 1971, a rising awareness of the transnational nature of environmental degradation since the 1970s, and the debt crisis of less developed countries of the 1980s resulted in calls for new thinking about the management of global problems, one that would rely less on the support of a hegemonic state. It was against this background that the notion of global governance emerged.[20]

The process of globalization that picked up steam after the demise of Communism in the former Soviet Union and Eastern Europe has further accelerated the shift from inter-state relations to global governance.[21] Globalization is a product of two processes, one deliberate and one unintentional. With the advent of revolutions in transport and communications technology, the deliberate process grows out of a conscious strategy of removing at-the-border barriers to the movement of people, goods and services, capital and ideas, and of promoting behind-the-border policy harmonization or convergence to enhance market integration. But this deliberate process of economic deregulation, liberalization and privatization has intensified the fast expansion of unintended cross-border spillover effects or global challenges, apart from the positive effect of boosting global aggregate economic growth.[22] The global challenges or trans-sovereign problems[23] include, but have never been restricted to, the proliferation and transboundary movement of weapons of mass destruction and terrorist groups endangering international peace and security; the spread of communicable diseases; climate change due to increased and wanton energy use; financial instability and trade imbalance; the growth of transnational organized crime; widespread poverty due to the ever greater divide between the haves and the have-nots; and heightened concern about human suffering because of the 'CNN effect' which gives people easy and instantaneous access to information around the globe. Such challenges and problems straddle the border between domestic and foreign policy with the interests of domestic constituencies involved.[24] Some of them fall into the social and economic sectors over which the pro-liberal states in the West have reduced power, necessitating that the public sector harness the expertise of non-state actors. The said technological revolution has also increased the mobilization capacity and interconnectedness of non-state actors, empowering them to exert greater influence on other actors in international society. Some of the challenges thrive in the power vacuum left by sovereignty under siege. Sovereignty is challenged externally by the globalizing forces and/or internally by state decay or collapse due to poverty and internal conflict.[25] Weakened sovereignty and trans-sovereign challenges create a new security dilemma which differs from the old version in which threats came from aggressive powerful states.[26] While 'dark networks' of terrorist groups and transnational organized crime may be problematic developments, international organizations and transnational communities (e.g. civil society organizations and networks of experts) have received increased attention for their functions of providing global public goods, facilitating international cooperation and socializing other actors.

Table 1.1 shows the proliferation of both IGOs and international non-governmental organizations (INGOs) since the early twentieth century.[27] Although some of the INGOs run counter to government policies, many of them have worked cooperatively with governments and IGOs in various areas. In fact, there has been a fusion of public authority and private power, giving rise to the salience of public–private partnerships. For example, the UN Global Compact has called for the inclusion of private global regulations into global governance due to the fact that states, economies and even social lives fall increasingly under the regulations of global-level 'private authorities'. John Gerard Ruggie suggests that 'a fundamental reconstitution of the global public domain' in international politics is now under way, based upon the 'growing significance of global corporate social responsibility initiatives triggered by the dynamic interplay

14 *Global governance: the building blocks*

Table 1.1 The growth of IGOs and INGOs, 1909–2008

	IGOs	INGOs
1909	37	176
1951	123	832
1960	154	1,255
1968	229	1,899
1976	252	2,502
1981	337	4,265
1985	378	4,676
1991	297	4,620
1998	254	5,766
2003	245	7,261
2008	247	8,003

Source: Union of International Associations, *Yearbook of International Organizations* (Munich: K.G. Saur), 1988/89, Vol. 2, Appendix 3, Table 2 (for 1909, 1951, 1960, 1968, 1976 and 1981); 1999–2000, Vol. 2, Appendix 3, Table 2 (for 1985, 1991 and 1998); 2004–2005, Vol. 5, Fig. 0.1.2 (for 2003); 2009–2010, Vol. 5, Fig. 0.1.2 (for 2008).

Note
The figures refer to the total number of 'conventional international bodies' (i.e. Types A–D in the *Yearbook of International Organizations*).

between civil society actors and multinational corporations'.[28] States are enmeshed into a complex network of international institutions and have to work with non-state actors in matters involving control and resolution of collective problems. With a broadened range of actors, global governance is no longer understood as a phenomenon of intergovernmental or international relations under the control of states.

This gives rise to a key question: Could globalization undermine the modern state system? Answers to this type of question can be grouped into three lines of thinking: the 'retreat of the state' in the face of globalization; the 'state-centric' argument; and the 'state transformation' view.[29]

Those who pursue the argument of the 'retreat of the state' view nation-states as victims of globalization and contend that state sovereignty is at stake in the process. Previously state authority in society and the economy was supreme and exclusive but now it has shrunk and has to be shared with other loci or sources of authority.[30] This idea of a 'retreat of the state' holds that the power to make and enforce rules has been reallocated to a variety of institutions, public and private, above and below the level of the state. The world system has become multi-centric and multi-layered. An implication of this 'retreat' view is that the relative power of the state is eroding. The state exercises little power over economic activity, with multinational corporations (MNCs) being increasingly free to set up their business across the globe. Pressurized by the need to reduce taxation and regulations to attract globally mobile capital, the state, notably in the Third World, is left with less leeway to intervene in the national economy to maintain the provision and regulation of social services and welfare.[31] In addition, because of economic globalization, national economies have been 'denationalized'. The statist mode of governance over a bounded territorial space has been regarded as impracticable and obsolescent. Rather, it is replaced by multilateral or trans-state governance developed through regional and global regimes. Susan Strange gave the vivid description that 'where states were once masters of markets, now it is the markets which, on many crucial issues, are the masters over the governments of states'.[32] In short, for the 'retreat' school, global governance is characterized by a relocation of authority upwards to regional and global organizations, downwards to sub-national units and sideways to a host of non-state actors, resulting in a dispersal of the loci of governance, a situation that has been aptly described as 'governance *without* government'.[33]

However, those who uphold the state-centric worldview insist that globalization has not undermined the sovereign authority of states. The state retains substantial capacities to govern its domestic affairs and global activities. 'State-centric' scholars assert that it might be true that there are new challenges to the state but states have enough capacities to respond to them and to enforce rules and regulations. Stephen Krasner takes the view that the norm of Westphalian sovereignty has since its inception been routinely compromised through coercive intervention, conventions, agreements and treaties whenever the ruling elites believe that it suits their rational self-interest to surrender it. Given that states have never been as 'sovereign' as many have assumed, there is little reason to believe that current cases of violation under the influence of globalization indicate a retreat of the sovereign state.[34] Both Robert Gilpin and Kenneth Waltz argue that despite the phenomenal growth of regimes and institutions, they are constructed on the basis of principles espoused by the dominant great power or hegemon. The hegemon facilitates international cooperation and prevents defection from the rules of the regimes through the use of side payments and sanctions or even by coercing recalcitrant states to play by the rules of the game. The nation-state is still the only institution that has the capability to enforce decisions. Governance itself cannot deal successfully with the global issues created by globalization.[35] Given that global governance cannot overcome the anarchic nature of the international system, neo-realists assert that states and the distribution of capabilities among them still matter and that the importance of institutions of global governance has been exaggerated. Kenneth Waltz argues that the world is less interdependent and globalized than is usually supposed. The most path-breaking events in international politics are caused and explained by differences in the capabilities of states. International institutions are an extension of great power interests, with weak states having little or no alternative but to jump on the bandwagon. Less powerful states have little role to play in international cooperation.[36] In John Mearsheimer's words, 'the most powerful states in the system create and shape institutions so that they can maintain their share of world power, or even increase it'.[37] In a system without central government, there are no effective laws and institutions to guide and constrain states with greater capability in the pursuit of their national interests. Powerful states have the ability to bring pressure on less powerful ones and shape international political and economic institutions according to their will.

16 *Global governance: the building blocks*

In contrast to the 'retreat' and 'state-centric' arguments, state transformists are of the view that accelerated globalization has not yet spelt the end of the state. It has rather ushered in a transformation from Westphalian to post-Westphalian statehood. In a globalizing world, states are increasingly interconnected with each other. Previously, nation-states only needed to regulate the issues at or within their defined territorial borders. However, as a result of globalization, a growing list of issues has been shifted from the national and inter-state domains to the global realm. These global problems, particularly those regarded as non-traditional security issues, as discussed in individual chapters below, defy national solutions and may not even be amenable to region-wide solutions. Not only are national policy-makers not well equipped to tackle these global issues, but also the associated state-centric approach is no longer useful for analysing and suggesting solutions for the global problems. This generates an increasing demand for cross-border political cooperation. Consequently there is a rapid growth of inter-state, transgovernmental and transnational relations.

Transgovernmental relations have progressively increased through a dense web of governmental policy networks or globe-spanning networks formed by government ministries or units such as courts, executives, regulatory agencies and legislatures interacting with each other on matters of common concern. Foreign relations of nation-states are no longer conducted exclusively by the ministries of foreign affairs or the heads of state or government. Transgovernmental relations have become the most widespread mode of international governance nowadays. Under the globe-spanning networks, the state is not disappearing but rather disaggregating into functional systems. These transgovernmental relations may occur without any formal treaties, though states still act as the primary, if not the sole, player in the web of transgovernmental system.[38] In addition, the expansion of transnational relations between non-state actors (i.e. individuals and civil society groups) has generated multi-level governance, as evidenced by the growth of INGOs and international organizations of a hybrid nature, with members coming from the government as well as non-governmental sectors.

In other words, the primary difference from both the 'retreat' and 'state-centric' arguments is that states still matter but they are no longer the sole actor in global governance. States are enmeshed in a complex network of international institutions and have to work with non-state actors in matters involving control and resolution of collective problems. That is why global governance is said to be concerned with 'the evolving system of (formal and informal) political coordination – across multiple levels from the local to the global – among public authorities (states and IGOs) and private agencies seeking to realize common purposes or resolve collective problems'.[39]

In summary, the modern sovereign state had once focused on the rules within a well-defined territory, upholding the principles of non-intervention and reciprocity. However, owing to the transformative force of globalization, the focus of global governance has shifted to transnational relations in regulating global issues. This cross-border cooperation is taking place in three ways: through intergovernmental organizations, through governmental policy networks and through non-state actors. The major debate among different global governance theorists is about whether or not the conventional understanding of sovereignty has been transformed into something new. 'Retreat' and 'state-centric' scholars provide opposite answers to that question. In contrast, the transformist theorists argue that while it is true that the actual substance of sovereignty has been changed in such a way that the capacity for state action and control is no longer absolute and non-state actors have become increasingly vocal and indispensable in addressing transnational issues, a gain of power for those non-state actors is, however, not necessarily equal to a loss of power for nation-states. A new game of sovereignty is emerging in the West where states, especially those in the European Union, accept in the first place regulated external intervention into their domestic affairs in return for influence on the internal affairs of other states, and preferential treatment in accordance to needs.[40]

Alongside the changing role of the state, we witness the changing nature of national sovereignty. As will be elaborated in detail in Chapter 5 below, in the wake of a sequence of atrocities committed against humanity in Africa, southeastern Europe and Southeast Asia in the 1990s, the notion of national sovereignty has undergone a process of reconceptualization. The conventional understanding of national sovereignty was based on two key elements: internal hierarchy and external autonomy.[41] F. H. Hinsley defines it as 'the idea that there is a final and absolute political authority in the political community ... and no final and absolute authority exists elsewhere'.[42] Georg Sørensen says that at the core of sovereignty is constitutional independence, which entails the principle of juridical equality of members in the international society of states and the regulative rules of non-intervention and reciprocity or equal treatment, although in substantial terms states are highly unequal in capacity for action and control in both internal and external affairs.[43] However, this organizing principle was no longer seen as absolute in the wake of a series of humanitarian crises that happened in the 1990s in Somalia (1992–94), Rwanda (1994), Srebrenica (1995), East Timor (1999) and Kosovo (1999). These 'conscience-shocking atrocities' called into question the credibility of the United Nations and eventually led to a redefinition of sovereignty from sovereignty as right of exclusivity to sovereignty as responsibility.[44] As early as 1992 UN Secretary-General Boutros Boutros-Ghali asserted in his *An Agenda for Peace* that 'the time of absolute and exclusive sovereignty ... has passed; its theory was never matched by reality'.[45]

In view of the contested nature of humanitarian intervention into Kosovo by the North Atlantic Treaty Organization (NATO) without the authorization of the UN Security Council, the Canadian government sponsored the establishment of the International Commission on Intervention and State Sovereignty (ICISS) to examine the guiding principles of humanitarian intervention. In its report entitled *The Responsibility to Protect*, the Commission held that sovereignty implies responsibility and that the right to non-intervention is conditional and constrained. As a sovereign entity, every individual state has the primary responsibility to protect its citizens from life-threatening dangers. In joining the United

Nations and signing its Charter, states indicate their acceptance of this accompanying responsibility. However, if a state is unable or unwilling to fulfil its responsibility, the international community of states has a residual or fallback responsibility to respond and the principle of non-intervention yields to the international responsibility to protect.[46] The rationale is that the modern states system is only a means to achieving the overriding goal of promoting the wellbeing and freedom of individuals. As soon as sovereignty per se becomes an impediment to this goal, sovereignty 'can, should and must be discarded'.[47] The notion was adopted by Kofi Annan, the UN Secretary-General (1997–2006), and the United Nations General Assembly in its World Summit in September 2005.[48]

In a closely related development, the subject matter of international relations has also undergone changes. Traditionally the object of security was the state and the principal threat to a state's security came from another state. With the end of the Cold War and the rise of internecine conflicts, concerns about human security and non-traditional security threats, including the trans-sovereign problems mentioned above, have been in the ascendancy, and the state has been increasingly viewed as a principal source of threat to human security. As a result, there is an expansion of what is to be governed by the global norms, rules and institutions. The state is no longer necessarily perceived as a solution to the newly emergent threats but as a problem.

While global governance has emerged from the limitations of inter-state relations under anarchy, many Third World states, however, perceive international relations as hierarchical relations between dominant and subordinate powers instead of anarchy.[49] They have a firm belief that in reality relations between *de jure* equal states are never equal or fair and that they are still subordinate to the major powers of the West, as evidenced in the frequent discussions of the American empire in the post-Cold War period. It is open to question whether developing states, including China, are willing to live with the new rules that the post-Westphalian order, a continuing Western-dominated order, imposes on them. Instead, they may understand the relative decline in state power (or escape from anarchy) as a much sought-after opportunity to renegotiate relations with, if not challenge the interests of, the dominant powers. They may therefore be committed to defending, consolidating or even augmenting sovereign control, be less likely to embrace and celebrate transnational processes that threaten it, and resist recognizing that non-state actors, particularly those based in the West, are legitimate players in global governance. We will examine this possibility in the study of China's engagement with the emergent global governance and its institutions in subsequent chapters.

Transformation of global governance institutions

Volker Rittberger *et al.* argue that there have been major historical shifts in global governance since the end of the Second World War, from the first stage of executive multilateralism to the second stage of advanced executive multilateralism in the wake of the Cold War, and then to the third stage of inclusive institutions at the turn of the twenty-first century.[50] Executive multilateralism took the form of intergovernmental organizations such as the United Nations and the Bretton Woods institutions. While it facilitated multilateral cooperation and behind-the-scenes negotiations among the executive branches of member states, policy-making remained the prerogative of the executives of various states. It denied civil society organizations opportunities and the right to take part in the activities and the decision-making process, resulting in a dubious input legitimacy of international policy-making. In view of the growth in the number and the power of civil society groups and movements since the end of the Cold War (see Table 1.1 above), major IGOs like the UN Economic and Social Council (ECOSOC), World Bank and the World Trade Organization began to recognize the need to engage and consult NGOs and business corporations, ushering in the second stage of advanced executive multilateralism in which public sector actors opened up to private sector or civil society actors to narrow the participatory gap.[51] As the latter group are increasingly active and aspire to be major players on the world stage, public–private partnerships are created in the third stage of inclusive institutions to manage the growing list of global problems.[52] Typical examples include the Global Alliance for Vaccines and Immunization (GAVI), the Global Fund to Fight AIDS, Tuberculosis and Malaria, UNITAID, the United Nations Global Compact, and the World Commission on Dams. At the time of writing (January 2011), there are twenty-eight members in the GAVI Alliance Board: nine independent individuals, five representatives from developing country governments, five from industrialized country governments, the Chief Executive Officer, and one representative from each of the following entities: the Research and Technical Health Institute, the industrialized country vaccine industry, the developing country vaccine industry, civil society organizations, the Bill and Melinda Gates Foundation, the World Health Organization (WHO), the United Nations Children's Fund (UNICEF) and the World Bank. China has, however, never been on the board and has not made any contributions to it.[53]

As will be discussed in the next chapter, China has adopted a state-centric approach to global governance. Studying China's involvement in it and its institutions sheds interesting light on whether or not the country is willing to cooperate with private sector actors in regulating various trans-sovereign issues, especially the institutions that endow private sector actors with voting rights, and how the interaction process takes place.

Global challenges, global public goods and collective action

In the previous section we have pointed out that the proliferation of non-state actors and trans-sovereign issues calls for global governance and collective action to manage threatening problems and hence to maintain collective order. What is at issue is how to do so. The collective action of providing global public goods by a host of actors is a means to confront and tackle these global challenges as well as the new security dilemma.

Global public goods are characterized by non-rivalry and non-exclusivity in consumption and by the fact that their benefits are quasi-universal, reaching across countries, population groups and generations. Pure non-rival goods can be used by numerous people because of the zero marginal cost of extending the consumption of the goods to additional users. Their enjoyment by, for instance, rural populations or less developed countries does not detract from their benefits for urban populations or more advanced countries. Pure non-exclusive goods are those whose benefits are available to all, contributors or non-contributors, once the goods are provided. Stated in non-technical parlance, global public goods are the results of actions that improve the wellbeing of people throughout the world and across generations (i.e. goods that are public in consumption) and that are provided by a multitude of actors (i.e. public in production).[54] International peace, a clean environment and public health constitute typical examples of global public goods.[55]

Two defining features collectively present a dilemma to policy-makers. On the one hand, exclusion of non-contributors, whose enjoyment of the goods does not reduce the benefits available to contributors, leads to a gross welfare loss. On the other hand, inclusion of non-contributors creates powerful incentives for many to free-ride on others' contribution. This 'free-riding' nature of public goods raises a crucial question as to who should provide them. Market mechanisms alone cannot address this problem adequately.

At the national level, owing to market failure, it is often the state or the public sector that bears the responsibility to supply public goods. Without a world government, the increasing demand for and undersupply of global public goods give rise to calls for their provision either by the hegemon or by global collective action, bearing testimony to the importance of global governance.[56] Following the pioneering work of Charles Kindleberger, an economic historian, about the prime causes of the Great Depression of 1929, International Relations scholars have paid attention to the important role of a single world leader in providing public goods so as to stabilize the international order. According to Kindleberger, Britain was unable to exercise the leadership in supplying the desirable public goods while the US was unwilling to do so due to the overwhelming influence of isolationism at home.[57] Conventional wisdom, however, has it that the hegemon bears the cost of providing public goods disproportionately and that smaller states reap disproportionate gains from free-riding on the service of the hegemon. This harks back to the neo-realist concerns over the relative distribution of gains from international cooperation. An interesting question is: If the hegemon falls into decline and can no longer provide the goods without help from others, will other leading states share the contribution to their provision?[58]

Whereas economists tend to single out the problem of free-riding to account for underprovision, students of international political economy also emphasize that global public goods are undersupplied because of the contested nature of some of them. The goods are contested for two main reasons. First, the provision of public goods (or bads) by one state has external effects (i.e. externalities) on other states. For example, during the 1980s, the production and use of chlorofluorocarbons by wealthy countries affected other countries, including less developed ones, through long-term depletion of the ozone layer. The resultant distribution of costs and benefits across countries and regions was highly uneven. Climate change mitigation is another case in point. Second, some public goods (or bads) are imposed on the developing world by more advanced countries in the West. The agreement on Trade-Related Aspects of Intellectual Property Rights (TRIPS) is a typical example.[59]

In the absence of effective mechanisms for collective action as well as a hegemon, all actors are reluctant to provide public goods adequately. An option is the setting up of alternative forms of governance to encourage states to provide collective goods by establishing organizations with effective power to enforce and monitor actors to behave in a mutually beneficial manner. Through binding contracts with international institutions, such as treaties and agreements, actors' preferences for global public goods can be restructured or reframed.[60] If global governance is understood as the sum of formal and informal rules to steer various actors at the global level to pursue common goals, then the rules should be developed and implemented to support the collective provision of global public goods. However, given the overarching principle of national sovereignty and the absence of an overarching central authority at the global level, global public goods cannot be supplied by coercion. Collective actions must be taken voluntarily. Who then might take the lead in providing global public goods? Why are they willing to do so? How would they put in place the rules in support of such provision? Why are some attempts to supply global public goods more successful than others? How would the costs and benefits of the provision be distributed or shared among the actors? Who would foot the bill for the provision? How could free-riding by individual actors be prevented?

The above discussions have highlighted some salient points in an enormous and still growing literature on what constitutes global governance. In order to attain some coherence, an attempt is made here to give a simple working definition of the concept behind this book:

Viewed as a dynamic process, global governance is about the making and implementation of global norms and rules by the joint effort of various actors in an anarchical world to provide global public goods (or regulate global public bads). It aims to tackle a host of trans-sovereign problems and to create a stable and responsive political order.

This book attempts to bring into sharper focus the making, maintenance and transformation of the global norms and rules that define the ends of global governance and the means – the provision of global public goods – to achieve them, as well as the role that China plays in the process. Before moving on to the study of China in global governance, it is appropriate to cite in full a caveat about global governance made by Chris Brown and Kirsten Ainley:

> the relevance of 'global governance' varies quite dramatically from issue to issue, and from one part of the world to another. It would be a mistake to

see the growth of global governance as a steady process encroaching on all areas of international life and all regions of the world. There are many parts of the world where a savage Hobbesian realism is the most accurate way of theorizing politics, both domestic and international, and there are some aspects of international politics where no states have proved willing to give up their sovereign prerogatives. In short ... global governance is not the same thing as global government – and much less, responsible and representative government; the extent to which the world as a whole is orderly and norm-governed should never be exaggerated.[61]

We need to bear in mind that the contributions made by China to the regulation of various issues to be examined in the following chapters may vary case by case. That is, China can be a problem or it can be a solution, and China may still harbour strong reservations about institutional multilateralism and may not be willing to surrender its sovereign control over rule-making and implementation.

2 Chinese perspectives on global governance

> The world will come to see that the constructive role China has played in global governance is helpful in getting the world economy back towards full recovery and prosperity.... China will remain conscientious in fulfilling international responsibilities consistent with its status as a major developing country.
>
> Li Keqiang, 2011[1]

There is little dispute that China has increasingly integrated itself into the international system and has remarkably increased its presence in various international organizations. Outside observers wonder whether China will behave in a cooperative way with other actors in the world. Inside China, a new centre of attention on the country's engagement in global governance has evolved since the dawn of the twenty-first century, focusing on what long-term goals Chinese participation in the multilateral international community should envisage.

China's leading scholars discuss the possible impacts the country could have on the global community. For them, the policy of multilateral engagement in the immediate post-Cold War years was largely made on the basis of Deng Xiaoping's admonitions of 'hiding one's capacities and biding one's time' and 'not seeking leadership' (*taoguang yanghui*; *buyao dangtou*). Hence China was preoccupied with merely increasing the breadth of participation in international institutions with little intention of seeking a leadership role or proactively setting the agenda of the policy-making process. To counter the rise of the 'China threat' arguments, China's policy-making elites and their think-tank advisers see the need for open expression of China's overall thinking about its roles in global affairs.[2]

Gaining a better understanding of how China interprets the concept of global governance is a critical first step towards explaining its participation in global governance in the twenty-first century. This chapter aims to examine how the Chinese conceptualize global governance so as to provide a context in which China watchers can assess the country's participation in various issue areas of global governance. The chapter consists of four sections. Based on the discussions of the changing role of the state vis-à-vis other non-state actors and the reconceptualization of national sovereignty in the previous chapter, the first section lays out the Chinese perspectives on these crucial issues. The second

24 Chinese perspectives on global governance

section explains how China came to such a conception of global governance. The third section shifts the focus from perspectives to praxis by examining how China applies its thinking to Third World development. The fourth section concludes by exploring the implications of such Chinese perspectives for its external behaviour, in particular its relations with the West.

Chinese perspectives on global governance

While there is no national blueprint for China's participation in global governance, the counry's perspective can be traced by examining how academic and policy-making elites address the key issues of the changing role of the state in the process of globalization and the changing nature of sovereignty.

Using *quanqiu zhili* (全球治理; 'global governance') as a keyword to look for articles in the 'China Academic Journals Full-text Database: Economics, Politics and Law' (中國期刊全文數據庫：經濟、政治與法律專檔), we have constructed Figure 2.1.

More than 98 per cent of the 698 articles identified were published in 2000 and thereafter, and 93 per cent were published after 2002. In other words, the subject of global governance entered the Chinese discourse only about a decade ago. In the West, in contrast, a vast amount of literature on the subject has been generated since the early 1990s.[3]

The evolution of Chinese perspectives on global governance has influenced by a 'new security concept' advocated by Chinese elites since 1996 when China presented a report to the 1996 ASEAN Regional Forum (ARF) Inter-sessional Support Group on Confidence-building Measures in Tokyo.[4] There, China outlined its security concerns such as external imposition of values and ideologies, the splitting of China, indiscriminate sanctions against China over international

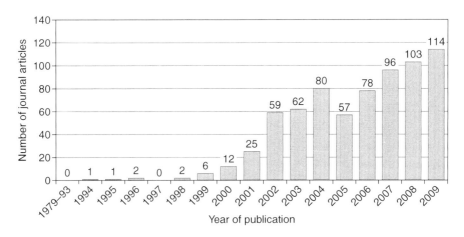

Figure 2.1 Number of Chinese journal articles on global governance, 1979–2009.

Note
Search done on 2 August 2007; updated on 7 March 2010.

issues, conflicts and wars in the region, and encroachment on its sovereignty, maritime rights and national interests.[5] With American 'hegemony' as its implicit target, the new security concept calls for using cooperative means to deal with security issues without diluting its state-centric version of international relations.[6] It stresses the importance of 'common security' as well as a multilateral approach to managing issues such as economic security, food security, energy security, financial security and environmental security. With this new security concept, China began to demonstrate a preference for a multilateral approach to participating in international affairs and for taking an active part in international forums, working with various IGOs and NGOs. To put flesh on the bones of this new security concept, the Chinese Ministry of Foreign Affairs published its Position Paper on Enhanced Cooperation in the Field of Non-Traditional Security Issues in 2002.[7] The discourse of global governance among Chinese scholars has, therefore, started to flourish since the beginning of this century.

Key figures in the study of globalization and global governance in China include Cai Tuo, Yu Zhengliang, Wang Yizhou and Yu Keping. The former three are said to be distinct from their national colleagues in that they share a globalist (*quanqiu zhuyi*) approach by virtue of their embrace of idealism, liberalism and non-statism.[8] In the first Chinese article that directly addresses the issue of global governance, Cai Tuo, Director of the Research Centre on Globalization and Global Problems at China University of Political Science and Law, defines global governance as:

> A set of new regulations, mechanisms, methods and activities for the administration of the public affairs of man, with the doctrine of holism of mankind and its common interest as the value orientation, and with dialogues, consultations and cooperation on equal footings among multiple actors as the approach so as to deal with global changes as well as global problems and challenges facing the contemporary world.[9]

This definition reveals some interesting understandings of the concept of global governance. The term 'administration of the public affairs of man' apparently refers to the subject matter of practical politics. ('Man' [*ren lei*] here presumably means humankind, including both genders.) The 'doctrine of holism' derives from some Chinese philosophical appreciation of the comprehensiveness of and balance in nature. It is interesting to point out that approaches such as 'dialogues, consultations and cooperation' are suggested, which tie in well with China's contemporary diplomatic approach to resolving international problems through peaceful means, and harmonize with the desire for the development of a peaceful environment, both international and domestic, for national modernization to proceed smoothly. Furthermore, Cai envisages five trends in global governance:[10]

1 from government to the non-governmental sector;
2 from state to society;
3 from territorial to non-territorial politics;

4 from an administration that is coercive and hierarchical to one that is based on equality, consultation, voluntariness and networks; and
5 global governance as a special political authority.

The first three refer to the growing prominence of non-governmental actors, including civil society organizations and MNCs, in global politics and their cross-border activities in what Rosenau has referred to as 'spheres of authority'. The fourth transformation signifies the making of collective decisions by a multiplicity of actors using non-hierarchical negotiations and agreements. As a result of the fourth factor, global governance has its own special political authority which tends to undermine the authority of the state but has yet to completely deprive it of authority.[11] It seems that China is adjusting incrementally to these trends, with some people moving more readily than others. For example, those working in the theoretical domain of politics and international relations such as academics are more flexible and liberal than those working in the practical domain such as policy advisers and government officials. As with Western conceptions of global governance, Cai emphasizes the significance of compliance with norms in global governance. He says that 'to meet the challenges [of governing global problems], norms and mechanisms acceptable to all nations have to be created through dialogues, consultations and cooperation, to be followed by coordinated joint actions.'[12]

Yu Zhengliang and his associates in Shanghai have coined the complex notions of 'global co-governance' (*quanqiu gongzhi*) and 'state co-governance' (*guojia gongtong zhili* or *guojia gongzhi*). In the former, a wide array of actors, not restricted to nation-states, manage issues of common concern in multilateral institutions and international treaties. To achieve this goal, state co-governance is the primary form of governance. Amounting in practice to no more than interstate multilateral cooperation, state co-governance is to be achieved by multilateral institutions, which have to be reformed in 'democratic' ways, with great powers assuming principal responsibilities for institutional redesign.[13]

Influenced by Anthony McGrew of the University of Southhampton, UK, Yu Keping, Deputy Director of the CCP Central Bureau of Translation, associates global governance with the legally binding international regimes used to resolve global issues such as military or non-military security threats so as to maintain a proper international political and economic order.[14] Sun Kuanping and Teng Shihua, of the CCP Central Bureau of Translation and East China University of Political Science and Law respectively, are of the view that global governance is characterized by four defining features: involvement of many actors; participation, cooperation and consultation based on widely accepted regimes; commitment to resolving common human problems; and compliance with institutions and rules on the basis of a common set of values.[15] Thus the focus of global governance is seen to be moving from the government to the non-governmental sector, and from the state to society.

An interesting question is: When Cai, Sun and Teng refer to 'on equal footings among multiple actors' and 'involvement of many actors', do they imply that the Chinese approach to international relations is moving away from a state-centric focus?

A diminished role for the nation-state in global governance?

According to Cai, China's vision of global governance differs from that of the West in several ways. First, due to its rising and yet limited power in global politics, China tends to take a prudent and low-profile position in international affairs and to work within the established frameworks of international organizations and multilateralism. This is echoed by Yang Jiemian of the Shanghai Institute of International Studies, who agrees that the Chinese government should adopt a prudent attitude towards global governance because of the thorny issue of likely infringement on national sovereignty and on the traditional role of the state in world affairs.[16]

While admitting that it is in China's national interest to participate actively in global governance, Cai argues that since Chinese participation has been 'in the name either of the government or of the state', for China there is little difference between global governance and international governance.[17] He points out that developing countries, being relative novices in the architecture of global governance, are apprehensive of both Western developed nations and global civil society because of the challenges they pose to the state and national sovereignty.[18] Using the Kurds as an example, Wang Yizhou argues that a nation without the capability to establish a corresponding sovereign state is unable to protect itself from foreign encroachment and intrusion.[19] This national concern with foreign coercion and intervention conjures up the calamitous experience that China suffered at the hands of foreign powers for more than 100 years from 1839 until the end of the Second World War (we will return to this point later) and the problem of control over ethnic minorities at its periphery, let alone the unresolved issue of Taiwan. For the Chinese leadership, contemporary China has to deal with the twin demands of state building and economic development. Hence, the state is required to play a leading role in global governance, particularly in the light of the nascent development of domestic NGOs. Implicit in this approach is the understanding that all non-state actors have to rally behind and coordinate with the state in order to keep foreign forces at bay. For Cai, it is more rational to view state–NGO relations as cooperative and complementary rather than confrontational.

Yu Keping also emphasizes that international organizations, global civil society and international regimes and regulatory mechanisms are often subject to enormous influence and even manipulation by the powerful West led by the US. Developed states tend to use their influence to impede effective global governance. Therefore, he warns against any move that would infringe on national sovereignty or undermine the role of nation-states in domestic and global governance.[20] This view is echoed by Liu Jinyuan of Nanjing University who maintains that powerful states have dominated and shaped the conduct of international institutions in order to promote their own foreign policy goals. He calls on developing states to ally together to resist a monopoly on governing international institutions by the powerful states.[21]

Some tend to equate global governance with the activities of IGOs in managing global transborder issues. In her study of the role of the WHO during the outbreak of severe acute respiratory syndrome (SARS), Wang Miao of the Renmin University of China associates global governance with the management of global issues by IGOs. She argues that research on global governance should focus on globalization and national sovereignty.[22] A more realist view about the role of the state in globalization and global governance is expressed by Tang Xianxing and Zhang Xiang of Fudan University. They maintain that global governance is simply a myth. It cannot change the anarchic nature of the international system and is therefore unable to take over the role of the nation-state.[23] Bates Gill notes the subtle difference between the notions of 'world order' (*shijie zhixu*) and 'international order' (*guoji zhixu*) in the Chinese discourse, saying that Chinese analysis in general prefers the latter statist concept to the former.[24]

The demise of the Westphalian notion of national sovereignty?

The above survey of the Chinese discourse on global governance indicates that the sovereign state still plays a paramount role in Chinese thinking. However, in its deepening engagement with global institutions, has China reconceptualized the notion of sovereignty? More importantly, how has China responded to the United Nations' efforts to redefine sovereignty as responsibility?

Allen Carlson of Cornell University argues that China conceptualizes sovereignty as a bundle of rights, which are pursued unevenly in the country.[25] Its desire to boost its domestic economic development and to enhance the legitimacy of the Communist regime, as well as its growing interest in portraying itself as a responsible state, have pushed China to modify its stance on economic sovereignty and human rights intervention. However, at the same time, China is not to be budged on such territorial and jurisdictional areas as the questions of Taiwan and Tibet. Overall, he demonstrates that China's stance on sovereignty is dynamic and malleable rather than static.[26] Bates Gill also shows China's increased flexibility and pragmatism in its changing approach to sovereignty, peacekeeping and anti-terrorism.[27]

Chinese scholars in the country tend to 'unbundle' national sovereignty into two broad categories: economic and trade matters on the one hand, and political and security issues on the other. Chu Shulong, Director of the Institute of Strategic Studies at Tsinghua University, has stated that if the country wants to integrate into the international community and benefit from that integration, then 'China has had to give up some of its sovereign rights'.[28] A typical example is its membership of the WTO. In order to benefit from membership, China not only has to adhere to the rules of the organization but also needs to rewrite some of its domestic regulations in order to fit in with the WTO's requirements. Su Changhe of Shanghai International Studies University argues that the increased need to address global public issues whose resolution requires global cooperative action is pushing China into accepting multilateralism and international regimes. In the engagement process, China has modified its exclusive view of national sovereignty. Although he does not elaborate on the change, he refutes the allegation that China is the staunchest fortress of the Westphalian world order.[29] Liu Dongguo of the Renmin University of China holds that the demand for global governance is in conflict with the prevailing world order. To establish global governance, new ideas have to be constructed. The first step towards establishing a new world order is to reform the age-old doctrine of national sovereignty and to allow the participation of an extensive array of non-state actors. However, Liu does not seem to have dwelt at length on whether and how new ideas about global governance are to be developed in China.[30]

In his discussion of the relationship between infectious diseases and non-traditional security issues, Wang Yizhou points out that it would be sensible to adopt a flexible approach to understanding the meaning of sovereignty in the age of globalization. While the traditional concept of security needs to be enriched, the notion of sovereignty likewise needs to be enhanced. The traditional notion of sovereignty proclaims the centrality of the principle of non-intervention in internal affairs without considering that the authority of a state is derived from the consent of its citizens.[31] Therefore, the concept of sovereignty should be understood at two different levels. First, domestically it should be bound to the obligation to protect the human rights of the local populace. Failure to respect, defend and promote human rights within one's territory would call into question the legitimacy of the state. This position is closer than those of many Chinese analysts to the UN notion of the 'responsibility to protect'. However, at the external level, particularly regarding inter-state relationships, Wang contends that China needs to maintain a defensive approach, according to which the principle of non-intervention still 'remains the foundation stone of the world politics'. While taking a 'progressive' approach to the notion of sovereignty, Wang warns that China needs to be mindful of the dangers of the erroneous idea that human rights can 'replace sovereignty' or that 'human rights matter more than sovereignty', which has been ardently promoted by Western powers in order to maintain their dominance.[32]

The Chinese government in general accepts the principle of humanitarianism, but it is adamantly opposed to interventionism. In preparing its report on humanitarian intervention, the ICISS held a number of round-table consultations around the world. According to Ramesh Thakur, a member of the ICISS, the strongest opposition against intervention was expressed by the Chinese in its Beijing consultation in 2001.[33] China's apprehension about the norm of the 'responsibility to protect' is shown in a Position Paper on the United Nations Reforms released by the Chinese government in June 2005. China maintains that the reforms should safeguard the principles of sovereign equality and non-interference in internal affairs. Even if a massive humanitarian crisis takes place, it says, the opinions of the country in question and the regional organization concerned should be respected, and it is eventually the responsibility of 'the Security Council to make the decision [to ease and defuse the crisis] in the frame [*sic*] of [the] UN in light of specific circumstances'.[34] In other words, interventions must be authorized by the Security Council and must not be unilaterally made by great powers, notably the US, at their will. A Chinese survey of the national literature on the study of national sovereignty in the period 1995–2005 makes little mention of the notion of 'responsibility to protect'. Neither is the background to the emergence of the new norm of humanitarian intervention given much attention.[35]

In spite of the evolution of new thinking on sovereignty in scholarly circles, the Westphalian understanding of sovereignty still carries much weight in Chinese official views. Humanitarian intervention and the responsibility to protect are believed to have the potential to threaten the survival of the Communist regime and to pose dangerous precedents for Tibet and Taiwan. In addition, common to the Chinese studies is an argument that power in the existing international order lies in the hands of the Western states, particularly the most powerful ones, for the major extant IGOs are the creation of Western states, with the rules of the game serving their national interests and favouring Western values. Wary of intervention by major powers through IGOs on the pretext of sustaining global governance, China is opposed to the idea of the 'pooling of sovereignty'. Sun Hui and Yu Yu argue that the United Nations should shoulder the principal responsibility for global governance, even though in the short run it is still subject to manipulation by the US-led Western powers. That is why they paradoxically call for the inclusion of non-state actors in the practice of global governance and for giving developing countries a stronger voice in the decision-making process of international organizations.[36]

Since the 1990s, Chinese external behaviour has largely reflected these theoretical discussions about global governance. On the one hand, China has embraced multilateralism and global governance and largely abided by international norms and rules. For instance, China proactively founded the Shanghai Five in 1996 and the succeeding Shanghai Cooperation Organization in 2001, and the Bo'ao Forum of Asia in 2001. It approved the Kyoto Protocol to the UN Framework Convention on Climate Change in 2002. In the economic arena, since joining the WTO in 2001, China has steadfastly reformed its trading system, making it more compatible with WTO rules and norms. Although some commentators and officials in the West have cast doubt on its compliance record, particularly in the areas of intellectual property rights and market access, China has demonstrated a will to adhere to the rules of the game by enacting and amending legislation and regulations with the aim of setting up a legal system that is agreeable to the WTO.

On the other hand, Beijing has expressed deep concerns about humanitarian interventions in sovereign states and about the alleged quest for global 'hegemony' by the United States, as evident in its reactions to the Kosovo crisis. Zhang Yunling of the Chinese Academy of Social Sciences in Beijing revealed that China was worried that 'what happened yesterday in Yugoslavia could occur tomorrow in Asia, especially in China, whose minority and human rights policies are always criticised by the United States and its allies'.[37] The Chinese were annoyed not only by the 'accidental' bombing of the Chinese embassy in

Belgrade by a US warplane in May 1999, but also by the fact that without authorization from the UN Security Council, the US-led NATO used armed forces against the former Yugoslavia, a sovereign state which was not a member of the organization and posed no direct threat to it. To counter American influence, China has reiterated its new security concept and called for remedying the damaged credibility of the UN Security Council. When the UN and major stakeholder states were debating how to respond to the outbreak of political violence in East Timor in the wake of a referendum on the relationship of East Timor with Indonesia in late August 1999, China (and Russia) stressed the need for the consent of the Indonesian government – although Indonesia's claim to sovereignty over East Timor and its occupation of it in 1975 were not recognized by the UN or many of its member states – and a mandate from the Security Council. Both conditions were fulfilled in mid-September 1999.[38]

Constructing Chinese perspectives

Why and how does China come to have such preferences and interests about global governance and what would be their possible impact on the world order?[39] The central focus of enquiry is on why China behaves according to the dictates of *realpolitik*. Why is the doctrine of sovereignty enshrined in China's worldview? Why does China consider its perspectives on global governance to be prescriptive guiding rules for a peaceful international order?

Social learning theory asserts that an actor learns new norms and practices in its interactions with other actors. The learning process involves the questioning of previous beliefs, the reconceptualization of problems and the articulation of new goals.[40] World order in China's imperial era was characterized as a hierarchical one in which unequal partners were 'integrated into a system of reciprocal relations'. Underlying this hierarchical system was the Confucian idea of harmony or universal community (*da tong*) whereby the seniors bestowed benevolence from above while the junior members practised obedience from below.[41] The Westphalian world order was also hierarchical in nature. On the one hand, it recognized the equal legal status of the 'civilized' sovereign states in Europe; on the other, it legitimized the expansion by force of the 'civilized' European system into the 'uncivilized' non-European world.[42] China began to be internalized into such a state-centric, *realpolitik*-dominated world order in the mid-nineteenth century when it suffered humiliating defeats at the hands of the Western and Japanese powers, which forcibly brought it into the Westphalian international system and subjected it to the principle of 'extraterritoriality'.[43] Since then, Chinese leaders – both republican and Communist – have steadfastly maintained that the international system is composed of juridically independent and equal but materially unequal states. Chinese perspectives on world order are thus informed by both its relative position in the order and its attempts to improve that position. China defines a just world order in terms not only of anti-imperialism but also of a militarily and economically strong China, showing 'a mixture of victimology and aggrandisement'.[44] When rhetoric is translated into practice, China, by instinct and by learning, attaches primary importance to the norms of national sovereignty, territorial integrity and peaceful coexistence among nation-states, as epitomized in the Five Principles of Peaceful Coexistence.[45] The 'siege mentality' was reactivated as soon as the Chinese Communist Party (CCP) experienced internal and external legitimation crises in the late 1980s.[46] To fend off alleged attempts by foreign powers, notably the US, to change or 'overthrow' its Communist political system, China has resorted to the Westphalian notion of world order, notably the sanctity of the principle of non-intervention.[47]

Inherent tensions exist between China's grave misgivings about the West's intentions towards it and the view held by the Chinese leadership that increased involvement with globalization remains the most viable way for the country to modernize itself. Cai Tuo explicitly states that 'the existing international order [is] profoundly unjust.'[48] The Chinese view on global governance holds that the world economy is highly unequal in the distribution of the fruits of development, resulting in a huge wealth gap between the world's rich and poor.[49] This highly unequal world also results from the fact that decision-making power in international institutions is held firmly by the developed world.[50] China, therefore, calls for a democratization of international relations as a way to remedy this problem. The measures for doing so have, however, not yet been spelt out in any detail by Chinese officials or scholars. But it would be a mistake to equate this with the views in the West that the world structure is undemocratic and that the development of a global civil society should be encouraged as one way to deal with this democratic deficit at the global level.[51] The latter view is not shared by Chinese officials. China's scepticism about global civil society and for that matter most major INGOs derives partly from the fact that they are dominated and controlled by the West. Also, for reasons that are apparent, China puts a lot of hope in the role played by the UN, since it holds a veto power in the Security Council. China's influence in other major international organizations pales in comparison with its status in the Security Council and the UN as a whole.

Seen in this way, the debate as to whether China is a status quo power or a revisionist power misses the crucial point that the key issue here is not whether China would present any threat to the age-old, established Westphalian system and notion of world order, but rather that China is adamantly opposed to the ongoing American campaign to create a new world order based on the solidarist values of individual sovereignty and liberal democracy.[52] China's socialization into the Westphalian, *realpolitik* norms of international order is now at odds with US endeavours to promote a value-based security community that imposes checks on national sovereignty. China is at pains to maintain the Westphalian international order while the US behaves as a revisionist hegemon, moulding new rules. Strictly speaking, it is China rather than the US that harbours a 'Cold War mentality' about the international order in its perception of the emerging global governance complex. As Rosemary Foot argues, as soon as China began to be aware of the need to increase its integration into the international system, the criteria of membership in the club of responsible states changed from pluralist concepts that emphasize respect for national sovereignty and non-intervention in the internal affairs of other states to solidarist concepts that rest on notions of common values and democratic governance.[53]

From this point of view, the idea of a 'harmonious world', which will be discussed below, shares the same logic of the prevailing Westphalian international system. In spite of its distrust of the transnational solidarist agenda of the post-Westphalian world order, China has nonetheless largely abided by international norms and been party to all major international treaties and organizations in addition to the UN. This forms part of China's grand strategy to assure other members of international society that it is a responsible and benign rising power.[54]

From perspectives to praxis: promoting governance with Chinese characteristics?

In defiance of the once-prevalent prediction of an imminent collapse of the Chinese economy and political system in the wake of the Tiananmen crisis, China's economic development regained momentum in 1992 after registering slow growth in 1989 and 1990. This gave rise to the 'China threat' theory in the US and Japan.[55] To counter it, China has adopted a two-pronged strategy regarding its involvement in global governance. First, it has joined all major international treaties and organizations and largely abided by international norms.[56] Second, it has been proactively playing the role of protagonist in the international arena. Among its various new roles, the following stand out:

- as a defender of the existing international order with an emphasis on maintaining the central role of the United Nations;
- as a constructive critic of unjust international rules and regimes offering alternative options for reforms, of which one is a proposal to 'democratize' international relations; and
- as a leading force fostering the formation of regional communities, particularly in Asia.[57]

However, it is said that what China now lacks is not a stance, but rather the capacity to exert widespread influence and the experience of exercising its power skilfully. With the foregoing discussion of the Chinese perspectives on global governance as a backdrop, the following sections explore how China translates its perspectives into practice. The discussions surrounding the 'Beijing Consensus' and Hu Jintao's notion of a 'harmonious world' are illustrative and deserve special attention.

Beijing Consensus vs. Washington Consensus

Following its successful economic reforms and rise in hard power, it is not surprising that China wants to project its model of development and governance abroad, thus presenting a challenge to the once dominant model advocated by such international financial institutions as the International Monetary Fund (IMF) and the World Bank, the White House, Wall Street and the US Treasury, commonly known as the 'Washington Consensus' or neo-liberal economic order.[58] The Washington-based financial institutions portray themselves as the 'exclusive holders of legitimate knowledge about development', leaving little room for alternative paths to development. With little respect for the national sovereignty of the recipient countries, they imposed uniform policy prescriptions onto Latin American, African and Southeast Asian countries suffering from economic turmoil between the 1980s and the Asian financial crisis of 1997–98, even though the indebted countries experienced economic problems of different kinds.[59]

In the wake of the demise of socialism in the former Soviet Union and Eastern Europe, the Washington-based financial institutions (and the UN) showed reduced tolerance for the dismal performance of the authoritarian or state-led models of economic growth in the Third World and in the former socialist countries. The effort of the financial institutions to promote good governance was designed to address the dual problems of unrepresentative and corrupt governments and the inefficiency of non-market systems.[60] The concept of good governance is an extension of the Washington Consensus with added emphases on the Western cultural values of the rule of law, transparency, accountability and democracy.[61]

These values, however, seem to matter little in China's success story. Joshua Cooper Ramo summarizes China's success as the 'Beijing Consensus' and frequently compares it with the Washington Consensus.[62] According to Ramo, the Beijing Consensus is characterized by three features. First, economic growth is led by innovation. By innovation, he means experimentation with new ideas and institutions and the notion that failures are deemed acceptable. However, this requires the state to exercise some degree of control over the new experiments in order to contain the damage caused by unsuccessful reform measures. Second, development has to be balanced and sustainable. That explains why the Chinese authorities are paying ever-increasing attention to the environmental costs of economic growth and to the social costs of regional and rural–urban inequalities. Finally, and more importantly, China's path to development is a quest for self-determination, without copying verbatim any blueprints for economic development from other countries. His publication has prompted ongoing discussions among China scholars inside and outside the country.[63] However, the term 'Beijing Consensus' has not acquired widespread approval or agreement among China scholars, who prefer to use 'China model' in their discourse. They argue that consensus is normally understood as an 'ideal model' which other states can recognize and promote. By contrast, the China model is one which tells others about China's developmental experience. Over the past three decades, China has made its own path of development, including the notion of 'socialist modernization with Chinese characteristics' since the 1980s. This can be claimed as a strategic policy for development under the opportunities and challenges of globalization. Other countries might develop their own paths with reference to China's experience, but the China model should not be treated as a consensus or universal blueprint for others to follow.[64]

Akin to Ramo, Randall Peerenboom asks whether or not China presents a new paradigm for developing states.[65] The China model favours gradually undertaking economic reforms led by the state as opposed to big-bang shock therapy. By attaching significance to self-determination and national sovereignty, it defies the policy prescriptions handed down by the IMF, the World Bank and governments in the West. It is worth noting that Chinese analysts only disagree with Ramo over the use of terminology to sum up China's experience. By and large, they resonate with Ramo by putting emphasis on the claims that the state should play a predominant and independent role in gradual reform and development. They also point out that there should not be any universal blueprint for development imposed by external actors from above.[66]

Following on from the idea of the Beijing Consensus and the succeeding notion of the China model, Chinese leaders began to realize the increasing importance of 'soft power' in world affairs. In early 2004 the CCP Central Committee promulgated the 'Opinions of the CCP Central Committee on Further Developing and Bringing about Flourishing Philosophy and Social Sciences'. In May of the same year, members of the CCP Politburo gathered to study the building of China's soft power in the context of debates about the Central Committee document as well as the Beijing Consensus/China model.[67] Accordingly, it is argued that the promotion of China's development model is a viable means for the country to build up its soft power. At the core of the China model are the values of economic development, social stability and harmony.[68] Treating the Beijing Consensus/China model as a major component of its soft power, Beijing began to make a spate of diplomatic forays into the developing world, particularly Africa, in a bid to win more friends and allies and counter the predominance of Washington. With rising criticisms of the Washington Consensus, the discourse on the Beijing Consensus/China model serves to strengthen the voice of the developing world in global governance.

An issue that could have far-reaching effects on global governance is the question of whether Beijing is proactively promoting an international order that is at odds with the West by strengthening economic ties with and extending its normative influence to developing countries.[69] Naazneen Barma and Ely Ratner of the University of California at Berkeley assert that the China model, which combines illiberal capitalism and illiberal sovereignty, 'could set scores of developing nations away from the path of liberal democracy, creating a community of countries that reject Western views of human rights and accepted standards of national governance'.[70] Indeed, for the leaders of the developing world, China's soft power lies in its espousal of the doctrine of non-intervention in domestic affairs, the provision of 'no-strings-attached' financial and technical aid – including health diplomacy[71] – to Third World countries, the expansion of commercial opportunities, and the ability of the CCP to sustain rapid economic growth under an authoritarian regime. For example, Angola has found China 'a more supportive and less critical partner' than the IMF.[72] Nigeria's Olusegun Obasanjo once said that the twenty-first century is 'the century for China to lead the world' and 'when you [i.e. China] are leading the world, we want to be close behind you'.[73] Iran reportedly looked to China for ways to stimulate the economy without losing political power.[74]

The appeal of the China model is, however, constrained by the fact that Chinese values and practice run counter to global norms which now attach much weight to liberalism, democracy and the accountability of political elites to the people, respect for human rights and ecological balance. The former President of the World Bank, Paul Wolfowitz, has pointed out that China and its big banks have not yet subscribed to the 'Equator Principles'. This voluntary code of conduct, launched in 2003, is designed to introduce good corporate governance by pledging that private bank-financed projects should meet certain human rights and environmental standards.[75] The Group of Seven industrialized states have been concerned that China's 'opportunistic' lending practices may result in burdening impoverished countries with a new wave of unsustainable debt, undermining their debt relief efforts.[76] The West is also prodding China into supporting the Extractive Industries Transparency Initiative, which aims at strengthening transparency and accountability – in short, good governance – in resource-rich countries through 'the full publication and verification of company payments and government revenues from oil, gas and mining'.[77] China's robust economic growth is being achieved at the expense of income equality and the environment. Political and legal reforms in the direction of promoting democracy and the rule of law lag far behind economic transformation. It is equally questionable whether the people of Africa would support the Chinese assertion that Third World countries and their people side with them against Western intrusion into their territorial integrity and national sovereignty. In the failing states of Africa which often lack a common identity capable of unifying the people, foreign interventions are sometimes appreciated by the competing groups as well as the ordinary people. Their views of non-intervention are rather contingent and the so-called principle of national sovereignty is, in their view, distorted by the ruling dictators into no more than elite sovereignty.[78] That is why even when America's reputation and soft-power influence in liberal democracies is on the wane as a result of its unilateral actions in Iraq and elsewhere, China's attempts to build up soft power do not seem to have convinced sceptics in the West, in global civil society, or among democrats in the developing world.[79]

A pluralist 'harmonious world'

Following the Fourth Plenum of the sixteenth CCP Central Committee, held in Beijing in September 2004, which proposed, among other things, the building of a 'harmonious socialist society' in China, the country began to expound the concept of a 'harmonious world' (*hexie shijie*), culminating in Hu Jintao's address to the United Nations Sixtieth Anniversary Summit in September 2005.[80]

It is said that the new notion represents China's overall goal and theory of global governance.[81] The harmonious world is to be built on the basis of sovereign nation-states that respect a plurality and diversity of cultures, ideologies and politico-economic systems and handle their relations with 'respect for sovereignty and territorial integrity, as well as respect for countries' right to independently choose their own social systems and paths of development'.[82]

Based on the official doctrine, both Lu Xiaohong of China Foreign Affairs University and Yu Keping have expounded the Chinese perspective on global governance. For them, the principal actors in global governance are nation-states and the United Nations.[83] From this point of view, the idea of a harmonious world shares the same logic as the Westphalian international system. China's advocacy for strengthening United Nations-based multilateralism and for constructing a harmonious world is obviously targeted at the 'hegemonic' role of the US and its neo-conservative mission to transform the prevailing Westphalian international system into what it regards as a 'more peaceful' world based on the solidarist values of liberty, human rights and democracy.[84] On a theoretical level, the Chinese notion bears a resemblance to the English School's pluralist conception of international society, in which sovereign states can maintain international order, in spite of the fact that they hold varying conceptions of human rights and global justice.[85]

By emphasizing the right of all states to choose their own paths of development while integrating with the global polity and economy, China, on the one hand, rejects a liberal political order imposed from the outside and, on the other hand, tries to develop and exercise soft power in dealing with global issues that require multilateral cooperation as well as in recruiting support from developing countries. One can argue that key to the Chinese approach to global governance is for the state actor to use soft power in a multilateral setting. To avoid a frontal attack on Washington, Beijing is careful to use soft balancing to counter US interests.[86] Its reserve about using the term 'Beijing Consensus' is part of a strategy to avoid being seen as challenging the Washington Consensus directly. On the international front, it uses multilateralism and reciprocal engagement to offset American hegemonic influence. In view of the changing norms of national sovereignty and role of the nation-state in global governance, China promotes the notion of a harmonious world which upholds the principle of non-intervention and stresses the predominant role of the state in governance.

Conclusion

One can summarize Chinese perspectives on global governance by addressing the questions of who makes the rules of governance, how, in whose interests and for what ends. China's approach to global governance remains fundamentally state-centric. It has developed a view of governance that posits that international order is to be produced and shaped by dominant states, with non-state actors playing at best epiphenomenal roles. Among the many comments about China's approach to global governance, a highly consistent theme, which constitutes the core of the mainstream perspective, is their concern about the ulterior motives behind the Western efforts to promote global governance. Wary of the possible loss of the country's national sovereignty, the Chinese view tends to attach significance to *intergovernmental* organizations, while admitting a multiplicity of actors, in managing global issues. Its embrace of multilateralism and its grudging inclusion of non-state actors are better understood as parts of its adaptive *realpolitik* strategy to reap the material benefits of economic globalization and to hedge against US-dominated global governance in a non-adversarial way. China's rationalist conception of global governance prompts it to deal with globalization and its impact by participating in multilateral institutions and by seeking to adhere as far as possible to the underlying norms and rules of the institutions. Benefits accruing to the country from increased membership of these institutions are believed to outweigh the costs involved. Despite displaying signs of greater flexibility in dealing with rule-making in the economic realm, the Chinese notion of national sovereignty insists on the principle of formal equality among states and their 'endowed' rights to non-intervention in their internal affairs. Only very recently did the concept of responsibility to protect enter the Chinese discourse on sovereignty. The new thinking has not yet been reflected in any observable changes in its national policy. Under the ingrained influence of the Westphalian conception of sovereignty as well as concern about the association between the promotion of good governance and the building of a pro-West liberal political order, China refrains from making its offers of aid and loans to Third World countries conditional on liberal reforms being undertaken. In sum, China perceives global governance as an international means to building an inclusive international society in which nation-states of diverse cultures, ideologies and politico-economic systems can coexist in peace and harmony. Behind a façade of deepening participation, China does not share many of the West's fundamental norms and rules that underpin global governance. Two implications follow from this.

First, a formidable challenge to China's aspiration to be a responsible great power is that its statist conception of the rules and values governing the management and resolution of global problems clashes with the emerging international norms of human security and individual sovereignty. Due to their dynamic interactions with international organizations and global civil society, powerful Western countries' conception of global issues is ever changing: their view of sovereignty is becoming contingent on certain conditions and a new sovereignty game is in the making.[87] In contrast, without an equally heavy engagement with non-state actors, internationally and domestically, China is often accused of intransigence, for failing to respond to global crises proactively and innovatively.[88] Since its founding, the People's Republic of China (PRC) has firmly clung to the Westphalian conception of international politics, which looks increasingly anachronistic in the current globalizing era. Its agenda-setting power is undermined by its inability to propose creative alternatives to the American and European preferences which rest on notions of common values and democratic governance.

The second implication is that as soon as China feels confident enough in its status as a great power, it may no longer feel totally obliged to comply with the established norms and rules of Western-dominated international institutions. Its intention to bend the rules if feasible is evident from its criticism of the injustice of the prevailing international order and its advocacy of a democratization of international relations. Tensions arise over who can legitimately define what constitutes the dominant norms of the day that guide global governance and international order. At issue is whether or not China can harness enough soft power to modify the existing norms in its favour, convincing others to follow the Chinese way of thinking. This will be the prime focus of the following chapters, which examine China's evolving role in the governance of various issue areas.

3 Peace and security

> If we had not possessed nuclear and hydrogen bombs, and launched satellites since the 1960s, China would not be regarded as an influential world power, nor would it have the international position it occupies today.
>
> Deng Xiaoping, 1988[1]

> If China likes denuclearization so much, why did it develop nuclear arms in the first place? Would China say it had to have nuclear arms to develop itself because it had special conditions?... Why is North Korea different from China?
>
> A North Korean diplomat, 2006[2]

Embedded in the above saying by Deng are two possible assumptions: one is that the possession of nuclear weapons is regarded by China as conferring on it the status of great power;[3] the other is that the possession of such weapons helps to enhance China's comprehensive power. If Chinese leaders think in this way, then it would not be too surprising if leaders of other countries thought likewise. So it would not be wrong to assume that non-nuclear states such as North Korea, as shown in the second quote above, will endeavour to develop nuclear capability if they can. Indeed Yale Professor Paul Kennedy has estimated that the number of nuclear powers will reach twenty by 2020 and thirty-five by 2050.[4]

The proliferation of weapons of mass destruction (WMD), in particular nuclear weapons, has been a major concern for many countries since the advent of the Cold War. The general belief is that the more nuclear weapons there are in the world, the more dangerous it will be for the world.[5] China did not share this belief until the 1990s when it gradually entered into various global arms control regimes. In fact, during the Cold War, China chastised the two superpowers – the United States and the Soviet Union – for monopolizing the production and possession of nuclear weapons. Indeed, in the 1960s, it even declared its support for nuclear proliferation as a means to 'break the hegemony of the superpowers'.[6] Now as China has largely identified itself with the global security status quo, being one of the few nuclear weapon states and one of the beneficiaries of the current globalization process, from the 1990s it started to change its nuclear thinking and become concerned about the proliferation of WMD, especially in its neighbouring countries.

The issue of peace and security has therefore figured prominently in the thinking of Chinese leaders, not least because a peaceful and stable external environment would be conducive to its development and modernization. In fact, peace and security have been among China's major global and domestic concerns since the establishment of the People's Republic in 1949, although the relative importance of peace vis-à-vis security has varied over time. From the 1950s to the 1970s, national security – the protection of the country's territory-based sovereignty from external aggression – was the most important issue in China's foreign policy. Since the 1980s, China has felt that its territorial sovereignty is largely safe, except as regards Taiwan and to a lesser extent Tibet and Xinjiang, and so the issue of security has gradually given way to the pursuit of peace and development.

What is the meaning of peace and security to the Chinese? How do they perceive these two closely related issues? What have they done to enhance peace and security, not only for themselves but also for others? In other words, what has China contributed to the global governance of peace and security? If we treat peace and security as public goods, how has China contributed to providing such goods, in particular to Northeast Asia, where North Korea has made clear its intention to build nuclear weapons?[7]

To answer these and other related questions, this chapter will concentrate on China's involvement in the United Nations and some major security regimes in the world, including those in the Asia-Pacific region. The United Nations is by far the most important global institution dealing with issues of peace and security. China, being one of the five permanent members of its Security Council, carries special responsibility for the maintenance of global peace and security. In terms of issue areas, it would be useful to consider China's changing attitude and practice in UN peacekeeping operations, and its evolving policy and practice in arms control and non-proliferation, especially in dealing with WMD. In regional affairs, Beijing's active participation in the Six-Party Talks aimed at stopping North Korea from developing nuclear weapons is a useful measure for gauging China's peace and security governance in Northeast Asia.

In the main this chapter examines: How is China involved in the promotion of *collective* action and the delivery of *collective* solutions to address pressing global security issues in the early twenty-first century? And what motivates China to increase its participation in global security governance and compliance with international obligations? The chapter is divided into two major parts: on China and the UN, in particular UN peacekeeping operations (UNPKO); and on nuclear non-proliferation.

China and the UN

Samuel Kim argued as late as the end of the 1990s that post-Mao China adopted a maxi/mini diplomacy to reap maximum benefits from the UN agencies while taking minimum financial responsibility. He backed up his claim by pointing to China's meagre contributions to the budgets of the UN systems between 1971 and 1985 which were at their highest in 1979.[8] Is China still a free-rider in the early twenty-first century in the UN, despite its rapid ascent to great power status?

Table 3.1 shows that China's share of the UN regular budget for 2010 was 3.189 per cent, behind France, the United Kingdom and the US among the five permanent members of the UN Security Council (UNSC), which together account for nearly 40 per cent of the budget. China's contributions were also lower than those of regional powers such as Canada (3.207 per cent), Italy (4.999 per cent), Germany (8.018 per cent) and Japan (12.53 per cent). Historically, China's current assessment rate is still below its level in 1973–74, shortly after its entry into the global organization.

Jin Yongjian, then president of China's UN Association, defended China's low percentage contribution, saying that its share of the UN budget for 2004–2006 was 35 per cent more than in the previous three years. In 2005 China paid $41 million.[9] Its gross contributions for 2010 rose sharply to $74.96 million. With an assessment rate just below the benchmark of 1 per cent in 2000, China's contributions have more than trebled in only ten years.

China and the UNPKO

China's participation in UNPKO offers another good indicator of its involvement in, and contributions to, the global governance of peace and security, as well as its monetary contributions to the UN peacekeepng budget. Against the background of a decline in contributions by Western countries to UN peace operations,[10] this section asks whether China now plays an increasing role in these operations. This is followed by an examination of how and why China has increased its personnel and monetary contributions to UNPKO. Does China also participate in 'hybrid missions' or non-UN peace operations?[11] And, finally, what impacts does it have on international peace and security? Here we will ask if China's engagement enhances the UN's legitimacy as the principal source of authority for peace operations, and is conducive to sustainable peace.[12]

Table 3.1 The assessment rates (%) of the permanent five for the UN regular budget

Country	1974	1984	1995	2000	2005	2010
China	5.50	0.88	0.72	0.995	2.053	3.189
France	5.86	6.51	6.32	6.545	6.030	6.123
USSR/Russia	12.97	10.54	5.68	1.077	1.100	1.602
UK	5.31	4.67	5.27	5.092	6.127	6.604
US	25.00	25.00	25.00	25.000	22.000	22.000
Total	54.64	47.60	42.99	38.709	37.310	39.518

Sources: For the years 1974 and 1984, Samuel S. Kim 'China and the United Nations', in Elizabeth Economy and Michel Oksenberg (eds), *China Joins the World: Progress and Prospects* (New York: Council on Foreign Relations, 1999), p. 68; for the rest, Committee on Contributions, United Nations General Assembly, www.un.org/ga/contributions/budget.shtml (accessed 19 December 2010).

China's personnel contribution to UNPKO has surged since 2003. As of September 2002, China contributed only 139 troops, observers and police officers to the ongoing UNPKO. As of December 2006, the number increased to 1,666.[13] As of the end of November 2010 China dispatched a contingent of 2,040 troops, police and civilian personnel to UN peace operations (Table 3.2), ranking first among the five permanent members. But its share of the peacekeeping budget for 2010, 3.94 per cent, was far below those of the US (27.17 per cent), the United Kingdom (8.16 per cent) and France (7.56 per cent) as well as Japan, Germany and Italy (12.53 per cent, 8.02 per cent and 5.00 per cent respectively).[14] Why is China reluctant to contribute a higher percentage to UN regular and peacekeeping budgets while its involvement in UNPKO personnel is growing? China maintains that its capacity to contribute is limited by its relatively low level of economic development.[15] The focus of China's contribution in personnel is on sub-Saharan Africa: for example, in Sudan, the Democratic Republic of Congo (DRC) and Liberia (Table 3.2). More than 68 per cent of China's personnel have been dispatched to Liberia and Côte d'Ivoire in the oil-rich Gulf of Guinea and to Sudan, including its Darfur region.[16]

Policy shifts towards UNPKO

In the 1970s China adopted a non-participation approach to UN peacekeeping operations. It did not vote on peacekeeping resolutions in the Security Council; neither did it pay its dues for the peacekeeping budget or contribute any personnel to the operations.[17] Its rationale was that China fought against UN forces in the Korean War (1950–53) and that, according to Maoist anti-imperialist revolutionary ideology, peacekeeping operations were plainly tools for the US or the USSR to intervene into the domestic affairs of weak states.[18] China's stance

Table 3.2 China's personnel contribution to UNPKO (as of November 2010)

	Military observers	Police	Troops	Total
MINURSO (Western Sahara)	11	–	–	11
MINUSTAH (Haiti)	–	28	–	28
MONUSCO (DRC)	16	–	218	234
UNAMID (Darfur, Sudan)	2	–	323	325
UNFIL (Lebanon)	–	–	344	344
UNMIL (Liberia)	1	18	564	583
UNMIS (Sudan)	12	22	444	478
UNMIT (Timor-Leste)	2	24	–	26
UNOCI (Côte d'Ivoire)	6	–	–	6
UNTSO (Middle East)	5	–	–	5
Total	55	92	1,893	2,040

Source: UN Department of Peacekeeping Operations, 'UN mission's summary detailed by country', 30 November 2010, www.un.org/en/peacekeeping/contributors/2010/nov10_3.pdf (accessed 19 December 2010).

began to modify in the early 1980s, as evidenced in its partial negation of the previous non-participation policy and in its application in September 1988 for membership of the UN Special Committee on Peacekeeping Operations which reviewed peacekeeping issues.[19]

However, since the end of the 1980s, UNPKO has transformed itself from performing a buffer function, to keeping apart belligerent groups along common borders, to dealing with new challenges ranging from state-building to humanitarian intervention and to peace enforcement. In addition to new principles laid down for UNPKO,[20] more operations have been established since 1988. In view of this normative change, China went to great lengths to defend the Cold War principles of peacekeeping operations, particularly about the necessity to secure the consent of the parties involved and the non-use of force. It was opposed to, or had serious reservations about, the peacekeeping operations formed in the 1990s under Chapter VII of the UN Charter based on the new principles, despite the fact that many operations posed little security threat to its territorial integrity. A typical example was its attitude towards the expanded mandate of the UN Protection Force in the former Yugoslavia initially established in 1992. China did not approve of the inclusion of the protection of the delivery of humanitarian relief and the setting up of safe havens within the sovereign state of the former Yugoslavia into the mandate. China also abstained from voting on UNSC Resolution 929 (1994) which authorized the establishment of Operation Turquoise led by France to tackle the civil war in Rwanda.[21]

China's long-standing principles are that internal conflicts must be solved by the people of the country in question and that external bodies, including the UN, should play 'only a supplementary and facilitating role in the promotion of a final settlement'.[22] China's adherence to the principle of national sovereignty also led it to cast a veto in January 1997 and in February 1999 on the extension of a peacekeeping operation in Guatemala and of the UN Preventive Development in Macedonia respectively, because the latter two countries had diplomatic relations with the Republic of China.[23] Taylor Fravel argues that this conservative stance stemmed from China's normative opposition to any attempt to erode the legitimacy of state sovereignty in international relations and the United Nations. The stance reflected China's uncertainty as to its position in the post-Cold War 'new world order' and about the rise of multilateral intervention into the internal affairs of other states when the US became the sole superpower.[24]

On the whole, UN peacekeeping since the 1990s has changed from a traditional understanding of keeping the peace once agreed on by all sides involved to a more intrusive and interventionist approach. China was initially reluctant to go along with this change because of its strict adherence to the supremacy of state sovereignty and the non-intervention principle. Its behaviour in the area of UNPKO in the 1990s demonstrated that although China was formally a player in global security governance, its commitment and participation were modest. Holding a Cold War mentality, it showed indifference to the subtle changes in the nature of post-Cold War international conflicts which did not often emanate from inter-state military confrontations. Without offering any feasible alternatives other than calls for 'peaceful settlement' of the disputes, it was not active in making and taking collective action to safeguard or establish international peace and security.[25]

However, since the turn of the new millennium, China has shown increased flexibility towards the hitherto sacrosanct principle of state sovereignty and its involvement in the UNPKO has subsequently been growing.[26] More remarkably, it joined the UN Standby Arrangements System (UNSAS) in January 2002.[27]

A turning point in China's changing attitude was the 2000 Report of the Panel on United Nations Peace Operations, otherwise known as Brahimi Report (named after Lakhdar Brahimi of Algeria, chairman of the Panel), commissioned by the UN Secretary-General Kofi Annan to review the UNPKO.[28] According to Stefan Stähle, the Report made four recommendations which were agreeable to the Chinese:[29]

1. Peacekeepers should be specifically mandated to use force to defend themselves, their freedom of movement, their mission and civilians under imminent threat of attack.
2. The United Nations should not mandate a mission before it has the resources available to fulfil it, which means in fact that pivotal states can be deployed first, to be followed by a UN force.
3. Better consultation should be established between the UNSC and the troop-contributing countries.
4. The United Nations should pursue a multidimensional approach in peace-building as an integral part of UNPKO, including the disarmament, demobilization and reintegration of former combatants, training of police forces, supervision of elections, and the strengthening of the rule of law and the protection of human rights.

Following the release of the Report, China called for greater participation by developing countries in the running of the UN Department of Peacekeeping Operations. Shen Guofang, then China's representative to the UN, said in November 2001 that 'special attention should be paid to the concerns of countries that are underrepresented in some departments' and 'what the Secretariat has done is far from enough and we hope it can do a better job in the days yet to come.'[30] China lobbied hard at the UN to appoint more Chinese officials in senior positions in the institution.[31] It also welcomed the recommendation that cooperation between the Security Council and the peacekeeping contributors be strengthened. By contributing more personnel to peacekeeping operations, China expects to be given more room to articulate its views about the operations, enhancing its capacity to set the agenda of the crucial functions and activities of the UN.[32]

Several factors have helped to modify China's attitude towards UNPKO. First and foremost, with growing national power, China can afford to allocate more resources – human and financial – to peacekeeping operations, and concomitantly wants to have a greater say in UNPKO.[33] Second, China desires to demonstrate to the outside world that it is a 'responsible great power', especially since the Asian financial crisis of 1997–98.[34] It wants to utilize its participation in UNPKO to assure other major powers as well as its neighbouring countries of its goodwill. Concern for its international reputation was a principal reason why China pressed Sudan into accepting the deployment of a hybrid UN–African Union peacekeeping force in Darfur.[35] Third, feeling uneasy about American 'hegemony', China desires to strengthen the United Nations, especially since the NATO unilateral intervention in the Kosovo conflict. Fourth, China can make use of the opportunity to train its military and police forces abroad. Finally, China has altered its interpretation of the legitimacy and efficacy of peacekeeping operations, and to a certain extent the changing nature of UN peacekeeping has helped to accommodate China's principles. China shares security interests with the rest of the world in fighting international terrorism arising from failed states.[36] These sets of changes are mutually interactive. China has been more accommodating to the use of small-scale force to protect civilians, to defend peacekeepers, and to maintain the freedom of the scope of peacekeeping activities.

It is often said that China is motivated by its quest for scarce natural resources in sub-Saharan Africa to increase its presence in the continent. While there is an element of truth that China's corporate interests in the Democratic Republic of Congo (copper and cobalt) and Sudan (oil) may motivate it to play an enhanced role in conflict resolution, there is no evidence to suggest that the Chinese central leadership has a grand strategic plan to use its peacekeeping operations to serve business interests. Instead the two sectors act quite independently of each other.[37] Rather, China believes that its friendship with both Islamic and Christian countries in Africa gives it an advantage over Western countries in mediating and resolving conflicts in the war-torn region.[38]

Also, the Taiwan factor now plays a reduced role in China's decisions as to whether or not to support individual UN peace operations. Despite its strict adherence to the norm of national sovereignty, China was alarmed by the adverse effect on its international image of its veto on the extension of the peace missions in Guatemala and Macedonia. After China's disapproval of sending UN military observers to Guatemala, Mexico and other countries threatened to put forward the same plan to the General Assembly, which would likely embarrass China in front of all member states. With regard to Macedonia, many Security Council members expressed their regret at China's veto, arguing that the withdrawal of the UN force could destabilize the Balkans. All the Security Council members other than China lent their support to the mission, although Russia abstained. China's handling of the establishment of a peace mission in Haiti in April 2004 was, in contrast, more flexible than in the Guatemala and Macedonia cases. Not only did it vote in favour of the establishment of the mission, it also dispatched police to it. It was the first time China sent peacekeeping forces to a country with which it had no diplomatic relations.[39]

Unlike Western countries, especially the US, China does not work through other international or regional organizations for peacekeeping purpose.[40]

Peace and security 47

Its participation in UNPKO has positively endorsed the UN's status as the principal authority for keeping international peace and security. China has, however, been loath to connect the notion of 'responsibility to protect' to peacekeeping and put it into practice. As discussed in Chapter 2 above, China's apprehension about the responsibility to protect was evident in the Position Paper on the United Nations Reforms released by the Chinese government in June 2005 (see Chapter 2, Note 34). China maintains that the reforms should primarily safeguard the principles of sovereign equality and non-interference in internal affairs. China's preferred state-centric approach has also undermined the effectiveness of its participation in international peacekeeping because of its reluctance to deal with non-state actors involved in the conflicts.[41]

A more active role in UNPKO notwithstanding, in the foreseeable future China is likely to refuse to send combat troops to peacekeeping operations. It is likely to endorse selectively the establishment of – but not necessarily participate in – peacekeeping operations under Chapter VII, contingent principally on having obtained the prior consent of the host country and under the authorization of the Security Council.

Governance of nuclear weapons and proliferation

The governance of arms control, disarmament and non-proliferation largely falls into the hands of the West, the US in particular. This is especially the case since the breakdown of the Soviet Union. This area of global governance has recently witnessed a two-track development: one is a multilateral track; and the other is what can be regarded as a Western cartel. These two tracks are strongly linked. China has become a member of the former, that is, a member of various multilateral institutions that include as their members a vast number of states, both developed and developing. The most prominent institution in this regard is the International Atomic Energy Agency (IAEA). Within the second track are four major international conventions or treaties and four related institutions or regimes. The four major conventions and treaties are:

1   the Treaty on the Non-Proliferation of Nuclear Weapons (NPT), 1970;[42]
2   the Biological and Toxin Weapons Convention (BTWC), 1972;[43]
3   the Chemical Weapons Convention (CWC), 1992;[44]
4   the Comprehensive Nuclear-Test-Ban Treaty (CTBT), opened for signature in 1996, but not entered into force.[45]

Their five accompanying institutions or regimes are the following.

1   The Nuclear Suppliers Group (NSG), established in 1975 and with a membership of forty-six countries as of December 2010, aims to coordinate nuclear export policies to prevent non-nuclear weapon states from exploiting peaceful nuclear cooperation as a way to develop or obtain nuclear weapons.[46]

48 *Peace and security*

2   The Australia Group (AG), formed in 1985 as a voluntary, informal arrangement among forty countries plus the European Commission (as of December 2010), regulates exports that could contribute to chemical and biological weapons.[47]
3   The Wassenaar Arrangement (on Export Controls for Conventional Arms and Dual-Use Goods and Technologies), which entered into force in 1996 and has a membership of forty countries as of December 2010, seeks to enhance cooperation in preventing sales of conventional arms and sensitive dual-use products to countries or regions of concern.[48]
4   The Missile Technology Control Regime (MTCR), established in 1987 and grouping together thirty-four member countries as of December 2010, controls the spread of delivery systems of WMD.[49]
5   The Hague Code of Conduct against Ballistic Missile Proliferation (HCOC), introduced in 2002, aims to prevent and control the proliferation of ballistic missiles capable of delivering WMD. As of August 2010, 131 states subscribed to it.[50]

None of these five accompanying institutions is based on any international arms-control treaties. Instead, they were established by Western powers.

China and non-proliferation regimes

To what extent does China support and comply with the prevailing norms and regimes about non-proliferation? How does China take on, strengthen and fulfil its nuclear and missile non-proliferation commitments?

As well documented elsewhere,[51] in the Mao period China argued that all sovereign states possessed the right to develop nuclear weapons. It expedited its nuclear weapon programme in the wake of the Sino-Soviet rift in the late 1950s. Despite the declarations in the 1960s that even with nuclear weapons, China would not undertake any nuclear proliferation beyond its borders, it argued alongside non-aligned developing countries that arms-control treaties served the sinister purpose of consolidating the two superpowers' monopoly of nuclear weapons. China made an about-turn on non-proliferation regimes in the early 1980s. Signs of its increased engagement with the regimes began to emerge in 1980 when it entered the Conference on Disarmament, which was founded the year before. Following that, China joined the IAEA in January 1984, thereby accepting to subject its civilian nuclear facilities to an external institution's oversight;[52] agreed to abide by the then guidelines of MTCR in February 1992; acceded to the NPT in March of the same year; signed the CWC in January 1993 and ratified it in April 1997; signed the CTBT in September 1996 (still subject to ratification by the National People's Congress as of late 2010);[53] became a member of the Zangger Committee, an institution on nuclear export control, in October 1997; and finally joined the NSG in May 2004.[54] However, there are gaps in China's participation.

China rejected an American invitation offered in May 1997 to join the AG. Despite that, in 2004 China began dialogues with both the AG and the

Wassenaar Arrangement, and the latter held outreach activities with China in 2008.[55] China applied in 2004 for MTCR membership, but the plenary session held in Seoul in October 'failed to reach a consensus' on Beijing's bid, and the plenary session held in Madrid in September 2005 decided not to take up the question of inviting China to join the group.[56] The US National Security Council under the presidency of Bill Clinton proposed in March 1998 that the US support China's membership in the MTCR in return for China's exercise of effective controls over its missile exports. Nevertheless, there have been concerns in the US that China's membership in the MTCR would undermine US national interests by exempting China from certain sanctions, giving it access to intelligence, allowing it to obstruct the normal decision-making process and relaxing missile-related export controls to China.[57] China's road to acceding to the Wassenaar Arrangement is more complicated. According to Wang Jun of China's Southwest Jiaotong University in Chengdu, applicant countries have to abide by the control lists established by the Zanggcr Committee, NSG, AG, MTCR, NPT, BTWC and CWC. In addition, they are required to submit reports on arms transfers to the United Nations Register of Conventional Arms (UNROCA). China had not submitted its reports to UNROCA between 1998 and 2006 in protest over US reports that revealed its arms sale to Taiwan. China began to resume the submission in 2007. But together with Russia and the US, China is reluctant or unable to reveal information on sales of small arms and light weapons (SALW) to UNROCA.[58] What are the main points of contention in China's engagement with the various non-proliferation regimes?

China has accused the US of applying a double standard in non-proliferation. On the one hand, the US acquiesces in the possession of nuclear weapons by Israel and India. On the other, it imposes sanctions on Iran, North Korea and Pakistan. In addition, the focus of the US, China argues, is on how to prevent the horizontal spread of nuclear weapons without considering the need for nuclear disarmament (i.e. an end to the vertical proliferation of nuclear weapons).[59] That partly explains why China has been lukewarm about reining in nuclear and missile proliferation to Pakistan and Iran. China was suspected of assisting Pakistan and Iran in developing their nuclear and chemical weapons and ballistic missiles. For Pakistan, the most typical case was the report in 1996 of a transfer of unsafeguarded ring magnets from the China Nuclear Energy Industry Corporation (CNEIC), a subsidiary of China National Nuclear Corporation. The two latest controversial transactions were a Sino-Pakistani contract to build a nuclear power reactor in Chashma, Pakistan, known as Chashma-2, in May 2004, just before the NSG was to decide on China's membership application, and the agreement in 2010 to provide Pakistan with two new nuclear reactors.[60] Critics have been suspicious about whether China had prior knowledge of, or even was involved in, the clandestine network of nuclear trade set up by Abdul Qadeer Khan, the noted Pakistani nuclear scientist. Khan's transfers of nuclear materials involved Iran, Libya and North Korea.

China was allegedly involved in assisting Iran's uranium enrichment programme. CNEIC was reported to be planning to sell Tehran a facility that could convert uranium ore into uranium hexafluoride gas, which could be further enriched to weapon-grade material. In addressing America's concerns, China promised in October 1997, just prior to a Jiang–Bush summit in Washington, that it would halt all future nuclear cooperation with Iran and cancel the sale of two power reactors and the uranium hexafluoride plant. But US intelligence reports continued pointing out that some Chinese 'entities' did not fully comply with the high-level commitment. Questions remain as to whether China has indirectly assisted North Korea's embryonic nuclear weapons programme through Pakistan or whether China has had knowledge about nuclear deals between Pakistan and North Korea.[61] Obviously China's assistance to Pakistan forms part of its strategy to balance India, its arch-rival. The triangular relations among China, India and the US over nuclear proliferation therefore deserve a closer look.

No first use, FMCT, PAROS, CTBT and PSI

China put forward in January 1994 a draft international treaty on no first use of nuclear weapons against each other to the other four nuclear weapon states. But negotiations on the treaty have never started. What China has achieved so far are that both China and Russia pledged in September 1994 no first use and detargeting of their nuclear weapons against each other and that China and the US reached an agreement in June 1998 not to target their nuclear weapons against each other. The five nuclear weapon states declared in April 2000 that their nuclear weapons would not target any state.[62]

China suffered a setback in initiating negotiations on a Fissile Material Cut-off Treaty (FMCT) and the Prevention of an Arms Race in Outer Space (PAROS).[63] In 1998 all the five permanent members of the UNSC (P5, in short) favoured opening negotiations on FMCT. China, in particular, called for setting up an ad hoc committee at the Committee on Disarmament (CD) to negotiate the FMCT. The P5 states reached a consensus that the treaty would only ban the *future* production of fissile material for weapon purposes without affecting their use of the *existing* stocks of the material. It was in China's interest to have such an international treaty because it would set limits on India's nuclear weapons development. However, China began to turn its back on this proactive approach in 1999 when the Clinton administration took steps to expand the American National Missile Defence system and the US Congress was promoting an increase in arms sales, including missile defence, to Taiwan. In the CD, China proposed that an ad hoc committee be immediately established to negotiate a treaty on the prevention of an arms race in outer space. In response to US opposition to the start of formal negotiations on outer space in the CD, China's strategy had been to link the FMCT negotiations to those for PAROS. China adopted a more hard-line stance in the wake of the announcement in December 2001 of US withdrawal from the Treaty on the Limitation of Anti-Ballistic Missile Systems (ABM Treaty), signed by the US and the USSR in May 1972.[64] But it received a rebuff from the US, and the US–China impasse lasted four years until 2003 when China delinked the two issues. But China (and Russia) reiterated that the FMCT negotiations had to be accompanied by the establishment of a body to discuss – if not to negotiate – PAROS. The US, however, did not pay heed to this request. Other obstacles to the opening of negotiations on FMCT included two demands from non-aligned states (G21): that FMCT should deal not only with non-proliferation but also with disarmament and that the scope of the treaty should cover existing stocks of fissile material. China accepted the first demand but opposed the second.[65] The US put forward in May 2006 a draft FMCT treaty which did not enjoy widespread support by CD member states because it did not have any verification provisions.[66] In an alleged attempt to press for a negotiation with the US of the outer space treaty, China launched a secret anti-satellite (ASAT) missile test in January 2007. The ambassadors of South Africa, Sri Lanka, Spain, Sweden, Switzerland and Syria (known as the P6), who served as presidents of the CD in 2007, put forward in March 2007 a draft proposal calling for the start of negotiations on the FMCT while allowing the contentious issues of the scope of the treaty and the verification regime to be resolved in the negotiation process. But this proposal was opposed by China, Iran and Pakistan. China insisted that a formal verification regime must be in place.[67] The years of deadlock ultimately ended in June 2009 when CD member states agreed unanimously to first negotiate the FMCT, and to enter into 'substantive discussions' on nuclear disarmament, the PAROS, and security assurances to non-nuclear-weapon states by nuclear-weapon states.[68] China's commitment to non-proliferation of WMD is contingent to a large extent on US arms sales to Taiwan and on the progress of the deployment of US missile defence systems in East Asia. Some bargaining power notwithstanding, China has limited ability to set the agenda of arms-control negotiations in the CD.

China also refuses to ratify the CTBT and to join the Proliferation Security Initiative (PSI). According to Alastair Iain Johnston, the US played little role in pressurizing or persuading China into signing up to the CTBT in September 1996. Playing a pivotal role in China's decision was displeasure from non-nuclear developing states about its nuclear test in May 1995, which was undertaken merely two days after the conclusion of the NPT review and extension conference. The imperative to portray itself as a 'responsible great power' spurred China to decide to join the treaty. After conducting eleven nuclear test explosions between 1990 and 1996, China first declared a moratorium on nuclear testing in July 1996 and acceded to the treaty two months later.[69] However, following the bombing of China's embassy in Belgrade by NATO in May 1999 and the US Senate's disapproval of US accession to the treaty five months later, China expressed reservation about ratification by its legislature, the National People's Congress.[70]

As a US counter-terrorism measure, the Proliferation Security Initiative was announced by George W. Bush in May 2003 to track and interdict suspected shipments of WMD in international waters. Strongly influenced by the *Yinhe* incident in 1993, which has been perceived in China as a prime case of bullying by the 'hegemonic' power, China asserts that military interception is 'beyond the limits of international law'.[71] On the one hand, China's sensitivity about any diminution of national sovereignty accounts for its stiff opposition to the imposition of sanctions as a means of fighting proliferation; on the other, China has a tacit agreement that it will cooperate with the US in countering illicit transfers of nuclear weapons.[72]

In sum, the factors that affect China's cooperation with non-proliferation regimes include:

- fluctuations in US–China relations;
- the external strategic environment, including instances of US unilateralism since 2001, in particular the US plan for missile defence shields and PSI;
- reciprocal compliance by other nuclear weapon states;
- sensitivity about possible diminution of sovereignty, and hence China's opposition to the imposition of sanctions as a means of combating proliferation;
- acceptance or internalization of non-proliferation norms: a deepened understanding of the dangers of proliferation;
- concern about its international reputation as China wants to demonstrate its peaceful and law-abiding intentions.

All in all, China's road from detachment from the nuclear non-proliferation regime to an active engagement with it is fraught with difficulties, as it has to weigh up different considerations and to strike a proper balance between its conflicting interests.

China and the North Korean nuclear crisis

North Korea (officially known as the Democratic People's Republic of Korea or DPRK) provides a critical case to test China's role in global security governance. What has China's evolving attitude been towards North Korea's attempts to acquire nuclear weapons since April 2003 when the latter withdrew from the NPT? How does China participate in international collective action to maintain an effective international non-proliferation regime and how far does it contribute to managing an imminent threat to non-proliferation emanating *outside* China?

The Six-Party Talks, involving the two Koreas, China, Japan, Russia and the US, can theoretically be assumed to be a security regime, for its role in defining both norms for the behaviour of the participating states and ways to observe, implement and verify those norms. Initially the Talks were not a preferred approach of the Americans. As Charles Pritchard, US special envoy for negotiations with North Korea in the first term of the George W. Bush administration (until August 2003), said, 'The original rationale for holding six-party talks was negative, not positive.'[73] As the Bush administration was loath to deal bilaterally with the 'rogue' Kim Jong-il regime, the US opted for a multilateral approach and 'outsourced' the management of North Korea's suspected nuclear weapons programme to China.[74] But Pyongyang was adamantly opposed to multilateral talks and instead demanded direct discussions with the US.[75] North Korea also rejected China's mediation in the crisis, warning Beijing in 2003 that 'You'd better mind your own business. If you would want to get involved in the matter, please ask the United States to provide security guarantees to DPRK.'[76] China had once wished to observe the issue from a distance. In February 2003 Colin Powell, then US Secretary of State, made a suggestion to China that it hold the multilateral talks. Meeting initial resistance from North Korea about the talks, both the US and China eventually reached an agreement with North Korea about holding trilateral discussions in April 2003, with China becoming the sole channel for communications between the US and North Korea.[77] However, the trilateral talks collapsed after the first round in the month when North Korean negotiators walked away because the US delegation was not allowed to meet its North Korean counterpart.[78] When China tried in July of the same year to convene the second round of the tripartite talks, the US insisted that discussion should be expanded to five parties including both Japan and South Korea.[79] Initially Beijing was hesitant about launching multilateral talks that would include both Japan and Russia for fear that its influence over the Korean Peninsula would diminish.[80] But North Korea made a counter-proposal that Six-Party Talks be held, so as to claim 'authorship' of the process.[81] China has since August 2003 assumed the role of convenor and host of the Six-Party Talks aimed at resolving the crisis by diplomatic means.[82] Though accepting the multilateral framework, Pyongyang insisted that bilateral negotiations between Washington and the DPRK take place during the multilateral talks, and China was well aware of this request. In the second half of 2009 North Korea went further to coax the Obama administration into direct bilateral discussions and the latter was open to this possibility provided that the former returned to the Six-Party Talks.[83] However, US–DPRK relations deteriorated seriously after the alleged sinking of the *Cheonan*, a South Korean naval vessel, by a North Korean torpedo and the artillery shelling of the South Korean island Yeonpyeong by North Korean armed force in March and November of 2010 respectively.[84] Has China played a constructive role in the multilateral talks in reining in Pyongyang's nuclear ambitions? Has China brought about any collective solution and action to alleviate a common security problem?

As seen from the results of the Six-Party Talks so far, in spite of a formal commitment to a nuclear-weapons-free Korean Peninsula by all parties, a Joint Statement of September 2005 and an Action Plan of February 2007 for the implementation of the Joint Statement, little progress has been made on various fronts and apparent diplomatic breakthroughs have been short-lived.[85] North Korea has neither dismantled its nuclear weapons programme nor returned to either the NPT or IAEA safeguards; it instead staged two tests of nuclear device in October 2006 and May 2009; US–North Korea relations have not been normalized; economic and humanitarian assistance to Pyongyang has been limited and intermittent; and the US offer of security guarantees to North Korea lacks any concrete form other than verbal assurance that the US will not invade North Korea. In short, the process of denuclearization is in limbo.

In explaining why there has been limited improvement in the regional security governance in Northeast Asia, we focus on examining China's stance and role in the crisis. In general, China is in favour of denuclearization of the Korean Peninsula, opposing North Korea's nuclear weapons ambitions, a goal shared by the US, South Korea, Japan and Russia. It, however, frets about any US unilateral push to initiate regime change or even collapse in North Korea, which would likely spur a massive influx of refugees across a 1,400-km frontier into northeast China, inundating one of China's economic heartlands, spreading democracy into China from Northeast Asia, and extending US influence up to its border. With regard to the Korean Peninsula, China's *first* priority is not to denuclearize North Korea but to prevent a war in the region and the collapse of the North Korean regime. Some Chinese diplomats were not convinced that North Korea possessed nuclear deterrent power whereas others believed that the country would not abandon its nuclear weapons. What has worried China much is a 'nuclear domino' theory by which Japan would seek nuclear weapons capability on the pretext that North Korea has gone nuclear.[86] Beijing has therefore made it be known that the use of force to resolve the crisis is unacceptable to it and has called on Washington to provide Pyongyang with security guarantees and economic aid.[87] It is in Beijing's interest to bring Pyongyang to the negotiating table and to resolve the crisis through negotiation. However, the matter is somewhat complicated by the fact that since the Korean War China has connected the Taiwan issue with North Korean affairs.[88] Although there are debates as to whether the level of Chinese pressure on North Korea is dependent on the US posture on Taiwan, the last thing China wants is a war in Korea, which would give Taiwan an opportunity to go independent.

A change in Chinese senior leadership in 2002–2004 also mattered. Jiang Zemin highlighted the imperative of improved Sino-US relations for enhancing regional peace and security. China was consequently focused on restraining North Korea's nuclear ambitions and capabilities. China–North Korea relations were tense in the 1990s when Jiang was the leader of the CCP, particularly after China decided to normalize relations with South Korea in September 1992, despite opposition from the North.[89] In contrast, Hu Jintao, who assumed the post of CCP General Secretary in November 2002 and began to consolidate power after becoming the chairman of the CCP Central Military Commission in November 2004, is sympathetic towards North Korea's growing sense of strategic vulnerability and is in favour of engaging the country. He reportedly devises four guiding principles for engagement: more summit meetings, closer economic ties, more regional cooperation, and enhanced coordination in dealing with common adversaries.[90] Between October 2003 and February 2005 at least three senior Chinese leaders and officials – Wu Bangguo, Li Changchun and Wang Jiarui – visited North Korea with promises of economic assistance.[91] During his visit to Pyongyang in October 2005, Hu persuaded the reclusive state to undertake economic reforms, invited Kim to pay a visit to southern China, including Shenzhen, and reportedly offered economic aid worth $2–3 billion.[92] Sino-North Korean commercial trade has since burgeoned.[93] Instead of taking collective action with the other four countries in the Six-Party Talks,[94] China promotes its own approach to stabilizing the crisis, emphasizing political stability and economic reforms in North Korea and regionalism, while continuing efforts to bring Pyongyang to the talks.[95]

But it seems that the Chinese pro-reform approach did not succeed in reducing the powerful influence of 'military-first' politics (sŏngun chŏngch'i) in North Korea. On 4 July, American Independence Day, of 2006, North Korea test-fired a total of seven intercontinental, medium- and short-range missiles into the Sea of Japan. The UNSC passed in the same month Resolution 1695 banning any transfer of missile and missile-related items to North Korea.[96] According to Shi Yinhong of Renmin University, the missile test was provoked by the imposition in September 2005, just four days before the announcement of the Joint Statement, of financial sanctions on North Korea by the US Treasury over alleged North Korean money laundering and currency counterfeiting activities through North Korean accounts in the Banco Delta Asia (BDA), a bank in Macao, a Chinese special administrative region, which Kim Jong-nam, Kim Jong-il's eldest son, is believed to visit often.[97] Beijing's ties with Pyongyang deteriorated sharply as a result of the latter's displeasure at Beijing's cooperation – if not conspiracy – with Washington in freezing the suspected accounts and the passage of the Security Council resolution. Having learned from the US invasion of Iraq in 2003 of the critical importance of a nuclear deterrent force to safeguarding its national security,[98] North Korea carried out its first – though not fully successful – underground nuclear test explosion, showing a total disregard for Chinese warnings, in October 2006, three months after the missile test.[99] After the test, North Korea wanted to return to the negotiating table as a nuclear weapon state, but it was adamantly opposed by other parties.[100] China rebuked North Korea for the nuclear explosion and threatened to cut off its oil supplies.[101] In defiance of external pressure, North Korea carried out in April 2009 a test of its long-range Taepodong-2 ballistic missile, and its second underground nuclear test a month later. This was followed by UNSC Resolution 1874 in June 2009, calling on UN member states to inspect and destroy suspected cargo travelling to or from North Korea. This demand is in line with the PSI, which China has not joined. In response, North Korea vowed to commence a uranium enrichment programme.[102]

Despite claims inside China that North Korea's behaviour has harmed Chinese interests and international reputation,[103] Beijing holds little sway over either North Korea or the US. Hence it maintains that the two countries must make compromises with each other in order to make progress in resolving the issue of denuclearization. In short, the crisis is largely a bilateral issue between Pyongyang and Washington.[104] The failure to preserve the status quo, as evidenced by the two North Korean nuclear tests, brings into question the usefulness of the Six-Party Talks. It is plain that an agreement to end the nuclear crisis peacefully must be made between North Korea and the US. The multilateral institutional framework is more a mechanism for endorsing the bilateral deal than a way to make, observe, implement and verify the pact, as a security regime is assumed to do. This cannot be shown more clearly than in the fact that until the bilateral negotiations between North Korea and the US in Berlin in January 2007, the stalemate in the Six-Party Talks since September 2005 had been unable to be resolved. Following on from the breakthrough in the Berlin talks, the six parties issued the aforementioned Action Plan of February 2007. A consequence of the breakthrough is, however, that since 2007 China has been marginalized in the Six-Party Talks.[105]

China is also unwilling to take collective action with the other four to deal with North Korea. According to Resolution 1718, adopted by the UNSC in October 2006 to address North Korea's first nuclear test, member states were 'called upon to take ... cooperative action including through inspection of cargo to and from [North Korea]'.[106] But, as mentioned above, China was expressly opposed to formal participation in the US-led PSI. As a continuation of Hu Jintao's pro-engagement approach, a flurry of high-level visits to Pyongyang by Chinese leaders began to take place after the February 2007 agreement on the Action Plan. Liu Yunshan, a Politburo member and the director of the CCP Propaganda Department, paid a visit to the North in October 2007, followed by Wang Jiarui, head of the CCP International Liaison Department, in February 2008. In particular, when Xi Jinping, Vice-President of the PRC, and Wang Jiarui were in Pyongyang in June 2008 and January 2009 respectively, they offered the host a huge amount of economic aid.[107] During Chinese Premier Wen Jiabao's visit to Pyongyang in early October 2009, the first such visit since 1991, the two countries signed a series of agreements whereby China promised aid to and economic cooperation with North Korea.[108] South Korean Foreign Minister Yu Myung-hwan promptly responded to the agreements by asking if the Chinese aid violated UNSC sanctions against the reclusive regime. Both Japan and South Korea have vowed to enforce the sanctions until North Korea abandons its nuclear weapons programme. The US State Department also said that it was awaiting more detailed information from the Chinese government.[109] A US Congressional Research Service report points out that China has not fully complied with the UN economic sanctions against North Korea. Beijing has continued selling sanctioned luxury goods to Pyongyang after the passage of UNSC Resolutions 1718 (2006) and 1874 (2009). The shipments amounted to $100–160 million in 2008 and about $132 million in 2009.[110]

At the end of 2010 the US accused China of 'enabling' North Korea to start a uranium enrichment programme and to launch deadly artillery attacks on South Korea in November of that year, and urged China to deliver a strong message to North Korea that 'its provocations are unacceptable'.[111] Pyongyang showed a visiting U.S. nuclear scientist in November a secretly built facility to enrich uranium.[112] Leaked US State Department cables, released in the same month, showed that the US had expressed continuing concern about China's reluctance to crack down on the transfer of missile components from North Korea to Iran via Beijing as well as about Chinese firms' complicity in supplying North Korea with precursors of chemical weapons. The same cables also demonstrated that China was often kept in the dark about the North Korean nuclear programme and that South Korea grumbled about China's pro-status quo attitude towards a nuclear North Korea.[113] US President Barack Obama told Hu Jintao in December 2010 that if Beijing failed to constrain North Korea, the US would redeploy its military forces in East Asia. Obama reiterated this warning when Hu was in Washington one month later. Until then China had not expressed concern over the uranium enrichment programme.[114] Obama also highlighted that the rise of China is partly attributable to the public goods of regional peace and security the US provides in Asia, hinting that China has been a free-rider in the past decades.[115]

If China is unable or reluctant to elicit collective action, can it facilitate the search for a common solution between North Korea and the US?[116] What is the role of China in the likely bilateral discussions between the two foes? Since neither the George W. Bush administration nor North Korea genuinely favoured or believed in multilateralism in handling the nuclear crisis, China became more active in promoting bilateral negotiations between North Korea and the US as soon as Bush stepped down from the presidency in 2009, probably with the acquiescence of the Obama administration. China is fearful of losing its influence over its neighbour. During his aforementioned visit to the North in January 2009, Wang Jiarui presented Kim Jong-il with a letter from Hu Jintao, inviting him to visit China.[117] Shortly after the former US President Bill Clinton's visit to Pyongyang in August 2009 to seek the release of two American journalists stranded in North Korea, during which he allegedly asked Kim Jong-il to invite Stephen Bosworth, US special representative for North Korea policy, to visit North Korea,[118] Hu Jintao dispatched Dai Bingguo, a Chinese state councillor and his special envoy, to North Korea in the following month. When meeting Dai, Kim Jong-il said the North is 'willing to resolve the [denuclearization] problems through *bilateral* and multilateral talks' (emphasis added).[119] Dai's encounter with Kim was immediately followed by Chinese Premier Wen Jiabao's visit in October. Kim Jong-il went further to stipulate that his country would return to the Six-Party Talks 'depending on the outcome' of its prior bilateral discussions with the US. There could be other forms of multilateral discussions, as Pyongyang said that it 'is willing to attend multilateral talks, *including* the six-party talks, based on the progress in the DPRK–U.S. talks' (emphasis added).[120] Shortly after returning to Beijing, Wen discussed the issue with Japan's then Prime Minister, Yukio Hatoyama, and South Korean President, Lee Myung-bak, and called for the US to engage in a 'conscientious and constructive' dialogue with North Korea.[121] After Barack Obama's Asian tour in November 2009, he dispatched Steven Bosworth to Pyongyang in December. Bosworth was in talks with Kang Sok-ju, the first vice foreign minister and a close aide to Kim Jong-il, and Kim Gye-gwan, the leader of the North Korean delegation to the Six-Party Talks. After the bilateral meetings, both the US and North Korea announced that they shared an understanding of the need to reconvene the Six-Party Talks and implement the 2005 agreement to dismantle the North Korean nuclear weapons programme, without mentioning the two-phase Action Plan concluded in 2007 or agreeing on when and how Pyongyang would return to the negotiating table.[122] However, North Korea's belligerent behaviour towards the South in 2010 terminated the momentum towards reconciliation between the two countries. Unwilling to get involved in the inter-Korea conflicts, China's response was tepid, refusing to publicly criticize North Korea's provocations.[123]

Since its inception in August 2003, the Six-Party Talks have largely failed to take collective action using carrots and sticks to manipulate the cost-benefit calculus of the Kim Jong-il regime and entice it into compliance with the norms and rules of denuclearization. The Talks have failed to socialize North Korea into believing in the moral legitimacy of the accepted norms of behaviour, for several reasons. First, the US has been loath to play the leadership role in coordinating other actors because of its inherent refusal to negotiate directly with North Korea. Second, as the only capable actor, the US has been hesitant about providing the best-shot public goods to neutralize the imminent threat from the North by mounting a direct attack on it. This is partly due to opposition from both China and South Korea and partly due to the aftermath of the Iraq War of 2003, which paradoxically socialized Kim Jong-il into believing in the utility of possessing nuclear weapons. Third, multilateralism is not China's (and North Korea's) preferred approach to conflict management. China's overriding concerns for regional stability and for maintaining its influence over North Korea make it unwilling to impose punitive sanctions on the North. While both the US and China agree that joint action is required to confront the threat emanating from North Korea's nuclearization, they do not want to bear the burden of punishing the culprit. The consequence is simply multilateral inaction.[124]

Conclusion

This chapter has covered China's activities in the UN in general and UNPKO in particular, as well as in non-proliferation regimes. Having abandoned its revolutionary ideology, China's phenomenal economic growth in the last three decades and its greater exposure to international diplomacy have helped to increase the confidence of Chinese leaders in reaching out to deal with global issues of peace and security. China has gradually moved from being self-centred to being a participatory, integral part of the world.

However, China's non-proliferation practice has been largely reactive and timid. The country has yet to accede to many regimes in the area, although circumstances are changing as China becomes more aware of the global concern and practice involved, and as an increasing number of countries, both developing and developed, expect China to play a greater role in this and other areas as a responsible member of the international community.

While China strives to make its voice heard in the international community, its capacity to create international norms, principles and rules in the realm of peace and security is fairly small. This chapter has amply demonstrated that China has had limited capacity to promote *collective* action or deliver *collective* solutions to get rid of the dangers posed by the possible use of nuclear weapons, a potential arms race in outer space, and nuclear proliferation in Northeast Asia.

4 Finance and trade

The world shrinks as China grows.

Ted C. Fishman, 2005[1]

To maintain the basic stability of the Chinese renminbi on a reasonable and balanced level ... is not only in the interests of China but also the world economy.

Wen Jiabao, 2009[2]

China's ability to play a significant role in global governance depends very much on its continuing economic growth. The fact that China's behaviour in foreign affairs now attracts so much international attention is due mainly to its phenomenal economic rise and its increasing mesh with the global economy (see Table 4.1). Barely significant in the global economic system when Mao died in 1976, the country has now become the second largest economy and trading nation after the United States.[3] In 2005, China's GDP soared past France's, Britain's, and Italy's.[4] By mid-2008 it had surpassed Germany's.[5] Despite the global economic downturn in 2007–2009, China's economy has the enviable record of growing 9.1 per cent in 2009 and 10.3 per cent in 2010.[6] Because of the world financial crisis, China's trade in 2009 was expected to fall and its trade surplus to drop to $185 billion in 2009 from the record $295.5 billion in 2008,[7] but it overtook Germany to become the world's biggest exporter during the year.[8]

China has an extraordinarily high savings ratio, currently standing at about 40 per cent of the average income, which means that it has the potential to sustain its growth momentum for an extended period of time based on its domestic and neighbouring markets.[9] Not only has China become the most attractive destination for foreign direct investment, surpassing the US in 2002 by attracting $50 billion that year,[10] but it has also started in recent years to invest abroad, as a way to secure natural resources to fuel its industries. Its overseas direct investment (ODI) grew from $3 billion in 2003 to $19 billion in 2007,[11] and then jumped to $56 billion in 2008, only to fall to $45 billion in 2009.[12] Its cumulative outward investment at the end of 2008 amounted to $183.97 billion, of which $131.32 billion (71.38 per cent) was in Asia, especially Hong Kong. The second largest destination is Latin America ($32.24 billion or 17.52 per cent),

Table 4.1 Selected indicators of China's economic growth, 1978–2008

	1978	1991	2001	2008	Average annual growth rate (%)		
					1978–91	1991–2001	2001–2008
GDP (billion yuan)	364.52	2,178.15	10,965.52	30,067.00	14.74	17.54	15.50
GDP ($ billion)	148.18	379.50	1,324.50	4,327.00	7.50	13.32	18.42
Exports and Imports ($ billion)	20.64	135.70	509.65	25,632.60	15.59	14.15	75.01
Foreign exchange reserves ($ million)	167.00	21,712.00	212,165.00	1,946,030.00	45.42	25.60	37.25
Actually utilized foreign investment ($ million)	1,029.20*	4,666.00	49,672.00	95,253.00	16.32*	26.68	9.75

Sources: *Zhongguo tongji nianjian* (*China Statistical Yearbook*) (Beijing: Zhongguo tongji chubanshe) (China Statistics Press), 2009, pp. 37, 724, 745; World Bank, 'GDP (current US$)', http://data.worldbank.org/indicator/NY.GDP.MKTP.CD (accessed 3 May 2010).

Notes
1 The Chinese Communist Party decided to launch economic reforms in December 1978; Deng Xiaoping paid a visit to southern China in January and February 1992 to revive the reform momentum stalled in the wake of the Tiananmen incident of 1989; and China joined the WTO in December 2001;
2 Actually utilized foreign investment excludes foreign loans.
* This is the annual average of the total foreign investment of $5,146 million in 1979–84 and the annual growth rate is assumed to be between 1981 and 1991.

concentrating in the Cayman Islands and Virgin Islands, with Africa trailing behind ($7.8 billion or 4.24 per cent). Although ODI only forms a very small part of the Chinese economy (about 1.3 per cent), it has become a pivotal economic force, sustaining and, in some cases, lifting the economic growth of some countries. This chapter argues that this global economic shift is leading China to demand a greater say in global economic governance, as a way to protect and promote its national interests and as a way for the country to be seen to be acting responsibly in world affairs.

To assess China's evolving role in global economic governance, this chapter addresses three interrelated issues. The first concerns China's admission to such major multilateral financial institutions as the World Bank, the IMF, and the WTO. Does China's membership of these organizations herald its coming of age as one of the major economic powers in the world? If China's integration into global economic governance is beneficial to the country's economic development, does it mean that China has a vested interest in strengthening the role of these international financial institutions rather than challenging them from within or promoting another platform to govern global economic affairs? Second, can China use its growing wealth as a means to enhance its influence (and that of the developing world) in international financial institutions vis-à-vis the US? Finally, and more importantly, will China provide the global public good of international financial stability by taking the lead in rectifying the imbalanced global trade? In this respect, many economists and policy-makers in the West argue that the Chinese government should take on the global responsibility of allowing an appreciation of the Chinese renminbi against the US dollar in order to reduce its current account surplus.[13]

To address these three sets of issues, this chapter first scrutinizes China's increasingly active participation in such major international organizations as the Bretton Woods system, the G7, and the G20. The purpose is to gauge China's involvement in the governance of finance and trade in the world and its potential role in the global economic order. The second part of this chapter looks at the imbalance in global trade and China's response to the demand by the West that it appreciate its currency. At issue is whether or not China is willing to provide some form of public goods to sustain and promote global economic governance.

China and the global economic order

Since the early 1980s, China has adopted an increasingly cooperative approach to working with major international institutions. In addition to the United Nations, the Bretton Woods system (the World Bank, the IMF, and the GATT/WTO) has featured prominently in China's engagement with global economic governance. Apart from joining these principal organizations, China has also played an increasing role in the G20 in the wake of the global economic crisis of 2007–2009 and has begun to initiate a large number of free trade agreements bilaterally and regionally.

The World Bank

China joined the World Bank in 1980. Since then it has benefited from the Bank's cheap loans for developing many projects in the initial phase of its opening up to the outside world, subsequent to the adoption of a reform policy in 1978. In addition, the Bank has transferred much technology and information to China to help it build up its structural capacity. In 2007/2008 the Bank extended $1.5134 billion to support ten development projects in the country, making a total of $43.688 billion covering 296 projects.[14]

As China's economy continues to grow, it has resumed substantial bilateral aid to some African countries, seen by many observers as a way to secure valuable raw materials. In so doing, China has been accused by the West of turning a blind eye to some flagrant human rights violations committed by certain African governments while the World Bank faces questions as to why it continues to offer loans to China.[15] The American President of the World Bank, Robert Zoellick, called on China to coordinate its support to the world's poor with the rest of the international community. China's increasing bilateral assistance extended to poor developing countries around the world with little or no strings attached has begun to pose a challenge to the work of the World Bank since these recipient countries can now turn to an alternative source of help without having to abide by the stringent conditions of good governance set by multilateral financial institutions. These conditions include transparency, corruption eradication, the opening up of the market to foreign investments, the adoption of democratic practice and neo-liberal economic measures. At the end of 2007 China said it would start donating to the World Bank's main concessional loans fund for poor countries by joining the Bank's International Development Association. Some observers see this move as an indication of Beijing's increasing readiness to engage with the Bank.[16]

The appointment in June 2008 of Justin Yifu Lin, a Chinese economist, to the post of Chief Economist of the World Bank signified a subtle shift in the Bank's free market orthodoxy, as Lin, though trained at Chicago, is a firm believer in the important role of government in the economy.[17] Lin's appointment is seen by some observers as a welcome move which was long overdue. It was welcomed by many African countries which see the development recipe handed down by the Bank – the Washington Consensus – as ill-conceived and condescending. Such an appointment is long overdue as China's place in the world economy has grown dramatically during the past three decades. Robert Zoellick's remark in 2005, while serving as US Deputy Secretary of State, that a rising China should become a 'responsible stakeholder' in the global system, is a telling indicator.[18] Lin's appointment, though attracting high publicity, is a small change which may not mean a lot to the way the World Bank conducts its business (as usual). His appointment may pave the way for China's increasing identification with and involvement in the Bank's activities.

According to a UN University report on global governance, a very large proportion of the voting rights in the World Bank is vested in a very small number of industrialized countries, the principal shareholders, in terms of their paid-up capital.[19] As of November 2010 China holds 2.85 per cent of the Bank's shares and 2.78 per cent of its voting power, ranking sixth among the 187 member states of the Bank.[20] In contrast, a large number of developing countries and transitional economies are vested with a small proportion of the voting rights even though they are the principal stakeholders as interest payments from them provide a large part of the Bank's income.

Subsequent to the financial crisis of 2007–2009, some major economies in the West invited China to increase its financial contribution to the Bank so as to enhance its liquidity and hence its capacity to lend. China seems willing to do so, on the condition that its contribution is reflected in increased voting power and a greater say in the Bank's decision-making process. At the World Bank spring meeting in April 2010, the 187 member states agreed to boost the capital of the International Bank for Reconstruction and Development (one of the four major institutions under the umbrella organization World Bank) by $86.2 billion, including $5.1 billion paid-up capital, in return for increasing the voting rights of developing and transition countries at the expense of Japan and some European countries. China's voting power has subsequently risen to 4.42 per cent, ranking third after the US (15.85 per cent) and Japan (6.84 per cent) (see Figure 4.1). Taken together, the voting rights of Germany, France and the UK have been reduced to 11.5 per cent from 13.08 per cent. But the Group of 24 developing countries wished to have a system that would automatically revise voting rights in accordance with changes in the relative economic powers of the developed and developing worlds. Yan Fang of China University of Political Science and Law even argues that 'China should at least be above Japan in terms of voting

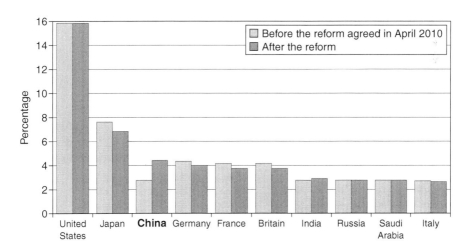

Figure 4.1 China's growing power in the World Bank (source: adapted from Xin Zhiming, 'China gains more say in World Bank', *China Daily*, www.chinadaily.com.cn/business/2010-04/27/content_9778666.htm (accessed 23 December 2010)).

64 *Finance and trade*

power', given that China is poised to overtake Japan to become the second-largest economy on the globe in 2010.[21] The next quota review, however, will not be due until 2015.

The IMF

The IMF was set up with the principal aim of stabilizing the financial situation of the world so as to provide an environment conducive to economic development and trade growth. In the Fund, the influence of members (as consolidated in terms of their voting rights when the Fund was first formed) is in proportion to their financial contributions. This arrangement is coming under increasing challenge as the IMF now faces two related problems: one is the maintenance of the financial stability of the world in terms of exchange rate adjustments; the other, closely connected with the first, is the pressure put on the IMF to reform its power structure as a result of the economic power shift in the world.

The year 2006 saw the beginning of some fundamental changes to the way the IMF is run. The annual meeting of the IMF coincided roughly with the visit of Chinese President Hu Jintao to Washington, DC in April 2006. High on the agenda of the Sino-US meeting between Hu and Bush was the Bush administration's pressure on China to appreciate its currency so as to ease the rising trade deficit that the US had with China, some $200 billion in 2005 (see Table 4.2 below). Exchange-rate issues have been the core business of the IMF. In the past, decisions affecting exchange rate issues had been taken by the G8 countries, but in 2006 the IMF found it necessary to move away from this elite group to wider multilateral deliberation within the IMF. This was because of the rise of emerging economies, with China in the lead. They demand that decisions on exchange rates reflect their input. This reform within the IMF is a consequence of the change in the global balance of economic power. Rodrigo Rato,[22] then Managing Director of the IMF, said publicly in April 2006 that global economic imbalances should focus not only on exchange rate appreciation to boost consumption in emerging Asia but also on fiscal adjustments in the US to stimulate private saving and structural reforms that could promote demand and improve productivity in Europe and Japan. He called for 'coordinated action by the major players in the global economy'.[23] The IMF, not surprisingly following the US line, suggests that China should appreciate its currency, notwithstanding the fact that it had revalued the yuan *nominally* by 2.1 per cent in July 2005. By the end of 2007 the Chinese currency had gained 11.9 per cent against the US dollar since mid-2005,[24] and 21 per cent by September 2008.[25] China was reluctant to take further steps to revalue after 2008. (This exchange rate issue will be discussed again later.)

Another major issue that reflects the shift in the global economic balance is the pressure exerted on the IMF to change its governance and voting structure. The credibility of the IMF has suffered as a result of the advice it gave Asian countries during the financial crises of 1997–98, which led to further economic downturn in some cases. The broadening of the IMF decision-making structure is seen to be necessary in order to accommodate a wider representation of countries beyond the world's rich so as to rescue the institution's reputation and enhance its legitimacy. Also, the role of the IMF as a lender of last resort has been eroded, as middle-income countries have built up large reserves and as private investment flows have become increasingly prevalent. In the case of China, as of December 2010, the country has amassed $2.85 trillion in foreign reserves,[26] enabling it to exercise increasing influence over the global financial situation. This means the IMF should extend the share in its decision-making power held by emerging economies. At present the IMF is only accountable to finance ministries and central bankers of major economies and not to governments in general, much less to the peoples of the world. Many of its decisions often seem to be shrouded in secrecy.[27]

Inviting China to make a bigger contribution to the Fund would mean rearranging the weight of voting rights and diminishing the influence wielded by some European members, a change which will not be easy to achieve. As in the World Bank, a realignment of voting shares in the IMF was initiated in 2008.[28] At the G20 meeting of finance ministers and central bank governors in the UK in March 2009, China, together with Brazil, Russia and India (the BRIC countries), argued that the voting rights of emerging economies in the IMF should be increased.[29] At the equivalent G20 meeting in October 2010, the participating countries agreed to transfer more than 6 per cent of IMF quota shares, which determine (but are not the same as) the voting power of individual countries, to dynamic 'emerging market and developing countries' and to under-represented countries from over-represented countries, without affecting the voting share of the least developed countries. It was agreed that on the Executive Board, which comprises twenty-four directors and the nanaging director and which conducts the daily operations of the IMF, European nations would give up two seats to emerging market and developing countries. Brazil and India, which at present share seats with other countries, are expected to have their own seats on the new Board. A pledge was also made to elect all members of the Board.[30] Until the proposed reforms become effective by the end of 2012, which will require approval by many members' legislatures, the quota shares and voting rights of these four BRIC countries are 9.76 per cent and 9.6 per cent respectively, amounting only to 57 per cent of those the US holds (see Figure 4.2). The IMF has declared that following the quota shift, the ten largest members of the Fund will be the United States, Japan, the BRIC countries, and the four largest European countries (France, Germany, Italy and the UK), with China becoming the third-largest shareholder after the US and Japan. It is likely that the shares of Canada (2.93 per cent and 2.88 per cent), the Netherlands (2.37 per cent and 2.34 per cent) and Belgium (2.12 per cent and 2.08 per cent) will be reduced accordingly.[31] While China is prepared to make a greater monetary contribution to both institutions in order to boost its share holding, and in turn its voting rights and its say in them, it also calls for continuing reforms in the selection of the managing director of the IMF, which by convention is always an European, and in the

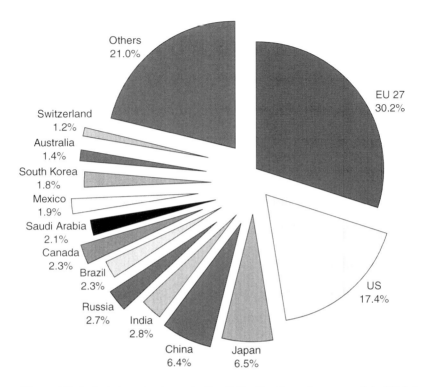

Figure 4.2 Projected quota shares in the IMF after the reform agreed in 2010 (source: International Monetary Fund, 'Quota and voting shares before and after implementation of reforms agreed in 2008 and 2010', www.imf.org/external/np/sec/pr/2011/pdfs/quota_tbl.pdf (accessed 19 April 2011)).

calculation and readjustment of the quota with the aim of stemming 'any country [read the US] from accessing to a veto power'.[32]

At the G20 summit held in London in April 2009, heads of governments agreed to take a number of steps to tackle the global financial crisis. These included a pledge to jointly fund a $1 trillion package to provide the necessary credit to stimulate the global economy, to boost world trade, and to discourage excessive risk-taking by investment banks. The IMF was to receive an additional $500 billion for lending to countries in financial difficulties. Japan and the EU each pledged to contribute $100 billion to the IMF, and China pledged $40 billion.[33] Although China's pledge was apparently made without any condition regarding its IMF quota, its pressure on the institution to reform was palpable.[34] But later China decided to buy up to $50 billion of IMF bonds rather than making a financial contribution to it. In addition, some of the bonds were to be denominated in special drawing rights (SDRs), the IMF's artificial reserve currency, which in turn would be based on a basket of currencies including the renminbi. This decision probably had both domestic and international political purposes. Externally, it would help China to bargain for stronger representation in the IMF before the latter completes the review by January 2011; internally, it could address domestic opposition to using Chinese foreign exchange reserves to finance an international financial institution.[35] China also calls for its currency to be included in the basket of SDRs. In response France, as the chair of the G20 in 2011, advised the IMF to study the widening of the basket from the euro, the yen, British sterling and the dollar to include the renminbi. This change has received backing from the US.[36]

The G20 meeting of finance ministers and central bank governors in 2010 to double the IMF's quotas to SDR 476.8 billion (or $755.7 billion at the prevailing exchange rates). But it was uncertain who would foot the bill. At the same meeting, the IMF was given a new mandate to examine the 'persistently large imbalances' and to play the role of arbitrator or mediator in trade and currency disputes.[37] However, China wants the IMF to go further, and 'enhance its surveillance over countries issuing major reserve currencies' so as to promote financial stability, obviously targeting the US once again. China's demand for change was at its most explicit when Hu Jintao said before his state visit to the US in January 2011 that '[t]he current international currency system is the product of the past'.[38]

In order to gain more say in the organization, China also had its eye on a senior position at the IMF. Zhu Min was groomed by the Chinese government in 2009 for an IMF appointment when he was transferred from the Bank of China to the People's Bank of China (the former is a state-owned bank while the latter is China's central bank). China initially hoped that Zhu would become a deputy managing director at the IMF, taking over the place occupied by a Japanese official as Asia's most senior staff member in the institution. But eventually Zhu was only given the position of special adviser to the Managing Director of the IMF, Dominique Strauss-Kahn. Succeeding Strauss-Khan as the new chief, Christine Lagarde in July 2011 nominated Zhu to be one of the four deputy managing directors of the IMF.[39]

The WTO

The WTO remains the only major organization within the Bretton Woods system in which China can play a more significant role, given the country's growing trading power and the organization's more egalitarian power structure. Traditionally China has been, and is likely to continue to be, shut out of major decisions made in the World Bank and the IMF. However, the WTO is more egalitarian than they are in terms of membership rights: member countries strive to reach decision by general consensus; voting, if called for, is based on one country, one vote. Small countries can take big trading partners to arbitration through the Dispute Settlement Mechanism if they feel that they are being unfairly treated by the big powers. China claimed in its *China's Peaceful Development Road*, a white paper released by the State Council in December 2005, that the country's economic growth in the period 2000–2004 contributed 13 per cent to world economic growth.[40] China has made substantial contributions towards freeing up world trade. For example, it cut its tariffs by 72 per cent from 1992 to 2005, compared with a 36 per cent decrease by developed countries and a 24 per cent drop by developing countries.[41] For agricultural produce, its tariffs stood at 15.3 per cent at the end of 2005, dropping from 54 per cent when it joined the WTO in December 2001, compared with a world average of 62 per cent.[42] The country has enacted or revised over 1,000 laws and regulations to help bring its trading system into compliance with WTO rules.[43] Arguably no positive global trading change during peacetime has been felt as acutely as China's entry into the world's trading system through the WTO. But how active a part will China play in shaping the global trading order?

Because of the WTO's power structure, which is different from that of the World Bank and the IMF, there is no need and indeed no room for China to work towards increasing its voting power in the organization. China is certainly becoming an increasingly big trading nation, but it remains to be seen whether the country can add value to the WTO system by making policy contributions to render the organization more effective. China's behaviour during global trade discussions (trade rounds) should provide valuable clues.

The Doha Round of trade negotiations and the WTO trade ministerial meeting held in Hong Kong in December 2005 provided a good opportunity for China to showcase its policy contributions to global trade. But observers were largely dismissive of China's performance at the time, saying that the country played a very low-key role in the negotiations and shied away from the limelight. Chinese officials, however, rebutted such observations, saying that China had done a lot of work to prepare the Hong Kong meeting, mostly quietly and behind the scenes, and had participated in nearly all the 'green room' meetings,[44] where most of the important discussions take place among twenty to thirty major players.

Chinese officials put forward several reasons for China's reticence in these negotiations. First, China is still new to multilateral trade diplomacy; it is still in the process of feeling its way through the intricacies of the WTO working procedures.[45] In addition, limited resources are available to Chinese trade officials to carry out their work. The WTO section of China's Commerce Ministry is not only responsible for implementing the numerous changes needed to comply with WTO rules, but also has to deal with an increasing number of cases of developing bilateral and regional free trade areas. China concluded its first bilateral free trade agreement with Chile in November 2005. Since then it has negotiated with a further twenty-seven countries, including Australia, New Zealand and the ten members of the Association of Southeast Asian Nations (ASEAN), in a bid to reach bilateral or regional free trade agreements (FTA).[46] All these and other trade projects place a severe strain on Beijing's trade bureaucracy. China signed its FTA with Pakistan on 24 November 2006. Its FTA with New Zealand entered into force on 1 October 2008, and that with ASEAN on 1 January 2010. According to a 2009 China report by PriceWaterhouseCoopers, as of 2009 nine FTAs had been implemented, six were under negotiation and three were receiving feasibility studies.[47]

Second, China is at present in a somewhat awkward situation: while it is a developing country with a self-imposed moral and ideological obligation to help other developing countries, especially in dealing with agricultural issues arising from farm subsidies in rich countries, it is also a fast emerging industrial country, and so is motivated to protect the interests of industrialized countries in seeing further tariff cuts for industrial goods.[48] This dual identity means that China has to tread a fine line between the developed (mainly industrial) and the developing (mainly agricultural) world.

Third, Chinese reticence is not unique. While China seems to be absent from the great debates on trade issues, other big Asian trading nations like Japan and South Korea and groups like ASEAN have also kept a low profile, despite their growing participation in world trade.[49] So reticence seems to be an Asian-wide cultural feature and perhaps a non-Western rather than a uniquely Chinese characteristic, something more to do with the global economic system and political power structure and stages of development as well as social and ideological traditions rather than simply a lack of interest in contributing globally or a desire to free-ride.

From G7 to G20

Beyond the Bretton Woods institutions, another sign of a global power shift is the enlargement of the G7 industrialized countries to form a wider discussion group. According to Yu Yongding, a research fellow at the Chinese Academy of Social Sciences, China is interested in the work of G7, but feels that the influence of the Group should not overshadow that of the UN or the Bretton Woods institutions.[50] Apparently China prefers to deal with international affairs in a wider multilateral setting than a small group of rich countries headed by the US.

To China, the G20 is more representative than the G7 in global affairs. Established through the initiative of the G7 in 1999, the G20 brings together heads of government, finance ministers and central bank governors of the G7 and of emerging economies (Argentina, Australia, Brazil, China, India, Indonesia, South Korea, Mexico, Russia, Saudi Arabia, South Africa and Turkey) and the EU. The managing director of the IMF and the president of the World Bank, plus the chairs of the International Monetary and Financial Committee of the IMF and of the Development Committee of the World Bank, also participate in G20 meetings on an exofficio basis.[51] Thus the G20 represents a diverse group of four Asian countries, three Islamic, three Latin American and one leading African country, in addition to those in the West.

In October 2005 the finance ministers and central bank governors from the G20 held their annual meeting in Xianghe in Hebei province of China. They released two interesting statements: one relating to development and the other to the reform of the Bretton Woods institutions. On development, the statement recognized that 'each country has primary responsibility for its own economic and social development, and for this reason it is important to respect the development of country-owned strategies.'[52] On the reform of the Bretton Woods institutions, the statement said that the world economy had changed, and so both the quota system and the representation system within these institutions should be adjusted to mirror such changes.[53]

Signs of collective or global economic governance, in which the global economy is governed not by a single hegemon but by a group of powerful actors collectively, emerged at the G20 summit held in South Korea in October 2010. Initially the US proposed that the surplus or deficit of each country's current account balance should not exceed 4 per cent of its GDP by 2015. Failing to overcome opposition from Germany, Russia and Italy, in addition to China, the US could agree with other G20 members only to pledge to curb 'excessive' imbalances.[54]

In the rather scant Chinese scholarly analyses of the grouping, the general view seems to be that the G20 is more representative than the G7. However, the latter is still very much in control of the former.[55] The G20 offers both challenges to and opportunities for China, although there appear to be more opportunities than risks.[56] The G20 can be seen as a successful co-optation by the G7, allowing a wider scope of representation in global economic governance while still giving the rich countries a major say in important global economic matters. The increasing involvement of the emerging economies in the G20 and their increasing bargaining power mean that some structural changes are likely to affect the way major decisions to handle the global economy are taken.

China's potential leadership role in the Third World as well as the G20 has met with some difficulties as its economic competitiveness has made other countries like India and Brazil reluctant to open up their markets. As discussed in detail below, China's refusal to appreciate its currency has caused uproar in some export-oriented developing countries, as its economies competitiveness tends to stifle the growth of their labour-intensive industries. However, China's economic growth has also stimulated their economies by increasing two-way trade and Chinese investments. For example, some of the initial fears that ASEAN countries had of China's economic rise have proved to be unfounded precisely because of mutual benefits as a result of increasing economic integration. They all thrive in an economic chain of production. Asian economies have accumulated over $2,000 billion of foreign reserves,[57] partly because of all round economic growth and partly because of lessons learned from the Asian financial crisis of 1997–98 (to be discussed below). Countries in the region have been working towards further economic integration.[58]

Sino-US trade relations

Table 4.2 shows that the US began to register a trade deficit with China in 1985, amounting to a tiny $6 million. It surged to $1.66 billion the following year, soared past $10 billion in 1990, reached $50 billion in 1997, and went through the benchmark of $100 billion in 2002 and of $200 billion in 2005. Despite the shrinking of international trade during the global economic downturn, in 2009 the US trade deficit with China stood at $226.8 billion.

Table 4.2 US trade with China ($ million)

	Exports	Imports	Balance
1985	3,856	3,862	−6
1986	3,106	4,771	−1,665
1990	4,806	15,237	−10,431
1997	12,862	62,558	−49,696
2000	16,185	100,018	−83,833
2001	19,182	102,278	−83,096
2002	22,128	125,193	−103,065
2003	28,368	152,436	−124,068
2004	34,428	196,682	−162,254
2005	41,192	243,470	−202,278
2006	53,673	287,774	−234,101
2007	62,937	321,443	−258,506
2008	69,733	337,773	−268,040
2009	69,576	296,402	−226,826

Source: US Census Bureau, Foreign Trade Division, 'Trade in goods (imports, exports, and trade balance) with China', www.census.gov/foreign-trade/balance/c5700.html (accessed 24 April 2010).

The ballooning trade surplus with the US has led China to accumulate sizeable foreign exchange reserves (see Table 4.1 above). About two-thirds of China's reserves are held in US Treasury securities and other dollar assets.[59] With this apparently favourable creditor position, will China be able to turn its financial advantage into geopolitical advantage vis-à-vis the US? While admitting that China can exercise some influence over how interest rate and exchange rate adjustments are made in Washington, DC, in a preliminary analysis Daniel Drezner does not think so, for several reasons.[60] First, the US still holds a very strong economic position in the world. Although it runs fiscal deficits and trade deficits with the rest of the world, its debt ratio is estimated to be only 37 per cent of its total GDP, a ratio far smaller than those of either Japan or many of the Eurozone economies.[61] Second, the US can gain easy access to other sources of finance, through either the private sector or the public sector. So its position is relatively stable and assured. Third, America's strong position in the international financial architecture means that it can afford to resist Chinese leverage with relative ease. It is also in a strong position to take retaliatory action to deter potential threats to its position. In this respect, there is no safe haven for trade surpluses other than US dollar-denominated securities and assets. The fact that the US, backed up by its huge domestic consumer market, can put pressure on China to appreciate its currency serves as a neat example to illustrate the two countries' relative economic positions.

China and global financial imbalances

Believed to be the most severe economic crisis since the Great Depression of the 1930s, the global financial crisis of 2007–2009 was triggered by the bursting of the housing bubble and the subprime mortgage crisis in the US. However, the build-up of the bubble is often attributed, among other factors, to China's huge trade surplus with the rest of the world, in particular the US. China's overall trade surplus soared to $102 billion in 2005 from merely $32 billion a year before.[62] The rise continued to $298 billion in 2008.[63] The bulk of China's total trade surplus derives from trade with the US, its largest trading partner, as shown in Table 4.2.

As a proportion of GDP, China's current account surplus reached its peak of 10.6 per cent in 2007 (Table 4.3). This global current account imbalance and the lopsided distribution of capital have created a huge demand for US assets as emerging economies, notably China, and commodity-producing states do not have comparable investment opportunities.[64] With growing foreign exchange reserves, China supplied funds to the US by purchasing US Treasury bonds. While the influx of foreign funds helped to depress US real interest rates after 2000, it motivated American households to invest in housing assets, generating a housing and building boom as well as increasing household debt relative to disposable income. Ever-increasing housing equity further encouraged private consumption. In view of the availability of cheap credit and the housing frenzy, banks not only lowered their lending standards but also transformed the traditional model in which they hold loans in their portfolios until these are fully refunded. To seek higher yields and to spread financial risks, they bundled the loans into mortgage-backed securities and sold them to institutional investors. The latter repackaged the securities into collateralized debt obligations (CDOs), and divided them into at least three 'tranches' or classes of risk.[65] The CDOs were then sold to dispersed investors with varying appetite for financial risk, including hedge funds and multinational banks, which in turn used them as

Table 4.3 Current account balances of selected countries (percentage of GDP)

	China	South Korea	Russia	Saudi Arabia	US
1985	−3.72	−0.82	N/A	−12.45	−2.97
1990	3.36	−0.76	N/A	−3.55	−1.37
1995	0.22	−1.68	1.76	−3.73	−1.54
1997	3.88	−1.62	−0.02	0.18	−1.70
1998	3.09	11.69	0.08	−9.01	−2.46
1999	1.95	5.51	12.57	0.26	−3.23
2000	1.71	2.30	18.04	7.60	−4.21
2001	1.31	1.59	11.07	5.11	−3.88
2002	2.44	0.94	8.44	6.30	−4.33
2003	2.80	1.86	8.23	13.07	−4.70
2004	3.55	3.90	10.07	20.74	−5.34
2005	7.13	1.77	11.07	28.54	−5.94
2006	9.34	0.57	9.56	27.78	−6.02
2007	10.64	0.56	5.98	24.31	−5.11
2008	9.64	−0.62	6.22	27.85	−4.65
2009	5.96	5.13	4.01	6.17	−2.68

Sources: IMF, International Financial Statistics Database; World Bank, 'GDP (current US$)', http://data.worldbank.org/indicator/NY.GDP.MKTP.CD (accessed 29 December 2010).

'assets' to borrow short-term funds.[66] (For some details about CDOs and the US housing market, see Appendix A.)

Some economists and former Treasury officials have argued that what lie at the root of the financial crisis are the global macroeconomic imbalances across major countries that started in 2004.[67] The first driver was the American expansionary or accommodative monetary policy after the bursting of the dotcom bubble in 2000 and the terrorist attacks of 11 September 2001. The US Federal Reserve argued that deflation was a real threat to the American economy. Other contributing factors were the rise of global oil and gas prices which generated surpluses for the oil-producing states in the Middle East and in Russia and Central Asian states; China's growing current account surplus and its exchange rate policy (Table 4.3); and financial innovation in the US.[68] A key to the rebalancing of the global economy, the argument goes, is for the Chinese government to allow the renminbi, the Chinese yuan, to appreciate in order to encourage domestic consumption in China as imports become less expensive, leading to a reduction of its trade surplus.

Like Japan and the newly industrializing economies in East Asia, China has relied on export-oriented industrialization to sustain high economic growth. Following the Asian financial crisis of 1997–98, it (and such newly industrializing countries in Asia as South Korea; see Table 4.3) began to accumulate foreign exchange reserves as a precautionary buffer against any future financial crisis, contributing to the growth of a global saving glut, as mentioned by Ben Bernanke, the Chairman of the Federal Reserve, in 2005.[69] To maintain an exchange rate that is favourable to its exports, the Chinese monetary authorities must intervene in the foreign exchange market by buying the current account surplus from the sellers, resulting in a growth of money supply in the Chinese economy. To offset or 'sterilize' the inflationary effects of the build-up of foreign exchange reserves on the domestic monetary base, the authorities have to issue domestic bonds to absorb the growing money supply *and* to invest the foreign exchange reserves they hold in dollar-denominated assets to offset the cost of redeeming the domestic bonds.[70] This has generated a flow of financial capital from China into the US, fuelling the availability of cheap credit and eventually the financial crisis.

The above account shows that the allegedly undervalued Chinese currency is believed to be one of the culprits of the global economic recession. It is argued that there should be greater international coordination and cooperation among national macroeconomic policies, including exchange rate policies, due to their impacts on global financial stability. The G20 meeting in Pittsburgh in September 2009 made references to it. Furthermore, the argument goes, China has room to and should take the lead in addressing the global imbalances. Coupled with the fact that Chinese private consumption is below 40 per cent of GDP, about half that of the US, its huge domestic market, which does not exist in other surplus countries, allows China to reorient its growth towards boosting domestic demand and to reduce its holding of foreign reserves.[71] It is argued that the renminbi has become increasing undervalued since 2002. The scale of appreciation after July 2005 was so moderate that the degree of undervaluation by December 2008 was up to 19 per cent.[72] There have been renewed calls from the US and other major developing countries such as India and Brazil for a large and rapid revaluation of the renminbi.[73]

How does China perceive the macroeconomic problem of global imbalances and its managed exchange rate regime? Does it concede that its holding of US Treasury bonds helped to fuel the housing bubble? In his writing on 'Global imbalances and China' in October 2006, Yu Yongding, then Director of the Institute of World Economics and Politics at the Chinese Academy of Social Sciences, did not directly address the issues. However, he pointed out that while China provided the US with $80 billion a year by selling inexpensive goods to American consumers and buying US. Treasury bonds which helped keep US interest rates at a low level, 'China's good deed fail[ed] to achieve much appreciation from the Americans'.[74] He offered an answer to this puzzle by citing Phillip L. Swagel of the American Enterprise Institute, a conservative think-tank that had a close relationship with the George W. Bush administration. Swagel wrote in 2005 that,

> if there is short-term pain ... for the United States, why pressure China to revalue? U.S. policymakers surely understand the downsides of a yuan revaluation for the U.S. economy. And they certainly must realize that their very public campaign only makes it more difficult for the Chinese to take action ... the push for a Chinese exchange-rate change ... is instead a devious attempt to prolong the enormous benefits the United States derives at China's expense from the fixed dollar–yuan exchange rate.[75]

In other words, Yu believed that Washington, at least the George W. Bush administration, did not genuinely want an appreciation of the renminbi.[76] He recognized, however, that China's current account surplus would not be sustainable because the Chinese central bank's sale of low-yield bonds to commercial banks would undermine the latter's profitability and the surplus was earned at substantial cost. This included the dominance of lower-end processing output in China's exports and the associated environmental damage, and the policy dilemma the central bank was facing as to whether it should hold US assets or not. So Yu concluded that China would need to reduce the surplus. A possible measure would be to increase government expenditures on public goods in social security, healthcare and education, and in infrastructure. For example, during the global economic downturn, the Chinese government announced that it would invest 850 billion yuan ($125 billion) in improving the medical and healthcare system in the country.[77] This initiative is not only a response to the increasing public dissatisfaction with poor quality healthcare (see Chapter 7 below), but also part of an economic stimulus package designed to alleviate the negative impact of the global financial crisis on the country. With the aim of reducing medical costs for individuals, the government hopes that citizens will be willing to spend more on consumer goods. The export-led development policy should also be adjusted. However, he was sceptical of the positive effect of the revaluation of the renminbi on balancing the current account. He warned that not only did the Plaza Accord of September 1985, which started the appreciation of the Japanese yen against the US dollar, fail to reduce the US trade deficit with Japan but also plunged the Japanese economy into recession in the decade of the 1990s.[78] Zhou Xiaochuan, the Governor of the People's Bank of China, refutes the claim that the global imbalances were the dominant cause of the financial crisis by stressing that both macro- and micro-factors were at work.[79] This view was echoed by Jiang Yaoping, Chinese Vice-Minister for Commerce, who argues that the exchange rate is not the major cause of China's trade surplus with the US. Rather, the processing trade, from which global companies including American companies benefit, is the chief reason and so renminbi appreciation will not contribute much to addressing the trade imbalance.[80]

One may conclude that China is highly sceptical about the role played by its accumulation of current account surplus in the crisis. A large-scale appreciation of the renminbi is very unlikely, partly due to the rise of nationalism in the country.[81] The Chinese leadership refuses to be seen as bowing to external pressure. China will adjust the value of its currency at its own pace. A leading Chinese banker, travelling with Chinese Vice-President Xi Jinping's party to New Zealand in June 2010, reportedly indicated that China's currency could appreciate by about 20 per cent in the next five years.[82] On 19 June 2010 the People's Bank of China indicated that it would adopt a flexible approach towards the appreciation of the yuan, a piece of news widely reported in the global media (see Figure 4.3). However, American officials were not satisfied with the slow pace of the appreciation, as the value of yuan had risen only 1.9 per cent by 1 October 2010.[83]

In view of the fact that some countries, including China, refused to allow the value of their currencies to rise in order to boost export competitiveness, Brazil's Finance Minister, Guido Mantega, warned in September 2010 before G20 meetings in South Korea, 'We're in the midst of an international currency war, a general weakening of currency'. When Mantega made his remarks, the Brazilian real had risen by 25 per cent since the beginning of 2009. He also pointed out the difficulty in undertaking collective action among various economic powers to address economic downturn.[84] The threat of competitive devaluations reminds us of the danger of the 'beggar-thy-neighbour' policies that many countries in the West pursued in the late 1920s and 1930s, which were believed to be a major cause of the Great Depression in the 1930s.

As the holder of the rotating presidency of the G20 in 2011, France proposed at a February 2011 meeting of G20 finance ministers and central bank governors that certain economic indicators should be used to monitor global imbalances and avert economic crises in the future. Two sets of indicators were suggested to gauge imbalances within countries and between countries. The former comprised public deficit and debt, and private savings and debt, whereas the latter was composed of current account balance or trade balance, and foreign currency reserves or real exchange rates. China had little disagreement with other members over

76 *Finance and trade*

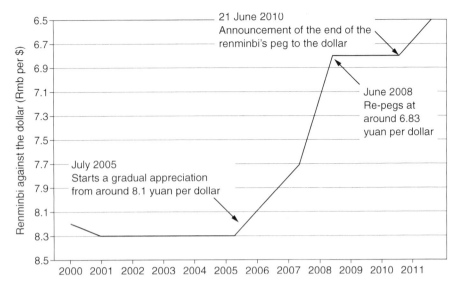

Figure 4.3 The appreciation of the yuan (sources: International Monetary Fund, *International Financial Statistics* (electronic version) (accessed 15 April 2011); Alan Beattie and Geoff Dyer, 'Sceptics await more policy shifts in China', *Financial Times*, 21 June 2010, www.ft.com/cms/s/0/1fb4390a-7d62–11df-a0f5–00144feabdc0.html (accessed 23 June 2010); Xinhua, 'China's yuan sets new high against U.S. dollar Friday', *Global Times*, 15 April 2011, http://business.globaltimes.cn/china-economy/2011–04/645015.html (accessed 15 April 2011)).

the internal indicators but was defiantly opposed to using current account balance, foreign currency reserves and real exchange rate as indicators. The ministers broke the deadlock and reached a compromise only after China made a concession on the exchange rate, allowing it to be taken into consideration, among other factors, in assessing whether a country's policies would lead to global imbalances. Although China won significant concessions on current account balance and foreign currency reserves, it was in effect isolated in the meeting, as not only industrialized countries but also other emerging economies did not side with it on the issue of the exchange rate.[85]

Nor has China initiated any practical measure to prevent a repeat of the crisis. Zhou Xiaochuan's proposal for using SDRs as the new global currency was not well received except by Russia.[86] A small shift of voting power in the IMF and World Bank from industrial countries to developing nations offers no immediate solution to the underlying causes of the global financial crisis. It is unlikely that the minor readjustment will improve the IMF's relations with the Asian developing countries from damage done in the wake of the Asian financial crisis.[87] Paradoxically, it was the US rather than China that forced a realignment of the quota shares and voting rights. The Executive Board of the IMF has only twenty members. The decision to enlarge it to twenty-four has to be renewed periodically. The US threatened in August 2010 not to vote in favour of the extension so as to force European nations to give up two seats on the Board. It is also said that the realignment has only symbolic significance because the Board makes decisions mainly by consensus instead of by voting.[88]

In addition, China has played a fairly marginal role in the formulation of the IMF's proposal for levying charges and taxes on financial institutions.[89] Rather, it relies more on domestic restructuring, for instance by improving its social safety net so as to encourage more spending and less saving, and on East Asian regional cooperation. Hu Jintao emphasized in the G20 summit held in Washington, DC, in November 2008 the need to promote regional financial cooperation and to enhance an Asian regional assistance funding mechanism. But Hu's proposal was not included in the statement of the summit. One month after the G20 meeting, China, Japan and South Korea held their first-ever regional summit to strengthen regional measures to counter global financial turmoil.[90] In short, it is open to dispute whether China is yet able or ready to offer any *global* public goods to stabilize the *global* finance and economy.

Conclusion

There is little doubt that China has benefited tremendously from its growing participation in the global economy. Its economic rise since its entry into the WTO in December 2001 has been phenomenal. So it is fair to assume that it is in its interest to lend support to the working of international financial institutions while looking for ways to augment its presence and decision-making power within them. There are, however, constraints on the conversion of China's financial power into political power vis-à-vis the US. While China's hunt for increased power in the Bretton Woods institutions has been moderately successful, its capacity for stabilizing the global economy is rather limited. It dismisses the claim that it should take on responsibility for rectifying the global imbalances.

Of the three financial institutions – the World Bank, the IMF and the WTO – the WTO is constitutionally and structurally more egalitarian, in the sense that member states are more equal in status and influence within the organization than is the case in the other two institutions. The decisions made in the World Bank and the IMF are controlled by the West, especially by the US, because of the weighted voting system and there is little that the developing world can do to change this power structure in a major way in the foreseeable future. China has a stronger position in the WTO than in the other two because of its rising trading power on the one hand and on the other its relatively weak position compared with developed countries in the World Bank and the IMF. The rise of China and other emerging economies like India, Brazil and South Africa may help to change the situation somewhat, but they are still relatively small in influence in comparison with the existing powers in the G7. There is no apparently strong leadership emerging in the developing world ready to take on the task of fundamentally altering the existing power structure. China is not in a position to take the lead because of its mild political will and its lack of experience, for cultural, historical and diplomatic reasons. Despite China's quest for increasing its say and sway in the Bretton Woods system, its policy contributions towards making the system more representative and stable are likely to be limited, for reasons deriving from the country itself and beyond.

In the end, in spite of an emerging collective governance, any major change in global economic governance depends very much on rich countries and big multilateral corporations, which are not surprisingly slow to respond to moves that are seen to be taking away their power and interests. Global economic governance seems to be a monopolistic game among the global rich and powerful; it is neither a representative nor a democratic game that extends to the developing world.

Samuel Kim of Columbia University has referred to China as a Group of One, meaning that it often acts unilaterally for its own interests with token respect for the rules and norms of international society. However, it is interesting to note that a UN University report on global governance points out implicitly that the US *is* a Group of One, acting unilaterally out of self-interest and paying scant attention at times to international rules and norms. In a way both countries are very jealous in guarding their sovereignty and independence, they seem to approach the unilateralism–multilateralism continuum from opposite ends. While the US shows signs of moving away from multilateralism towards greater unilateralism in general (with a slight reversion initiated under the Obama administration), China moves in the opposite direction, from isolation and self-help to gradually but guardedly embracing multilateralism. Both share some commonalities as a Group of One and intend to use international institutions to discipline and rein each other in, but adopt different approaches because of their different strategic interests and stages of development.

China has opted to work with the US in managing global affairs rather than to challenge American supremacy headon, a deliberate policy adopted by Deng Xiaoping which has largely been followed by his successors. Although China works unceasingly to enhance its power in global economic institutions, it does so within the existing system rather than outside of it. It strives to learn and adjust to outside constraints rather than to redesign or reconstruct the existing system, much less to overthrow it.

5 Human rights and humanitarian intervention

> Do not mistaken [sic] China, we are opposed to political confrontation, not because we are scared of it but because it does not bring about a culture of peace. Do not mistaken [sic] China, we are opposed to country-specific resolutions, not because we are afraid of them but because they do not contribute to promoting and protecting human rights. Whoever provokes confrontation, we will have to fight to the end.
>
> Sha Zukang, April 2003[1]

This chapter first discusses the role of the United Nations in establishing the standards and rules of human rights, starting from the adoption of the Universal Declaration of Human Rights (UDHR) in December 1948. It focuses on the UN Commission on Human Rights (UNCHR) (1947–2006) and its successor, UN Human Rights Council (UNHRC). They have played a key role in standard setting, drafting and preparing international human rights conventions and regimes, and promoting three 'generations' or 'dimensions' of human rights – civil and political rights; economic, social and cultural rights; and the collective rights of peoples.[2] Following a string of atrocities in the 1990s, humanitarian intervention was undertaken and a new concept of 'responsibility to protect' was advanced to protect human rights in conflict-torn societies. Consequently the UN Security Council has assumed an increasingly prominent role in dealing with human rights issues, as the linkages between human rights violations and threats to international peace and security have become clearer.

Second, the chapter examines China's role in the UNCHR/UNHRC, as well as the universal human rights regime. Emphasis will be placed on whether China promotes collective action to deal with human rights violations or whether it challenges the universalism of human rights. Attention will also be given to the weight China puts on state sovereignty relative to human rights, and on the first generation of rights relative to the second and third ones. Finally, the chapter assesses China's reaction to the new wave of interventionism based on the grounds of protecting human rights.

The evolution of human rights discourse: an overview

The UNCHR was created under the UN Economic and Social Council in accordance with Article 68 of the UN Charter. Following the 1945 UN Conference on International Organization in San Francisco, promotion of human rights was given more weight than their protection.[3] In the first two decades of its existence (1947–66), the UNCHR largely focused on setting and promoting human rights norms and practices instead of enforcing them. As Eleanor Roosevelt, the first chair, declared, the Universal Declaration of Human Rights was neither a treaty nor an international agreement, but 'a declaration of basic principles of human rights and freedoms ... to serve as a common standard of achievement for all peoples of all nations'.[4] This was largely because the then major powers – France, the United Kingdom, the US and the USSR – violated human rights standards to varying degrees.[5] Due to the US–Soviet confrontation in the Cold War, the initial vision of an international bill of human rights could not crystallize. The first two generations of human rights were respectively embodied in the International Covenant on Civil and Political Rights (ICCPR), adopted in December 1966 and put into force in March 1976, and the International Covenant on Economic, Social and Civil Rights (ICESCR), adopted in December 1966 and put into force in January 1976. Alongside the UDHR, they informally constitute the International Bill of Human Rights.[6]

Championed by developing states, the right to development, one of the most prominent third-generation rights, was adopted by the General Assembly in December 1986 in the form of the Declaration on the Right to Development.[7] The US was the only state that objected to it, with eight other countries abstaining from voting.[8] Two elements of it are controversial. First, according to Article 3 of the Declaration on the Right to Development, 'states have the primary responsibility for the creation of national and international conditions favourable to the realization of the right to development'; they 'have the duty to cooperate with each other in ensuring development and eliminating obstacles to development'; and they should 'promote a new international economic order based on sovereign equality, interdependence, mutual interest and cooperation among states'. The Declaration is associated with the attempt by the developing world in the 1970s to call for a new international economic order (NIEO). This focused on the structural inequalities between the North and the South and campaigned for debt relief, preferential access for trade and finance and transfer of resources from the North to the South. Second, the Declaration establishes the notion of the collective rights of a group, more than the sum of personal rights based on negative freedom. For some, therefore, the right to development is not a natural right, and hence not a human right.[9] Despite the adoption of the Declaration on the Right to Development, the right has yet to be codified in any legally binding international treaty or covenant.

The march of human rights continued, however, to the effect that discrimination on the grounds of race and sex were delegitimized by the UN adoption of the International Convention on the Elimination of All Forms of Racial

Discrimination (ICERD; 1966), the International Covenant on the Suppression and Punishment of the Crime of Apartheid (ICSPCA; 1973), and the Convention on the Elimination of All Forms of Discrimination against Women (CEDAW; 1979). Protection from torture, of the rights of children, migrant workers and disabled people and from enforced disappearance were codified in the Convention against Torture and Other Cruel, Inhuman or Degrading Treatment or Punishment (1984), the Convention on the Rights of the Child (CRC; 1989), the International Convention on the Protection of the Rights of All Migrant Workers and Members of their Families (1990), the Convention on the Rights of Persons with Disabilities (2006) and the International Convention for the Protection of All Persons from Enforced Disappearance (2006) (see Table 5.1). The normative human rights discourse was given a new impetus in 2005 when the UN World Summit endorsed the notion of 'responsibility to protect' which argues that state sovereignty implies a responsibility of states to protect their citizenry (as discussed in detail below).

The credibility of the United Nations as well as international society in addressing human rights abuses was called into question in the wake of a series of humanitarian catastrophes in the post-Cold War period, notably those in Somalia (1992–94), Rwanda (1994), Srebrenica (1995), Kosovo (1999) and East Timor (1999). After the humanitarian intervention by NATO in Kosovo, undertaken without authorization by the UN Security Council, the Canadian government sponsored the establishment of an independent International Commission on Intervention and State Sovereignty to examine the guiding principles of humanitarian intervention, in particular whether the international community has an obligation to remedy egregious human rights violations. In its report entitled *The Responsibility to Protect* (*R2P*), the Commission held that sovereignty implies responsibility and that the right to non-intervention is conditional and constrained. As a sovereign entity, every individual state has the primary responsibility to protect its citizens from life-threatening dangers. In joining the United Nations and signing its Charter, states have indicated their acceptance of this accompanying responsibility. However, if a state is unable or unwilling to fulfil its responsibility, then the international community of states has a residual or fallback responsibility to respond and the principle of non-intervention will yield to the international responsibility to protect.[10] This notion of R2P was adopted by Kofi Annan, the UN Secretary-General from 1997 to 2006, and after a watered-down compromise, by the United Nations General Assembly in its 2005 World Summit in September 2005.[11]

Institutional developments at the UN

As soon as the UNCHR and its Sub-Commission on Prevention of Discrimination and Protection of Minorities (known informally as the UN Sub-Commission on Human Rights until 1999, when it was formally renamed the Sub-Commission on the Promotion and Protection of Human Rights)[12] were endowed in June 1967 (in Resolution 1235) and May 1970 (in Resolution 1503) by

Table 5.1 Status of China's participation in major human rights instruments

	Date of adoption by the UN General Assembly	Date of signature by China	Date of ratification by China
Convention on the Prevention and Punishment of the Crime of Genocide	9 December 1948	20 July 1949 (by the Republic of China [ROC])	19 July 1951 (by the ROC) 18 April 1983 (by the People's Republic of China [PRC])
International Convention on the Elimination of All Forms of Racial Discrimination (ICERD)	21 December 1965	31 March 1966 (by the ROC)	10 December 1970 (by the ROC) 29 December 1981 (by the PRC)
International Covenant on Civil and Political Rights (ICCPR)	16 December 1966	5 October 1967 (by the ROC) 5 October 1998 (by the PRC)	
International Covenant on Economic, Social and Civil Rights (ICESCR)	16 December 1966	5 October 1967 (by ROC) 27 October 1997 (by the PRC)	27 March 2001
International Covenant on the Suppression and Punishment of the Crime of Apartheid (ICSPCA)	30 November 1973		18 April 1983 (accession)
Convention on the Elimination of All Forms of Discrimination against Women (CEDAW)	18 December 1979	17 July 1980	4 November 1980
Convention against Torture and Other Cruel, Inhuman or Degrading Treatment or Punishment (CAT)	10 December 1984	12 December 1986	4 October 1988
Convention on the Rights of the Child (CRC)	20 November 1989	29 August 1990	2 March 1992
International Convention on the Protection of the Rights of All Migrant Workers and Members of their Families (ICRMW)	18 December 1990		
Convention on the Rights of Persons with Disabilities (CRPD)	13 December 2006	30 March 2007	1 August 2008
International Convention for the Protection of All Persons from Enforced Disappearance (CPED)	20 December 2006		

Source: United Nations Treaty Collection Database, http://treaties.un.org/Pages/Treaties.aspx?id=4&subid=A&lang=en (accessed 18 September 2010).

ECOSOC with the authority to examine human rights abuses and enforce human rights practices,[13] states sought membership of the body not to enhance the human rights regime but to defend themselves from, or even block, other states' criticism, resulting in an erosion of its credibility.[14] The most widely cited occasions of embarrassment were the election of Libya to the chairmanship in 2003 and the inclusion of both Sudan and Zimbabwe into the Commission in 2005.[15] However, China counters that the credibility deficit of the UNCHR was due to the fact that the Western powers in the organization applied a double standard in dealing with human rights, with developing countries being disproportionately targeted by the resolutions while countries in the West were given immunity from scrutiny.[16]

Subsequent to the study of the UN Secretary-General's High-level Panel on Threats, Challenges and Change, and the follow-up report on it by Kofi Annan,[17] the September 2005 UN World Summit approved replacing the UNCHR with the Human Rights Council. Created in March 2006 and starting its first session three months later, the forty-seven-member UNHRC's membership is subject to scrutiny by the General Assembly (by simple majority vote, i.e. at least ninety-seven votes out of 192),[18] members will be subject to peer review during their first three-year term, and are not eligible for re-election after serving two consecutive terms.[19] Zimbabwe and Sudan did not stand for election and both Venezuela and Iran were rejected in the first election in 2006.[20] Membership can be suspended by a two-thirds majority of the General Assembly members who are present and vote. The slightly downsized new organization gives greater representation to Asian and East European countries.[21] There are thirteen seats for Asian states and six for Eastern Europe whereas they had twelve and five respectively in the defunct UNCHR. The new Council is no longer subsidiary to ECOSOC; it is now a subsidiary body – but not a principal organ – of the General Assembly, with its status being reviewed five years after its formation.[22] It meets more frequently than the UNCHR, with at least three meetings a year for no less than ten weeks in total. In contrast, there was only one annual six-week plenary meeting in March–April in Geneva for the UNCHR.

Universal periodic review (UPR), created by General Assembly Resolution 60/251, is another key innovative feature of the UNHRC,[23] whereby the human rights records of all 192 UN member states will be reviewed once every four years. There are three major sources of review: the state itself, the UN Office of the High Commissioner for Human Rights (OHCHR) and international human rights groups.[24] A controversial issue is whether the UPR should be the sole means to address human rights situations in particular countries or one additional layer of the special procedures (see below for details).[25]

In order to protect human rights better, the UNCHR established the Sub-Commission and treaty bodies or 'committees' to monitor compliance with the aforementioned UN human rights treaties by the member states. The treaty bodies are composed of experts in the fields who work as independent individuals and do not necessarily represent the interests of their own government. Corresponding with the eight treaties in force, there are eight treaty bodies.[26]

In addition, there are 'special procedures', i.e. the mandate given to a group of independent investigators who examine, monitor and publicly report on human rights situations in specific countries or on specific human rights issues. These special procedures are entrusted to either an individual (known as a 'special rapporteur', 'representative' or 'independent expert') or a group of five individuals (one from each of the five regions) (called a 'working group'). The experts are appointed by the UNCHR (and the succeeding UNHRC) to investigate countries or territories that had allegedly appalling human rights situations (country mandates) or particular global thematic issues (thematic mandates). In addition to the 1503 procedure mentioned above, they are the means whereby the UNCHR/UNHRC carries out the protection of human rights. As at 9 December 2010, there were eight country mandates and thirty-one thematic mandates.[27] The earliest one was the Working Group on Enforced or Involuntary Disappearances, established in 1980, whereas the latest ones are the Independent Expert on the Situation of Human Rights in the Sudan and the Independent Expert in the Field of Cultural Rights, both established in 2009. Every mandate has a mandate-holder or holders who undertake country missions or fact-finding missions and report back to the UNCHR/UNHRC.

Another vital UN human rights institution is the Office of the Higher Commissioner for Human Rights, based in Geneva and established by the UN General Assembly in December 1993.[28] The attempts to endow an individual with the authority to enforce human rights standards can date back to 1947 when the UNDHR was being drafted. Jewish organizations, Uruguay and Costa Rica had introduced proposals to establish either a human rights commissioner or a human rights attorney-general, but due to resistance from socialist countries, the General Assembly did not reach a consensus on the issue throughout the Cold War period. After the Cold War, Amnesty International promoted the same idea to the World Conference on Human Rights in Vienna in June 1993, which endorsed it in its Vienna Declaration and Programme of Action. As an Under-Secretary-General, the High Commissioner for Human Rights is a high-ranking officer in the UN. One of the mandates of the High Commissioner, which has turned out to be the most controversial one, is to promote and protect the right to development. While the US is strongly opposed to and the European Union is cautious about the right, a group of 'like-minded' African, Asian, Latin American and Middle Eastern countries, including China, India, Indonesia and Sudan is striving for an improvement of the conditions for their development (see below for more discussion). The Office's regular budget in 2004 was $27.1 million; it grew to $79.5 million for the biennium 2006–2007 and $115.3 million, or 2.89 per cent of UN's global budget, for the biennium 2008–2009. Voluntary contributions rose from $54.8 million in 2004 to $95.7 million in 2007 and $119.9 million in 2008.[29] In the belief that the primary responsibility for protecting human rights rests with national government, it provides technical assistance and advice in the form of training courses for judges and officials in the criminal justice system, assistance in elections and advice on constitutional and legislative reform. In addition, it promotes and monitors compliance with international human rights standards by national governments through its field presence, which includes eleven country offices and eight regional offices and gives support to both the UN country teams by deploying human rights advisers or supporting human rights components of UN peace missions.[30] It sponsors the establishment of national human rights institutions to enforce international human rights standards at the national level. It also serves as the secretariat of the UNCHR/UNHRC, provides research and secretariat support for the treaty bodies and assists the work of the experts of 'special procedures'.

Initially the UNSC was not involved in protecting human rights. Throughout the Cold War era, the UNSC only imposed coercive measures on two states for human rights purposes, namely Southern Rhodesia (1966) and South Africa (1977).[31] But the landmark Resolutions 688 (1991) and 794 (1992) on 'safe havens' in Iraq and Somalia respectively laid the way for the UNSC to intervene on humanitarian grounds.[32] The aforementioned humanitarian emergencies in the 1990s served to further strengthen the view that international peace ultimately rests on respect for human rights. Large-scale, systematic human rights violations, e.g. ethnic cleansing, genocide and other crimes against humanity, demand the intervention of the UNSC under Chapter VII. The humanitarian crisis in Darfur, Sudan, is a case in point. Consequently, the UNSC's involvement in human rights protection in the processes of peacekeeping and peace-building continues to grow.

China's engagement with the global human rights regime

Chinese involvement in the UN human rights regime started with the opening of China's society and economy to the outside world. Having attended as an observer for three years in 1979–81, China has been a member of the UNCHR since 1982.[33] It was a member of the UNHRC for two consecutive terms between 2006 and 2012, and hence is not eligible for re-election for 2012–15.[34] China was given a universal periodic review in 2009.[35] China's activities in the UN human rights regime have nevertheless been limited. Before 1989 its interests and involvement were largely restricted to the rights to self-determination and the right to development.[36] Chinese experts have never taken on the role of holder of country or thematic mandates.[37] Chinese specialists are present in five treaty bodies but not on the most important Human Rights Committee. By the end of 2009 a total of sixty-six countries issued standing invitations to special procedures. But China, Russia and the US have not extended such invitations.[38] In addition, China has not signed up for or ratified three major treaties. Despite the fact and claim that China has increased its participation in global governance and in international organizations since the 1990s, it has yet to become a signatory to two of the three conventions adopted since 1990 (see Table 5.1 above). Although China signed the International Covenant on Civil and Political Rights in 1998, it has yet to ratify it. Katie Lee indicates that while top Chinese leaders have on several occasions expressed their intention to do so, significant legal reform, especially in the criminal justice system, would be necessary before China can proceed towards ratification.[39] Several plausible explanations may be advanced for this Chinese procrastination. First, China is cautious about promoting civil and political rights at this stage of its development lest the Party's legitimacy and control be seriously challenged. Second, differences of opinion may exist within the Politburo as to the speed and intensity of political reform. Third, China does not want to be seen to be kowtowing to political pressure coming from the outside, especially the West. China's attention was rather focused on addressing the institutions of 'special procedures' and 'country-specific resolutions' in the transition from the UNCHR to the UNHRC.

From UNCHR to UNHRC

China deplored a 'quantum jump' in the country mandates under the special procedures.[40] China called for a reform in the mandates to the effect that they would deal only with large-scale, gross violations of human rights and that the UPR should be applied equally to all states regardless of their cultural and religious backgrounds and differences.[41] It was critical of the UNCHR mechanism of considering 'country situations', i.e. human rights abuses in particular countries, and decried the country-specific resolutions (*guo bie ti'an*) passed by the UNCHR as discriminatory and politically charged, arguing that it was a flaw in the Commission. On behalf of the Like-Minded Group (LMG) of twenty developing states, itself included, China expressed in November 2005 the view that 'the country specific review ... should either be abolished or applied strictly to address "gross and systematic violations" '.[42] A side note is that China often utilizes support from the LMG to resist human rights norms from the West. For example, as soon as the Norwegian Nobel Committee announced in October 2010 that it would award the 2010 Nobel Peace Prize to Liu Xiaobo, a jailed Chinese political dissident, China waged an intensive campaign to mobilize other countries to boycott the ceremony in Oslo in December 2010. Among the eighteen countries not represented at the ceremony, ten, China included, were members of the LMG.[43]

China's dislike of country-specific resolutions began to evolve in 1989 when its immunity from international criticism of its human rights record ended. The UN response to China's human rights failings post-June 1989 principally took three forms: the country-specific resolutions moved in the UNCHR and its Sub-Commission on Human Rights; the reporting activities required by the treaty bodies; and the special procedures.[44] In August 1989 the Sub-Commission passed with fifteen votes for and nine against a resolution expressing its concern over the Tiananmen killings and asking the Secretary-General to provide the UNCHR with information on China's human rights after the crackdown. This resolution was adopted despite China's intense and aggressive lobbying to dissuade members of the Sub-Commission from doing so, with threats of trade sanctions against countries in favour of it. China was dismayed by the fact that it was subjected to the first ever resolution critical of large-scale, domestic human rights abuses by a permanent member of the Security Council. The China debate also inadvertently resulted in an institutional change in the Sub-Commission, which decided to introduce secret ballot to consider all country-specific resolutions in order to prevent the more powerful states from using aggressive diplomatic pressures to manipulate the experts' voting decisions.[45] Almost every year between 1990 and 2004 the US sponsored a condemnatory resolution in the UNCHR or its Sub-Commission criticizing China's human rights record.[46] China had to strenuously mobilize support from members of the developing world, especially African states, in the Commission to defeat the introduction of the resolution by preventing debates through the procedural 'no-action' motion.[47] For instance, the Pakistan-led 'no-action' resolution was passed narrowly (with seventeen votes in favour, fifteen against, and eleven abstentions) in the 1990 meeting of UNCHR with some African and Latin American states abstaining. However, a resolution on Tibet was adopted by the UNCHR Sub-Commission in August 1991.[48] China pointed out in 1996 that among the fifty-eight country-specific resolutions passed by the UNCHR since 1992, almost all targeted developing countries.[49] Against this background, China advocated that sponsorship of country-specific resolutions be avoided.[50] The Islamic states, however, do not want to do away with the mechanism that they use to lash out at Israel for violating the human rights of the Palestinian people.[51] In the negotiation process leading to the adoption of the ground rules for the UNHRC, China demanded that country-specific resolutions only be passed after obtaining a two-thirds majority, but the move was found unacceptable by the West.[52] China dropped this demand at the last minute in return for a compromise worked out by the outgoing president, Luis Alfonso de Alba, that country-specific resolutions should gain 'broad support' from the forty-seven member states and have the signatures of at least fifteen of them before they are brought to the Council. It was argued that as the UN General Assembly Resolution 60/251 set midnight of 18 June 2007 as the deadline for reaching an agreement on the rules, China did not want to project a negative international image just one year before the Beijing Olympics. But Richard Howitt, the European Parliament observer, argued that the fifteen-member threshold would effectively prevent the Council from addressing human rights crises in Darfur, Chechnya or Burma.[53]

China has often featured in Special Rapporteurs' annual reports. In 1995 it was the subject of all Special Rapporteurs' and Working Groups' reports. Early that year, China called for a 'comprehensive reform' of the UNCHR, questioning the mandate and impartiality of the Special Rapporteurs and Working Groups. Rosemary Foot notes that the 'reform' was not aimed at strengthening the UN human rights machinery but rather undermining its legitimacy.[54] China did not allow the visit to the country by the Special Rapporteur on Torture until December 2005 after ten years of trying.[55] China expressed concern in the early days of the UNHRC that the UPR 'may overlap with the work of human rights treaty bodies and special mechanisms, thus increasing report burdens for developing countries'. It opined that the new UNHRC should be a forum for 'dialogue and cooperation', which was included into the General Assembly Resolution 60/251.[56] However, China's preference for the special procedures was at odds with the views of many other states which regarded the system of special procedures as an asset of the old Commission and therefore meriting preservation in the new Council.[57] Having come under criticism for focusing disproportionately on Israel,[58] the new Council was at pains to be seen as serious about dealing with human rights emergencies in the world. After deliberating in the first three sessions on Palestine and Lebanon,[59] it held a special session on Darfur in its fourth meeting in December 2006, and adopted unanimously – with China's support – a decision to dispatch a High-Level Mission to assess the human rights situation there.[60] It also discussed human rights situations in some Beijing-friendly states, including North Korea, Myanmar, Sri Lanka and Zimbabwe, although concrete results have hardly been apparent. Although work relating to special procedures continues, the ability of the Council to effectively act on country situations by special procedures or country-specific resolutions is open to dispute, given that the Asian and African states now have a comfortable majority after occupying twenty-six seats on the Council (or 55 per cent of the votes).[61] The UN Special Rapporteur for Human Rights in Myanmar, Tomás Ojea Quintana, wrote in his March 2010 report that 'some of these human rights violations may entail categories of crimes against humanity or war crimes under the terms of the Rome Statute of the International Criminal Court'. After the release of the report, China launched a diplomatic campaign to block a US-backed international probe into possible war crimes by the military junta. China heavily lobbied European and Asian countries and the UN leadership against the US proposal.[62]

China was in favour of a membership of the new Council similar to – if not larger than – the old one whereas the US called for a much leaner membership of twenty states. Eventually they decided on a compromise whereby the new Council would be composed of forty-seven states but, as explained above, China was pleased that the share of Asian countries in the body had increased.[63] To address one of the major shortcomings of the UNCHR, which met annually for six weeks, Kofi Annan proposed that the new Council be a standing body, 'able to meet regularly and at any time to deal with imminent human rights crises and allow for timely and in-depth consideration of human rights issues'.[64] Due to the huge financial burden of deploying personnel in Geneva permanently, some developing countries, including China, were opposed to this proposal. General Assembly Resolution 60/251 (para. 10) therefore decided that the Council 'shall be able to hold special sessions, when needed, at the request of a member of the Council with the support of one third of the membership of the Council [i.e. sixteen member states]'. But as observed by Yvonne Terlingen, there has been a flurry of calls for special sessions. Between June 2006 and September 2010, there were a total of thirteen special sessions.[65]

Right to development

China attaches much significance to the right to development, claiming that it is the precondition for realizing other human rights.[66] The UN has long had minimal attention to integrating human rights into economic growth promotion programmes. During the final round of negotiations between states on the 2005 World Summit Outcome Document, the US demanded that all references to the right to development be removed because of the opposition from American conservatives. But the developing world was determined to add this right to Resolution 60/251 (2006), which established the HRC.[67] While this claim may contribute to the global diffusion of human rights by striking a balance among the three generations of human rights,[68] ambiguities abound and the focus of the West differs qualitatively from the developing world. Who are the rights holders? Who are the duty bearers responsible for securing the right? Can the right to development be interpreted in such a way that it can be demanded by developing countries from more developed ones or by peoples from their states? What specific steps or programmes of action should states take to realize the right to development?[69] China spoke on behalf of the LMG in the UNHRC on the relationship between globalization and the right to development, urging 'the international community to take stock of the slow progress with regard to the Millennium Development Goals' and 'broaden and strengthen the full and effective participation of developing countries in international economic decision-making and norm-setting'.[70] While China calls for an international economic order built on equity and justice, the knotty issues that have plagued the enforcement of the right to development remain unaddressed. Effective mechanisms to ensure that states comply with their commitment to realizing the right are lacking.

To promote both economic growth and respect for human rights, the West emphasizes the need for 'good governance', arguing that development means economic growth plus attention to civil–political and socioeconomic rights, including the empowerment of women and civil society.[71] Conditionality is usually imposed by the West on the granting of development assistance to developing countries whereas China insists on foreign aid with no strings attached. The Millennium Development Goals also actively promote civil, political, cultural, social and economic rights, rejecting any trade-offs between development and rights.[72] Against this background, the UN Development Programme introduced in 1990 an annual *Human Development Report* (*HDR*) and index. On the Human Development Index, China (at 0.772) has only achieved a medium level of human development. It was ranked ninety-second among 182 countries and territories in the *HDR* 2009, below Ukraine, Thailand, Iran and Georgia.[73] Many Chinese do not enjoy the right to development in their own country.

Post-Cold War humanitarian intervention[74]

As discussed in Chapter 3, the notion of humanitarian intervention was greeted by the Chinese government with much suspicion. China is deeply worried that outside humanitarian intervention may lead to foreign encroachment and national disintegration, a possibility that still haunts its leaders. The Chinese would not countenance a repetition of the intervention into Kosovo, which eventually led the minority region to seek independence from Serbia and has stirred up Taiwan's claim to statehood based on the principle of self-determination. After the International Court of Justice issued in July 2010 a non-binding opinion that Kosovo's secession from Serbia does not violate international law, the pro-independence *Taiwan News* stated in an editorial that '[t]he ICJ opinion on Kosovo also hints that a declaration or, more precisely, a formal affirmation by Taiwan of its independence would probably not "violate international law" especially since Taiwan has actually never been part of the PRC State.'[75]

Central to China's stance on humanitarian intervention in Darfur are the statist principles whereby military intervention for humanitarian purposes within the territory of a sovereign state cannot be made without the latter's consent, that the sovereignty and territorial integrity of the target state must be duly respected, and that the crisis in Darfur would best be handled by African countries.[76] When Chinese President Hu Jintao visited Khartoum in February 2007, he said that it was imperative to observe four principles in resolving the Darfur problem:[77]

- to respect Sudan's sovereignty and territorial integrity;
- to resolve the issue by peaceful means and by sticking to dialogue and coordination based on equality;
- to have the African Union and the United Nations playing constructive roles in a peacekeeping mission in Darfur; and
- to improve the situation in Darfur and the living conditions of the local people.

Under Chinese sponsorship, a new three-tiered rule on humanitarian intervention is being applied to Darfur, and is likely to set a precedent for future interventions. In essence, such a 'conditional' intervention may be undertaken by actors at three levels: the host country at the national level; international organizations at the regional level; and the United Nations at the global level. The distinctive features of the China-orchestrated humanitarian intervention are twofold. First, although it is sanctioned by the UNSC, the real agent for intervention is the African Union (AU), the regional intergovernmental organization. The presence of Western powers is almost non-existent. This stands in stark contrast to the minimal role played by the Organization of African Unity, the predecessor of AU, and ASEAN in the humanitarian crises in Somalia and East Timor respectively in the 1990s. Second, even though no prior consent from the Sudanese government was required under UNSC Resolution 1769,[78] in effect not only was host-country consent sought but Khartoum also dictates the terms of reference of the peacekeeping operation.[79] These new rules, which differ from the recommendations in the ICISS report on R2P, provide China with adequate de facto protection against external intervention into its internal affairs in the name of human rights. However, it is open to question whether the new rule can protect endangered people in a timely manner, as it requires the sanction of the host government.

Conclusion

While the UNCHR/UNHRC has been the centrepiece of the promotion and protection of human rights since 1946 and China joined it in 1982, China has not provided many global public goods in forms of protecting human rights by strengthening the institutional machinery of the UN body. Instead, it has primarily been concerned about how to shield itself, and 'like-minded' developing states, from UN monitoring and criticisms. While rhetorically championing the cause of the developing world in debates about the right to development, it has made minimal contributions to the formulation and clarification of norms or to monitoring their enforcement. It is also disputable whether the new three-tiered state-centric rules about humanitarian intervention can contribute to addressing humanitarian crises promptly.

Two observations can perhaps be made from this situation as regards global human rights. First, why is China in this situation? An explanation may be found in China's late development and late engagement with the outside world, especially with the existing norms and rules of international association at the human and the state levels. Does China's late development justify different, more lenient treatment or should China be pressured and forced to change by international sanctions, led by the liberal Western government or non-governmental sectors? There seems to be no easy answer. Much depends on power relationships, China's learning process, and outside admonition and help. Second, China has often argued that the ability of the Chinese state to lift a large proportion of its population out of abject poverty is an achievement not to be ignored: China's ability to feed a fifth of humankind is a fulfilment of basic human needs at the global level. China is thus making a significant contribution to the world. It is not very clear how many people are persuaded by this kind of argument, especially since the international community witnessed in the 1990s that disrespect for human rights by nationalist, authoritarian regimes constitutes a significant threat to international security and peace. Some would regard China's contributions as passive if not negative, rather than positive and active. Unless China models its actions and behaviour on those of the West, a gap will remain between China and the West in the theory and practice of human rights.

6 Environmental protection

> China, which will soon be the biggest economic power in the world, says to the world: Commitments apply to you, but not to us. This is utterly unacceptable. This is about the essentials, and one has to react to this hypocrisy.
>
> Nicolas Sarkozy, 2009[1]

> I heard President Sarkozy talk about hypocrisy. I think I'm trying to avoid such words myself. I am trying to go into the arguments and debate about historical responsibility. People tend to forget where it is from. In the past 200 years of industrialization developed countries contributed more than 80 percent of emissions. Whoever created this problem is responsible for the catastrophe we are facing.
>
> He Yafei, 2009[2]

Although an extensive literature has grown up on China's environmental woes and international environmental policy,[3] little attention seems to have been paid to the interplay between the domestic and the international aspects of China's environmental governance.[4] This phenomenon is intriguing, given that China's huge population means that a fifth of humankind is suffering serious environmental damage, a situation which ought to command the attention of the global community. What is China's participation in global environmental governance? What is the linkage between China's domestic environmental governance and its international environmental governance? How do they mirror each other with respect to China's concerns for environmental protection? As a rising power anxious to be seen as a responsible member of the international community, has China complied with the international rules and norms that govern environmental protection? In what way has it contributed to the governance of the global environmental commons? Does it aspire to do so? Is it capable of doing so? To answer these and other related questions, this chapter proposes to look at China from both the inside out and from the outside so as to chart the contours of the domestic–international linkage.

China realizes that it stands to benefit from taking domestic initiatives and joining international efforts to clean up its polluted environment, as long as its political authorities are not severely threatened. China can be expected to cooperate more fully with international environmental regimes than with other types of global regimes, as it has come to realize, albeit belatedly, that proper environmental protection constitutes an important part of its overall sustainable development. Also, the central government is more tolerant of domestic environmental NGOs than of those working in areas such as human rights and infectious diseases.

Chinese leaders seem to think that if the country can clean up its own environmental act, then it will be making a significant contribution to the international effort to combat global environmental problems. The supply of global public goods in terms of a clean environment is partly contingent on the availability of the same public goods domestically. Indeed, China's environmental protection, or the lack of it, has exerted a significant impact on the environments of its neighbours. Air carrying a high concentration of sulphur dioxide from the burning of coal has spread from mainland China to Hong Kong, South Korea, Japan, and the west coast of the United States and Canada,[5] bringing with it acid rain. Such pollution goes as far as New Zealand, which is distant from most of the world's industrial centres.[6] China's heavily toxic rivers have caused pollution problems not only to its own habitat, but also to the lakes of neighbouring countries in Central Asia. The hydro-electric dams in southwest Yunnan province have severely affected the people living downstream of the Mekong River in Laos, Thailand, Myanmar and Vietnam.[7] China has overtaken the United States as the largest carbon dioxide emitter in the world,[8] as it consumes a lot of hydrocarbons such as crude oil and coal. It is also the largest importer of tropical rainforest timber in the world, consuming about 50 per cent of the world's annual output.[9]

The sheer aggregate size of China and its increasing integration with the rest of the world mean that what it does or does not do in the environmental sphere will increasingly impact the world. China has, to all intents and purposes, become an integral part of the world. If China enjoys a clean environment, then all will stand to benefit. This line of thinking suggests an intimate relationship between China's ecology and the global ecology, and between China's domestic governance and its emerging role in global environmental governance. As climate change mitigation has the properties of a global public good, it would be interesting to find out whether or not China is free-riding in the global campaign to prevent global warming.

China's environmental involvement can be scrutinized at the international, regional and domestic levels. The main Chinese actors involved include the State Environmental Protection Administration (SEPA)/Ministry of Environmental Protection (MEP)[10] and other central and local government agencies, green NGOs and some environmentally concerned individuals. The functions of these actors will be discussed in the following assessments of China's global and domestic environmental governance, and of the domestic impact on the global scene and then vice versa.

Assessing China's global environment governance

China's environmental governance at the global level can be gauged from three related areas of activities: agenda setting, rule negotiation, and rule compliance. In terms of agenda setting, China's role in international environmental programmes seemed to be small, probably until the 2009 Copenhagen Summit on Climate Change (discussed in detail later), as it was still at a relatively early stage of learning from others about international diplomacy in general and international environmental protection in particular, although its engagement with global environmental governance can date back to the early 1970s, shortly after its accession to the United Nations in late 1971. In 1972, at the close of the Cultural Revolution, PRC officials attended the United Nations Conference on Human Environment held in Stockholm, Sweden. Since then, however, China's level of participation in international environmental diplomacy remained low until its adoption of the reform and opening policy. Its contributions to these international conferences have been confined to general statements about its view of the world or to the signing of international treaties. As of 2009, 313 out of 348 (or 90 per cent) international treaties and conventions of various kinds, including those on the environment, that the country has signed or ratified since its establishment in 1949, date from after 1978.[11] China has entered into some fifty international environmental treaties.[12]

China's green NGOs started to participate in international environmental conferences in 2002, when delegates from dozens of them, supported by external funds, attended the World Conference on Sustainable Development held in Johannesburg, South Africa. Chinese NGO delegates were reported to have been rather quiet there, reflecting to a large extent their inexperience in international conferencing and their lack of confidence. The learning process of China's NGOs is expected to gather pace, as many delegates have brought home useful information which they have subsequently incorporated into work programmes for domestic implementation. Some of these NGOs have continued to keep in contact with their overseas counterparts. In October 2002 the Global Environment Facility (GEF) – the designated financial mechanism for international agreements on biodiversity, climate change and persistent organic pollutants – held its second general assembly in Beijing. Some forty Chinese NGOs joined overseas NGO representatives in a forum organized by Friends of Nature, a prominent Chinese green NGO. In November 2005 an international conference on renewable energy was held in Beijing, and Chinese NGOs were active in a parallel non-governmental forum. (We shall return to the activities of these NGOs later.)

Information about China's involvement in international rule negotiation is sketchy. However, the country has instituted with Japan and South Korea regular meetings among environment ministers to discuss issues of common concern, such as air pollution and sandstorms. China has also entered into similar discussions with ASEAN. It has established with the EU a programme to improve environmental governance. In addition, it has joined a US initiative to form an

Asian Pacific Partnership involving four other countries[13] – Australia,[14] Japan, South Korea, and India – to develop technology to control environmental pollution, as a way to complement the 1997 Kyoto Protocol. (Together these six countries account for half of the world's emissions of greenhouse gases.) The US and Brazil initiated in 2007 an International Biofuels Forum to explore the possibilities of wider use of biofuels, including ethanol derived from sugar cane and corn. China, together with India, South Africa and the European Commission, were parties to the forum.[15] China also works within the G20 to tackle environmental problems. Apart from these activities, China has also entered into numerous multilateral and bilateral discussions on environmental cooperation. As the world's top greenhouse gas emitters as well as its top energy users, both the US and China recognize the importance of their relationship not only to themselves but also to the rest of the world. Increasingly high-level discussions – bilateral or multilateral, formal or informal, regular or occasional – have taken place in recent years in areas of economic cooperation, energy use and environmental protection.[16]

In terms of rule compliance, China has committed itself to complying with the terms and conditions of some fifty or so international environmental treaties that it has signed or ratified, to observing the relevant international environmental standards, and to taking measures to halt environmental degradation. In 1994 the country adopted Agenda 21, a comprehensive programme of environmental protection activities first proposed at the United Nations Conference on the Environment and Development in Rio de Janeiro, Brazil, in 1992. It has also passed a lot of domestic legislation to protect its environment and to increase the strength and punitive powers of its Environment Ministry (to be discussed further in the next section).

It would be difficult to make an accurate assessment of the compliance of any country with international environmental law, as the meaning of compliance is controversial, as environmental norms and mechanisms are diverse and lack coordination,[17] and as most international environment treaties do not have a robust system of monitoring and enforcement to make compliance effective. An exception to this general situation is the Kyoto Protocol. Despite its relatively short, controversial history, the Protocol offers a basis for making a preliminary assessment. China is exempted from reducing its emissions of greenhouse gases because of its status as a developing state. The principle of 'common but differentiated responsibility' allows developing countries to catch up with the West in industrialization. The work of the UNDP and the UN Environment Programme (UNEP) has been important in raising China's environmental awareness and standards, but they take an advisory and supportive rather than a judicial role and they work under very tight budgets.[18] In addition, the UNEP has a narrow mandate and small staff, and its work is often hampered by rivalries between the developed and the developing worlds.

China and the Kyoto Protocol

The Kyoto Protocol is the most stringent environmental treaty so far established because of the formal legal requirements made of signatory states to abide by its rules under penalties and cut back their emissions of greenhouse gases. China signed it in May 1998 and ratified it in August 2002. An examination of China's relationship with the Kyoto Protocol serves as an important indicator of its attitude towards global environmental governance.

Because of its developing country status, China is exempt from the Protocol's legal requirement to reduce emissions of greenhouse gases, including carbon dioxide, methane, chlorofluorocarbons and other gases.[19] In the UN Climate Change Conferences of 2009 and 2010 in Copenhagen and Cancún, Mexico, respectively, the fate of the Protocol when its emissions targets come to expire at the end of 2012 was a matter of heated debate. The United States has not ratified the Protocol and has demanded that the preferential treatment given to major developing countries in the Protocol be discarded. But China, Brazil, South Africa and India, collectively forming an alliance known as BASIC, have countered that more emissions reduction by the US is required if they are to sign up to a new global climate regime.[20] The Copenhagen summit ended in deadlock, failing to agree on a legally binding post-Kyoto treaty on emissions reduction. The issue became more prominent in the Cancún conference when Japan led Russia and Canada in opposing the extension of the Protocol beyond 2012. Instead, Japan asked for a new framework in which all major emitting countries, including China and India, would be committed to emissions reduction. At the same time, developing states demanded a second commitment period of the Protocol from 2013. China agreed to negotiations provided its conditions were met, of which one was the extension of the Protocol. The other BASIC countries also said that the continuation of Kyoto was non-negotiable.[21] As a compromise, the Cancún Agreement gives another year for states to decide if the Protocol will be extended.[22]

Assessing China's domestic environmental governance

Since 1949 the National People's Congress, China's legislature, has formulated nine laws on environmental protection and fifteen laws on the protection of natural resources. And since 1996 the State Council has formulated or revised over fifty administrative regulations relating to environmental protection. By the end of 2005 the country had promulgated over 800 national environmental protection standards and thirty local standards, dealt with over 75,000 cases of environmental law violations, and closed down 16,000 enterprises illegally discharging pollutants.[23] By that time there were 3,226 environmental protection administration departments at various levels all over the country, with 167,000 people engaged in environmental work, research, education and publicity. In addition, there were 3,854 environmental supervision and environmental law enforcement organs with more than 50,000 staff members. Another 300,000 people worked in enterprises and government departments dealing with the environment.[24]

The above figures and statistics, reported in China's white paper entitled *Environmental Protection in China (1996–2005)*, give a useful but static picture of China's domestic environmental governance. They do not tell us how effective the laws, regulations and standards are, or how well the staff involved in monitoring and enforcing compliance perform their tasks. And the white paper has little or nothing to say about involvement in environmental protection by NGOs, an increasingly vocal sector in China's environmental management.

Due to its fast economic growth and industrial development, China has become the world's largest emitter of sulphur dioxide. The resulting creation of acid rain causes havoc to China's environment, in terms of economic costs and human welfare, and to a lesser extent to that of its neighbours. In 2005 China emitted 25.5 million tonnes of the gas, which was a 27 per cent increase since 2000, of which coal- and oil-fired power plants accounted for eleven million tonnes. The emissions increased to twenty-six million tonnes in 2006.[25] According to the World Bank, China has twenty of the world's thirty most air-polluted cities, and a study by the Blacksmith Institute, New York, reveals that China was home to two of the most polluted places in the world in 2007.[26] A total of 357 – more than half – of the 696 cities and counties in China were affected by acid rain in 2005 due to sulphur dioxide pollution.[27] Nationwide, a third of the country suffered from acid rain.[28] In September 2006 SEPA and the State Statistics Bureau issued a Green GDP report saying that pollution cost the country an equivalent of 3.05 per cent of its economic output and that it would take a one-off direct investment of about $136 billion – nearly 7 per cent of GDP – to clean up all the pollution pumped into the country's air, water and soil in 2004.[29] Health costs formed a major part of the economic losses.

In view of the huge ecological cost, three years after SEPA was elevated to become an agency under the State Council, the Tenth Five-Year Plan (2001–2005) set ambitious emission reduction targets and boosted environmental spending to 700 billion yuan ($85 billion), equivalent to 1.3 per cent of GDP, up from 0.93 per cent in the Ninth Five-Year Plan (1996–2000) and 0.73 per cent in the Eight (1991–1995) (though still below the 2 per cent threshold suggested by the World Bank).[30] However, by early 2005, actual spending was 30 per cent short of the target.[31] Also, the Tenth Five-Year Plan failed to meet 40 per cent of its environmental targets.[32] SEPA estimated that the country would need 1.4 trillion yuan ($175 billion) in its Eleventh Five-Year Plan (2006–2010) to tackle environmental problems,[33] representing about 1.5 per cent of GDP. (In comparison, developed countries already spent about 1–2 per cent of their GDP on environmental protection even in the 1970s, with the US spending 2 per cent and Japan 2–3 per cent.)[34] Chen Bin, the vice head of SEPA's planning and finance department, said that the percentage needed to rise to about 3 per cent before noticeable improvements could be made to the environment.[35]

In 2004 China recorded more than 74,000 incidents of protest and unrest, up from 58,000 a year earlier.[36] In 2005 there were 51,000 pollution-related disputes, up 30 per cent from a year earlier.[37] Zhou Shengxian, head of SEPA, said in July 2007 that his agency had received 1,814 petitions from citizens 'appealing for a better environment' in the first five months of the year, an 8 per cent increase from the corresponding period of the previous year.[38] A mass protest against the construction of a chemical plant in Fujian's Xiamen in June 2007 was widely covered by international mass media.[39] Apparently these figures and events have alarmed the leadership, as social stability forms a foundation of legitimate governance in the country. However, there seems to be little or no systematic analysis of the scale of these conflicts and whether they were directed at polluting factories or local governments or both. Suffice to suggest a close correlation between riots and environmental issues. In May 2006 China announced the establishment of three more environmental supervision centres, in addition to two recently established, in order to strengthen the enforcement of environmental protection law.[40] Six offices will also be set up to monitor civil and military nuclear security across the country. These centres and offices will report directly to SEPA so as to streamline procedures for dealing with environmental issues and disputes by bypassing resistance from local governments and inter-provincial rivalries.[41] Although SEPA has been elevated to central agency level, its importance in China's domestic environmental structure has not gone unchallenged. Powerful ministries such as those in the economic and industrial sectors have often put immense political pressure on SEPA, which has sometimes had to respond by using 'name and shame' tactics, exposing serious breaches of environmental law to the public.[42]

One of the recent measures taken by the government is a package of taxes dubbed 'chopsticks taxes', aimed at reducing the use of wood products and increasing levies on luxury cars and yachts that consume a lot of fuel.[43] Other measures include the closing down of factories that produce heavy pollutants, and the monitoring of some 300,000 factories;[44] the cleaning up of rivers and lakes; the imposition of heavy fines on polluters; the strengthening of the legal system; and stringent adherence to the requirements for industries to submit environmental assessment reports to the government before major infrastructural works can start.

Of the many serious environmental mishaps in China, the Songhua benzene spill in late 2005 may have served as a major wake-up call to the top Chinese leadership that something drastic needed to be done to clean up the country's environment. The poisonous chemical came from an explosion in a plant in Jilin run by China National Petroleum Corporation. The Songhua River incident, which led to the cutting off for five days of normal supplies of running water to Harbin, the capital city of Heilongjiang province in northeast China with over three million inhabitants, and affected more than half a million people living downstream in Russia's Far East, became a turning point in the official Chinese thinking on environmental protection. Not only did China apologize to Russia for the leak and Xie Zhenhua, head of SEPA, resign following the incident, but the clean-up of the Songhua over the following five years was estimated to have cost $3 billion.[45] Subsequent to the Songhua spill, the central government began to inspect 21,000 plants that line China's major waterways and to review old environmental assessment reports.[46] More than half these plants were found to be located along the Yangtze and Yellow rivers.

Realizing the fragility of its one-sided economic growth, the country's Eleventh Five-Year Plan (2006–2010) aims to cut energy consumption by 20 per cent in terms of per capita GDP growth,[47] and emission of major pollutants by ten per cent, and to increase forest coverage from 18.2 per cent to 20 per cent.[48] Also, by 2010, 70 per cent of city sewage and 60 per cent of non-toxic domestic waste are to be treated.[49] However, Premier Wen Jiabao revealed in March 2010 that in the first four years of the 2006–2010 period China's energy intensity fell only 14.38 per cent, far below the stated target.[50] Stephen Howes of the Australian National University, however, questioned the Chinese claim of an improvement in energy intensity. Based on China's official data, he found that the energy intensity had fallen only 8.2 per cent by 2009 relative to 2005. He called on the Chinese government to explain how the 14.38 per cent claim was derived.[51] More alarmingly, Wen revealed in September 2010 a rise in energy intensity in the first half of the year, principally due to the Chinese government's four trillion-yuan fiscal stimulus package, launched in 2008, which promoted investment in the heavy industry sector. In response to his declaration that he would spare no effort in meeting the target, various local governments ordered power cuts not only to high-emission industrial plants but also to hospitals and schools.[52] Obviously, ordinary people in China continue to suffer from environmental damage. So what can they do to help themselves apart from taking violent protest action?

The role of non-state actors[53]

Recent publications on environmental protection in China have suggested that public participation should be reciprocal; that is, it should involve public input into government processes as well as government-initiated consultations with private citizens and groups.[54] Also, such inputs and consultations should be open and transparent, and should be conducted in a 'scientific way', that is a rational way devoid of ideological pressure. Furthermore, decisions made must be acceptable to those who are affected by them, directly or indirectly.

A subtle indicator of China's compliance with commonly accepted environmental standards is the government's policy towards the growth of environmental NGOs.[55] In 1997 only a handful of NGOs of various kinds existed in China. Most of them were based in the capital, Beijing. The precise number of NGOs in China at present is unknown. However, according to some Chinese official statistics, as of 2008 there were 229,681 *shehui tuanti* (or social organizations), 182,382 *minban feiqiye danwei* (private non-enterprise units, such as research and educational institutes and foundations) and 1,597 foundations, totalling 413,660 NGOs. In contrast, there were only 4,446 NGOs (and all were social organizations) twenty years ago.[56] Since the 1990s, concerned Chinese individuals, mainly intellectuals, have started to organize NGOs to promote environmental awareness. The first one,[57] Friends of Nature, was formally registered in March 1994 with the Ministry of Civil Affairs. This was followed by another well-known NGO, Global Village of Beijing, founded in 1996. The programmes and activities of these and some NGOs are funded by overseas agencies, with foundations like Ford, the Rockefeller Brothers Fund and Winrock International annually contributing millions of dollars.[58] According to Yang Dongping, a vice-president of Friends of Nature, there are about 1,000 indigenous green NGOs in China, of which more than 100 are grassroots groups, 500 are student groups, and the rest receive some form of government subsidy.[59] A survey conducted by the All-China Environment Federation, an NGO established in 2005 under the sponsorship of SEPA, reveals that there were 2,768 environmental NGOs in China at the end of 2005,[60] with a total individual membership of 224,000.[61] About 90 per cent of these NGOs were initiated by government departments and student volunteers, and only 20 per cent had registered with the government.[62] Most of them are poorly resourced and too small to have any significant impact.

Chinese environmentalists made their debut on the international stage when they attended the UN-sponsored World Summit on Sustainable Development, held in Johannesburg, South Africa, in late August 2002.[63] The summit was attended by leaders and representatives of over 100 countries as well as delegates from 1,000 NGOs around the world. Apart from Chinese government officials, some forty social organizations were present, including eleven grassroots NGOs from different parts of the country.[64] The twenty delegates from China's environmental NGOs were sponsored by the British Embassy, the Ford Foundation and Canada's Civil Society Project.[65] Although the voice of Chinese environmentalists was said to be feeble at the international forum,[66] they have started to link up with international NGOs and to lobby or work with their government, especially with SEPA. They have also worked with the industrial sector at home to help alleviate environmental problems. The UN conference was an eye-opening experience for many Chinese grassroots NGO workers, as they were exposed to a flood of information on global environmental issues. They also realized how far behind China's NGO development was, even in comparison with other developing countries like Indonesia, the Philippines and Malaysia.[67] In addition, they had the rare opportunity of meeting their own colleagues from other parts of China. After the Johannesburg Summit, Chinese delegates held a conference in Nanjing in September 2002 to brief their colleagues in China and, as a result, they drew up an action plan outlining their future work in the country, stressing the importance of NGO contributions and promoting the ideas of sustainability and public participation.

Unlike other types of NGOs, green groups in China are seen in an ambivalent light by the authorities. On the one hand, they are seen as less threatening, as they tend to work with the government to alleviate environmental damage which the government sometimes finds difficult to tackle on its own. These NGOs work more efficiently to motivate common folk to take steps to protect their environmental interests. The existence of NGOs can, apart from helping to improve China's environmental record, enhance the country's international image.[68] On the other, the fact that they can raise the level of public awareness over some rather volatile social and environmental issues poses a potential threat to the authority of the government. Furthermore, the government is worried that such groups may eventually evolve into political parties, as has happened in many overseas countries. Somehow, the government and the emerging NGO sector have to learn to live and work with each other. During the campaign to compete for the hosting of the 2008 Olympics, the Beijing Olympic Organizing Committee, a semi-governmental body, for the first time invited environmental NGOs to attend proceedings as advisers, in order to promote a green image for the Beijing Games.

A courageous and adventurous non-governmental initiative was the setting up in 1999 of the Centre for Legal Assistance to Pollution Victims in Beijing, with substantial financial support from the Ford Foundation. The director of the Centre is Wang Canfa, an environmental lawyer and a professor at the China University of Political Science and Law, Beijing. The Centre provides a channel for citizens to voice their grievances against the authorities. Through legal proceedings, ordinary people can seek compensation from the government and business corporations. Up to 2002 the Centre had received thousands of phone calls and taken the twenty-two cases it deemed most worthy to the courts. The number of cases rose to over eighty by mid-2006.[69] Beginning with two or three part-time volunteers in 1999, in 2007 its 270 or so volunteers received 9,000 requests for help.[70] In a landmark case raised by the Centre in 2002 on behalf of 100 peasant families against a paper factory which had dumped toxic chemicals into Shiliang River in eastern Jiangsu province, a local court ruled against the factory and awarded compensation amounting to 5.6 million yuan to the affected families.[71] According to the influential green activist Liang Congjie,[72] this was a landmark case, as almost nobody in China had ever used environmental law to protect his or her rights before 2002.

A new non-governmental effort to combat environmental problems has come from the business sector. Originally triggered by their concerns over the annual sandstorms that blow from northern China to Beijing, around 100 business people (including twenty or so from Taiwan working in China) met in mid-2004 to form an environmental group called Alxa SEE Ecology Association (Alxa or Alashan is the name of a place in the Mongolian plateau, a seedbed of sandstorms, and SEE stands for society, entrepreneur and ecology).[73] By the end of 2005, this association had collected some 100 million yuan ($12 million)[74] to fund works to combat sandstorms. Over the years it has diversified its activities to cover public environmental education and international networking. This is perhaps the first time that Chinese entrepreneurs have used their corporate social responsibility in a collective way to forge a public-private partnership to deal with environmental issues.

Another unique feature of China is the development of government-organized NGOs or GONGOs. These organizations enjoy three advantages over grassroots NGOs in that they are better resourced as they are funded by the government, they can attract a relatively large number of specialists and experts to work for them, and they can serve as effective and efficient conduits between international organizations or donors, civil society and the government.[75] Two such organizations with strong links to SEPA stand out: the China Environmental Culture Promotion Association (first established in 1993), whose work was revived by

102 *Environmental protection*

Pan Yue when he joined SEPA as vice minister in 2003; and the All-China Environment Federation,[76] a nationwide mass organization established in April 2005, with the aim of bringing the public and the government together to achieve sustainable development. According to Ru Jiang, who did doctoral research on China's environmental issues at Stanford,[77] GONGOs are generally more effective in performing tasks related to the official responsibilities of their supervisory organizations, such as policy consultation and information exchange; in contrast, citizen-organized NGOs are more effective in engaging in public education, environmental advocacy, and grassroots environmental activities. Although GONGOs mushroomed as a direct result of the administrative reform of 1998, which was aimed at downsizing government bureaucracy, they are increasingly independent of government agencies. This is due not only to their exposure and access to international rules, resources and technology but also to the fact that their second-generation leaders and staff members are no longer recruited from the government.[78]

Many international environmental NGOs work, sometimes in close collaboration with local NGOs, to promote environmental protection by introducing programmes and management techniques and by bringing in much needed funding. Groups such as WWF, Ecologia, Pacific Environment, Friends of the Earth, and Greenpeace have set up projects or opened offices in China.[79] It was estimated that in 1996–2000 15 per cent of total spending on the environment originated from multilateral and bilateral lending programmes and aid budgets.[80] For example, by June 2006 GEF had extended or approved over $500 million to fund forty-five projects in China.[81]

The role of local governments

As the bulk of environmental pollution takes place in the localities, it is imperative to study why local authorities fail to address the problem. The incentive structure that local officials face helps us understand more about the mounting difficulties in remedying pollution at the local level. First, there are competing interests between environmental protection and the maintenance of production and employment. For local officials, whose performance is assessed by higher-level authorities and local people principally on their records of economic growth, the economic goal is always accorded higher priority than the environmental goal. Even with a pollution fee system in place, local governments tend to offer their enterprises tax exemptions or grants to offset penalties.

Second, government officials' thinking about environmental problems is influenced by a hypothesis known as the 'environmental Kuznets curve' (EKC).[82] The hypothesis asserts that environmental degradation increases in the early stages of economic development (as indicated in higher emissions per capita) until the process reaches a turning point or threshold at a higher level of economic development; thereafter the overall levels of degradation gradually fall and stabilize at a relatively low level. In other words, the relationship between economic growth and its environmental impact shows an inverted U-shape. The reasoning is that at higher levels of development, the economy is transformed into one based on information technology and services, thereby reducing the rate of resource depletion. Additional favourable factors would include increased environmental consciousness and enforcement of environmental regulations, increased use of cleaner and more energy-efficient production technology, and enhanced commitment to environmental expenditures. A policy implication of the EKC hypothesis is that economic development is not a threat to the environment. Rather, it should be conceived as a means to environmental improvement. So there is no need to curtail economic growth to protect the environment. This hypothesis was once believed to be applicable to China. Between 1997 and 2001 China's GDP grew by 33.7 per cent while carbon dioxide emissions rose 0.2 per cent only and sulphur dioxide emissions even fell by nearly 40 per cent. However, there were controversies surrounding the remarkable drop in emissions. In addition to falsified data, the closure of a large number of small-scale, inefficient coal mines was an important factor. Economic development, however, has not brought with it a decrease in environmental degradation.[83]

Third, the efforts of local governments to curb environmental pollution are undermined by the fact that the wanton dumping of hazardous waste and measures to safeguard the environment possess the properties of externality and public goods.[84] With no charges being made for the harm done to the environment, the market system cannot discourage individuals and firms from discharging waste into the air and water. Given that within a threshold level non-payers' consumption of public goods is not at the expense of payers and that it is extremely difficult or costly to exclude non-payers from consuming public goods, individuals and firms tend to free-ride with respect to the provision of public goods (i.e. environmental clean-ups in this case). Both result in an oversupply of polluting goods and an undersupply of public goods.[85]

Following this logic, local county officials in China are inclined to free-ride on others' investments in environmental clean-ups because while the county would have to bear the full cost of the investment, it would share the benefits with people downstream who contribute little to the clean-up but cannot be excluded from its benefits. Analogously, environmental pollution is a 'public bad' whose harmful effects are experienced by all who use the environmental resource. To minimize a local population's exposure to pollution, local officials are tempted to push polluting firms close to the downstream boundaries of local jurisdictions. In so doing, local people are 'minimally' hurt by toxic wastes, and local firms are not charged for damaging the environment while their industrial production can be maintained. The decentralization of economic powers to subnational governments is consequently at odds with the collective action necessary to achieve environmental goals. This is one of the reasons why environmental experts have called for the power to combat environmental problems to be vested in a regional or central agency. Pan Yue of SEPA has demanded that environmental officials be given real power to implement existing laws and regulations and that environmental inspectors in different sectors be brought under a unified administration.[86]

The central government is putting mounting pressure on local governments and enterprises to rein in pollution. In a SEPA inspection campaign launched in October 2006, it was found that only 30 per cent of the investigated projects obtained a pass in pollution control design before they were allowed to begin construction. The environmental watchdog blacklisted a total of eighty-two projects worth 1.12 trillion yuan that had allegedly seriously violated environmental protection assessment rules. In a Politburo study session in December 2006 Hu Jintao urged local authorities to conserve the environment, linking energy use and pollution control with national and economic security.[87] In January 2007 SEPA stripped four cities in Shanxi province of the power to approve new construction projects on the grounds of their failure to take measures to protect the environment.[88] Working with the People's Bank of China, the central bank, and the China Banking Regulatory Commission, SEPA can refuse polluting firms bank credit. However, it remains to be seen whether this 'green credit' policy is enforceable at local levels where officials attach primary importance to economic growth.[89]

Domestic impact on global environmental governance

As the largest and fastest-growing developing country, China's domestic experiences in environmental governance may be of some use to other developing nations and have impacts on its neighbours. The fact that China shares land borders and fifteen rivers with fourteen countries means that its environmental damage can easily pass on to them, as evidenced by the Songhua incident, increasing the potential for environmental conflict. These issues have a clear impact on China's diplomacy, not least in terms of environmental justice. China jealously guards the principle of common but differentiated responsibility, for its own benefit as well as for the developing world. It has chastised some developed countries for using environmental grounds to delay Third World development by imposing trade barriers, tying development aid to environmental standards, exploitating the natural resources of the Third World, and transferring polluting industries to poor countries. These acts constitute what the Chinese government regards as environmental imperialism.[90]

China's stance on a key issue that tends to divide the more developed countries from the less developed countries is worthy of note for its direct impact on the working of global environmental governance. It is: How should the burden of tackling environmental deterioration be shared fairly among countries with uneven levels of economic development?

While China has indicated its willingness to participate in talks on fighting global warming beyond 2012, it maintains that more developed countries should take the lead in addressing the problem of environmental pollution and that it will not accept any mandatory quotas of reductions in greenhouse gas emissions.[91] Instead, it argues for improving its relatively low energy efficiency to *slow* the growth of emissions. Shortly before the Copenhagen meeting, China set a 'voluntary' target of reducing the carbon intensity of its economy by 40–45 per cent by 2020, from a 2005 baseline.[92] Its arguments are threefold. First, China's per capita emissions are low in comparison with the world average and with those of the industrialized countries in particular.[93] Second, as a developing country, China lacks the financial and technological resources to shift to the use of environmentally friendly energy technology. Finally, developed nations are more responsible for the accumulation of greenhouse gases than developing ones (see Appendices B and C).[94] But it can be countered that emissions by the emerging economies of China, India and Mexico have risen rapidly in recent years.[95] Therefore, the US has declared that it will not be a party to a new climate change treaty if it is not applicable to China, India and the rest of the Third World.[96] In response, China and four developing states have not committed themselves to the goal pledged by the eight largest industrialized countries in July 2008 of halving global greenhouse gas emissions by 2025 (from the 1990 level).[97] At the Copenhagen conference, developed nations were willing to pledge that by 2050 they would slash their emissions to a level 80 per cent below what they were in 1990. This was dubbed the '80 per cent by 2050' formula. However, due to China's resistance, the promise was not given in the Copenhagen Accord. Since there were separate targets for developed and developing countries, marked 'x' and 'y' in the draft agreement, China (and India) resisted any attempt to introduce a formal commitment to emissions reduction by developing states. The initial goal for reaching a legally binding treaty in 2010 was also dropped.[98]

Moreover, due to its concerns over sovereignty, China strongly resisted international monitoring and verification of its pledge on emissions mitigation, which the US expressly requested. Towards the end of the Copenhagen Summit, the US and the BASIC countries sealed a deal whereby each country was to submit its emission reduction or mitigation target to the UN Framework Convention on Climate Change (UNFCCC) by 31 January 2010; the information would then be subject to international consultations and analysis (ICA), a verification programme.[99] Joanna Lewis argues that China's reservation about the measurement, reporting and verification (MRV) of national mitigation measures is due largely to its concerns over the quality of its energy statistics and transparency.[100] By the deadline, fifty-five developed and developing states, including the US, the twenty-seven member states of the EU, China, India, Brazil and Japan, submitted their emission goals to the UNFCCC. However, China still insisted that its efforts to slow the growth of emissions were voluntary and non-binding.[101]

As argued by neo-realists, global public goods can only be provided by great powers (hegemons). The effectiveness of global environmental governance depends to a large extent on whether the US and China, the two biggest emitters of greenhouse gases, could both assume a leadership role and reach a compromise on a new protocol beyond 2012. The climate change conference in Cancún in December 2010 restored some momentum to the negotiation process largely because the two powers found room for compromise. Unlike the conference in Copenhagen a year before where it displayed great power diplomacy in negotiations, China played a low-profile role in Cancún. Xie Zhenhua, head of the

106 *Environmental protection*

Chinese delegation, conceded that his team 'had been instructed to avoid saying "No" at the talks'.[102] Instead, India took the lead in mustering political support for ICA whereby states submit their emissions reduction targets and provide regular reports on their measures to achieve the stated goals and to evaluate progress towards them.[103] Consequently, a more formalized mechanism of reporting and verification has been brought into the UN process. In the words of Todd Stern, the US special envoy for climate change, the Cancún Agreement 'successfully anchors mitigation pledges of the Copenhagen Accord and builds on the transparency element of the accord with substantial details and content.'[104]

Why did China change its stance and strategy on the negotiations? Politics matter in China's calculation. First, China's international image was battered by accusations that it sabotaged the Copenhagen talks. While China portrayed itself as a defender of the interests of the developing world in the talks, some of the least developed countries blamed China for the deadlock. In mid-2009 Bangladesh set up an informal group of 'most vulnerable countries' including some island states and other impoverished countries to press for bolder, binding measures to cut emissions by all large economies, including China and India. Bowing to pressure from China and India, African states withdrew from the group in December 2009. The setback in Copenhagen caused a split among developing nations. The Group of 77 also felt betrayed at not being a party to the deal struck at the eleventh hour between the US and the BASIC countries. At Cancún China wanted to be seen as a positive force.[105] As the US made it abundantly clear that unless there was progress on the verification regime, it would not endorse any deals on the proposed Green Fund, which would amount to $100 billion annually by 2020, or on technology transfer and deforestation, the issues high on the agenda of many developing countries, China did not want to be seen as the wrecker of a global agreement.[106] Second, Chinese President Hu Jintao was scheduled to visit the US in January 2011, one month after the Cancún meeting. China was at pains to build up good working relations with the US before the state visit. The value of the Chinese currency and North Korea's provocative behaviour towards the South had already put strains on their mutual relations.[107] Finally, the Norwegian Nobel Committee announced in October 2010 that it would award the Peace Prize for 2010 to Liu Xiaobo, a Chinese political dissident sentenced to eleven years in prison. The award ceremony was held when the Cancún Conference was under way. As long as a binding commitment to reduce emissions was out of reach, China felt that climate change was less of a threat to its national interest than Liu Xiaobo and the endorsement bestowed on him by the West as well as domestic human rights activists. The Chinese leadership focused on how to stave off the negative impact of the award on the legitimacy of the ruling Communist Party.

Global impact on domestic environmental governance

In examining the international sources of environmental policy change in China, Robert Falkner has identified two dynamics at work: one is international socializing and learning through China's political integration with the world, for example participation in international organizations and entering into international treaties; the other is China's economic globalization through trade, which is helping to upgrade China's environmental standards to meet the higher standards set by the developed world with which China has substantial trade.[108]

By mid-2006, China had entered into bilateral environmental cooperation agreements or memorandums of understanding with forty-two countries.[109] Its participation in global environmental governance seems to serve at least two purposes. First, China uses global environmental governance as a platform to present its argument that developing countries should be given 'common but differentiated treatment', a principle which would allow these countries greater flexibility in complying with internationally agreed standards so that they can have more time to catch up with the West in their industrialization.

Second, the Chinese government can use the signing and ratification of international treaties relating to environmental protection to put pressure on domestic manufacturers and consumers and on those with vested interests to take steps to improve the environment. The measures taken in this respect include legal, economic and administrative means, and the introduction to China of expertise and financial support from international organizations and rich countries. China's membership of the WTO serves as a good way to improve the quality of its manufacturing products so as to meet certain environmental standards. Its close working relationships with the World Bank and the UNDP help to secure the necessary funding and technology to enhance its environmental work. With financial and technical aid from the UNDP and Norway worth $2.4 million, China introduced a pilot scheme to analyse and study ways to mitigate environmental change in provinces and regions that would be sensitive to climate change and use fossil fuel intensively.[110] China is the largest recipient of grants and loans from the World Bank for environmental work. In a similar vein, China's interactions with various global environmental actors at various levels serve to break down domestic inter-agency obstacles that might stand in the way of bureaucratic coordination.

The hosting of the 2008 Olympic Games pushed China to improve its environmental protection standards.[111] The Chinese government vowed to run a green Olympics. Under mounting pressure from the International Olympic Committee, whose President, Jacques Rogge, issued a grim warning in August 2007 that Beijing's poor air quality could cause a postponement of some endurance sports events,[112] China went to great lengths to improve the environment ahead of the Games. Polluting factories along Beijing's rivers were either relocated or closed; Capital Iron and Steel Group, Beijing's largest polluter, was partially closed and relocated to Hebei province.[113] The Chinese authorities announced in June 2008 that it would order 45 per cent of Beijing's 3.29 million vehicles off the city's streets for two months between 20 July and 20 September 2008 during the hosting of the Olympics and the Paralympics.[114] The impact of a trial car ban in August 2007 on air quality was, however, not apparent because about one-third of the particulate matter in Beijing originated outside the city. The Ministry of

Environmental Protection unveiled in late July 2008 emergency measures in and around Beijing in the event that Beijing's air quality remained persistently poor. They included an extension of the odd–even car restrictions to Tianjin, a metropolitan coastal city 120 km southeast of Beijing, and to four urban areas in Hebei province which surround Beijing. On top of the initial car ban system, vehicles whose number plates' last digit matched the last number of the date were also forced off the streets.[115] Furthermore, a total of 105 factories in Beijing and 117 plants in Tianjin and Hebei province shut down their production totally or partially. International scientists examined which of the anti-pollution measures Beijing took were eventually successful and at what cost. China's experiment carried wider implications for other industrializing countries, particularly India.[116] The global economic downturn from late 2008 further helped to improve the environment. The Chinese government, however, acknowledged in 2010 that pollution levels had resumed and the country's industrial sector was producing far more waste than previously reported.[117]

Conclusion

Domestically China has done quite a lot of work to combat environmental degradation in recent years, but because of the sheer size of the problem and its general neglect since 1949, the country faces an uphill struggle. With an environment that is likely to get worse before it gets better, China will continue to export its environmental problems to neighbouring countries through river pollution, air pollution and acid rain. It will also continue to import heavy pollution-producing industries through foreign direct investments made by multinational corporations and to disseminate these industries together with their pollution to its rural areas. Ironically, the international community has had to make use of both international pressure and assistance to help China to help itself.[118] China's green NGOs can potentially play an important role, not only to link up with international NGOs and multilateral institutions to deal with the problem, but also to relate more directly with grassroots problems than government agencies.

Neil Carter and Arthur Mol have concluded that the decisions and actions of Chinese leaders – at home and abroad – 'strongly reflect well-perceived domestic interests and priorities (sovereignty and security being among the most important), and there is little evidence of an acceptance of a wider global environmental responsibility as a future global hegemon'.[119] The success or otherwise of China's environmental policies, according to Elizabeth Economy,[120] lies with a broader and more fundamental set of institutional reforms that would promote transparency, the rule of law and official accountability. In other words, unless political rights are properly respected and protected, it will be difficult to make significant progress on environmental rights.[121] To be sure, China has made some progress, but more needs to be done quickly in order to deal with a fast-deteriorating environment. Domestically, there is a pressing need for the central government to establish a governance framework containing incentives for local officials to embrace the idea and practice of environmental protection rather than relying on the present costly command-and-control style of domestic environmental governance.

Obviously, China's domestic approach can hardly be applicable to the management of global environmental governance, because of international anarchy and competition among big powers. China has also shown little sign of contributing to the setting of a global agenda for environmental protection, due to its limited capability and its lack of international experience and political will. What it could do is try to eliminate the Chinese sources of global environmental problems as much as possible so as to reduce adverse effects on the global commons, using self-help or assistance from the outside. While China changes itself, at its own pace, in order to change the world, the world can help China to help itself to enhance environmental protection. Since China's pollution is so serious, any significant improvements made in any sector of its environment would be greeted with applause by other stakeholders. China has accumulated a lot of experiences in its development, including those in combating environmental problems, some of which could be of use to the developing world. That said, with a self-proclaimed aspiration to be a responsible great power and with the privileged position of holding permanent membership in the UN Security Council, China is obliged to demonstrate by deed how it is going to assume responsibility for the provision of global public goods in proportion with its growing political and economic power.

7 Public health

> I believe that in a globalising world, in a world where countries like *China* are joining, and want to join, world governance, at a time when the G8 is becoming the G20, it is right for these countries to take up a share of the burden [in facing global health challenges].
>
> Michel Kazatchkine, 2010[1]

Globalization has changed the landscape of public health. A fundamental change is that people can no longer assume that a nation's public health is a within-the-border domestic issue that has no impact on other nations. Public health is now widely considered to be a non-traditional security issue with global implications. Given this deterritorialization, a key issue is how to control the spread of micro-organisms in a borderless world. Health issues are at the forefront of the study of global politics and global governance. Global health governance is broadly understood as the system of rules used by various actors, acting collectively at sub-national, national and international levels, to control, regulate and mitigate the adverse effects of globalization on the health of populations.[2] For the purpose of this book, the system refers to those rules embodied in health-related international institutions that govern global public goods for health. The prime focus of this chapter is on China's emerging role in global health governance.

Since the turn of this century, it has been observed that China has increasingly embraced multilateralism in global health governance.[3] This engagement was intensified during and after the outbreak of SARS of 2002–2003. This chapter examines China's role in the current global health regime, particularly in three major areas of containment, control and cure of infectious diseases. It first provides a brief overview of China's health governance since the establishment of the PRC. What have the major changes in China's healthcare system been and why does China now care about health governance inside the country and want to improve its health system in terms of disease containment, control and cure? The second section examines China's evolving role in global health governance, focusing on the three key areas that underpin global health governance, namely China and the international health regulations (containing disease), China's health aid to Africa (controlling disease) and its position on access to essential drugs (curing disease). The third section turns to the role of China within the G20 and the health-related Millennium Development Goals (MDGs). How can we account for China's health aid? If health diplomacy is simply a means, then what are the ends of China's health aid?

Domestic health governance: how and why China cares

Providing basic medical care for most people in urban and rural areas, China's healthcare system in Mao's revolutionary era was more equitable and preventive than it is at present. Built on a network of 'barefoot doctors', healthcare workers with rudimentary training, developed at the commune level, China's public health system provided more than 90 per cent of China's population with life-long government-subsidized healthcare. Various public projects and educational campaigns were carried out, aimed at improving hygiene and preventing outbreaks of disease. As a result, this 'cradle-to-grave' system was often praised as a model for the Third World. Not only did the system largely reduce the incidence of communicable diseases, it also significantly raised life expectancy from thrity-five years in 1952 to sixty-eight years in 1985. Infant mortality dropped from about 250 per 1,000 to thirty-four per 1,000 live births during the same period.[4]

However, alongside economic reforms that disbanded both the communes and the associated cooperative medical scheme, China's public health system in the early 1980s switched to a user-pay, market-oriented system. While it is true that scientific and medical skill has improved as a result of the reform, overall, China's medical reform has been a failure in terms of public access to medical care. Under the user-pay health system, people's basic health rights are no longer guaranteed. In many rural areas, public health services have almost collapsed. As a consequence, China's public health system has sadly degenerated into one of the most backward in the world.[5] One of the biggest problems facing China's healthcare system today is inequality in health outcomes, which has increased since the 1990s. Private health (out-of-pocket) payments increased from 20 per cent in 1978 to nearly 60 per cent in 2000,[6] making health services increasingly unaffordable for most citizens. Furthermore, the bulk of medical resources is spent in urban areas, particularly in the coastal regions of Beijing, Shanghai, Zhejiang and Jiangsu.[7] According to the 2006 National Health Survey, conducted by the Ministry of Health, 48.9 per cent of those who needed medical care did not seek it from a doctor because of the cost involved, and 29.6 per cent of those who needed to be hospitalized could not afford it.[8] Overall, more than 90 per cent of the population were not satisfied with the health system.[9] Because of falling public health spending in the reform period, China's health system was unable to handle (re-)emerging infectious diseases. As discussed further below, the SARS outbreak fully exposed the shortcomings and failures of the prevailing public health system to meet the challenges posed by globalization. Consequently it pushed the governance of health firmly back onto the government's policy agenda. Apart from that, the changing norm about the nature of health — treating it as a human rights issue – and the institutional weakness of China's health system gave further impetus to China to undertake healthcare reform at the turn of the twenty-first century.

Curing disease: changing norms on access to healthcare

At the turn of the millennium, a global norm of health shifting the focus of public health discourse onto the needs of the most disadvantaged people in society began to emerge. Dubbed the human rights approach, it regards public health as a human right. The constitution of the WHO explicitly states: 'The enjoyment of the highest attainable standard of health is one of the fundamental rights of every human being without distinction of race, religion, political belief, economic or social condition.'[10] The right to health requires 'government and public authorities to put in place policies and action plans which will lead to available and accessible health care for all in the shortest possible time'.[11] In other words, access to primary healthcare and services are fundamental rights. Equitable access to healthcare is the primary criterion used to evaluate a country's public health system.

Furthermore, with the end of the Cold War and the steady decline of interstate wars, security has no longer been narrowly understood as the absence of military threats to a state emerging from another state. Threats that cannot be resolved or mitigated through the threat or use of military force began to attract the attention of national leaders and the public. As a result of the 'broadening' and 'deepening' approaches, the security agenda migrates away from concerns about state-centric values and is open to both non-military sources of threats and threats to society and human beings. With the advent of globalization, there is an ever-increasing interdependence or mutual vulnerability among states and societies. States have less ability to control the flow of viruses and pathogens across borders. Even the more developed states admit that despite spectacular advances in medical science, they have lost control of the incidence and spread of communicable diseases within their own territories on their own. They recognize that it is in their interests to help improve the provision of public health facilities in developing nations. Against this background, concerns for health security have frequently appeared in the discourse on security studies in the early twenty-first century.[12] The first meeting of the United Nations Security Council in 2000 – the first in the new millennium – discussed the impact of the Human Immunodeficiency Virus/Acquired Immune Deficiency Syndrome (HIV/AIDS) pandemic on peace and security in Africa. It was of much political significance because it was also the first Security Council meeting that addressed a health issue. It paved the way for the Security Council to adopt Resolution 1308 in July that year. Although China was not proactive in the Security Council debate, the UN activities triggered a learning process in the country which reached its climax in 2003 when it had an unforgettable and traumatic experience of the security threat from infectious diseases. Since then the security perspective has had powerful influence on Chinese public health policy.[13]

In order to remedy its ailing healthcare system and to provide a universal and affordable medical service to Chinese citizens, Beijing endorsed in 2009 a three-year plan for medical reform, whereby the government would invest 850 billion yuan ($125 billion) improving the country's healthcare system.[14] However, just one year after the reform, during the eleventh Standing Committee of the National People's Congress in December 2010, members expressed scepticism about the achievement of the reform in improving the provision of accessible and affordable medical care in China. They argued that uneven distribution of quality medical resources is at the root of the current public health problem. According to Chinese government statistics, while 42 per cent of medical doctors possess a bachelor's or higher degree, more than 80 per cent of these work in hospitals in cities. As a result, patients from rural and suburban areas have little confidence in community and rural clinics. They tend to visit better-resourced hospitals in the cities. A typical example is Beijing where about seventy million patients have no fixed abode in the capital but come from other parts of the country.[15] This finding is echoed by those who offer medical services to the rural people. They claim that money alone cannot resolve the problem adequately. A major hurdle to expanding healthcare to rural people is the dearth of skilled medical practitioners in the countryside who know how to use the medical equipment bought by the newly built or refurbished rural clinics.[16] The situation of *kanbing nan, kanbing gui* ('getting healthcare is difficult, seeing a doctor is expensive') is still widespread in China.

Controlling and containing disease: institutional weaknesses

Another motivation for China's shifting stance on public health is the institutional weakness of its health system in controlling infectious diseases. Apart from the above-mentioned difficulties in offering accessible and affordable medical care for all, another serious problem for the current Chinese health system is disease surveillance and control inside the country. The primary reason for this is that public health was removed from the national development agenda under the economic reform initiated by Deng Xiaoping in the late 1970s. Owing to a lack of government commitment and a shortage of funds for public health, many anti-epidemic stations and preventive care institutions have been cut back.[17] As a consequence, some infectious and parasitic diseases, such as tuberculosis and schistosomiasis, have been resurgent in rural areas.[18] With fee-driven incentives, China's health system has been transformed into an emergency system, failing to control (re-)emerging infectious diseases effectively.[19]

In the midst of the SARS outbreak, the WHO pointed out on 9 April 2003 in its Mission Report to the Ministry of Health in China that the prevention work in Beijing 'was not so well organised'.[20] In a work plan of provincial visits, the WHO further stressed that '[t]here was an urgent need to improve surveillance and infection control' in the country.[21] China's tardy report on avian influenza (H5N1) in 2003 led WHO officials to criticize the government further for 'not yet [coming] around to [putting] global interests ahead of its own'.[22] The WHO advised that 'great effort to develop options for the New CMS [cooperative medical scheme] must be made'.[23] Furthermore, in July 2005, a joint report issued by the State Council's Development Research Centre and the WHO pointed the finger directly at China's public healthcare system for its failure to prevent and control both serious chronic diseases and infectious diseases. The report concluded that China's health reform over the past twenty years had been 'basically unsuccessful'.[24] China came under mounting pressure to remedy the deficiencies of health surveillance and control of infectious diseases in its healthcare infrastructure at all levels.[25]

In a nutshell, the SARS epidemic has had lasting effects on China's conceptualization of the global nature of public health and national security. Witnessing the severe deficiencies of its healthcare system and the loss of 'face' in the international community, China began to be more determined than ever before to forge ties with institutions of global health governance in order to improve its failing healthcare infrastructure and repair its tarnished international reputation.

China's evolving role in global health governance

Despite having been a member of the WHO since its entry into the United Nations in 1971, China had not had much interaction with the organization until the full-blown outbreak of SARS. Since then, China has strengthened its engagement with the WHO in combating such infectious diseases as HIV/AIDS, avian flu and more recently influenza A(H1N1) (commonly known as swine flu).

As soon as it began to be involved in global health governance, China found itself confronted with two crucial debates high on the global health agenda. First, the prevention and containment of infectious diseases is considered a global public good for health.[26] Any belated response or negligence in their prevention and containment is deemed to be global public 'bad'. Second, states are expected to take collective action and to cooperate with each other in a multilateral setting to provide global public goods for health. However, the incentive to free-ride in the supply of global public goods begs a crucial question as to who should be responsible for their provision.

Following increasing participation in global health governance,[27] China has played a more proactive role in various international and regional forums, such as the Global Fund to Fight AIDS, Tuberculosis and Malaria (hereafter the Global Fund), the ASEAN Plus Three Seminars on Enhancing Cooperation in the Field of Non-Traditional Security Issues, the International AIDS Conference, and the International Congress on AIDS in Asia and the Pacific. In addition, a new understanding of the importance of public health as well as encouragement of the WHO led the Chinese government to give its full support to Dr Margaret Chan, a Hong Kong Chinese who worked in Hong Kong's Department of Health before she joined the WHO in 2003, for her election campaign to become Director-General of the World Health Organization. Her successful election in November 2006 marked the first time a Chinese assumed leadership of a United Nations organization. The Chinese campaign team was led – albeit informally – by Wu Yi, the then Vice-Premier with the portfolio for public health. The team included Cui Tiankai, an Assistant Foreign Minister; Gao Qiang, Health Minister; and Sha Zhukang, Chinese Ambassador to the UN in Geneva. China preferred Chan to Liu Peilong, a senior mainland Chinese health official, because of her professional training in the West and technocratic work experience in Hong Kong, which was believed to be an asset to China in its campaign to rebuild its reputation as a responsible state and to enhance its international status as a great power.[28] Below we scrutinize China's evolving role in three key areas underpinning global health governance: disease containment, control and cure.

Containing disease: China and the International Health Regulations

The outbreak of SARS and the re-emergence of H5N1 in 2003 brought the issue of institutional reform of global health governance to the fore. As the successor to the International Sanitary Regulations (ISR) of 1903, the International Health Regulations (IHR) of 1969, with minor revisions in 1981, only required states to report outbreaks of three diseases that had threatened the Western world in the nineteenth century, namely cholera, plague and yellow fever. Because of medical advances since the First World War, more advanced countries had once thought that infectious diseases were conquered. With proper border control, they saw little need to strengthen international cooperation on combating contagious diseases. In the 1980s the initial optimism turned out to be misplaced after the emergence and identification of HIV/AIDS in that decade. In 1996 the WHO began the process of revising the IHR, but member states did not perceive the imperative to strengthen the rules until the world witnessed the birth of such deadly new diseases as SARS and H5N1. After the release of a provisional draft in January 1998, it took six years to establish an interim draft in January 2004. Eventually, in May 2005, the WHO completed the revision which came into force in June 2007.[29] Instead of covering only three diseases, the new IHR focus on all 'public health emergencies of international concern' (PHEIC).[30] The IHR (2005) confer greater power on the WHO, such as the power to use data from non-official sources rather than relying on its member states and the power to govern a broader range of public health emergencies of international concern, including those caused by new or (re-)emerging diseases, chemical agents, contaminated food and radioactive material. Under the new IHR, the WHO will create an IHR Expert Roster, an Emergency Committee and a Review Committee. Every member state shall create a national IHR focal point to facilitate communication with other states and the WHO.

An ensuing question is whether China is able to comply with the WHO's new demands for disease surveillance while it does not have a functioning basic health system at grassroots level. Given that China had a history of not being open in handling infectious diseases, its failure to acknowledge the problem of HIV/AIDS inside the country for more than fifteen years until June 2001 serving as the most typical example, one has reasonable grounds for doubting that China will abide by this new health regime.[31] The Ministry of Health was assigned as the national IHR focal point, and the Chinese Frontier Health and Quarantine Law was revised in December 2007.[32] However, these institutional and legal reforms per se cannot ensure China's full compliance with the IHR. Compliance was put to the test in 2008 in the contamination of Chinese milk products. As discussed in detail in Chapter 8, there was a lapse of two months before the Chinese government took steps to handle the dairy products adulterated with melamine, a nitrogen-rich chemical used illegally to inflate protein levels. Up to 300,000 children fell ill from the tainted products and six died. It was supposedly an issue of international concern because the dairy products of Sanlu Group and Mengniu, two dairy product companies involved in the scandal, were sold overseas and the chemical showed up in various products that used Chinese dairy ingredients, resulting in a ban on food imports from China in some countries.[33] Fonterra, a New Zealand dairy company that had a 43 per cent stake in Sanlu, failed to persuade Sanlu and the local authorities to recall the product. Later, Fonterra informed the New Zealand embassy in Beijing of the contamination. With the intervention of Helen Clark, then New Zealand's Prime Minister, New Zealand foreign affairs officials drew Beijing's attention to the problem in September 2008.[34] But it was apparent that China did not treat it as a PHEIC and accordingly did not notify the WHO in a timely manner.[35] While Chinese health officials countered that prior to the food scandal there were no standards for allowable amounts of melamine in food and blamed Sanlu for not reporting the incident to the government,[36] critics argued that the Chinese government covered up the health crisis in order not to disrupt the Beijing Olympic Games in August 2008.

Another contentious issue in the implementation of the IHR is whether states can adopt regulations and measures that are more stringent than those stipulated in the IHR.[37] In the Influenza A(H1N1) (2009) outbreak, China was criticized for putting in place overly stringent and restrictive measures on travellers. But even the developed world now tended to side with developing countries in asking for increased freedom to tackle exogenous life-threatening viruses.[38] The fact that the incidence of Influenza A(H1N1) was comparatively low in China may strengthen the Chinese claim that the control measures, albeit inhospitable to visitors, were necessary to curtail the international spread of the disease, contributing to the provision of a global public good to the international community.

However, China's concern over national sovereignty and the resultant state-centric approach to global governance, discussed in Chapter 2, may be inimical to the universal implementation of the IHR. China declares that the IHR apply to the 'entire territory' of the PRC, including Hong Kong, Macao and Taiwan.[39] However, Taiwan is de facto independent of the PRC. Not accountable to China's central government, Taipei is under no obligation to report disease outbreaks to Beijing. Taiwan was excluded from the two meetings of the Intergovernmental Working Group convened by the WHO Executive Board for the revision of the IHR.[40] How can China fulfil its IHR responsibility if there is a disease outbreak in Taiwan, which was seriously affected by SARS? As the new health regime relies less on reports from governments, China may run a risk of losing 'face' again should the world learn of any outbreak in Taiwan via non-official channels of communication. China's sovereignty claim has impaled it on the horns of a dilemma. It faces a daunting challenge of how Taiwan can be informally included in the IHR without being treated as a signatory. While the motives for the Chinese decision in 2009 to drop its objection to Taiwan's application for observer status in the World Health Assembly remain unclear, as the process has been cloaked in a shroud of secrecy,[41] it is tempting to suggest that this move helped China to enhance its international standing in the health regime by informally shifting the reporting obligations to Taiwan while leaving the cardinal 'One China' principle unscathed. It is likely that the informal inclusion of Taiwan, a territory with a population of twenty-three million, into the WHO as well as the IHR may contribute to the building of an effective regime of global health governance, although this may not be the primary concern of China.

Controlling disease: China's health aid to Africa

International health assistance has a relatively long history, dating back to the early twentieth century when the International Sanitary Bureau was established in 1902 to provide medical aid and advice to states of the Americas. A, if not the, principal rationale has been the view that the best way to protect the developed world from the attacks of deadly diseases originating in developing countries is to treat and curtail them at their source. Traditionally, colonial powers and non-governmental institutions were the main providers of health assistance.[42] In the case of China, political and economic factors may have provided stronger motives for medical aid than fear of the spread of infection. As a victim of imperialism in the past, China may have an advantage over the West in offering aid to the developing world.

Externally China's health policy under Mao could be seen as 'strategic health diplomacy'.[43] In order to expand its political influence in the developing world and to carve out some international space for development, all of China's health aid was delivered to developing countries, mostly in Africa. It began in the 1960s to send 'angels in white' (nurses) and 'barefoot doctors' (doctors) to the African continent to show its goodwill to the people there. Since its first medical team went to Algeria in 1963, China has dispatched more than 20,000 medical practitioners and given 240 million medical treatments to seventy-one developing countries, forty-five of them in Africa, the others in the other four continents.[44] This South-South medical cooperation has formed the backbone of China's growing health diplomacy aimed at spreading its political influence among developing countries.

Under Deng's leadership, China's extension of health aid continued to be in line with its foreign policy objectives. Beijing continued its goodwill gestures by providing health assistance to the developing world after embarking on economic reforms. However, the scope was more restricted than was in Mao's era. The number of countries to which China sent its medical teams reduced substantially. In the course of economic reforms up to the end of the 1990s, the Chinese government placed economic development at the top of its policy agenda, giving a relatively low priority to health in the government's national development plan and international aid programmes. Health was assigned to the less crucial realm of 'low politics'.

Towards the end of the last century, China began to resume forging close ties with Africa. In spite of problems with its health system at home, the Chinese government reiterated in its *China's African Policy*, published in early 2006, its commitment to help to improve Africa's public health service.[45] Indeed, its aid to Africa played a pivotal role in Margaret Chan's WHO election campaign discussed above. When the campaign was drawing to a close, Beijing held in early November 2006 the Beijing Summit and the Third Ministerial Conference of the Forum on China–Africa Cooperation (FOCAC). There, Chan was introduced by Chinese leaders to key African health officials, particularly those on the WHO Executive Board. In addition, China offered to provide $2 billion in preferential export credits and $3 billion in concessional loans to the African countries.[46] Beijing was alleged to have pledged to throw weight behind an African candidate in the next election for the director-general.[47] Likely as a goodwill gesture to Africa, Chan emphasized the need to improve the health of African people, notably women, in her inaugural speech as the newly elected head of the WHO.[48]

It would be interesting to find out whether China is acting out of brotherly altruism in providing health aid to Africa or whether health aid is being used as an instrument to advance such foreign policy interests as the quest for natural resources (see Chapter 9). The next section will analyse China's policy on access to essential medicines, particularly antiretrovirals (ARVs). By investigating China's position on generic drugs and its contribution towards helping African countries gain access to them, the section aims to explore the extent to which China is willing to promote the development of its African allies in their fight against the HIV/AIDS pandemic.

Curing disease: access to essential drugs

A global health issue on the agenda of curing disease is access to essential, affordable medicines. Given the '10/90 gap' – only 10 per cent of the worldwide health-related research budget is spent on research and development into the problems that afflict 90 per cent of the world's population – the call to engage the world's marginalized people since the turn of this century has been of tremendous importance.[49] For example, while more than 33.4 million people worldwide were infected with the HIV virus at the end of 2008, only four million in low- and middle-income countries – less than 12 per cent – received life-prolonging ARV drugs due to their prohibitive price.[50] Since large populations in the poorest parts of the world cannot afford to buy existing essential medicines, the debate between public health and intellectual property rights becomes a 'life versus profit' issue. Should HIV/AIDS drugs be protected by patents? Do the poor have the right to gain access to essential life-sustaining drugs? The problem of access to antiretroviral treatment, care and support remains the subject of heated debate in the global health regime in the twenty-first century.

With regard to access to essential drugs, the WHO declares that 'essential drugs are those that satisfy the health care needs of the majority of the population; they should therefore be available at all times in adequate amounts and in appropriate dosage form'.[51] However, the TRIPS agreement under the WTO is often blamed by civil society organizations for favouring and protecting the big pharmaceutical companies' interests. Although the TRIPS agreement allows developing countries to override drug patents by issuing 'compulsory licences' to manufacture cheaper copy ARVs, the capacity of developing countries to issue a compulsory licence is still unresolved. A hotly contested claim among international relations scholars and HIV/AIDS activists is that the crises of this pandemic are not due to unavailability of drugs but rather to the fact that patients are denied access to the drugs.[52]

A study of China's position on drug patents and the WTO's TRIPS agreement shows that China is failing to adequately support the developing world in curbing HIV/AIDS. While China is lending verbal support to developing countries in the post-TRIPS negotiation within the WTO, it is not taking the leader in demanding the overthrow or revision of 'US-style patent law'.[53] An examination of its investment in pharmaceutical research and development over the last decade clearly shows that China shares few immediate interests with many African countries in the matter of patents. China has opened its door to admit foreign investment. Pharmaceutical industries are among the fast growing inside China. Some typical examples are the cooperation between GlaxoSmithKline (GSK) in China,[54] Shanghai Clinical Research Centre[55] and BGI (formerly known as Beijing Genomics Institute).[56]

China's applications to the World Intellectual Property Organization (WIPO) under the Patent Cooperation Treaty (PCT) have been growing rapidly, from 2,512 in 2005 to 7,906 in 2009, or from 2 per cent to 5 per cent of all applications. In 2009, while the number of PCT applications filed by some advanced countries, such as the US, Germany and Sweden, fell by more than 10 per cent over the preceding year, China had the astonishingly high growth rate of 29.1 per cent (see Table 7.1).[57] This high growth rate can be explained partly by the fact that China started at a very low base: in 2005 it had the smallest number of applications among the countries under comparison, and partly by the fact that China is eager to protect its commercial interests against competition with other innovation-intensive countries. It is anticipated that China will become a major force in producing patented products, including medicines, in the coming years.

Beijing is also showing its overriding ambition to register and protect patents. The State Intellectual Property Office released in November 2010 a National Patent Development Strategy, in which China sets the annual filings of two million domestic patents as its target for 2015. Total patent filing in China in 2009 were only about 600,000, roughly half of them 'utility-model patents' and the other half 'invention patents'. However, this number increased to 743,779 in the first eleven months of 2010.[58] Owing to its rapidly growing research and development and the potential commercial benefits, China (and India) has little incentive to lend support to African countries over relaxing patent requirements

Table 7.1 Top ten Patent Cooperation Treaty applications by country of origin, 2005–2009

	2005	2006	2007	2008	2009	2009 share (%)	Changed compared to 2008 (%)
US	46,858	51,296	54,044	51,673	46,079	29.6	−10.8
Japan	24,870	27,023	27,749	28,785	29,807	19.1	3.6
Germany	15,987	16,734	17,825	18,854	16,732	10.7	−11.3
South Korea	4,689	5,946	7,065	7,900	8,049	5.2	1.9
China	2,512	3,937	5,465	6,126	7,906	5.1	29.1
France	5,756	6,264	6,570	7,073	7,163	4.6	1.3
UK	5,096	5,093	5,539	5,513	5,326	3.4	−3.4
Netherlands	4,504	4,550	4,422	4,341	4,445	2.9	2.4
Switzerland	3,294	3,613	3,814	3,749	3,673	2.4	−2.0
Sweden	2,887	3,334	3,658	4,136	3,581	2.3	−13.4

Source: World Intellectual Property Organization, *The International Patent System Yearly Review: Developments and Performance in 2009* (Geneva: WIPO, 2009), p. 15.

in the TRIPS agreement. Unlike Brazil, Thailand and those African countries with high HIV prevalence rates, China has largely complied with the rules of intellectual property rights since its entry into the WTO in 2001. The fact that China has not issued any compulsory licences, although it has the right to do so, is another sign that it has no intention of overturning the current patent regime on medicines.

China, the G20 and the Millennium Development Goals

China's rising power and accumulated wealth over the past three decades have raised international concern about its share of responsibility for global governance. This section aims to gauge China's contribution in the field of global health and analyse how it can address the global health challenges, in particular in relation to the MDGs.

In September 2000, the United Nations General Assembly adopted Resolution 55/2 whereby all member states vowed to achieve by the year 2015 eight development goals, collectively known as the MDGs. The sixth goal is to provide access to treatment for HIV/AIDS by 2010 and to halt and reverse the spread of HIV/AIDS, tuberculosis and malaria by 2015.[59] However, while progress has been made, new infections outpace prevention efforts. For example, in 2008, among the 8.8 million people who needed life-prolonging treatment for HIV, only 42 per cent of them in low- and middle-income countries received it. In other words, 5.5 million people in need still did not have access to medication. In addition, while the number of patients receiving treatment has increased in the past few years, the new infection rate has far outstripped the expansion of treatment. So, for every two people who start treatment in the world, five become infected.[60] It has been argued that states are 'unlikely to achieve Goal 6'.[61]

Historically, developed countries, especially the G8 and the EU countries, have been the largest donors to international health programmes. Their tremendous financial power has allowed them to extend their leverage over agenda-setting in global health governance, particularly on the priority given to different health issues. For example, during the G8 Summit in Okinawa, Japan, in 2000, the group committed itself to advancing the fight against HIV/AIDS, tuberculosis and malaria. Their commitment subsequently set the stage for the formation of the Global Fund in 2002 and led to the allocation of considerable resources for the prevention and treatment of these diseases globally. In 2005 the group further pledged in Gleneagles, Scotland, an extra $50 billion in aid for development. Including with its previous $80 billion commitment, the group made a pledge of nearly $130 billion in total for international development assistance by 2010.[62] Although as of June 2010 there was a $10 billion shortfall in the group's delivery of their commitment, there is no doubt that the G8 and the Global Fund are the dominant financiers in the fight against HIV/AIDS, tuberculosis and malaria. For example, of the $8.7 billion's worth of total international assistance on HIV/AIDS in 2008–2009, more than 82 per cent ($7.6 billion) came from the G8 countries.[63]

However, with the onset of a global recession in 2008, international donors, particularly the most developed countries, are cutting back on AIDS support, directly weakening the fight against the epidemic across Africa. In 2008–2009, the G8, EU and other donor governments provided $7.6 billion for AIDS relief to developing nations. Compared with $7.7 billion disbursed in 2007–2008, the funding remained essentially flat.[64] Concomitant with the global economic downturn is a power shift from the more developed industrialized countries in the North to the emerging economies in the South. The focus of global health governance has correspondingly shifted from the G8 to a larger group, the G20, created in 1999 (see also Chapter 4).[65] The original concern of the G20 was primarily financial stability and sustainable economic growth with scant attention to global health or social development.[66] However, in October 2010, in the initiative of the South Korean President Lee Myung-bak, a G20 working group on development was established.[67] It is the first working group that emphasizes development assistance and strives for achievement of the MDGs, in particular Goal 2 on improving the quality of education. Considering that there are deep political divisions among the member states, it is still uncertain whether the pro-development approach can be sustained within the group.[68] Nevertheless, it is an important step forward and contributes to the provision of global public goods, in line with the growing influence of this group. While international donors are reducing their pledges of AIDS support, will the emerging economies of the G20, especially China, become significant new players in global health governance?

Paradoxically, although most of the major emerging market economies are comparatively unscathed by the global economic downturn and have maintained robust economic growth, they remain major recipients of aid for their domestic health programmes. According to the Institute of Health Metrics and Evaluation, India and China were among the top ten recipients of health assistance between 2002 and 2007.[69] Despite the fact that China's economy has overtaken that of its nearest competitor, Japan, to become the second largest in the world, with foreign exchange reserves of $2.85 trillion at the end of 2010,[70] it is the fourth-largest recipient of the Global Fund, after Ethiopia, India and Tanzania. Between 2002 when the Global Fund was launched and 2010, China received $964 million, of which 40 per cent went to combat HIV/AIDS in the country.[71] It is little wonder that Michel Kazatchkine, the Executive Director of the Global Fund, asked China (and India) to increase their contributions to the fight against the HIV/AIDS pandemic. Based on a country's national income and the amount that donors are expected to contribute, the Global Fund suggested in 2010 that the Chinese government should contribute $96 million to the Fund over the next three years, or sixteen times its current annual donation.[72] However, during the Global Fund's donors meeting in October 2010 in New York, China pledged only $14 million to the Fund for the 2011–13 funding cycle, slightly more than Nigeria ($10 million), a new donor to the Fund, but far less than Kazatchkine's expectation.[73] Overall, the Global Fund will need $13 billion to $20 billion in 2011–13 to fulfil Goal 6 of the MDGs on time.[74] In the Fund's meeting in October, donors committed $11.7 billion in total for the three years. While it is claimed to be the largest ever financial pledge for a collective international effort to fight the three pandemics, the Global Fund has noted that there is still a huge financing gap to cover the expected minimum demand for health. This shortfall 'could slow down the effort to beat the three diseases'.[75] The Global Fund was disappointed that 'hopes for contributions from several emerging nations from the G20 group have not materialised', although some African countries such as Nigeria, Namibia and Tunisia made commitments for the first time.[76]

While China is now the world's second largest economy, its donations to the WHO, the principal intergovernmental health organization, are not generous at all (see also Chapter 3 for the UN in general). Between 2008 and 2009, its voluntary contributions to the WHO were a mere $4.23 million, less than 0.3 per cent of the total contributions from member states, far less than the US or many members of the G8 (see Table 7.2). China also lagged far behind some medium and even small powers such as Norway ($103.92 million), the Netherlands ($81.61 million), Spain ($59.11 million), Australia ($58.25 million), Sweden ($54.60 million) and Luxembourg ($32 million).[77] A comparison with 1992–93, when the Chinese economy began to take off, reveals surprisingly that China's contribution has been decreasing over time. In 1992–93, it paid $5.80 million to the WHO, accounting for 0.77 per cent of the total contributions from member states.[78]

While China has utilized multilateral cooperation to mobilize international health aid to tackle its mounting internal AIDS crisis,[79] its contributions to global health do not seem to measure up to its growing economic wealth and status. This may be another incidence of the maxi/mini principle, described by Samuel Kim in the 1990s, whereby China wants to maximize its rights while minimizing its responsibilities and commitments. One has valid grounds for asking whether China is a system-exploiting power, tending to free-ride on multilateral efforts to manage global diseases. On the other hand, Chinese officials have often referred

Table 7.2 China and G8 contributions to the World Health Organization in 2008–2009

	Voluntary contributions (US dollars)
	(% of the total contributions from member states)
United States	$424,540,852 (29.56)
United Kingdom	$205,510,011 (14.31)
Canada	$96,356,532 (6.71)
Germany	$48,150,583 (3.35)
Italy	$37,157,862 (2.59)
Japan	$24,520,679 (1.71)
Russia	$20,050,000 (1.40)
France	$19,401,505 (1.35)
China	$4,232,333 (0.29)

Source: World Health Organization, 'Voluntary contributions by fund and by donor for the financial period 2008–2009', Sixty-Third World Health Assembly, A63/INF.COC./4, 29 April 2010; http://apps.who.int/gb/ebwha/pdf_files/WHA63/A63_ID4-en.pdf (accessed 11 January 2011).

to China's development status and its low per capita GDP. The country faces a lot of well known domestic problems. They also claim that 'the biggest contribution China can make to global health is to provide adequate healthcare to its 1.3 billion people'.[80] The small contributions to the Global Fund may also reflect China's reservations about engaging non-state actors in global governance.

Conclusion

Infectious diseases do not recognize or respect national boundaries and can move from one country to another within hours. In order to secure the health of the population of a highly globalized world, states have to take collective action and work with each other as well as with non-governmental organizations to provide global public goods for health. By examining China's domestic health governance and its evolving role in global health governance, this chapter finds that China has now come to an understanding of the importance of good health governance which is more in line with the prevailing global norms than was the case in the pre-SARS period. It is now more proactive in engaging with various actors both inside and outside the country in order to deal with its health challenges. HIV/AIDS and other infectious diseases are cases in point. Externally, China is willing to participate in global health forums and it is among the top ten recipient countries in terms of total global health dollars. Nevertheless, its compliance record in observing the IHR is not unblemished. As to the issue of access to essential medicines, this chapter finds that China fails to support the developing world adequately in tackling the spread of HIV/AIDS. It pays lip service to Africa's calls for extending access to essential HIV/AIDS medicine to ailing patients in the continent. Although it is the second largest economy in the world, China's contributions towards resolving global health problems are far from generous. One has valid grounds for suspecting that China may be taking a 'free-riding' approach to global health. Its health aid to African countries is channelled mainly through bilateral state-to-state deals and concessional loans. More importantly, in comparison with the voluntary contributions of other member states to the WHO, China's contribution is not commensurate with its increasing economic power.

To cite a popular slogan in China – *gaibian ziji yingxiang shijie* ('transforming oneself to influence the world')[81] – if China really wants to portray itself as a 'responsible state', it should take on more global responsibilities, heighten its presence in the global health realm and make greater contributions to global health.

8 Food safety

> Food is essential, and safety should be a top priority. Food safety is closely related to people's lives and health, economic development and social harmony.
>
> Li Keqiang, 2010[1]

China has already overtaken Germany as the world's largest merchandise exporter, accounting for 9.6 per cent of world exports in 2009 (see also Chapter 4).[2] China is now one of the major food exporters. According to the WTO's *International Trade Statistics 2009*, China exported in 2008 $35.9 billion worth of food to the world, accounting for 3.2 per cent of world food exports. This compares with only 1.4 per cent in 1980.[3] China is a leading producer and exporter of farmed seafood in the world. As shown in Figure 8.1, China has since 1984 been a net exporter of foodstuffs. Its (net) exports have grown rapidly

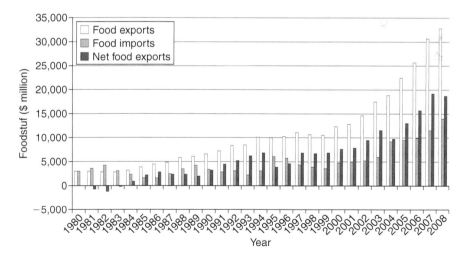

Figure 8.1 China's foodstuff exports and imports, 1980–2008 ($ million) (sources: *Zhongguo tongji nianjian* (*China Statistical Yearbook*), 2000, pp. 589–90 (for 1980–89); 2009, pp. 726–7 (for 1990–2008)).

126 Food safety

since it joined the WTO in December 2001. In 2008 foodstuffs contributed 6.3 per cent to China's total trade surplus, making it a key export product of the country. Japan and the United States are the leading markets for China's food exports (see Figure 8.2). Its export boom has made it the largest source of US imports since 2007, with 19.1 per cent of all US imports in 2009 coming from China.[4] In particular, China is the third largest supplier of food imports into the US.[5] This growth is consistent with the impressive growth in global food exports in the last decade, particularly in processed food.[6]

With the growth of Chinese exports and the globalization of food production and consumption, there has been increasing worldwide concern about the quality and standards of Chinese products. There has been a spate of food and drug safety scandals involving Chinese goods since 2007, affecting toothpaste, fake infant milk powder, melamine-tainted pet food, fake green peas and bleaching pistachios, as well as excessive pesticide residues in vegetables, fruit, teas, domestic fungi, animal products and seafood. The latest incident was about melamine-tainted milk powder that caused six fatalities and almost 300,000 cases of children with kidney damage, of whom more than 53,000 were hospitalized, in 2008.[7] All these food scandals have sparked worldwide debate on China's consumer product safety, bringing the quality of Chinese food under the spotlight of the international community. Given increasing interaction with the world and being a new player in global food governance, China's product safety is not only crucial for its people's wellbeing but also salient to the rest of the

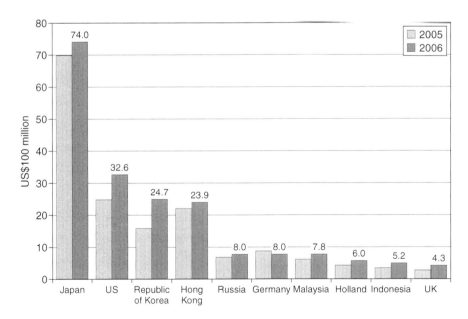

Figure 8.2 Top ten destinations of China's food exports, 2005 and 2006 (source: 'White Paper on Food Quality and Safety', China.org.cn; 17 August 2007; www.china.org.cn/english/news/221274.htm (accessed 28 September 2010)).

world. China has come under pressure from the rest of the world, especially the major consumer countries in the West, to transform its present food regulatory regime into a more effective food safety governance institution. This highlights not only the imperative of improving China's consumer product safety standards but also the pressing need for a concerted international effort to establish an effective regulatory governance regime to unify Chinese safety standards with those of the more advanced West, as China has now become an integral part of globalized food supply chains. Harmonization of the national regulatory regimes of exporting and importing countries is deemed necessary in the age of globalization in order not to impede normal international trade.[8] At issue is whether China is a player in this inclusive process or whether it feels that the evolving global food governance system encroaches on rather than supplements its national regulatory practices.

While we acknowledge that China's product safety is relevant not only to food products but also to other commodities such as toys, tyres and so on, this chapter focuses on food and drug safety issues as they have attracted the most attention both domestically and internationally. It first examines and identifies the flaws in China's food safety governance. Why is the quality of China's food products so inferior? Why does it appear that product safety problems are largely restricted to products manufactured in China? We then highlight some of the actions that the Chinese government has taken so far to improve its food safety. Attention is paid to the extent and limits of China's engagement and cooperation with the outside world, both bilaterally and multilaterally, in providing global public goods for food safety. The chapter concludes by summarizing the challenges that the Chinse government is facing in managing food safety issues.

China's food safety: a rising global concern

China is not only the largest food-consuming country but also the largest food-producing country in the world. Increasingly intertwined in global trade and with a string of safety breaches, Chinese food safety has often been identified as not yet conforming with international standards. This has not only put China's food safety under the global spotlight but has also rendered the label 'Made in China' a symbol for shoddy goods among consumers, to be equated with 'buyer beware'.[9] A series of food safety breaches have made consumers paranoid about the quality of Chinese products. Some attribute them to China's authoritarian political system and bluntly proclaim that the Chinese system is 'without rule of law'.[10] As early as 2002 the EU banned imports of a wide array of Chinese animal products, including poultry, livestock and honey. This stringent restriction began to ease two years later only after China had made considerable improvements in its veterinary standards.[11] The EU's Rapid Alert System for Food and Feed (RASFF) reported 260 food safety problems related to Chinese food products in 2006.[12] China has received the highest number of notifications from the RASFF: 355 in 2007, 500 in 2008 and 345 in 2009.[13] The US Food and

128 *Food safety*

Drug Administration (FDA)'s rejection rate of food imported from China is much higher than that from other trading partners.[14] In February 2008, just six months before the Beijing Olympics, when Beijing's grocery chickens tested positive for hormones, the US Olympic team announced that it would import its own food and cook its own meals during the games for fear of failing the drug tests if they had been eating food containing excessive amounts of hormones. This decision damaged China's international image and perceptions of its capacity to organize a global event.[15] Serious incidences of contamination in China's food industry have caused many life and health implications around the world.

China's response to the criticism from the West about the safety of its food exports is sometimes rather defensive. It often claims that the mass media in the West have exaggerated the violations of product safety standards in order to demonize China.[16] During a US–China Strategic Economic Dialogue meeting held in Washington, DC, in May 2007, Wu Yi, the then Vice-Premier and leader of the Chinese delegation, openly lashed out at the critics, stating that 'confrontation does no good at all to problem-solving'.[17] Beijing officials emphasize that it is impossible to achieve 'zero risk in terms of food safety' and that 99 per cent of its food exports to the US are safe and meet quality standards.[18] Probably as an act of retaliation against growing international criticism, China has strengthened its inspections of foreign products entering China and has seized some American and European imports. For example, China complained that some US products such as oranges failed to meet Chinese standards;[19] and suspended imports of some US chicken and pork after finding excess chemical residues, including antibiotics, in 2007.[20] In addition, in early 2007, the Chinese government blocked imports of Evian water from France, claiming that the bacteria levels exceeded its national standards.[21] In response to the seizure, Danone, the producer of Evian water, claimed that the bacteria in the mineral water were harmless and met the standard set by the WHO. The company further asserted that China did not align its domestic standards with international health regulations.[22]

Nevertheless, China's inferior food is not only found in exports. Chinese citizens often encounter inferior food in their daily life. Owing to constant food safety incidents, the level of Chinese consumers' trust in food safety has fallen dramatically. While shopping, food safety is a major concern and 'what to eat' has become a question for many Chinese.[23] Several national surveys, carried out by different organizations between 2005 and 2010, came to the same conclusion: food safety and unsafe food ingredients are the issues that worry the Chinese the most, and more than half of them do not have confidence in the country's food safety system.[24] According to an Asian Development Bank estimate, food-related disease costs China $14 billion a year in lost lives and healthcare expenditure.[25] The government has made strenuous efforts to improve food safety after a series of contamination and health scares. For example, in 2006, the government conducted more than ten million inspections, and 152,000 unlicensed food producers and retailers were shut down for making and selling fake and low-quality products.[26] However, in an official nationwide inspection in 2007, nearly 15 per cent of foods still failed quality checks.[27]

Flaws in China's food safety governance

Although China has been able to lift some 400 million people out of abject poverty in the past thirty years,[28] substantial income inequality between coastal and inland regions and between cities and the countryside remains. It is said that a dual food system is evolving in China which leaves the rural population exposed to most of the country's hazardous food.[29] Suppliers tend to produce food in accordance with the more stringent standards of the intended recipient countries. However, this 'export driving' scheme does not help to improve food safety inside China, particularly in the countryside, or in foreign markets where regulations are less tight. While suppliers tend to provide food of higher standards to urban and international markets, the rural areas may receive or produce only second-rate or even unsafe products. With lower living standards and lower literacy, many rural Chinese lack consumer knowledge and consumer rights. Under the 'dual food system', they are perhaps the most vulnerable to the unsafe food products inside the country. Therefore, strengthening the Chinese food safety system would not only benefit other countries but would also provide an essential public good for all Chinese. Ideally, harmonization of national food standards to tighten the food safety regulatory system across the board, which would reduce the cost of monitoring, should be the long-term goal of the reform of the food governance system. However, before looking at the reform measures aimed at achieving that goal, one must understand why the quality of China's food products is so inferior and where the flaws of its food safety governance lie. Three major flaws in China's food safety governance are identified here: a disjointed production system; a fragmented and corrupt regulatory system; and growing but limited civil society participation.

A disjointed production system

As a result of the decentralized economic structure, which was given further impetus by the post-Mao economic reforms, the production of food and drugs is scattered across China among hundreds of thousands of small-scale collective and private firms that employ fewer than ten workers. The Chinese government has encountered great difficulty in ensuring product safety. While the top three slaughterhouses of the US account for 65 per cent of the meat sold domestically, China's top three slaughterhouses process only 5 per cent of the meat in the country. According to China's Administration of Quality Supervision, Inspection and Quarantine (AQSIQ), 78.7 per cent of the country's food processing industries are small-scale food workshops, with fewer than ten employees and occupying less than two acres of farm land. These workshops only make up 9.3 per cent of the market share,[30] reflecting the very low cost of their production compared with other big producers.

Because of poor production conditions and quality control, these small food workshops become a major source of threats to food safety. Common threats include pesticides, fungicides, illegal veterinary medicine, and contamination during processing and transport. Owing to the sheer size of the country and the enormous number of small-scale farms and food processing plants, it is very difficult for the government to monitor and manage food safety effectively. The government tried to address the problem by initiating a market access system in 2002 by which food producers would be issued production licences only if they met official standards. However, this system collapsed after forcing many small-scale workshops to close down and pushing up local unemployment rates. Local authorities, tasked with regulating food safety, had little incentive to comply with the regulations. They were unwilling to promote food safety at the expense of employment opportunity and tax revenue accruing to local coffers.[31]

According to a national survey of 448,153 food producers carried out by AQSIQ in 2007, nearly half of China's food processors (49.8 per cent) had improper licences and 36.6 per cent had no licence at all.[32] In other words, less than 15 per cent of the food plants were licensed. More seriously, some major food companies sub-contract parts of their production to small- or family-sized producers. They rely on several sub-contractors to provide food ingredients or services. As a result, it is very difficult to regulate food safety and keep track of the origins of the raw materials.[33] In a State Council white paper entitled *China's Food Quality and Safety*, published in August 2007, the government openly admitted the problem, and explicitly indicated that these food workshops 'pose the most difficult problem for ensuring food quality and safety'.[34]

An underlying cause of the prevalence of sub-standard small-scale food plants is the lack of an insurance or compensation system. This induces farmers to overuse pesticides to prevent the loss of their crops, stock or vegetables. China is not only a major consumer of pesticides but also a large producer and exporter of the chemicals. That there is no insurance scheme in place to compensate for losses to farmers incurred by animal disease or food-borne illnesses gives little incentive for farmers to report any unusual situations affecting their stock or vegetables.[35] In order to minimize or avoid losses, farmers tend to overuse antibiotics or pesticides in the hope of maintaining the 'health' of their livestock and vegetables when they enter the retail markets.

Another contributing factor is the shortage of cold storage and logistics systems. China only had about 30,000 refrigerated trucks for transporting food by mid-2007, while the US had about 280,000. An international management consulting firm, A. T. Kearney, advised in a report published in 2007 that China would need to invest about $100 billion over the next ten years to upgrade its refrigeration capacity to meet international standards.[36]

A similar production structure can be found in China's drug industry. Due to the high profitability of the pharmaceutical industry in China, local authorities went to great lengths to promote the growth of the sector in their area. One study shows that China had 2,731 drug manufacturers in 1985; this grew to 5,100 in

1997. The number of drug sellers rose from 53,269 to 86,000, of which over 90 per cent were small firms, in the same period.[37]

A fragmented and corrupt regulatory system

The second weakness of China's food safety governance is its fragmented and overlapping authority and responsibility among diverse regulatory bureaucracies. In the Maoist command economy, China's food industry was led and supervised by several industrial ministries, including Light Industry, Food, Agriculture, Chemical Industry, and Commerce, resulting in a complex division of labour among them. But due to the fact that food enterprise managers were not required to be responsible for the profit and loss of their enterprises, they had little incentive to produce counterfeit products or to contaminate food in order to earn higher profits. Food safety was understood as a matter of *food hygiene* rather than deliberate food adulteration under the Mao era.[38]

As part of Mao's historical legacy, China's food safety regulatory regime is still managed by a couple of relatively independent agencies, of which the principal ones are the Ministry of Agriculture, AQSIQ, the Ministry of Health (MoH) and the State Administration for Industry and Commerce (SAIC).[39] They are assigned responsibility for different parts of the food supply chain. Between 2004 and 2008, the Ministry of Agriculture was in charge of planting and animal feed, AQSIQ was responsible for the food manufacturing and processing sector, while the SAIC and the MoH were responsible for food distribution and consumption (e.g. the catering industry and restaurants) respectively. The State Food and Drug Administration (SFDA) was tasked with regulating food and related products as well as investigating food safety incident and the subsequent prosecution.[40] The SFDA was moved back to the MoH in March 2008, losing its independent authority but still playing a monitoring role in food consumption. The recent Food Safety Law of 2009, however, does not fully redress this segmented regime.[41]

Poor enforcement of the rules laid down by the central government is often due to poor coordination and tugs-of-war among different agencies. For example, before 1998, the MoH and the State Pharmaceutical Administration (SPA) (*Guojia yiyao guanliju*) were the principal regulators in the drug industry. However, the two regulators did not always share information with each other and sometimes competed intensely for regulatory power.[42] In order to alleviate the governance crises in drug safety regulation, the central government created the State Drug Administration (SDA) within the MoH in 1998 as an attempt to consolidate drug regulation into a single body. As a result of the 1998 restructuring, all state pharmaceutical enterprises were in principle subordinate to the MoH while the SDA was solely responsible for drug safety regulation without any involvement in economic regulation or industrial promotion. In other words, at the national level the MoH 'had no say' in the safety regulatory process. However, it continued to issue licences in competition with the SDA. At the subnational level, things were even more complicated. The original SPA took over the role of the MoH and some provincial SPAs were even renamed provincial drug companies. Many officials played dual roles of regulation in government and production in enterprises, undermining the independence and authority of the regulator.[43] Indeed, for financial reasons, the primary task of local regulators was not to monitor the local pharmaceutical industry but to foster a business-friendly environment for the growth of the companies.

In addition, China made a distinction between prescription and non-prescription drugs in 2000. Since then, the sale of non-prescription drugs has grown substantially from $600 million in 1999 to $7.3 billion in 2005. Drug companies anxious to sell more non-prescription drugs tried to bribe SDA/SFDA officials to speed up approvals. This has given much room for bureaucratic manoeuvring and corruption. The most typical case of corruption in the food and drug safety system is that of Zheng Xiaoyu, the director of SDA/SFDA in 1998–2005. He was executed in July 2007 for accepting gifts and bribes worth more than $850,000 from eight pharmaceutical companies in return for expediting the approval of new drugs applications. During seven years at the helm of the SDA/SFDA, he approved more than 150,000 new medicines, or 21,428 every year on average. China's approval rate was 134 times higher than that of its US counterpart, which only approved 140 or so annually. At least six drugs that the SFDA approved during Zheng's seven-year tenure were said to be counterfeit.[44] Many regulatory officials were also stakeholders of various pharmaceutical companies, and were consequently more concerned about the companies' growth than the quality and safety of their drugs. After the Zheng scandal, the SFDA required all staff members to divest their shareholdings in the pharmaceutical companies, which amounted to 3.5 million yuan (approximately $526,400).[45]

Growing but limited civil society participation

Non-governmental organizations are emerging in China to raise consumer concerns about food safety and to self-regulate the food industry. Examples are: the Pesticide Eco-Alternatives Centre (PEAC) based in Kunming, Yunnan, southwest China, created in February 2002; Wang Hai's Consumer Protection Hotline; the China Consumers' Association, established in 1984; the China Condiment Industry Association; and the China National Food Industry Association. The PEAC is the sole Chinese NGO promoting reduced use of pesticides and the usage of alternative forms of pest control instead.[46] Wang Hai is dubbed the 'Ralph Nader of China': he followed in the footsteps of Ralph Nader in the US who set up a non-profit consumer advocacy group known as Public Citizen in 1971.[47] However, owing to various restrictions on the registration, operation and funding of genuine NGOs in China, they play minimal role in safeguarding food safety. The China Consumers' Association receives and handles complaints from consumers about food products, but it is a government-run organization. Like their counterparts in the US, the Chinese trade associations can regulate their member enterprises in order to raise the quality standards of their products. Nevertheless, due to their small size, they serve more as a conduit of information and regulations between the government and businesses.[48] Whistle-blowers are often given severe punishment by the Chinese authorities. An example is Tang Lin, a villager from Chongqing's Fengjie county. He launched an online chat group to advocate food safety after his one-year-old son died in August 2008 from milk powder contamination. He was sentenced in June 2010 to one year in a 're-education through labour' camp for 'posing a threat to public security by scare-mongering'.[49] Another victim, whose trial caught both domestic and international attention and commanded widespread sympathy, is Zhao Lianhai. After his son was made ill by tainted formula milk, he created a website to champion the cause of the affected parents and helped them to pursue lawsuits against dairy companies. He was given a two-and-a-half-year sentence in November 2010 for 'inciting social disorder'.[50] In an apparent move to give in to both internal and external pressures, the Chinese government reportedly released him on medical grounds at the end of December 2010 when he did not appeal against the verdict.[51]

Chinese measures to improve food safety

The food scares expose two shortcomings in the Chinese and international food safety systems. Not only do they show the potential threat to health that stems from deficiencies in Chinese foodstuffs, but they also indicate the limits of the importing countries' monitoring capacities to prevent inferior food from entering their territories. In order to resolve this problem, both China and the importing countries share a common interest in ensuring the safety of Chinese food products by engaging in bilateral or multilateral cooperation. This section examines what China has done internally and how Beijing, other major powers and international organizations can beef up the Chinese consumer product safety system without damaging normal international trade.

Domestic measures

Domestically, in the wake of the series of food safety scandals in 2007, China pledged $1.2 billion to address the problem and launched nationwide crackdowns to weed out unqualified producers and confiscate fake products. In the same year, the State Council established the Leading Group on Product Quality and Food Safety, headed by then Vice-Premier Wu Yi. The government submitted the Draft Food Safety Law to the National People's Congress, the legislature, at the end of the year.[52] The Food Safety Law (*shipin anquan fa*) entered into force on 1 June 2009, and in accordance with the Law an unusually high-level State Council Food Safety Commission (*Guowuyuan shipin anquan weiyuanhui*) was set up in February 2010. It is led by Li Keqiang, the executive Vice Premier, with Hui Liangyu and Wang Qishan, two Vice-Premiers, being vice-directors. Other members of the Commission include the Minister of Industry and Information, the Minister of Health, the Minister of Agriculture, and Directors of AQSIQ, SAIC, the SFDA and the State Grain Bureau.[53] The SFDA in December

134 *Food safety*

2010 ordered local food and drug administrations to tighten the monitoring of the trade and consumption of diary products. Restaurants are required to keep files on their suppliers of dairy products as well as documents to help the authorities identify the specifications of the products.[54]

External approach

Externally, in 2007 China joined the World Organization for Animal Health, a body responsible for fighting animal disease, and is active in the Codex Alimentarius Commission, an international food standard-setting body created in 1963 by the United Nations Food and Agriculture Organization (FAO) and WHO.[55] China is also a party to the WTO's Agreement on the Application of Sanitary and Phytosanitary Measures (SPS Agreement). The SPS Agreement helps member states to apply policies and measures relating to food safety as well as animal and plant health and encourages acceptance of the same food safety standards by member states.[56] The Chinese authorities understand the importance of cooperating with the more advanced importing countries to improve consumer product standards and to come up with collectively agreed minimum standards. As shown in Table 8.1, China's official standards match or are even higher than the standards of Codex in terms of the maximum residual limit (MRL) of chlorpyrifos in vegetables and the MRL of oxytetracycline in fish and aquatic products. However, Codex simply lays down minimum standards for states to follow. States under international law have the right to set up more stringent standards than Codex. In general, the food safety standards adopted by developed countries are higher than those adopted by developing countries. For example, Japan's chlorpyrifos standard in vegetables and onions is much higher than Codex or China's. Furthermore, MRL is only one of the standards used to safeguard food. Other benchmarks, such as quality of irrigation water, good agricultural practices, veterinary drugs, pollutants and spoilage organisms allowed in food, standards for food additives and their use, hygiene standards for food packaging materials, standards for signs or labels on food packages, and standards for food testing methods, are also important for food safety control.[57]

Another important international food safety regime is the International Food Safety Authorities Network (INFOSAN). It is an information network for the dissemination of food safety-related public health events that may have international implications.[58] It was developed by the WHO in March 2004 in cooperation with the FAO. It is operated and managed by the WHO's Department of Food Safety, Zoonoses and Foodborne Diseases. According to the International Health Regulations (IHR) (2005), member states of the WHO have the responsibility to inform the WHO through their National IHR Focal Points and INFOSAN Emergency Contact Point of any possible public health emergency of international concern, including food contamination and foodborne diseases, within twenty-four hours of assessment.[59]

As mentioned earlier, the melamine-tainted milk scandal in 2008 made up to 300,000 children ill and killed at least six infants in China. One may wonder

Table 8.1 The MRL of the chlorpyrifos standard in vegetables and the MRL of the oxytetracycline standard in fish and aquatic products

Importers	Vegetables (Chlorpyrifos)	Garlic (Chlorpyrifos)	Onions (Chlorpyrifos)	Spinach (Chlorpyrifos)	Fish (Oxytetracycline)
CODEX	0.52 ppm	–	0.20 ppm	–	0.20 ppm
China	0.36 ppm (2003–2005)	0.02 ppm (2003–2005)	0.02 ppm (2003–2005)	1.00 ppm (2003–2005)	0.10 ppm (2001–2005)
Japan	0.79 ppm (1992–2001), 0.11 ppm (2002–2005)	0.05 ppm (1992–2001), 020.01 ppm (2002–2005)	0.50 ppm (1992–2001), 0.05 ppm (2002–2005)	0.10 ppm (1996–2001), 0.01 ppm (2002–2005)	0.20 ppm (1992–2005)
United States	0.76 ppm (1992–2005)	0.50 ppm (1992–2005)	0.50 ppm (1992–2005)	0.05 ppm (1992–2005)	2.00 ppm (1992–2005)
EU	0.52 ppm (1992–2001), 0.10 ppm (2002–2005)	0.05 ppm (1992–2005)	0.20 ppm (1992–2005)	0.05 ppm (1992–2005)	0.10 ppm (1992–2005)
Australia	0.10 ppm (2002–2005)	0.01 ppm (1992–2005)	0.01 ppm (1992–2005)	0.01 ppm (1992–2005)	0.20 ppm (1992–2005)

Source: Chunlai Chen, Jun Yang and Christopher Findlay, 'Measuring the Effect of Food Safety Standards on China's Agricultural Exports', *Review of World Economics*, Vol. 144, No. 1 (2008), p. 93; with modifications.

whether the Chinese government regarded this as a 'public health emergency of international concern' and informed the WHO promptly through the INFOSAN Emergency Contact Point. As soon as the WHO learned of the tainted milk incident through the INFOSAN Emergency surveillance system, it requested further information from the Chinese authorities on 11 September 2008. China's INFOSAN Emergency Contact Point under the Ministry of Health confirmed this incident and provided the WHO with a description the following day. Four days later, the WHO sent out an INFOSAN Emergency Alert to member states, warning them of the event and of the possibility that the contaminated milk products could have entered their markets.[60]

Thus two months elapsed between the outbreak of the milk scandal in July 2008 and the triggering of the INFOSAN Emergency Alert in September 2008. According to IHR (2005), countries are required to report any food safety emergency to the WHO INFOSAN with twenty-four hours. A Chinese representative to the WHO in Geneva explained in November 2010 that before the incident of the contaminated milk powder, China did not have any national melamine standard for food products and, as a result, it was hard to decide whether the contamination constituted 'a public health emergency of international concern' from the Chinese perspective.[61] However, critics argued that the tardy response was not due to technical factors; instead, the Chinese government had covered up the outbreak in order not to disrupt the Beijing Olympics in August 2008.[62]

In the final analysis, the question at the heart of the various scandals is whether the country's food processing industries, of which 78 per cent are small-scale food workshops, can fully implement the food safety standards and whether the national SFDA can monitor the various producers and enforce the standards faithfully. Quality control becomes arduous work for the government. Consumers in China and the outside world have grounds for scepticism. At the end of December 2009 Chinese regulators announced the arrest of three executives of the Shanghai Panda Dairy Company and the closure of the company for selling melamine-contaminated milk products. However, the Shanghai government acknowledged days later that the arrests had actually been made in April 2009 and the investigation into the Shanghai dairy began in February 2009. No official explanation was offered for the ten-month delay in alerting the public. Despite the fact that the Food Safety Law and the corresponding Food Safety Act have been effective since June and July 2009 respectively, transparency in information disclosure was found wanting.[63] Being one of the major food exporters in the world, China's ability to establish successful food safety control can contribute greatly to the global public goods for food safety. To that end, it is far from sufficient for China to set up an official regime on food safety; more importantly, it needs to ensure that the regime is rigorously enforced to protect 'Made in China' food from adulteration or excessive chemicals such as pesticide residues. This prompts calls for closer bilateral or multilateral cooperation with major food-importing countries on food safety.

Bilateral cooperation

As mentioned earlier, Japan, the United States and the European Union are the leading markets for China's food exports. These governments have more grounds to be concerned about China's food safety than others. First, China is the largest source of food imports for Japan. Since the toxic dumplings incident that made ten people ill in Japan in 2008, the safety of Chinese-made food products has become a great concern. The two countries agreed to strengthen cooperation on food safety through a bilateral agreement in early 2010, which allows each country's government officials to carry out on-site inspections of food facilities in the other. Before 2002, 99 per cent of Japan's imports of spinach came from China, accounting for 40,000–50,000 tonnes annually worth $30–$35 million a year. However, in 2002, the Japanese government tightened the MRL of the pesticide chlorpyrifos in spinach from 0.1 ppm to 0.01 ppm (see Table 8.1).[64] After finding excessive pesticide residue in the spinach imported from China, Japan banned or restricted all such imports from China in July 2002.[65] It is not yet clear whether the 2010 bilateral agreement between Beijing and Tokyo has had any significant effect on improving Chinese foodstuffs.

Second, in relation to the United States, since 2007 China has overtaken Canada to become the largest source of US imports, accounting for 19.1 per cent of all US imports. This increasing bilateral trade has made China's food safety a matter of increasing concern for the US. The US Consumer Product Safety Commission recalls a lot of Chinese manufactured or produced goods every year and the number of these recalls rose sharply between 2000 and 2008 (see Figure 8.3). Although there are a lot of recalls from the FDA, the General Accountability

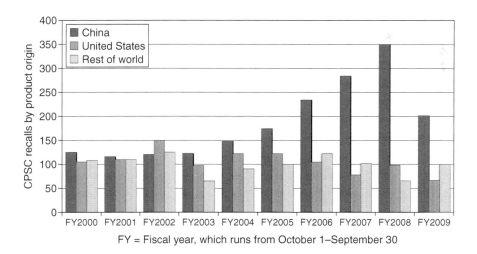

Figure 8.3 The number of recalls by the US Consumer Product Safety Commission (source: adapted from Michael J. Wagner, 'Product safety summit shows value of cooperation', *China Business Review*, January–February 2010, www.china-businessreview.com/public/1001/wagner.html (accessed 5 October 2010)).

Office, an independent US government auditor, admitted that the government's food safety management controls were weak. For a long time the FDA has suffered from 'an appallingly low inspection rate'. The FDA has fewer than 200 full-time inspectors to conduct and investigate all imported food and drugs in more than 300 US ports of entry.[66] The food safety scares in 2007 also brought to the fore the fact that the FDA can inspect only 1 per cent of food imports, and give only 0.2 per cent of the imports laboratory analysis, illustrating how the US monitoring system is underfunded.[67] Compared with Japan's 15 per cent inspection rate of all food imports from China,[68] the US rate is extremely low. This highlights a pressing need for China and the US to cooperate to improve the safety standards of Chinese food products.

In order to enhance bilateral regulatory cooperation in the areas of food, drugs, medical devices and animal feed, the Chinese AQSIQ and the US Department of Health and Human Services signed a binding Memorandum of Agreement on food and animal feed in December 2007, which allowed the US FDA to open offices in China. Three offices were formally opened in late 2008, in Beijing, Shanghai and Guangzhou. This was the first time that the FDA opened offices outside the US. The agreement provided that the two countries would 'establish a bilateral cooperative mechanism regarding food and feed safety'. However, in response to a probe by two US congressmen about contaminated Chinese-made heparin, a blood thinner allegedly linked to at least eighty-one deaths in the US in 2007 and 2008, an FDA official openly admitted that 'there are serious limitations on what the FDA can do to pursue civil and criminal investigations in foreign countries, especially without the cooperation of the foreign government'.[69] The US requested the Chinese government to investigate but after two years no investigation had been pursued according to the US congressmen. In a letter to the US Congress on 16 June 2010, the FDA wrote that it was 'denied full access' to manufacturers of raw heparin in China.[70] In an interview with the media, Margaret Hamburg, the FDA Commissioner, also conceded the limitations of her office in overseeing China's food and medicine safety.[71] The FDA has to rely on China to inspect the firms that produce food and medical-related products destined for the US market.

Multilateral cooperation

Apart from Japan and the US, China has also developed multilateral cooperation on food safety with other regional organizations, such as the EU and ASEAN. While China has become one of the EU's leading trading partners, more than half the sub-standard consumer products detected in the EU originated from China. In order to improve communication and collaboration between the Chinese and EU authorities, both parties signed a Memorandum of Understanding on product safety, including food products, in January 2006. This MoU was renewed and extended in 2009. According to the agreement, both sides consented to have joint meetings, exchange relevant information and follow up the problems identified.[72] As part of the EU–China Trade Project, an 'EU–China Food Safety Workshop' was held in Beijing on 4 November 2009 by the European Union delegation to China. The workshop facilitated the sharing of experiences and best practice in collaboration between governments, the food industry and consumers in order to improve the working of the food safety regulatory system in China.[73] With regard to the ASEAN countries, two China–ASEAN ministerial meetings on quality supervision, inspection and quarantine were held in China and Cambodia in 2007 and 2010 respectively.[74] The two sides also signed an MoU in Singapore in 2007 on strengthening sanitary and phytosanitary cooperation.. The question of how effective are the aforementioned bilateral and multilateral mechanisms in improving China's food safety remains a matter of guesswork. However, increasing the opportunities for international cooperation will likely help China to learn from other countries, especially those which have introduced more stringent regulations, to strengthen its capacity to regulate food safety.

Conclusion

In summary, China is facing a daunting twin challenge in food safety governance – to strengthen and unify national regulatory regimes and standards, and simultaneously to cooperate with the outside world in conforming to the norms and rules of global food governance. China is a new player to global food governance, which is evolving as a result of rising trade as well as the formation of globalized food chains and networks. It became a net exporter of foodstuffs in 1984 and its net exports have grown rapidly since it joined the WTO in 2001.

However, food governance is undergoing radical transformation in the era of globalization. While global food governance calls for involvement by state, sub-national, supra-national and non-state social actors in multiple layers of the institutions of governance, China's domestic reform is focused rather on building the capacity of a state-based regulatory framework, in the belief that food regulation should rest with the sovereign state. Accordingly, a more powerful regulatory body, the State Council Food Safety Commission, was created at the highest central level and a national Food Safety Law was enacted. This emerging regulatory regime is designed to supervise and control the country's food safety by introducing laws and regulations in a top-down approach. Compared with the time when food safety was understood as simply a matter of hygiene, this regulatory regime is at least one step forward. However, at issue is whether or not this state-based regulatory framework can adequately deal with the food safety challenges that China faces, especially given its sheer size and the number of its local small-scale producers. One year after the implementation of the law, the Vice-Minister of AQSIQ, Pu Changcheng, openly confessed at a forum on food safety in Beijing in 2010 that '[t]he current situation is not satisfactory', and '[d]espite there being sufficient room for the growth of food production and processing, China is full of small-scale companies.'[75] Obviously food quality control is still a problem haunting China.

The weaknesses of China's food safety governance also lie in its fragmented food production and regulatory system and limited civil society participation.

Given that many food hazard incidents happen at local levels and are caused by small firms across the country, some food experts in the West advocate that 'the best approach to reach manufactures is through local government initiatives rather than "through Beijing" '.[76] However, China's central government is reluctant to let local governments and civil society groups become embedded in the global governance arrangement and interact directly with external regulatory bodies, fearing the erosion of sovereign power and central authority. This is related to China's state-centric conceptualization of global governance, as a result of which its food governance is also primarily focused at the national level. Peter Oosterveer, an academic in environmental policy, claims that 'the conventional nation-state-based regulation of food production and consumption is less and less able to deal effectively with the complex challenges on food governance emerging in the context of global modernity'.[77] This points to the conflict between the state-based regulatory model and the enormous challenges of tackling global issues that affect the physical survival of human beings. Due to the strong protectionism of local industries by their governments and the lack of consumer watchdog organizations, China's food safety capacity at both the local and the national levels remains fragile.

9 Energy security

> China's economic growth is driving its thirst for energy. In response, China is acting as if it can somehow 'lock up' energy supplies around the world. This is not a sensible path to achieving energy security. Moreover, a mercantilist strategy leads to partnerships with regimes that hurt China's reputation and lead others to question its intentions. In contrast, market strategies can lessen volatility, instability, and hoarding.
>
> Robert Zoellick, 2005[1]

Since the first oil crisis in 1973, energy security has become a critical issue to oil-poor countries, as they have experienced worsening vulnerability to oil fluctuations. Oil prices have rallied to higher, sustained levels since the turn of the century (around March 1999), and were dramatically volatile throughout 2008, fluctuating between an all-time high of more than $147 a barrel in July and a low of less than $36 in December. They rebounded to $90 by the end of 2010.[2] Analysts attribute the escalating prices to the surging demands from China, India and the US (Figure 9.1), the depreciation of the value of US dollar,[3] and the declining productivity of mature oilfields.[4] China's demand for energy, particularly oil, rising sharply since the early 1990s, has led to the emergence of energy security as a key foreign policy concern for the world. China has replaced the more industrialized Japan as the second largest consumer of oil and the second largest oil-importing country in the world, after the United States.[5] The gravity of the problem has manifested itself most remarkably in the ever-widening domestic output–consumption gap from 1994 to date (see Figure 9.2). The International Energy Agency (IEA) said in its *World Energy Outlook 2010* that global primary energy demand between 2008 and 2035 would grow 1.2 per cent per annum on average. China (and India) would outpace other countries in the demand growth. According to IEA projections, the average annual growth rate of China's demand will amount to 2.1 per cent. China will lead the rest of the world in the rise of demand for oil between 2009 and 2035, representing almost half of the net growth.[6]

An equally alarming trend is that the capacity for oil production in the early twenty-first century is less than ever before. It is reported that the spare capacity

142 *Energy security*

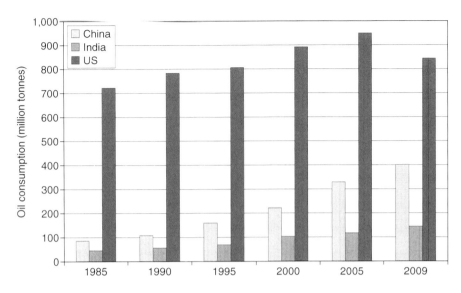

Figure 9.1 Crude oil consumption in China, India and the US (million tonnes) (source: BP, *BP Statistical Review of World Energy*, London: BP, various years).

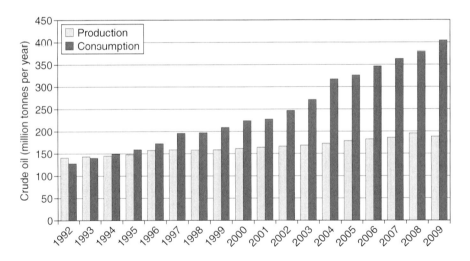

Figure 9.2 China's production and consumption of crude oil (million tonnes per year) (source: *BP Statistical Review of World Energy*, various years).

of the Organization of Petroleum Exporting Countries (OPEC) might fall to 3.9 per cent of world demand by 2015 from 6.8 per cent in 2010.[7] A historical factor was OPEC's decision to reduce upstream investments in 1998 in the wake of the Asian financial crisis of 1997–98, resulting in idled capacity shrinking from five million barrels per day in 1998 to 700,000 b/d in 2005. In addition, many of the deposits of 'easy oil' – those that can readily be exploited at low cost – are close to being exhausted. Reluctant to invest in the exploration of 'tough oil' reserves in inhospitable environments, oil-rich countries produce more oil than they find to replace it.[8] Thus, the IEA projected in 2009 that world oil production would only grow by 1 per cent on average in the 2008–30 period.[9]

A parallel development is the growing dominance of national oil companies (NOCs) vis-à-vis privately run international oil companies (IOCs) in the upstream sector. The majority of petroleum reserves are now concentrated in the hands of NOCs which have close and interlocking relationships with their national governments. They are often wielded by their governments as an instrument to achieve foreign policy goals. Nine of the ten largest liquid petroleum reserve-holding oil companies in 2006 were state-owned, accounting for more than 80 per cent of the global liquid reserves. It is widely argued that in comparison with IOCs, NOCs have lower production efficiency and are more focused on current production at the expense of capital investment.[10]

Against this background, energy analysts have been debating whether or not energy producers in the world will be able to increase supplies to meet the ever-growing global energy demand. More crucially, given that almost all of the more advanced industrialized countries are energy-importing, they are concerned as to whether China's growing energy demand and its efforts to meet that demand will threaten their primary interests. A commonly agreed objective of energy security is to 'assure adequate, reliable supplies of energy at reasonable prices and in ways that do not jeopardise major national values and objectives'.[11] What stirs debates, controversies and tensions among nations is the fact that they hold different 'national values and objectives', as will be elaborated below.

Energy security, public goods and global energy governance

Energy insecurity possesses the features of 'problem interdependence' across political boundaries in which the source of a problem lies in one political unit while the impact of the problem is borne by other political units.[12] The voracious demand and scramble for oil from both China and India has pushed up international oil prices. The weakening US dollar and the falling productivity of mature oilfields in OPEC member states have intensified the disorder of and volatility in world oil markets. Energy insecurity is becoming a transnational issue, calling for governance between oil-producing and oil-consuming countries in order to lessen the negative impact of tight oil markets. Provision of public goods is one of the means to promote energy security. In order to prevent energy from being wielded as a 'political weapon' or an instrument of foreign policy, it is argued that oil and gas should be traded on international markets free of quantitative constraints and tariffs instead of on a bilateral contractual basis. A public good could take the form of promoting and maintaining well-functioning, open international oil markets in order to maintain moderately stable supplies of oil and gas at market-determined prices. Stakeholders, including oil exporting and importing countries, NOCs and IOCs, are instrumental in devising and establishing global energy governance, briefly understood as the sum of all international and transnational rule systems about the production, exchange and use of energy, to govern the provision of the public goods.

Market vs. neo-mercantilism

Two broad approaches to safeguarding energy security are the liberal and the realist (or statist) approaches. The former focuses on getting more oil on the world markets by encouraging investment in producer countries. In addition, open access to the markets and multilateral cooperation are promoted.[13] The latter, in contrast, emphasizes strategic bilateralism in which a consumer country establishes special relations with a producer country or state companies of consumer countries seek access to equity oil of producer countries.

Since the oil shock of 1973, Western powers have been at pains to promote competitive world oil markets in an interdependent international economy. Until November 1973, international oil transactions were dominated by the 'seven sisters', an oligopolistic group of international oil companies, which were granted long-term concession agreements to explore and exploit oil in the oil-rich countries.[14] As integrated conglomerates, the IOCs also dominated the oil-refining and marketing sectors and formed joint ventures to explore foreign oilfields. With little price competition among them, international oil prices were principally determined by agreements between the IOCs and host governments. The world oil industry began to experience fundamental changes when oil-producing countries in the OPEC region and elsewhere nationalized oil assets, followed by the decisions by the Organization of Arab Petroleum Exporting Countries and OPEC in October and November 1973 to set oil prices unilaterally.[15] Despite the de-integration, due to the continued dominance of IOCs in downstream marketing, OPEC countries continued selling oil to the oil companies by long-term contracts. Oil companies were faced with a glut in supplies of oil due to the cumulative effects of four developments in the 1970s:

- the worldwide economic recession after the oil shock;
- the arrival on the market in the 1970s of non-OPEC oil-producing countries – including the UK and Norway (after North Sea oil was brought on stream in the second half of the 1970s), Mexico, the USSR and even China;[16]
- the tendencies of some OPEC member states, especially those with low financial and oil reserves and high populations, to produce above prescribed quotas; and
- energy conservation in developed countries, leading to slackened demand.

Coupled with oil-producing countries' nascent efforts to sell their oil abroad by their own international marketing networks, IOCs began to buy less oil on long-term supply contracts from OPEC countries. An increased share of oil has since then been traded on the spot markets, contributing to the formation of competitive world oil markets. By the end of 1970s, only about 10 per cent of internationally traded oil was in spot markets; the share increased sharply to more than 50 per cent at the end of 1982. To provide opportunities for hedging to reduce market volatility, at the end of March 1983 the New York Mercantile Exchange introduced crude oil futures contracts whereby both buyers and sellers could minimize risk. Since then a benchmark world oil price has been that of West Texas Intermediate light sweet crude oil.[17] Brent blend oil started trading in November 1983 on the International Petroleum Exchange (IPE) in London.[18] After the so-called 1986 crisis which precipitated a steep oil price fall, OPEC's leverage in determining the price of internationally traded oil was reduced, albeit not eliminated.[19] Major actors in the producing countries, notably Saudi Arabia, can still exert substantial influence on prevailing prices in the market by adjusting oil supplies.[20]

A collective-action policy response to the oil shock of 1973 was the creation of the International Energy Agency by the European and American members of the OECD. To address supply disruptions, the IEA has required its members to build up oil stocks – first equal to sixty days, later raised to ninety days of net imports. It has been empowered to trigger an oil-sharing mechanism if individual members or a group of member states face a 7 per cent shortfall in supplies. But oil-sharing is not supposed to be used to bring down the price of oil. It has been argued that the threat to initiate a coordinated release of oil stocks has contributed to moderating market instability and price rises by propelling OPEC, in particular Saudi Arabia, to increase output. Oil-producing countries are loath to let consumer governments earn the profits derived from selling oil at a high price.[21] Macroeconomic policy transformation in OECD countries in the 1980s, particularly after the rise of Ronald Reagan and Margaret Thatcher to power in the US and the United Kingdom, also facilitated the removal of state interventions in commodity markets. Both Norway and the UK gave up administered pricing in 1984. Thatcher's Conservative government abolished in 1985 the state-owned British National Oil Company, formed by the Labour government ten years previously to maintain adequate oil supplies.[22] National energy policy, price controls and bilateral deals on energy supplies largely disappeared.[23] In general, a pro-market notion of energy security began to take root in OECD states in the 1980s. In the wake of the fall of Communism, many in the West have gone to great lengths to espouse the liberal approach, in the belief that a single world order, of which a defining feature would be liberalization of the world economy with a reduced role for the state in it, would take shape.[24]

In the current globalization era, advocates of the pro-market approach to energy security call for 'the provision of affordable, reliable, diverse and ample supplies of oil and gas ... and adequate infrastructure to deliver these supplies to market'.[25] Key ingredients of this definition are the reduction of both price volatility and production disruption, and the assurance that energy-producing countries produce oil and gas for the global market. The IEA adopted in 1993 a policy statement that '[f]ree and open trade and a secure framework for investment contribute to efficient energy markets and energy security.'[26] Increased tightness in oil markets and the growing dominance of 'neo-mercantilist' NOCs have renewed energy security concerns in oil-deficient countries, and are likely to

146 *Energy security*

usher in a new international energy order.[27] Given that national oil companies and their governments are more inclined to use oil and natural gas as a lever for political ends by cutting off (or threatening to withhold) supplies to extract political and strategic advantages, energy security tends to be focused on 'reducing the vulnerability of [an] economy to the reduction or cut-off of oil [and gas] supplies from any given supplier or group of suppliers or to sudden large increases in prices of special energy commodities such as oil and natural gas'.[28] To prevent this from happening, pro-market proponents assert that oil and gas should be traded as a commodity on international markets.

In contrast, neo-mercantilists argue for achieving a maximum degree of self-sufficiency in energy supplies and state control over the strategic sectors or 'commanding heights' of the national economy. Neo-mercantilism or economic nationalism maintains that the pursuit of power and the pursuit of wealth are complementary: wealth is an essential means to power and power is necessary for the acquisition of wealth. Industrialization is key to the growth of military power and thus central to national security. Neo-mercantilists argue that economic self-sufficiency is crucial to industrialization, which, in turn, is conducive to political independence. Competition among states for scarce resources which are essential to industrialization is therefore inherent in international relations. It is of paramount importance for the state to seize and exercise control over the 'commanding heights' of the modern economy. Like neo-realists, neo-mercantilists are also more concerned about relative gain than about absolute or mutual gain in international cooperation or commerce. For them, dominant economic powers are determined to preserve a liberal economic order because the latter is of great benefit to them.[29] To secure adequate and reliable access to energy supplies, states engage in energy diplomacy, defined as 'the use of foreign policy to secure access to energy supplies abroad and to promote (mostly bilateral, that is, government to government) cooperation in the energy sector'.[30] Seen in this perspective, energy diplomacy per se is not new. Many industrialized countries employed the tool in their industrialization. But the result was at best mixed, revealing limits for late-industrializing countries to improve their access to energy by the same means.[31] There is one caveat: although the 'special relationship' between the US and Saudi Arabia is often understood as an exemplar case of the statist approach, the relationship does not provide for US oil companies to acquire equity oil in the Kingdom, nor to pursue long-term, bilateral supply contracts on preferential prices with it. Instead, it is built on the understanding that the US guarantees the national security of Saudi Arabia in return for the latter's cooperation in maintaining a steady stream of moderately priced oil to international oil markets.[32] The staunchest supporters of the neo-mercantilist approach are rather China and Russia.

China's neo-mercantilist approach

What does China do on the ground to enhance its energy security? How far does it take collective action with other actors in the provision of the said public goods? As part and parcel of its efforts to enhance its energy security, China has put much emphasis on mercantilist self-reliance. In line with the aforementioned discussion of neo-mercantilist thought, 'resource mercantilism' is defined by Flynt Leverett as 'the reliance of energy importing states on national energy companies to secure access to overseas oil and gas resources on more privileged bases than simple supply contracts'. The Chinese state is increasingly reliant on its national oil companies to acquire equity stakes in overseas oil and gas reserves, and provides various kinds of support to its NOCs to buy energy assets abroad.[33] The notion of 'self-reliance' should not be understood as advocating a reduction in energy dependence from imported hydrocarbons. It merely means that the Chinese oil security policy is to diversify the sources and supply routes of energy imports, reducing reliance on any single external power or source. As shown in Table 9.1, China relied heavily in 1995 on Southeast Asia and minor oil-producing countries in the Middle East (Oman and Yemen) for its oil imports. Major oil producers in the Middle East (Iran and Saudi Arabia) and Africa were the principal sources of China's oil imports in 2001. Iran, in particular, provided 18 per cent of China's imports. Six years later not only did China buy crude oil from the Middle East and Africa but also from the former Soviet Union (Russia and Kazakhstan).

China's energy diplomacy or 'going-out' strategy focuses on Russia and Central Asia, the Persian Gulf states, notably Saudi Arabia and Iran, sub-Saharan Africa, and Latin America. Central to China's neo-mercantilist approach to energy security are long-term bilateral oil supply contracts with Russia and equity investment in upstream oil exploration and production in Sudan, Nigeria and Angola. These contracts are entered into by its three NOCs, namely the China National Petroleum Corporation (CNPC), the China Petroleum and Chemical Corporation (Sinopec) and the China National Offshore Oil Corporation (CNOOC). In return for exploration rights, China has promised to offer huge multi-sector infrastructure investments in or export guarantee credits or low-interest loans to the oil-producing countries, which Western IOCs cannot do.

Table 9.1 China's top five crude oil supplying countries, 1995, 2001, and 2007 (share of the total imports as measured by volume)

1995		2001		2007	
Indonesia	30.89%	Iran	18.00%	Saudi Arabia	16.14%
Oman	21.38%	Saudi Arabia	14.57%	Angola	15.32%
Yemen	14.47%	Oman	13.51%	Iran	12.59%
Angola	5.84%	Sudan	8.25%	Russia	8.90%
Iran	5.45%	Angola	6.30%	Oman	8.38%
Subtotal	78.03%	Subtotal	60.63%	Subtotal	61.33%

Sources: *Almanac of China's Foreign Economic Relations and Trade*, 1996/97 and *Yearbook of China's Foreign Economic Relations and Trade*, 2003 (both published Beijing: Zhongguo duiwai jingji maoyi chubanshe (China Foreign Economic Relations and Trade Publishing House)); *China Commerce Yearbook*, 2008 (Beijing: Zhongguo shangwu chubanshe (China Commerce and Trade Press)).

China's oil extractive operations in sub-Saharan Africa are concentrated in the fields that were deserted by or are of little interest to the Western IOCs.[34] This practice can best be illustrated by China's energy diplomacy with Russia and Africa.

Discussions on a Sino-Russian energy pipeline connecting the Irkutsk and Yakutsk basins and Sakhalin Island in eastern Russia, believed to be the home of vast untapped hydrocarbon resources, to northeast China date back to 1994 when the late Boris Yeltsin was the Russian President.[35] Initially China secured in July 2001 an agreement with Mikhail Khodorkovsky's Yukos to build a 2,400-km oil pipeline from Angarsk to Daqing, which was to transport thirty million tonnes per year by 2010.[36] However, as a result of the intervention of Japan beginning in 2002 and the demise of Yukos following the arrest of Khodorkovsky in October 2003, the Russian government became hesitant about committing itself to the construction of the Angarsk–Daqing line.[37] It eventually decided in December 2004 to scrap the line. Instead, it would construct an oil pipeline *within* its territory, running from Taishet (in the Irkutsk region, about 500 km northwest of Angarsk) via Skovorodino (in the Amur region) to Perevoznaya near Vladivostok and Nakhodka on the Russian Pacific coast.[38] With a final annual capacity of eighty million tonnes, this 4,700-km trans-Siberia pipeline is known as the East Siberia–Pacific Ocean (ESPO) pipeline. But, geopolitical factors intervened. A re-examination of its energy relations with China and Japan led Russia to conclude that it was imperative to maintain good relations with China.[39] Accordingly, Russia unveiled in September 2005 a two-stage plan to build the ESPO pipeline, with the first stage, started in April 2006, going to Skovorodino only.

After the collapse of the Angarsk–Daqing project, China focused on lobbying Russia for a branch line to China from the ESPO pipeline in Skovorodino, the end-point of the first stage of the pipeline. From the Amur River on the Chinese–Russian border the spur is to be connected to a 992-km Chinese pipeline, constructed by the CNPC, to Daqing.[40] The construction of the branch line was initially meant to commence in July 2006. But once again there were repeated procrastinations. Despite the fact that both countries had been in talks for years over the spur line, and a bilateral protocol and MoU to build it were signed in July 2007 and October 2008 respectively, and that the branch line is merely 67 km long (or one-fortieth of the first stage of the ESPO line), it was not operational until the end of 2010.[41] Displaying his dismay at the slow progress, Zhang Guobao, head of China's State Energy Bureau, said in Moscow in October 2008, 'We've discussed this for many years, but the results do not correspond to what they should be for two neighbouring powers.'[42] Just one month after the signing of the MoU, bilateral negotiations over the terms of the agreement foundered. Only in February 2009 could a loans-for-oil deal be clinched. According to the agreement, China Development Bank would lend $15 billion to Rosneft and $10 billion to Transneft in return for an annual supply of fifteen million tonnes of Siberian oil for twenty years, starting in January 2011. The bulk of oil would be destined for a refinery in Tianjin, a 51–49 per cent Sino-Russian joint venture, which would buy more than nine million tonnes of the Siberian oil per year in

2012 when it was completed.[43] However, CNPC and Rosneft still disagree over the price of the Russian oil sold to China via the spur line. Rosneft insists that the price be based on the ESPO blend sold at the Pacific Ocean port of Kozmino while CNPC wants a reduced rate because Skovorodino is much closer to China than to Kozmino. It is apparent that Rosneft is prevailing in the dispute.[44]

The aid-for-oil approach is also applied to Africa when Chinese oil investment in the continent grows. China declared officially in a white paper entitled *China's African Policy* that it would provide financial assistance to African countries with neither political strings attached nor interference in the internal affairs of the host countries.[45] Accordingly, China contributed $1.8 billion to African countries as development aid in 2002. During his eight-country African tour in early 2007, President Hu Jintao pledged to double the aid to Africa by 2009, including $3 billion in loans and $2 billion in credits.[46] China set up a China–Africa Development Fund (CADFund), an investment vehicle, in June 2007 with an initial capital of $1 billion provided by the state-owned China Development Bank. The target would be to expand it to $5 billion. Nevertheless, China neither shares the same definitions of official development aid (ODA) as traditional donors in the OECD nor regularly releases data on its aid to the developing world, thus making a precise calculation of its contribution to Africa difficult.[47] A study by an economist at the IMF reckons that China had provided Africa with a total of $19 billion of loans and credits up to the end of 2006.[48] A US Congressional Research Service report says that China offered sub-Saharan African countries economic assistance totalling more than $33 billion between 2002 and 2007, with more than 80 per cent of it delivered in 2006 and 2007.[49] Based on detailed research on the composition of China's external aid as well as the sizes of the components, Deborah Brautigam estimates that China's annual development aid to Africa increased from $689 million in 2001 to $2,476 million in 2009, with an accumulated total of $10.52 billion by 2009.[50]

The CNPC's activities in Sudan, the first stop on China's foray into the African oil sector, date back to 1995 when the West began to ostracize the Khartoum regime. A year later it bought 40 per cent of the Greater Nile Petroleum Operating Company (GNPOC) in Sudan, which was granted in March 1997 a contract to develop three blocks in southern Sudan. The CNPC and Sinopec later combined to take a 47 per cent stake in the second largest oil consortium in Sudan, the Petrodar Operating Company (PDOC), to develop two blocks in northern Upper Nile. The CNPC also invested in infrastructure and refining. China announced in October 2009 that it would double its direct investment in Nigeria from $3 billion to $6 billion, with the majority in the oil sector.[51] China offered aid, not necessarily to be used in oil exploration, to both Nigeria and Angola.[52] In 2004 China granted Angola a credit line of $2 billion to be repaid over twelve years by sales of Angolan oil to China. Angola would set aside 15,000 barrels per day (or 747,000 tonnes per year), starting from the fifth year and the exports would increase to 40,000 barrels per day (or 1.99 million tonnes per year) until the loan was fully repaid.[53] A consensus among energy analysts is that Chinese NOCs receive substantial financial subsidies from state banks when making overseas investments. Therefore, despite technical inferiority to IOCs, they can secure oil deals in African countries by giving highly generous investment packages to the host governments. In addition, the Chinese government also provides pariah states, notably Sudan, with implicit political protection.[54]

Conventional wisdom therefore claims that Chinese NOCs lock up or gobble up huge oil reserves in Africa with low-cost financial assistance from the central government and that the investment displays a 'lack of a moral agenda'.[55] The Chinese respond that the quest for state control over the flow of the strategic resource of oil is necessary to protect the Chinese economy from the vicissitudes and instabilities of the world oil markets. With twin concerns over 'volume risk' and 'price risk', China shows little interest in promoting free, competitive global oil markets or participating in the emerging global energy governance.[56] By 'volume risk' is meant worry about the adequacy of oil and gas supplies on international markets. On the one hand, due to increasing integration of oil and gas trading in the past thirty years or so, the danger of supply disruptions as a result of exporting countries using energy as a political 'weapon' and suddenly cutting off supplies to selected customers has reduced; on the other, the possibility of supply stoppages due to terrorism or political turmoil within oil-producing countries has increased. With its deeply held beliefs that the oil markets have long been dominated by international oil companies and that the US will not allow the markets to work in favour of Chinese interests, China often worries about the security of energy supplies on international markets (we shall return to this topic later). That international natural gas markets are largely non-existent only serves to fuel further Beijing's scepticism about the viability of the market approach.[57] Its concerns over 'price risk' or price volatility have also heightened. As a result, China wants to insulate its economy from supply and price fluctuations by engaging in long-term supply contracts with, or buying equity oil stakes in, oil-producing countries, which it is believed will provide China with cheaper and more stable energy supplies.

China has not established any multilateral cooperative mechanisms with consumer countries either. While experts argue that regional energy cooperation centred on ASEAN, including ASEAN Plus Three (China, Japan and South Korea) and the East Asia Community, would enhance the energy security of China and its Northeast Asian neighbours, policy measures such as joint use of oil stockpiles on the basis of Japanese oil stocks and construction of regional energy transport infrastructure connections have yet to materialize. Despite the rapid growth of East Asian economies and their demand for energy, their strategic energy stockpiles remain at low levels except in the case of Japan, which holds about 120 days' worth of net oil imports. Due to the IEA requirement that its oil stocks can only be drawn down to replace domestic supply loss, Japan has been concerned about panic buying on the part of its neighbouring oil-importing countries in the case of regional or global oil market disruptions.[58]

Although China has in recent years been involved in regional and international energy-related regimes which call for the use of market forces and international trade to address energy insecurity,[59] as noted above, it is less inclined to rely on international oil markets to balance its demand for and supply of oil. Its participation in Russian Far East energy development does not contribute to expanding the supply base of the global energy markets. As seen from the negotiations over the Russian ESPO pipeline, China is focused on 'locking up' part of Russian oil for its own market at a discounted price. It is not involved in the second leg of the ESPO line which aims to export oil to a wider market in the Asia-Pacific or in the exploration and development of oil and gas resources in Russian Eastern Siberia. In other words, it is not prepared to play an exemplary role in creating the global public goods of enhancing energy security by maintaining or expanding the scale and smooth functioning of the global energy markets, although the claim that Chinese NOCs remove oil from the world market may not be valid.[60]

Why not the market?

Behind this parochial perspective lies its mistrust of global markets and of multilateral engagement with oil importers or companies. How has this Chinese mistrust of the global oil market come into being? The Chinese oil industry has felt that as latecomers to the international oil business, its corporations have been spurned by both major IOCs and NOCs in oil-affluent countries when the Chinese seek overseas investment opportunities. Evidence can be seen in the growth of 'resource nationalism' in both Russia and the US. The CNPC's bid for a 75 per cent stake in Russia's Slavneft in December 2002 was rejected due to opposition from Sibneft and TNK, the CNPC's Russian rivals, and political concern in Russia about Chinese ownership of a strategic resource.[61] This was followed by another, more severe, setback when US politicians scuppered the acquisition of Unocal by CNOOC in 2005.[62] CNOOC first approached Unocal in March 2005 with a non-binding offer price, targeting the latter's untapped reserves in Southeast Asia, the Caspian Sea and North America and its exploration technology. In April Chevron offered to pay $16.5 billion to acquire Unocal. Two months later, CNOOC announced its foray into the purchase with an all-cash $18.5 billion offer. The competition between CNOOC and Chevron over Unocal was eventually determined not by commercial forces but by geopolitics. In face of intense opposition from the US Congress, which urged the George W. Bush administration to review the bid thoroughly on vital national security grounds,[63] and from US public opinion, CNOOC withdrew its bid to purchase Unocal in early August 2005, although Fu Chengyu, CNOOC's chairman, maintained that the company was simply 'following a system that was set up by leading Western countries, especially the US'. Eventually Unocal was bought by Chevron at the latter's revised offer of $17.7 billion. Michael Klare has noted the implications of the Unocal episode for a new world order, arguing that 'a new chapter in the history of international politics' has begun. Under this emerging order of the twenty-first century, energy will be treated primarily no longer as a commodity traded on the international market but as a strategic resource, with the state rather than international oil companies taking a commanding role.

With the group of energy-deficient countries expanding, relentless international competition for oil and gas is likely to intensify.[64]

Behind China's rush to buy oil and gas from Russia is, however, a perception that Russia is only one of the available options. Having learnt from bitter experience not to trust Russians, China will not become a hostage to Russian fortune.[65] Russia's suspension of oil and gas supplies to Belarus, Latvia, Lithuania and Ukraine since 2003 exemplifies its use of oil as a weapon to punish its non-compliant brethren.[66] Although the Russian share of China's oil imports rose rapidly from a tiny 2.9 per cent in 2001, Russia is merely one of the major sources and the Russians do not dominate the market.[67] In contrast to an aggregate growth of 12.4 per cent in China's oil imports in 2007 over the previous year, its imports from Russia actually fell by 9 per cent in the same period. In the negotiations over the routing of the ESPO pipeline, China played Kazakhstan off against Russia.[68] Nevertheless, given the unpredictability of Russian policy-making, why has China expended so much time and effort on securing Russian energy supplies? Russian (and Central Asian) oil and gas hold a particular strategic value for China in that they do not have to be delivered to China in foreign-owned oil tankers by sea via the Strait of Malacca. Instead, they can be transported by overland routes without passing through any transit countries. China believes this makes them more secure because they are not under the domination of the American naval forces.[69] Inside China there is a popular belief that the US would set up a naval blockade in the Strait in the event of military confrontation with China over Taiwan, so China is at pains to avoid being held hostage to the US.[70] In addition, both Russia and China share a preference for long-term, bilateral state-to-state deals.[71]

In addition to the rise of 'resource nationalism', another factor is that Chinese NOCs lack the advanced exploration technologies needed to compete with the majors in drilling more promising deep-water blocks in, for instance, the Gulf of Guinea in West Africa. Chinese companies are also inexperienced in dealing with international oil markets, as China was self-sufficient in oil supplies from when the Daqing oilfield became fully operational in the mid-1960s until 1993.[72] In addition it is claimed that up to 40 per cent of US oil imports come from long-term supply contracts and from its equity oil assets abroad. What makes Japan particularly vulnerable to energy insecurity is that equity oil only contributes 10 per cent of its imports. With equity oil accounting for 15 per cent of China's total oil imports, this argument indeed justifies a more rigorous approach to pursuing long-term bilateral agreements in the areas where international oil companies have yet to establish a foothold.[73]

Joining the IEA is not high on China's agenda in its attempts to tackle the challenge of energy insecurity either. Without membership of the OECD, China is not a formal member of the IEA. The IEA discussed the membership of China (and India) at a ministerial meeting in March 2008 without coming to any decision.[74] Two months later the George W. Bush administration called on China to join the IEA, suggesting that the Agency's charter could be revised to include both China and India. Nobuo Tanaka, Executive Director of the IEA, in March

2010 called on China to join. He argued that without the participation of China the relevance of the IEA, especially its storage level reports, would be open to question.[75] Proponents have also argued that China's membership would alleviate its sense of strategic vulnerability, deterring it from hoarding oil and thus driving up global market prices. However, obstacles to China's admission are not easy to overcome. They include the requirements that members of the OECD must be committed to the free market economy and liberal democracy, that all members have to maintain strategic petroleum reserves (SPRs) equivalent to at least ninety days' worth of net oil imports and that they cannot release them without consultation with other members. Transparency in crucial decisions about emergency stockpiles is a matter of primary concern.[76] China has a three-phase plan for building up its strategic reserve facility. The first phase, the construction of oil tanks with a total capacity of 102 million barrels, in four bases along the coast was completed in October 2006 and they were filled by early 2009. This is allegedly enough to cover twelve to fourteen days of oil imports. The Chinese government formally unveiled the second phase in September 2009, the building of eight new reserves by 2011, but some of the tanks have reportedly been ready since the end of 2008. The designed capacity of the second phase is 170 million barrels. The largest phase is the third one with 204 million barrels and will likely be built by 2020. Chinese NOCs build and fill commercial petroleum reserves as well. Some oil analysts have been concerned that China could make use of its emerging SPRs to manipulate the oil market in its favour. If China were to join the IEA, they believe, it would be required to adhere to the norms and rules on the drawdown of the reserves.[77] Henry Paulson, then US Treasury Secretary in the George W. Bush administration, urged Beijing in a US–China strategic economic dialogue in June 2008 to be more open about its oil reserves as well as the policies guiding the use of its stockpiles. In particular, he called on the Chinese government to clarify whether it would use the oil reserves to manage the oil price.[78] At issue is not the proportion between the total oil reserves and its net imports, but the fact that the whole project is shrouded in secrecy. With little knowledge about the timing of China's purchases of oil to fill its reserves, industry analysts have been concerned that they are likely to destabilize the oil markets by spurring global oil demand and raising oil prices unexpectedly.[79]

China also harbours scepticism about whether the US and Japan would allow it to play a decisive role in the IEA, even if it joined, and whether major oil-consuming countries would cooperate with China in releasing oil stocks in the event of supply disruptions, given that the coordinated release of SPRs among IEA members has been quite rare. The current rules of the IEA which stipulate that new members are given weighted voting rights on the basis of their levels of oil consumption in 1974 are not at all appealing to China. China is not confident that IEA membership would help it gain access to the required technology to improve its energy efficiency due to the concerns in the West about intellectual property rights and industrial competition with Chinese firms.[80] China's state-owned oil industry and government officials are therefore convinced that 'energy diplomacy' is more conducive to improving the country's precarious energy security than engagement with global energy governance. One can therefore understand why immediately after Tanaka's call to China to join the IEA, Beijing indirectly rejected it by reporting in an official newspaper the view of a Chinese oil expert that conditions were not ripe for China to join.[81]

Transparency in oil data about China is also a matter of concern in another multilateral regime known as the Joint Oil Data Initiative (JODI), created in 2003 and run by the secretariat of the Riyadh-based International Energy Forum. A JODI assessment of members' records for data submission, timeliness and completeness for the period July–December 2009 reveals that China was only given a 'fair' evaluation for completeness while seventy countries earned a 'good' rating in the area.[82] As chair of the G20 in 2011, France intends to enhance JODI, claiming that 'the system had not been sufficiently updated and lacked data on oil stocks, because some countries, including China, had been reluctant to reveal that information'.[83]

This situation gives rise to a vicious circle of security dilemmas because this Chinese strategic thinking provokes the suspicion prevalent in the West that Chinese state-owned energy companies are policy instruments of the state for securing energy supplies and that China is trying to change the rules of the game.[84] Energy analysts point out that both the CNPC and Sinopec, created from the defunct Ministry of Petroleum Industry, are ministry-level corporations and CNOOC has the lower rank of a general bureau. The oil industry has long been a pathway to China's central leadership with patron-client relations running from Yu Qiuli, head of the Maoist 'petroleum faction', to the former Vice-President Zeng Qinghong and Zhou Yongkang, currently a Politburo Standing Committee member.[85] Believing that the political background of China's NOCs and the generous support they receive from the state are disadvantageous to the IOCs, the latter as well as public opinion in the West call for a level playing field, demanding careful scrutiny of China's open pursuit of oil assets in the West. This further reinforces the long-held impression in China that international energy markets do not serve Chinese interests.

The imperfect nature of the world oil market also matters. First, regionalization of the world oil market has given rise to various long-standing special relationships. Asian consumers buy oil largely from the Middle East; the US gets oil from North and South America (Canada, Mexico and Venezuela); and European countries receive supplies from Russia, the Caspian region and North Africa. The fragmented regional markets are not flexible enough to reroute the supply lines easily. Second, major producers do not respond to market forces in their investment decisions. Higher market prices do not prompt OPEC to increase its capital investment because it reckons that other oil-rich countries, which are producing at their capacity limits, cannot capture its established market. Foreign private investment into the energy industry is not welcome and energy-producing countries are not comfortable with international rules. Russia has yet to ratify the Energy Charter Treaty, though it signed it in 1994; Saudi Arabia sought exemptions from WTO rules for its energy sector. Due to political constraints, new investments in

Iran and Iraq are not forthcoming.[86] The cumulative result is that world oil prices tend to escalate and are highly volatile and that it is a daunting challenge for China to buy oil outside the Persian Gulf market, making China, a novice in the market, more vulnerable than other players. For the Chinese strategic planners, the Gulf and the sea routes to Asia are dominated by the US. China has to be aggressive in securing access to energy outside the Middle East by resorting to bilateral state-to-state deals. The natural gas market is also regionalized: there are three major regional markets – the North American, the European (west of the Commonwealth of Independent States) and the East Asian markets – with little overlap in suppliers. The main source of the North American market is Canada; the European relies heavily on Russia and Algeria; and natural gas for the East Asian market comes from Indonesia and Australia. In the former two markets, natural gas is traded by pipeline networks built on long-term bilateral agreements. This discourages competition and creates an asymmetrical dependence between suppliers and consumers, whereas natural gas reaches East Asian countries via liquefied shipments. Due to the fact that the world energy market has never been a well-functioning free market, major importing countries cannot afford to rely on market forces to enhance security of energy supply.[87]

Assessing the mercantilist energy diplomacy

In an assessment of China's mercantile approach to energy security, this section addresses the issue of how far Chinese oil investment abroad and bilateral government-to-government energy contracts contribute to enhancing China's energy security. There is evidence that it is less positive than Chinese leaders anticipated.

While details of the destinations of Chinese equity oil in sub-Saharan Africa are sketchy, it is commonly held that the majority of the equity oil is not delivered back to China but sold on the markets in Europe and North America. One study found that while China derives 225,000 barrels per day from Sudan, less than 100,000 barrels per day go to China.[88] Another suggested that the total African output of Chinese NOCs in 2006 was about 13.3 million tonnes, of which 81 per cent came from Sudan, but only 24 per cent of the oil in 2006 was shipped back to China while 65 per cent was sold to Japan, China's arch-rival in energy security.[89] A more recent study by FACTS Global Energy also pointed out the same phenomenon. While China's overseas equity oil production expanded remarkably from 140,000 barrels per day (or 6.97 million tonnes per year) in 2000 to 900,000 barrels per day (or 44.82 million tonnes per year) in 2008, no more than half reached China.[90] So although investment in equity oil abroad was initially intended to enhance China's energy security, in fact China's NOCs behave in an economically rational manner by selling their shares of the African oil in the more lucrative and nearby markets in Europe and North America.[91] Although the Sino-Russian pipeline has materialized after a chequered history, the pipeline can only deliver a little more than 10 per cent of China's crude oil imports. China has to continue to rely on seaborne oil imports.

The next issue is whether or not the bilateral energy deals are sustainable and can augment China's influence in oil-producing countries. Russia and African countries have been careful to ensuring that they maintain good working relationships with companies from a range of countries. This explains why Chinese negotiations with Russia aimed at securing oil supplies from the Russian Far East were so long and tortuous. One cannot rule out the possibility that the Russian government and oil companies may renege on the agreements as soon as they emerge from financial crises when oil prices rebound.[92] Russia has been leery of becoming a 'raw materials appendage' to China.[93] The CNPC was reportedly not given equal and fair treatment in its investment in the Sudanese oil industry. Khartoum rejected the CNPC's offer to purchase Talisman's stake in the GNPOC, when the Canadian company was pushed by human rights groups to sell its assets in Sudan in 2002–2003. Instead, the Sudanese government directed the sale of the 25 per cent share to India's Oil and National Gas Corporation, an Indian NOC as well as a major competitor with Chinese NOCs for global energy resources. In addition to China, India, Malaysia and other countries in the Middle East and the West are equity investors in Sudan.[94]

Sinopec and CNOOC made a joint bid for a 20 per cent stake in an offshore oil block in Angola from Marathon Oil for $1.3 billion in July 2009, but Sonangol, the Angolan NOC, later blocked the investment.[95] Energy diplomacy can by no means guarantee that China is a dominant player in energy-rich countries. Furthermore, foreign equity oil is never free from producer countries' political interference and is subject to the risk of nationalization and war in the host country.[96]

Another matter of concern is whether Chinese NOCs overpay for their access to oil. Experts often argue that in competition with other consumer countries for access to oil supplies, China offers above-market prices as cost premiums. Examples include the CNPC's investment in Kazakhstan and CNOOC's in Nigeria.[97] In the battle with India for oil in Angola in 2005, China's payment to the host government was ten times India's offer.[98] The effectiveness of this statist approach is open to question. Japan had employed this strategy since the oil crisis in 1973, but began to abandon it in the 1990s in the midst of its recession.[99]

Conclusion

The starting point of this chapter is that both China and the advanced industrialized countries of the West are unable to achieve energy self-sufficiency and they will have to continue relying on external supplies. The chapter has argued that in spite of the fact that all major industrial and emerging economies face the same challenge of energy insecurity, China is not addressing the problem jointly with other countries. A common thread running through various Chinese efforts to bolster its energy security is that it relies on a neo-mercantilist, realist approach, making state-to-state bilateral energy deals with selected producer countries which are not in close alliance with the US; it also downplays market-based solutions and multilateral energy cooperation with other actors. This is most evident in China's energy diplomacy with Russia and Africa. China's reluctance to utilize the pro-market approach to address its energy insecurity can be attributed to its distrust of the neutrality of international energy markets. China's scepticism of market forces is in turn derived from its suspicion of US intentions following its rapid rise. Despite their deepening political, economic and societal ties, China is under no illusion that the US would be a responsible partner to help it bolster its energy security. There are lingering doubts in China that the US might use energy as a weapon to constrain it, reinforcing its general distrust of the US.

Regarding oil and gas as geo-strategic commodities, China prefers to deal with the problem of energy insecurity on its own. Resorting to energy diplomacy, albeit not highly coordinated by the central government in Beijing, China does not feel the need to get involved in global energy governance. It shows limited interest in pursuing energy security through multilateral cooperation with oil-exporting and oil-deficient states as well as international oil companies. Rather, the post-Daqing energy security strategy is primarily built on a modified form of 'self-reliance' to seek long-term, state-to-state deals with oil-rich countries. While China's integration into the world economy is actively under way, the process has not allayed its suspicion that its core national interests cannot be well protected by the global energy market and that its oil companies are at a disadvantage compared to other oil majors. Therefore, as far as the energy sector is concerned, realism prevails over liberalism in Chinese foreign policy-making. At the heart of the matter is the differing perception between China and the West as to whether the global oil market is a level playing field. On the one hand, China harbours serious doubts about the fairness of the international oil market and its rules when the country's NOCs suffer setbacks in their quest for overseas oil assets. On the other, the West argues that the growing power of Chinese NOCs and their state-backed financial deals on oil assets undermine the proper functioning of a competitive oil market. Their 'grab' for energy assets from the market, or 'resource mercantilism', is believed to endanger the energy security of other countries and could also have a deleterious effect on the human rights policies of both US and European countries. China's efforts to improve its energy security is thus perceived as a threat to other major powers, provoking counter-measures from them, thereby ushering in a security dilemma on the energy front.

Whether the scramble for energy resources by China and the rest of the world could be transformed into multilateral cooperation based on an expanded club of energy importers and on norms and rules in support of open trade in energy is open to question.[100] At issue is an ideational gap between China and the West. Until China understands that importing directly from producer countries is not necessarily risk-free and could be costly, and that supply disruptions emanating from the use of energy as a political weapon can be mitigated by well-functioning international markets, it may not muster the political will to take collective action with major oil-consuming powers to expand international oil markets and reach a consensus on the rules of the game governing energy insecurity.

10 Transnational organized crime

> The [PLA Navy] commanders evidently are ... seeking to contribute, but in a parallel rather than integrated manner.
>
> Richard Weitz, 2009[1]

The spectacular rise of China's economy is one of the factors that feeds into the proliferation of transnational organized crime (TOC). China's economic ascendancy per se promotes global trade in goods and services, cross-border movements of people and transnational financial flows, including foreign direct investment in China and overseas direct investment from China (see Chapter 4 above). This chapter addresses the following issues about transnational organized crime: What is TOC? How and why has it acquired political salience among key institutions of global governance? What international efforts are being made to combat transnational organized crime? How can global actors develop viable, coordinated international policies in the face of growing transnational criminality? What is China's role in the emergent global campaign to deal with this issue?

The importance of 'cooperation'

One of the most authoritative definitions of organized crime was given in the UN Convention against Transnational Organized Crime (UNTOC), adopted by the UN General Assembly in November 2000. It defines an 'organized crime group' as

> a structured group of three or more persons, existing for a period of time and acting in concert with the aim of committing one or more serious crimes or offences ... in order to obtain, directly or indirectly, financial or other material benefit.[2]

This definition understands TOC as organized crimes that involve two or more sovereign jurisdictions; in short, they are cross-border organized crimes. But they are not necessarily in breach of international criminal law. The smuggling of genuine, but non-taxed, tobacco products across borders is a typical example of transnational organized crime that does not contravene international law. As pointed out by Frank Madsen, Andre Bossard argues in a similar vein that transnational crimes have two constitutive elements: (1) the crossing of national borders by people, objects, intent or will (e.g. cyber-attacks for the latter); and (2) the international recognition of the crimes through international conventions or treaties. The focus of the term TOC is indeed on the 'cooperation' aspect of the crimes and the counter-measures.[3] By the same reasoning, transnational organized crime groups are those that are based in one state, establish links with fellow criminals in several host countries, and conduct illicit activities with low risk of apprehension.

The technological advances in air travel and telecommunications since the 1960s, the political changes arising from the collapse of the socialist system in the former Soviet Union and Eastern Europe and the following expansion of the European Union, and the deregulation of the financial markets all have contributed to an increasingly mobile population around the globe as well as a big expansion of global trade. They have made possible a rapid growth of transnational organized crime, which includes illicit trades in goods and people across porous borders. However, there has been a long-term neglect of these criminal activities. As Louise Shelley has argued, 'it is only since the end of the Cold War that [transnational organized crime] has been addressed by so many countries and international bodies.'[4] This was largely because both security institutions (e.g. the CIA and the KGB) and international organizations (e.g. the UN and the Council of Europe) needed to redefine their missions in the new era when conflicts between the two superpowers or their proxies no longer existed.[5] TOC thrives and is more visible in transitional states, e.g. the post-Soviet states, in which the rule of law, the law enforcement apparatus and the judicial process are nascent and hence criminal groups can more readily evade detection and apprehension by the authorities.[6] It undermines the stability of international financial markets, as evidenced by the 1992 Bank of Credit and Commerce International scandal, and fuels the spread of narcotics, prostitution and HIV/AIDS.

The transnational nature of organized crime precludes any country from mounting an effective campaign against the criminal groups on its own. A successful policy must seek an internationally coordinated harmonization in legislation to combat crime in order not to allow the groups any room to exploit differentiated enforcement strategies. Following the adoption in December 1988 of the United Nations Convention against Illicit Traffic in Narcotic Drugs and Psychotropic Substances (the Vienna Convention), TOC was the subject of a special UN conference, known as the World Ministerial Conference on Organized Transnational Crime, in Naples in November 1994. A couple of international conventions were subsequently opened for signature by UN member states, including the UNTOC of 2000[7] and the Convention for the Suppression of the Financing of Terrorism after 9/11. In combating TOC, two new developments have emerged: (1) the increasing use of computer-aided intelligence in targeting crime and criminals, known as 'intelligence-led policing'; and (2) attempts to go after and seize the proceeds of crime. Money trails play an increasing instrumental role in prosecuting offenders of TOC.[8]

160 *Transnational organized crime*

This chapter focuses on money laundering through financial institutions and maritime piracy, principally because China has recently been active in participating in the international cooperative regimes and efforts aimed at combating them. We will examine how far China and other stakeholding states share intelligence, a global public good, in tackling piracy and money laundering and how effectively China goes after the proceeds of the crimes. Given that it is often the West, particularly the US and the European Union, that has taken the initiative in placing selected types of crimes on the global agenda and that China has not participated in the rule-setting process,[9] how far does China share the Western understanding of the nature of the problem? Does it jealously defend its national autonomy in law enforcement? As a corollary, we also explore the prospects for an 'internationalization' of the Chinese perspective on the issues.[10]

Money laundering

Money laundering can be defined as the process of transforming money from illegal to legal status by disguising its unlawful origin.[11] According to one IMF estimate, the total scale of money laundering worldwide accounts for 2 to 5 per cent of global GDP.[12] Money laundering operates through three processes: placement, layering, and integration. Placement refers to the breaking down of large sums of illegally generated funds into smaller amounts, followed by their entry into the financial system. In the layering process, the deposits are dispersed among international financial institutions away from the illicit sources, making detecting and tracking difficult. It often involves the use of 'shell companies' registered in offshore financial centres located in microstates with lax financial regulation and enforcement. Integration takes place when the money enters the legal economy and can be used for legitimate business purposes.

The US was the first country to take steps to criminalize money laundering; it did so in 1986. It has pushed ahead with standardization and harmonization of national anti-money laundering regulations.[13] To combat money laundering internationally, the Basel Committee on Banking Supervision, formed in 1974 by the governors of the Group of Ten countries' central banks, issued in December 1988 a non-legal statement on combating money laundering.[14] This was followed by the establishment of the Financial Action Task Force on Money Laundering (FATF) at the G7 Summit in Paris one year later. Initially it had sixteen members, mainly OECD member states; it later expanded to its current thirty-four members.[15] As the most specialized intergovernmental organization in combating money laundering, it drew up in April 1990 a total of forty recommendations, both at the national and the international levels. Eight special recommendations were added in October 2001 to deal with terrorist financing. A ninth special recommendation was issued three years later with the aim of strengthening international standards against money laundering and terror financing. In total they are now known as the '40+9 Recommendations'.[16] Though non-binding, the recommendations provide a framework for states to cooperate against financial crime. Failure to adopt these recommendations results in the public listing of recalcitrant states, known as the Non-Cooperative Countries and Territories (NCCTs). Fifteen jurisdictions were listed as NCCTs in 2000, and eight in 2001. Due to the opposition of the World Bank and the IMF, no new countries or territories have been added to the list. FATF's strategy has since been to seek voluntary compliance by persuasion.[17] While it has identified no NCCTs since 2007, it does identify 'high-risk jurisdictions' and issue public statements about the deficiencies in their anti-money laundering regimes.[18] Global financial governance in combating money laundering is, however, inhibited, among other things, by the uneven regulation and differing standards of enforcement between developed and developing countries, as cross-border crime networks tend to exploit differences between jurisdictions, shifting to countries with 'weaker links' of law enforcement.[19] Tightened rules in country X may drive money laundering out to country Y. How far are states willing to share intelligence concerning the activities of transnational criminal groups? Are there any limitations on the collective efforts to thwart the crime? As shown below, what is at issue in the case of China is not its determination to be part of the global anti-money laundering (AML) regime, but rather how far it can harmonize national AML arrangements, both legal and institutional, with the prevailing international standards and coordinate enforcement to bring about global collective action against organized crime.[20]

China in the global AML regime: process and limitations

The Chinese government began its campaign against money laundering in September 1989 with the ratification of the Vienna Convention.[21] Article 349 was introduced in December 1990 to the Chinese Criminal Law to criminalize the laundering of proceeds from drug-related offences.[22] The National People's Congress (NPC), the legislature, revised in March 1997 the Chinese Criminal Law to the effect that its Article 191 proscribes money laundering. The People's Bank of China (PBC), the central bank, set up an AML leading group in September 2001. China stepped up its fight against money laundering in 2003 when it signed the United Nations Convention against Corruption (UNCAC) and the State Council instructed the PBC to lead a nationwide institutional network to curb the crime. As the first step, the Bank promulgated three sets of AML regulations in January, commonly known as 'One Regulation, Two Measures', and set up an AML Bureau (*fanxiqianju*) in September 2003 and a Chinese AML Monitoring and Analysis Centre (or AML Centre; *Zhongguo fanxiqian jiance fenxi zhongxin*) in April 2004.[23] The former is to monitor the compliance of the banking sector with various AML regulations, while the latter is to collect and process crucial information coming from various banking institutions about money laundering activities and to act as a major avenue for information sharing with overseas Financial Intelligence Units (FIUs), specialized governmental agencies created to handle money laundering and other financial crimes.

The NPC began to draft the Chinese AML Law in March 2003. A revised People's Bank Law, in which Article 46 stipulates the penalty for money laundering, took effect on 1 February 2004. In the same month, on behalf of China, the PBC formally lodged an application to join the FATF. The first hurdle China had to clear was the membership requirement that the applicant 'should be a full and active member of a relevant FATF-style regional body'.[24] Although formally China is a founding member of the Asia/Pacific Group on Money Laundering (APG), founded in 1997, China had not participated in the APG (until 2009) due to the membership of Taiwan (in the name of Chinese Taipei), also a founding member, in the same organization. In order to qualify as an active member of a relevant FATF-style regional institution, China established in October 2004 a Eurasian Group on Combating Money Laundering and Financing of Terrorism (EAG) with Russia, Kyrgyzstan, Belarus, Kazakhstan and Tajikistan.[25]

With the backing of 'One Regulation, Two Measures', the PBC began to undertake nationwide anti-money laundering inspections. However, both the regulations and the inspections were applicable only to the banking sector. Under the chairmanship of the PBC, five financial institutions in China formed a leading group.[26] In July 2004 a fully fledged Joint Ministerial Conference on Anti-Money Laundering (*fanxiqian buji lianxihuiyi gongzuo zhidu*) comprising twenty-three ministries and commissions was set up, with the PBC in the chair.[27] China was accepted as an observer to the FATF in January 2005.[28] It asked the FATF to give a preliminary evaluation of it ten months later. The FATF advised that an AML Law should be enacted before it could properly assess the Chinese AML legal architecture.[29] The NPC passed the AML Law in October 2006, just before an on-site visit to China by the FATF.[30] A report summarizing and analysing the Chinese counter-measures against both money laundering and terrorist financing was adopted by the FATF plenary in June 2007. The report also gave recommendations on how to improve anti-money laundering and combating financing of terrorism (CFT) regimes in China.[31] Following on from the promulgation of the AML Law, the PBC revised the 'One Regulation, Two Measures'. With the FATF's recommendation that preventive measures be implemented in three major areas (customer due diligence, records retention and suspicious transaction reporting), China's PBC, the China Banking Regulatory Commission, the China Securities Regulatory Commission, and the China Insurance Regulatory Commission promulgated regulatory measures in the first two areas in June 2007.[32] After the US threw its support behind China's quest for membership, China acceded to the FATF as a full member in June 2007.[33]

Information on the scale or severity of money laundering in China, as well as on the effectiveness of Chinese AML measures, is sketchy because the means of detecting the crime have yet to develop.[34] Deficiencies and flaws have been found in both legislation and institution-building in China. The June 2007 FATF evaluation report shows that of the 40+9 Recommendations, China was totally compliant with only eight recommendations, largely compliant with sixteen (or collectively less than half of the recommendations), partially compliant with another sixteen and non-compliant with nine. In particular, self-laundering (*zixing xiqian*), in which the laundering is undertaken by those who have committed predicate offences, is not criminalized.[35] That is why the US Department of State recommends that the Chinese authorities should 'not simply treat [money laundering] as a subsequent by-product of investigations into predicate offenses'.[36]

The Chinese Criminal Law narrowly defines seven criminal offences as predicate offences for money laundering. They are drug trafficking, triad organized crime, terrorist crime, smuggling, corruption and bribery, disrupting the order of financial management, and financial fraud.[37] They form the focus of Chinese law enforcement and prosecutorial authorities. In contrast, the FATF has advised that countries 'should apply the crime of money laundering to all serious offences, with a view to including the widest range of predicate offences'.[38] Chinese local bank officials also acknowledge that the Chinese conception of predicate offences fails to comply fully with either the UNTOC or the UNCAC.[39] The UNTOC argues for an application of the Convention to the offences of 'participation in an organized criminal group', 'the laundering of proceeds of crime', 'corruption', 'obstruction of justice' and transnational serious crime, involving an organized criminal group;[40] for the UNCAC, 'bribery of national public officials', 'bribery of foreign public officials and officials of public international organizations', 'embezzlement, misappropriation or other diversion of property by a public official', 'trading in influence', 'abuse of functions', 'illicit enrichment', 'bribery in the private sector', 'embezzlement of property in the private sector', 'laundering of proceeds of crime', 'concealment' and 'obstruction of justice' should be criminalized.[41] In other words, the predicate crimes that the two UN conventions have identified are broader than those proscribed by Chinese law. The AML Law is slightly more inclusive than the Criminal Law by adding 'and others' at the end of the list of seven predicate offences for money laundering.[42]

The AML Centre refers suspicious cases to the AML Bureau, which in turn passes confirmed cases to the Ministry of Public Security. While the AML Centre was supposed to function as a Chinese FIU in accordance with an FATF recommendation that every member establish an FIU, it did not meet all the requirements set forth by the Egmont Group of Financial Intelligence Units.[43] As early as 1996 the FATF began to extend its rules to non-bank financial institutions. Although China's AML Law covers securities, commodity brokerage, fund management and insurance companies, AML activities in China, under the leadership of the PBC, are still focused on the banking system. The AML regime has not adequately been adopted in the non-financial commercial sector such as real estate, lawyers' service and accountancy.[44] China has not fully implemented United Nations Security Council Resolutions 1267 (1999) and 1373 (2001) on freezing terrorist assets. The regulations were distributed to Chinese financial institutions only.[45] Chinese law is silent on the sharing of seized narcotics assets with overseas jurisdictions. Bilateral agreements between the US and China are under discussion.[46] Banks at grassroots level still permit anonymous accounts, failing to exercise due diligence and 'know their customers'.[47] In order not to increase the operational costs of its financial institutions, China sets relatively high thresholds on the size of Chinese currency or foreign exchange transactions that would trigger obligations on the institutions to report to the PBC.[48]

164 *Transnational organized crime*

Since it has not been involved in making the FATF rules, why does China comply with them voluntarily, albeit with problematic effectiveness in prosecutions, convictions and deterrence? Chinese initiatives to join the FATF were largely due to material concerns. With epidemic corruption within the country and a growing inflow of foreign direct investment, the Chinese authorities are concerned that cleansed funds concealed as FDI would return to the Chinese market via offshore financial centres.[49] The Chinese government also has a strong desire to promote the presence of Chinese financial institutions in the international financial sector and to position itself as a 'responsible stakeholder' in the sector, i.e. portraying itself as part of the solution rather than part of the problem. Because FATF members are urged to guard against countries that do not sufficiently meet the FATF standards (i.e. higher-risk countries), so Chinese membership of the FATF is crucial for Chinese banks to internationalize their operations, particularly in the US. Due to the proliferation of illegal underground banks, the AML regime is required to safeguard the credibility of and confidence in Chinese banks when foreign banks are allowed to expand their business operations in China as a result of China's admission to the WTO.[50] Also, China does not perceive FATF membership as undermining or threatening its national autonomy. As an expert-based body, the FATF is a soft international institution without any constitution. The 40+9 Recommendations are soft non-binding regulations only, not incurring sanctions.[51]

An additional yet scarcely noticed factor may be China's close ties with the 'criminal state' of North Korea.[52] As briefly discussed in Chapter 3, in September 2005 the Terrorism and Financial Crimes Division of the US Treasury designated the BDA, a relatively small bank in Macao, a special administrative region of China, as a 'primary money laundering concern' because of its alleged role of laundering on behalf of North Korea illicit proceeds earned from the criminal activities of producing and distributing counterfeit US currency notes and smuggling counterfeit cigarettes and narcotic drugs. The American authorities began in the 1990s to suspect involvement of North Korea and the BDA in such illegal activities. It was alleged that the Seng Heng Bank of Macao, the Bank of China (Macao) and the Bank of China (headquartered in Beijing) were also the objects of the inquiry.[53] The investigations triggered a $40 million run on the BDA, and the North Korean Zhongwang Trading Company withdrew its funds from the bank and transferred its Macao-based staff members to Shenzhen, China, until mid-November 2005. The Macao government subsequently took control of the bank and froze $25 million in fifty-two accounts linked to the North Korean government. After an eighteen-month investigation, the U.S. Treasury formally put BDA on the US government's money-laundering blacklist in March 2007, barring all US banks from doing business with it.[54] After a series of negotiations, the funds were eventually returned from the BDA via the Reserve Bank of New York and the Russian central bank to an account controlled by Pyongyang in a Russian private bank, the Far East Commercial Bank, in June 2007.[55]

Until 2005 the US effort to enlist China's cooperation received a lukewarm response from the Chinese government.[56] It was generally believed that by moving against the BDA, the US wanted to send a political message to China, pushing it to keep a curb on North Korean illicit activities.[57] In his testimony to the Subcommittee on Terrorism, Nonproliferation, and Trade of the Committee on Foreign Affairs, House of Representatives, in April 2007, David Ascher, a former senior adviser on East Asian affairs in the State Department, argued that

> Banco Delta was a symbolic target. We were trying to kill the chicken to scare the monkeys. And the monkeys were big Chinese banks doing business in North Korea, and we are not talking about tens of millions. We are talking about hundreds of millions.[58]

When the BDA was under close scrutiny in 2005, the Bank of China was preparing for its initial public offering (IPO) on the New York Stock Exchange.[59] It was imperative for China to keep a clean sheet in combating money laundering.

China's increasing engagement with the AML regime is consistent with the two 'microprocesses' of socialization identified by Iain Johnston, namely mimicking and social influence, in his study of China's participation in international institutions.[60] As a novice to the global anti-money laundering regime, China wants to copy group behavioural norms as it seeks effective means to crack down on domestic money laundering with which the Chinese authorities lack familiarity. Concerned about its international reputation and status, China also desires to gain social rewards and avoid punishments. That explains why criticisms of US 'hegemonism' are muted and why China offers little ideational or policy inputs to the AML regime. Nonetheless, it may be premature to infer that China has fully embraced or internalized the concept of multilateral efforts to counter transnational organized crime, especially when the regime is principally driven by the US.

Piracy

In the broadest terms, piracy can be defined as 'unlawful depredation at sea involving the use or threat of violence'. It is not a lawful act of a declared or widely recognized war.[61] In practice, a narrower definition was adopted by the 1982 United Nations Convention on the Law of the Sea (UNCLOS) and the International Maritime Organization (IMO), the UN specialized agency responsible for maritime affairs. Article 101 of UNCLOS defines piracy as any of the following acts:[62]

a   any illegal acts of violence or detention, or any act of depredation, committed for private ends by the crew or the passengers of a private ship or a private aircraft, and directed:
    i   on the high seas, against another ship or aircraft, or against persons or property on board such ship or aircraft;
    ii against a ship, aircraft, persons or property in a place outside the jurisdiction of any State;

b any act of voluntary participation in the operation of a ship or of an aircraft with knowledge of facts making it a pirate ship or aircraft;
c any act of inciting or of intentionally facilitating an act described in subparagraph (a) or (b).

The focus of concern, according to this narrow approach, is on acts of maritime depredation in international waters and for 'private ends', excluding those for 'political ends', e.g. terrorism. A key issue is what international waters are. The areas outside territorial waters are considered international waters. Territorial waters are defined by UNCLOS as a belt of coastal waters up to 12 nautical miles (22 km) from the baseline (normally the low-water line). They are the sovereign territories of the coastal states. However, littoral states are given an additional 12 nautical miles as the 'contiguous zone'. The issue is made more complicated when the notion of exclusive economic zone (EEZ), extending up to 200 nautical miles (370.4 km) off the coastline, is introduced. This ocean enclosure movement has had much impact on multilateral responses to piracy.[63] It is uncertain as to whether contiguous and exclusive economic zones should be regarded as quasi-territorial waters.[64] One argument is that, as noted by Martin Murphy, '[m]ost modern pirates ... are land-based, venturing out to intercept shipping often no more than twenty miles from shore'. He says that piracy is 'a domestic criminal problem which should be dealt with under domestic law and in which the international community has no right to interfere'.[65] The international community, however, has an interest in halting piracy collectively because the victims are often international and some coastal states, particularly the failed ones, lack the political will and material resources to maintain freedom of navigation effectively.[66] International cooperation is necessary to deal with a more sophisticated form of piracy which occurs when transnational organized criminal syndicates are involved in creating 'phantom ships'. Pirates hijack entire ships, set adrift (or even murder) the crew, and unload and sell cargoes to either the gangs' partners or innocent buyers. The ships are then registered under new names and offer shipping services but never arrive at destined ports.[67] What is at issue is how state and non-state actors, e.g. ship owners or shipping agents, can devise effective global or regional maritime anti-piracy regimes to halt piracy while giving due respect to the national sovereignty of coastal states.

How serious is piracy?

Figure 10.1 shows that before 1994 the incidence of piracy and armed robbery against ships was low level, at fewer than 100 cases per year. It experienced several surges in 1994–97, 1998–2000, 2001–2003 and 2006–2009 whereas it fell substantially in 2003–2006. In 2009 the number of incidents was 406, a rise of 100 (32.7 per cent) over 2008. The most affected areas were East Africa (222 or 54.7 per cent) and the South China Sea (seventy-one or 17.5 per cent).[68] The Piracy Reporting Centre of the International Maritime Bureau (IMB), a non-profit-making organization under the International Chamber of Commerce, also

Transnational organized crime 167

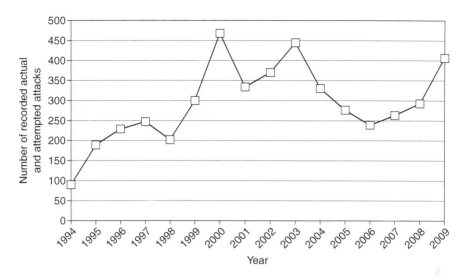

Figure 10.1 Incidence of piracy and armed robbery against ships, 1994–2009 (sources: (1) for 1994, Dana Dillon, 'Maritime piracy: defining the problem', *SAIS Review*, Vol. 25, No. 1 (Winter–Spring 2005), p. 155; (2) for 1995–2005, Martin N. Murphy, *Small Boats, Weak States, Dirty Money: Piracy and Maritime Terrorism in the Modern World* (London: Hurst, 2009), p. 63; (3) for 2006–2009, ICC International Maritime Bureau, *Piracy and Armed Robbery against Ships Annual Report 1 January–31 December 2009* (London: ICC International Maritime Bureau, 2010), pp. 5–6).

points to a similar pattern of incidence in which the number of cases of piracy and armed robbery rose steadily from 239 in 2006 to 406 in 2009 (see Table 10.1). Among the 406 incidents, 217 (53.4 per cent) were attributed to Somali pirates and 68 (16.7 per cent) took place in Southeast Asia and the Far East/East Asia. Before the rampant Somali piracy in the waters off the Horn of Africa became an issue of global concern in 2008, more than 30 per cent of recorded attacks in 2007 occurred in Southeast Asia and the Far East/East Asia. The attacks in Southeast Asia reached a climax at 53.7 per cent of the total in 1999.[69]

Table 10.1 Total number of Somali pirate attacks, 2005–2009

	Somali pirate attacks (S)	*World total attacks (T)*	*S/T (%)*
2005	48	276	17.39
2006	22	239	9.21
2007	51	263	19.39
2008	111	293	37.88
2009	217	406	53.45

Source: International Maritime Bureau, *Piracy and Armed Robbery against Ships Annual Report 1 January–31 December 2009* (London: ICC International Maritime Bureau, 2010), pp. 5–6.

168 *Transnational organized crime*

Pirates attacked forty-two oil tankers in 2009, a 40 per cent rise from 2008 or a 367 per cent growth from 2006. This was the highest level of attacks since the Centre started keeping records in 1992. The risk would push crude oil prices higher.[70] But specialists tend to agree that pirate attacks are under-reported because many ship owners or operators are reluctant to report for fear of the negative impact on the company reputation and of the cost of detainment in ports for investigation.[71]

Multilateral regimes on piracy

While piracy is a global issue, China is primarily concerned about piracy off Somalia and in Southeast and East Asia because the Gulf of Aden and the Strait of Malacca are parts of the strategic artery of Chinese international maritime trade. Although the total economic costs of piracy, estimated to be between $1 billion and $16 billion, are only equivalent to a tiny fraction of the total value of global seaborne trade, the real dangers of piracy off Somalia lie with its threats to the delivery of vital humanitarian assistance, especially food, to Somalia, Ethiopia and Sudan. With the annual average ransom paid to pirates escalating, piracy may also fuel regional armed conflicts and banditry.[72] Since 9/11 regional security analysts have linked the piracy threat with other maritime security threats, in particular maritime terrorism.[73] These concerns spark a need to initiate intensified international cooperation to counter piracy in dangerous regions. The following discussion focuses on how effective are regional cooperative agreements in the waters off Somalia and Southeast Asia, what are China's contributions to them, and what are the obstacles to inter-state cooperation.

The Horn of Africa

The year 2008 saw a steep rise in piracy off the Horn of Africa. In the following year, a total of 217 attacks in the waters off the Horn were attributable to Somali pirates, accounting for more than 53 per cent of the world total (see Table 10.1). Between January and November 2008, a total of 1,256 Chinese commercial vessels transited through Somali waters, of which 20 per cent came under pirate attack.[74] The United Nations Security Council passed a total of four resolutions (1816, 1838, 1846 and 1851) in 2008 to address the problem. The last two resolutions authorized states and regional organizations to use force to deter and repress piracy in Somali territorial waters and ashore, with the prior consent of the Transitional Federal Government (TFG) of Somalia.[75] The international shipping industry was shocked by the capture of *MV Sirius Star*, a Saudi oil supertanker, in November 2008 by Somali pirates some 450 nautical miles southeast off the coast of Kenya. The incident showed vividly the potential threats of piracy to the security of shipping lanes and energy supplies. Valued alone at $150 million, the supertanker was carrying crude oil worth more than $100 million. It was released in January 2009 after the ship owner paid an alleged ransom of $3 million to the pirates.[76]

Since October 2008, NATO has launched three missions, Operation Allied Provider (October–December 2008), Operation Allied Protector (March–August 2009) and Operation Ocean Shield (since August 2009), to counter piracy off the coast of Somalia.[77] Beginning in December 2008, the European Union has conducted a naval operation against piracy in the area, known as EUNAVFOR Somalia – Operation ATALANTA.[78] Pursuant to UNSC Resolution 1851 (2008), an international forum group, Contact Group on Piracy off the Coast of Somalia (CGPCS), was established in January 2009 to facilitate discussion and coordination of actions to suppress piracy. It is made up of forty-five states, seven regional and international organizations and two observers. Seven of the members are Asian countries, including China, India, Japan and South Korea.[79] The US Naval Forces Central Command's Combined Maritime Forces (CMF) set up the Combined Task Force 151 (CTF-151) in the same month solely for counter-piracy operations. As a multinational task force, it comprises naval ships and assets from more than twenty countries and operates in and around the Gulf of Aden, the Arabian Sea, the Indian Ocean and the Red Sea. In August 2008 the CMF created a Maritime Security Patrol Area (MSPA) in the Gulf of Aden as a more secure transit zone for merchant vessels. The MSPA includes the Internationally Recommended Transit Corridor (IRTC). Russia, China and India have deployed naval forces to the region to conduct anti-piracy operations. While they do not formally and fully coordinate with the CTF-151, they join the CTF-151, the EU and NATO in the monthly meetings of the Shared Awareness and Deconfliction (SHADE) group, held in Bahrain.[80] The IMO sponsored a meeting in January 2009 with seventeen regional governments in Djibouti, which adopted the Djibouti Code of Conduct. As an observer, Japan later made a contribution of $14 million to a fund created to support the Djibouti Code-related anti-piracy operations.[81]

The first attack on a Chinese vessel happened in November 2008. A fishing vessel, *FV Tianyu No. 8*, was seized off the coast of Kenya. It was released in February 2009 after paying an undisclosed amount of ransom.[82] A second cargo vessel, *MV Zhenhua 4*, fought off a pirate attack in December 2008.[83] China responded by dispatching in the same month naval escort fleets to patrol the Gulf of Aden, its first overseas combat operation in several centuries, and by signing up to the CGPCS. In October 2009, *De Xin Hai*, a Chinese bulk carrier delivering coal from South Africa to India, was hijacked 700 nautical miles to the east of Somalia, well beyond the IRTC. Before this incident, no ship had been captured so far from the Somali coast. At that time the Chinese task force – two frigates and a supply ship – was in the Gulf of Aden, operating relatively independently.[84] Rescue using force being too risky for the crew as well as the Chinese navy, the incident heightened the imperative for regional governance of piracy. China suggested in the UN one month later that the patrol area, IRTC, be carved up and patrolled by navies in accordance with set areas of responsibility, and that Beijing should assume the 'rotating chair' of the SHADE group.[85] Beijing also hosted in the same month a meeting with representatives of US, European, Russian and Japanese naval forces to boost anti-piracy efforts.[86]

To justify its leadership of SHADE, China eventually agreed to permanently deploy a ship in one of the sectors of the IRTC.[87] Furthermore, China made an offer to the EU to provide armed escorts for the World Food Programme's humanitarian aid shipments to Somalia, the likely consequence being that the People's Liberation Army Navy would deploy more warships to the region.[88] However, in stressing the guiding principles of independence and sovereignty, China has let it be known that it would neither lead other countries nor be led by any of them even when it assumes the chairmanship of SHADE.[89]

While China is more willing than ever before to offer global public goods by maintaining freedom of navigation, the Chinese flotilla has avoided coordinating with the American force under a single central command; the US hoped that the Chinese deployment of naval vessels 'could be a springboard for a resumed dialogue between the two countries' force' which terminated in 2008 in the wake of American arms sales to Taiwan.[90] China wants to contribute in 'a parallel rather than integrated manner'.[91] China's naval activism in the Indian Ocean has provoked Indian and Russian unease. Following in China's footsteps, India has sought the chairmanship of SHADE and Russia offered to increase its presence in the Ocean by helping to protect shipments of UN food aid to Somalia.[92] Although more countries have made contributions to the campaign against piracy off Somalia, a multilateral regional governance on piracy has yet to materialize. China continues to employ a 'go-it-alone' approach to handling pirate attacks. Although EU naval officials had warned that China might pay too much ransom, a subsidiary of the state-owned China Ocean Shipping (Group) Company allegedly paid more than $4 million to set the *De Xin Hai* and its crew free in December 2009. In June 2010 a Singaporean-flagged chemical tanker, *MV Golden Blessing*, was hijacked by Somali pirates. Nineteen Chinese sailors were held hostage on the coast of the Gulf of Aden. Negotiations between the Chinese and the pirates were protracted and difficult because, now treating Chinese crew as 'lucrative targets', the pirates reportedly demanded a ransom of up to $10 million for their release.[93]

Southeast Asia

The rise of Asia, especially China, has boosted both inter- and intra-regional trade in oil and manufactured goods and fast growth in shipping traffic. Accordingly Asian countries accounted for 38.8 per cent of the total tonnage of seaborne world exports in 2006, followed by European countries (21.8 per cent) and American states (21.1 per cent).[94] Many vessels going to or from East Asia transit through the Strait of Malacca and Singapore. It is said that more than 50,000 cargo ships transit through the Strait of Malacca and up to 80 per cent of oil delivered to Northeast Asia passes through the Strait.[95] Against this background, it is alarming to observe that piracy in Southeast Asia became more rampant and violent throughout the 1990s and the early years of the twenty-first century. Although piracy seems to have declined in the region, the problem persists with criminals using more advanced arms. Southeast Asia remains one of the areas most afflicted by piracy.[96]

One of the major obstacles to staging a successful attack on pirates in Southeast Asia is the concern of some coastal states, in particular Indonesia and Malaysia, about sovereign rights in their territorial waters and control over underwater resources in EEZs while they want to share the burden of providing the regional public goods of maritime security with other stakeholders. Regional states have overlapping jurisdictional claims to islands, EEZs and the archipelagos in the South China Sea, the Paracel and Spratly Islands being fiercely contested.[97] Hot pursuit of pirates across national borders or in waters under dispute is rare. There is a concern that multilateral piracy suppression may erode national sovereignty by internationalizing the Straits.[98] Indonesia is often accused of showing the least interest in combating piracy because the majority of the ships under attack are foreign-owned. The country does not allow foreign security guards to escort foreign vessels in its waters.[99] Regional states and other stakeholders tolerated this indifferent attitude towards piracy in the Strait of Malacca and near Singapore until external pressures mounted. In March 2004 Admiral Thomas B. Fargo, then commander of the US Pacific Command, proposed setting up a Regional Maritime Security Initiative (RMSI) to develop a partnership of willing regional nations to identify, monitor and intercept transnational maritime threats. To oppose patrols by extra-regional states, both Malaysia and Indonesia took steps to implement more effective measures to suppress piracy and other maritime crimes.[100] In addition, the Joint War Committee of the Lloyd's Market Association in July 2005 designated the Strait of Malacca and some areas in the southern Philippines as 'prone to hull war, strikes, terrorism and related perils'.[101] As a consequence, the marine insurance premium the shipping companies had to pay shot up. The listing was rescinded in August 2006 after regional states enhanced the security of the sea lanes.[102] The major measure was the Malacca Strait Security Initiative (MSSI), composed of the trilateral Malacca Strait Sea Patrol, MALSINDO (MALaysia–Singapore–INDOnesia), and the Eyes in the Sky (EiS) initiative, launched in July 2004 and September 2005 respectively. The MSSI has enabled the three countries to coordinate air patrols over the Malacca Strait. The Philippines has suggested that together with Malaysia and Indonesia it formalize a tripartite agreement to increase exchange of intelligence and information about piracy. Singapore was the first Asian country to join the Container Security Initiative, launched by the US in 2002.[103]

Although the new anti-piracy measures could have had deterrent effects on piracy and consequently led to an improvement in the maritime security of the region, progress towards a viable multilateral security regime is still slow. According to MALSINDO, the navies of the three countries are to patrol *within* their respective territorial waters without any provision for cross-border pursuit. A substantial reduction in piracy in 2005 compared to the year before was largely due to the effect of the December 2004 Indian Ocean tsunami on Aceh, Indonesia, where many pirates were allegedly located. While the EiS initiative itself represents a political breakthrough in which patrolling aircrafts are allowed to fly up to 3 nautical miles into the territorial waters of the three participating states, and the aircrafts have on board representatives from the states, the airborne surveillance is not supported by patrol vessels on the seas to investigate and interdict any suspect ships.[104]

Multilateral anti-piracy efforts have been blocked by the failure of both coastal and user states to reach an agreement on sharing the expenses of policing the waterways. Three major multilateral conferences were held in 2005 and 2006 in Indonesia, the US and Malaysia to address this knotty issue.[105] While ad hoc voluntary contributions were made by both Japan and China, various actors got bogged down by the issues of whether user states should be allowed to be involved in the security of the Strait and whether a user fee should be introduced to fund the costly anti-piracy programme. Littoral states in Southeast Asia steadfastly avoided any long-term institutionalization of sharing the responsibility for maintaining security in the Strait with the user states.[106] The US and many shipping companies were adamantly opposed to the introduction of any fees. Further signs of the failure of multilateralism in fighting piracy in East Asia include the fact that neither Malaysia nor Indonesia is party to two major multilateral anti-piracy regimes, namely the Convention for the Suppression of Unlawful Acts against the Safety of Maritime Navigation (SUA) and Regional Cooperation Agreement in Combating Piracy and Armed Robbery against Ships in Asia (ReCAAP).[107]

Entered into force in 1992 and with a current membership of 156 states, SUA is an attempt to address the inadequacies of the UNCLOS approach to piracy. Malaysia and Indonesia in particular are concerned about financial obligations on signatory states and possible infringements on national sovereignty if foreign vessels are allowed to exercise jurisdiction in their territorial waters. Akin to their response to RMSI, they have been highly sensitive to the possibility that the US might intervene in their domestic affairs under the cloak of combating transnational maritime crime. Being Muslim-majority countries, they have an additional reason to be wary about the hidden agenda of SUA, which was designed to tackle international terrorism, although it was presented as an anti-piracy document.[108] The idea of ReCAAP was initiated by then Japanese Prime Minister Junichiro Koizumi in November 2001 at an ASEAN Plus Three (China, Japan and South Korea) Summit in Brunei. The following negotiations led to the establishment of ReCAAP in November 2004 by a total of sixteen Asian states – the ten ASEAN member states, China, Japan, South Korea, India, Sri Lanka and Bangladesh. They also agreed to set up an Information Sharing Centre (ISC) in Singapore in November 2006. ReCAAP came into force in September 2006 after the tenth country ratified it. Neither Malaysia nor Indonesia joined it for fear that the organization would undermine their exclusive sovereignty over the area.[109] With substantial contributions from both Japan and Singapore, the ISC is also funded by voluntary contributions from the sixteen member states.[110] Japan has been active in proposing anti-piracy ventures in Southeast Asia, although not all of them bore fruit because of their perceived infringement of the sovereignty of the regional states. It also offers financial aid to the maritime forces of Malaysia and Indonesia and conducts bilateral anti-piracy exercises with them.[111]

Another hurdle to regional multilateralism is China's serious reservations about cooperation with the US and Japan in combating piracy in Southeast Asia.

It is concerned that both the US and Japan will strengthen their military presence in the Strait of Malacca and indirectly gain control over a major sea lane for oil delivery to China. Like Malaysia and Indonesia, China is opposed to RMSI.[112] China has for a long time claimed that the South China Sea is Chinese territory and Chinese security analysts seem to intentionally avoid discussing piracy in the South China Sea as well as the area known as Hong Kong–Luzon–Hainan triangle.[113] Territorial disputes in the South China Sea and China's strained relations with both Vietnam and the Philippines over the region since 2007 have hindered regional cooperation in combating piracy.[114] As a result, while incidents of piracy in the Strait of Malacca and near Singapore fell to only eleven in 2009 from a peak of eighty in 2000, no similar trend is observed in the South China Sea. Indeed the IMB recorded thirteen attacks in 2009, the highest level since 1994.[115]

China believes that it is expedient to maintain the status quo in the fight against piracy in Southeast Asia by letting Indonesia, Malaysia and Singapore shoulder the major responsibility for cracking down on the problem while largely ignoring similar issues in the South China Sea. This is because China shares their concerns over infringement of national sovereignty. In contrast, China is more committed to participation in the anti-piracy missions off the Horn of Africa. These are undertaken under the auspices of the UNSC with the consent of the Somali TFG. Piracy in waters off Somalia coresponds more with the UNCLOS definition than that in the Strait of Malacca and near Singapore, as many Somali pirates stage their attacks in international waters.

Conclusion

Based on the notion that international financial stability and freedom or safety of navigation through international waters are global public goods, this chapter shows that China's provides these global public goods to varying degrees: it also participates in global governance with regard to transnational organized crime. As a novice in global or regional multilateral regimes to combat money laundering and piracy, what motivates China to engage with the relevant governance institutions is its primary concern about the material interests of its banks and companies, which would be harmed by both money laundering and piracy. On the one hand, China does not want to miss any opportunity to demonstrate to the outside world that it is a responsible global stakeholder, pursuing policies that support the provision of global public goods; on the other, it keeps a wary eye on the potential negative impacts of integration into global governance on its sovereignty and operational autonomy. China is therefore reluctant to be fully embedded in the regional governance frameworks concerning piracy in both the Horn of Africa and Southeast Asia, although its engagement in the two regions shows a difference in style and in the degree of involvement, as has been demonstrated in this chapter. China even downplays or is in denial about the presence of piracy in the South China Sea which it claims to be part of its core interests and territory.

Conclusion

This book started off with two questions: (1) how powerful has China become? (2) What kind of world order is likely to emerge in the wake of a rising China? Drawing on the theory of global governance, the book has taken these two interrelated themes to assess China's increasing influence over how world affairs are governed, and what the consequences and implications will be for the evolving global order. As discussed in Chapter 1, the essence of global governance is the rules system that governs or steers the supply of global public goods by various actors to address various trans-sovereign problems in order to maintain a stable and responsive global order. At the first level, this book assesses whether China is willing and able to provide global public goods to address a wide array of global problems and whether China can craft new global rules to govern the provision of such goods. We have analysed various issue areas of global concern, ranging from peace and security to transnational organized crime (chapters 3 to 10). At the second level, it scrutinizes what implications China's increasing engagement with global governance would have for the world order.

To conclude this study, this chapter will first summarize the principal findings and major arguments about China's contribution to global public goods. What sort of international public goods does it supply and in what areas? Does it take collective action with other state and non-state actors through international institutions or does it free-ride on others' efforts instead? The chapter will then evaluate how powerful China is on the world stage in terms of its ability to provide global public goods and to make rules for the rest of the world to follow. Finally, it will assess whether a new world order is in the making with China's rising power as well as its increasing participation in world affairs.

Does China provide global public goods?

Before 1979, when a poor, isolated China was on difficult to hostile terms with the two superpowers, then the United States and the Soviet Union, it made little or no contributions to the world, except perhaps promoting or calling for revolutions, liberation and anti-imperialism in the developing world. Inside the country the Communist Party was at that time preoccupied with domestic upheavals of one kind or another, from the Anti-Rightist Campaign of 1957 to the Great Leap

Forward of 1958–61 and then to the Cultural Revolution from 1966 to the death of Mao in 1976. Beginning with the reform and opening up since 1979, China has been normalizing its international relations, improving ties with erstwhile enemies, increasing participation in a wide array of international institutions, and forging commercial ties with various business enterprises and countries around the world. It is often seen that China has benefited from the process of globalization in the last three decades or so, reaping huge economic returns under the Bretton Woods system and the relatively stable international political environment since the end of the Cold War. With its recent meteoric rise and accumulated wealth, attention has shifted to Beijing's share of responsibility for providing global public goods. Comparing the two periods of its development before and after 1979, one could easily conclude that China has begun to provide some public goods in a broad sense in the latter period. If we accept that China does provide these in a broad sense, what are they? In this book, we ask: Has China contributed to making and preserving international peace and security, to promoting world trade and maintaining global financial stability, to cleaning the environment, to safeguarding human rights, to ensuring food safety and public health, to sustaining energy availability and to clamping down on transnational organized crime?

As regards peace and security (Chapter 3), apart from its increasing engagement with arms control and non-proliferation treaties, China's growing contributions towards UN peacekeeping activities stand out. Beginning in the 1990s when China first started to contribute personnel to the UN peacekeeping operation in Cambodia, the country has over time increased its manpower support, to the extent that it is now the largest contributor among the five permanent members of the Security Council in terms of the size of its peacekeeping force to UN-sponsored operations. China's monetary contributions to the UN general revenue and peacekeeping budget have also increased steadily, although not at a high enough rate to satisfy some critics. However, the exact contribution of China to the resolution of the North Korean nuclear weapons crisis is unclear. On the one hand, there has not been a war or large-scale military confrontation on the Korean Peninsula even when North Korea's relations with both the United States and South Korea worsened during Pyongyang's development of its nuclear weapons and missile programmes. On the other hand, although Beijing has been hosting the Six-Party Talks on the crisis since August 2003, these have failed to stop Pyongyang from continuing to develop its nuclear weapons programme. Critics tend to blame China for its intransigence in not taking collective action with the other four parties, especially the US, South Korea and Japan, to rein in North Korea. China's primary concerns are rather the survival of North Korea's regime, the potential ramifications in the event of its sudden demise for China's own security, and China's privileged position in Northeast Asia. Nor has China succeeded in bringing about sustainable direct bilateral negotiations between the US and North Korea.

There is undoubtedly a great deal of truth in the claim that China is a major beneficiary of economic globalization. While the country has become the second largest economy and the largest merchandise exporter in the world, in the midst of the global financial crisis there was sharp disagreement between China and the US over the root cause of global financial instability and by extension over the solution (a global public good) to it. China is accused of free-riding on the open trading system and of deliberately keeping its currency, the renminbi or yuan, low in order to promote exports in a neo-mercantilist and unfair way and to amass enormous amounts of foreign exchange reserves. The United States, which has recorded a heavy trade imbalance with China for many years, especially since China joined the WTO in 2001, has been particularly critical, on several occasions coming close to labelling China as a currency manipulator meriting retaliatory action. The US therefore argues that China should take the lead in addressing the global imbalances by expediting the appreciation of the renminbi (Chapter 4). However, Beijing disagrees, claiming that overborrowing in the US was the culprit of the financial crisis. It thus shows marked reluctance to take collective action with deficit countries to rectify global economic imbalances.

The area of human rights is perhaps the most controversial, as it relates to human values and judgements, which not only are diverse across cultures but are also different across societies at different stages of development. The lack of an acceptable standard across nations often results in different interpretations, arguments and debates, and even finger pointing. To the Chinese government, if improvements can be made to promote the welfare of its people, such as the provision of food and housing, then it is fulfilling its responsibilities to one-fifth of humankind and hence to the world at large. In the West some fervent critics of China's record focus rather on political and civil rights and pay scant attention to the country's achievement in poverty alleviation, regarding the latter as less important than human rights or as a lesser kind of human rights. However, to the many poor and weak in the Third World, what China has done offers lessons to be learned, regardless of human rights. Although, at the international level, the Chinese government has signed and ratified many international human rights treaties, passed domestic legislation to mirror its international treaty obligations, strengthened in incremental ways its legal system, and engaged in human rights dialogues with the outside world, it provides little global public goods in safeguarding international human rights. In alliance with a group of like-minded states with dubious human rights records, China has tried to dilute the influence or undermine the functions of some key international human rights regimes, for example, the Special Procedures and the country-specific resolutions in the UN Human Rights Council. China also blocked a more comprehensive and sweeping reform of the UN Commission on Human Rights in 2006. Even in the treaties it has signed and ratified, China is often absent from the treaty-monitoring bodies.

Environmental issues are perhaps more global than most other issues, given the fact that, for example, air pollution has no regard for territorial border, as it goes wherever the wind blows. Domestically, China has taken a lot of measures to tackle its environmental problems, including legislative means, administrative steps, fiscal policies and the adoption of innovations such as the development of

Conclusion 177

green technologies as well as alternative and renewable energy, the setting up of green cities, and the mandating of the reduction of the intensity of energy use, among others. On the international front, however, China has been criticized by others for not agreeing to a binding, verifiable limit on greenhouse gas emissions. The United States and China are at loggerheads over who should bear the primary responsibility for addressing climate change and global warming. The US has been citing this Chinese intransigence as a reason for not ratifying the Kyoto Protocol and for insisting that China (and India) must be on board for a new globally binding environmental treaty. Claiming that it is a late-industrializing country with little historical responsibility for the current levels of pollution, China has invoked the 'common but differentiated responsibility' principle, provided for by the Protocol, to exempt it from setting limits on greenhouse gas emissions. For China, the maximum level of responsibility it can assume, and its contribution to the global public good of a clean environment, is merely to slow down its consumption of energy and hence its emission of greenhouse gases.

Akin to environmental degradation, public health is a major global concern. To improve its reputation tarnished by the SARS outbreak and to utilize international resources and technical assistance to tackle its internal health challenge, China has had no hesitation about multilateral cooperation with various actors inside China as well as in the international arena since the turn of this century. Beijing has taken measures to tackle the country's ailing health system and has attempted to provide an accessible and affordable healthcare system to its 1.3 billion people. However, it remains to be seen whether the health reform will be successful. In global health governance, China has made progress to varying degrees in the areas of containment, control and cure of infectious diseases or health risk, and has provided African states with health aid. However, due to its growing research and development in pharmaceuticals, it has done little more than pay lip service to support African states and their peoples in asking for a relaxation on HIV/AIDS drug patents. China also hesitates to take more global responsibility for making donations towards global health activities. Its contribution to global health institutions is a mismatch with its increasing might and accumulated wealth. Now the second largest economy in the world, its donation to the WHO is not only far less than that of the US but also comes behind some medium or small powers such as Norway and Luxembourg. China's stingy health donation has aroused concerns about its free-riding and its abdication of responsibility for providing global public goods for health.

A common feature of China's health governance and food safety governance is its willingness to cooperate with various actors to deal with its internal health and food safety challenges. A spate of food and drug safety scandals arising from Chinese goods since 2007 has highlighted not only the need for China to improve its consumer product safety standards but also the pressing need for a concerted international effort to unify Chinese standards with the international food safety regime. Domestically, China has taken measures to weed out unqualified or fake products and to implement enhanced food safety laws. Simultaneously it has adopted bilateral and multilateral cooperative measures to improve its food standards and to conform to the norms and rules of global food governance. However, due to its disjointed and fragmented food production and regulatory system, endemic corruption among officials, and limited room for civil society participation in monitoring, China is still facing daunting challenges in food safety governance. In addition, China has not stayed in step with the emerging needs of a responsive food safety regime arising from a globalized food production system. It continues to cling to a top-down and state-centric approach to food safety, which undermines the effectiveness of its governance in this area.

A well-functioning market in energy that can meet the ever-increasing demand of consumer countries and is buoyed up by an encompassing international institution is a global public good in the energy sector. One might have thus thought that China had a strong incentive to strengthen the role of the international energy market and join the International Energy Agency, as it has been an oil-deficient country since 1993 and is now the second largest oil consumer in the world. However, China's energy security strategy, especially its strategy about the crucial commodity of oil, is best characterized as neo-mercantilist and 'acting alone'. Through bilateral agreements with a host of oil-producing countries in Eurasia and Africa, China is attempting to acquire oil via long-term deals or equity investment without relying on the international market. The rationale for this neo-mercantilist approach is concern over national autonomy and deep mistrust of the supposedly impartial role of the international market and the role of the US in the operation of the market as well as the IEA. While this strategy serves to diversify the sources of China's oil imports, reducing dependence on the volatile Middle East, China has thus far not given due attention to the cost and deficiency of this state-centric approach.

One can say that China is most cooperative with the West in combating transnational organized crime in the various policy areas covered by this book. This should not be surprising, as material interests are at stake in money laundering and maritime piracy and China has little experience in tackling organized crime. That said, however, one can differentiate between China's approaches to money laundering and to piracy. In the former, China has been willing to revise its own domestic law and keen to join the FATF as part of global collective action to fight cross-border money laundering. This was most evident when some of its major state-owned banks were complicit in assisting North Korea in the crime. In the case of piracy off Somalia, while China is determined to contribute to the provision of the global public good of maritime security and freedom of navigation by, among other things, assuming the rotating chair of SHADE, it is loath to closely coordinate its anti-piracy operations with other stakeholders such as the US and NATO. Its preferred mode of cooperation is rather to work in parallel with other states or organizations in the area. China is also subject to muted criticism that it indirectly encourages piracy by paying excessively handsome ransoms to pirates.

How powerful is China?

The preceding section shows that in terms of membership and participation, China has done reasonably well in international institutions and regimes through which global public goods are provided, especially given that it started from a very low base in 1979. China is accorded great power status not simply because of its material preponderance in terms of its aggregate economic size but also because of its ever-deepening presence in the governance of a vast variety of issue areas of global concern. This can be seen from Table C.1, which compares China's participation in the policy areas we have examined with three other major emerging powers, namely Brazil, India and Russia. Apparently China's participation is much higher than the other major emerging powers. In the areas of peace and security, finance and trade, the environment and public health, China's increasing institutional presence is most remarkable. It contributes more than the other UNSC permanent members to United Nations peacekeeping operations; its voting rights in the World Bank and the IMF are the largest in the developing world; it is a key party to the G20 and the UN Framework Convention on Climate Change negotiations; and a Chinese national, Margaret Chan, is in charge of the WHO.

However, in terms of quality, there is room for debate as to whether China at this stage of its development has done or achieved enough in terms of contributing global public goods and making rules for global governance institutions. One case in which China has forged some new rules in governing global issues is its stance on humanitarian intervention, a subject we have discussed in some depth as regards Darfur, Sudan (Chapter 5). The West sees humanitarian intervention as a justifiable means to stop serious abuses of human rights and as inherent in the residual powers of outsiders (meaning the West in the name of the 'international community') to intervene. According to China, several conditions need to be satisfied before intervention should be allowed. Apart from the consent of the host government and the sanction of the UNSC, the case for intervention must be based on the existence of a threat to regional peace and security and regional organizations must be given the prerogative to make decisions on intervention. Whether or not these conditions, which were applied to Darfur, will be applicable to other cases remains to be seen and whether they genuinely contribute to regional peace and security is also hotly disputed. Nonetheless, these conditions put the power of authorization of peacekeeping more in the hands of the host and neighbouring governments than in the hands of Western powers. This situation reflects China's concern about national sovereignty and the significant role played by intergovernmental organizations in managing global issues. China has successfully crafted the rules it prefers in the area of humanitarian intervention.

However, aside from humanitarian intervention, there are few rules that China can make in its engagement with global governance. Rather China goes to great lengths to *defend* its currency, human rights and environmental policy. China also somewhat defiantly sets its own pace for adjusting the value of the renminbi, controlling greenhouse gas emissions, ensuring energy availability and

Table C.1 China's involvement in various issue areas in comparison with other emerging powers

Issue-area	China	Brazil	India	Russia
Peace and security	• One of the P5 • contributes more than other permanent members of the UNSC to UNPKO (2,039 personnel)* • a nuclear power but not a party to AG, Wassenaar Arrangement, MTCR and HCOC • a major actor in the Six-Party Talks on North Korea and the multilateral talks on Iran	• A moderate contributor to UNPKO (2,267 personnel)* • neither a P5 member nor a member of the Six-Party Talks, and not involved in Iran • more active than China and India in joining non-proliferation regimes except in AG, Wassenaar and HCOC • increasing attention to disarmament	• A major contributor to UNPKO (8,691 personnel)* • a nuclear power; but neither a P5 member nor a member of the Six-Party Talks, and not involved in Iran • joined BTWC and CWC	• One of the P5 • few contributions to UNPKO (258 personnel)* • a major nuclear power comparable to the US • plays a relatively marginal role in the Six-Party Talks, but more influential than China on Iran • a party to all major arms control and non-proliferation regimes except AG
Finance and trade	• The second largest economy and the largest exporter • huge trade surplus with the US and the largest foreign exchange reserves • a major destination of FDI • its renminbi appreciation is at the top of the agenda of economic governance	• Plays a less significant role than China, although pointing out the danger of 'currency war'	• Plays a less significant role than China, although has concerns over agricultural trade liberalization	• Plays a less significant role than China • has yet to join WTO

Human rights and humanitarian intervention (HI)	• Often wants to dilute the role of the UN special procedures and country-specific resolutions • a member of the Like-Minded Group (LMG) • has created new rules for humanitarian intervention in Darfur • its human rights are often a focus of external criticism	• Not a member of the LMG • less active and vocal than China in the issue area than China	• a member of the LMG • less active and vocal than China	• Sometimes sides with China • less active and vocal than China
Environment	• The largest CO_2 emitter • a key player in Conference of the Parties meetings • refuses to have mandatory cap on emissions • heavy investment in green technology	• Less active and vocal than both China and India	• A partner with China but with lower emissions	• Less active and vocal than both China and India
Public health	• The source of SARS • Taiwan was a key issue in IHR negotiations • Margaret Chan as the WHO DG • an emerging force in health aid to Africa and patent registration • its financial contribution to international health institutions is not commensurate with its aggregate economic wealth	• More active than China in calling for revisions in patent protection in TRIPS agreement • no financial contribution to the WHO in 2008–2009	• A major producer of generic drugs • less active or influential in WHO than China	• Financially contributes more than other BRIC countries to health institutions, e.g. the WHO and Global Fund

continued

Table C.1 Continued

Issue-area	China	Brazil	India	Russia
Food safety	• A major exporter of food products • with frequent reports of food scandals • a member of Codex Alimentarius and SPS Agreement	• Little role noted • a member of Codex Alimentarius	• Little role noted • a member of Codex Alimentarius	• Little role noted • a member of Codex Alimentarius • not a member of SPS Agreement
Energy security	• Though oil-deficient, a major oil and gas producer • the 2nd largest consumer of oil, after the US • the 2nd largest oil-importing country • not a member of IEA • engages bilaterally with oil-producing countries • believed to be a key actor in pushing up the world oil price	• One of the major producers of oil (2.6% of the world total in 2009)	• Produces little oil • the 4th largest consumer and importer of oil • not a member of IEA • a competitor of China in overseas oil exploration • also a key actor in oil price movement	• A major oil and gas producer (oil: 12.9% of the world total in 2009; gas: 17.6%) • selling oil to China after a long negotiation process • using energy as a diplomatic tool
Transnational organized crime	• A member of FATF • a partner with the US in combating North Korea's money laundering • a co-chair of SHADE in fighting piracy	• A member of FATF • less active in anti-piracy	• A member of FATF • following in China's footsteps, wants to strengthen its role in combating piracy in Somalia, but not a co-chair of SHADE	• A member of FAFT • following in China's footsteps, wants to strengthen its role in combating piracy in Somalia, but not a co-chair of SHADE

Note
* As of December 2010.

food safety, and combating piracy. It is against multilateralism as a way to strengthen the global human rights regime and cautious of endorsing multilateral force in humanitarian interventions and of putting collective pressure on North Korea. Contrary to the conventional thinking that Chinese foreign policy has become increasingly assertive and aggressive,[1] why is China still reactive, passive and defensive in so many policy areas and loath to take collective action? Is China a free-rider in its participation in collective activity?

While China may not be a strong candidate for a free-rider in international politics, as it has expended many resources and much manpower on addressing a wide array of trans-sovereign issues, it is not yet a genuine great power in terms of the capacity to change the architecture of global governance. One may argue that China has consciously chosen this. Yan Xuetong of Tsinghua University in Beijing may provide us with an important clue as to why China stays on the periphery of the global governance process. While the world may consider China a superpower and hence expect it to take more responsibility for resolving global problems, he says, 'No. This is a *trap* to exhaust our limited resources'.[2] Yan's colleagues in both the Chinese Realist school and the 'Selective Multilateralist' school also have a similar view.[3] This resonates with the neo-realist concern over relative gains and the conventional wisdom which holds that the hegemon bears the cost of providing global public goods disproportionately (discussed in Chapter 1). This is also closely related to a lively debate inside China on what international responsibilities China should take on. The mainstream thinking is that China's primary responsibility is towards its own people. It is imperative to lift its 150 million impoverished people (about 11 per cent of the total population) out of poverty.[4] This is echoed by Wang Jisi of Peking University who argues that '[i]f an organizing principle must be established to guide China's grand strategy, it should be the improvement of the Chinese people's living standards, welfare, and happiness through social justice.'[5] More importantly, our analysis has shown that China has not projected any values, norms and rules that are likely to be accepted and internalized by the international community. As shown in our analysis, the primary values and norms that China has been at pains to espouse are the statist principle of national sovereignty, non-interference in the domestic affairs of other states and the right to choose one's path to national development. While these values and norms helped to prevent inter-state wars in the Cold War era and may be agreeable to some political elites of developing countries, they are not conducive to collectively solving the various global issues that tend to threaten the wellbeing of the world population in the current age of globalization and growing interdependence. In terms of inducing others to conform to its way of thinking and behaving, China's power, though growing fast, especially in the economic realm, is still limited and constrained.

A new world order in the making?

Is a new world order in the making as a result of China's increasing involvement in global governance? This is our second puzzle here. It is now quite natural for other states to look towards China as a great power or even a strong candidate for a superpower. Surely China has a voice in deciding how global governance is managed. However, it will be debatable whether or not China should have a decisive voice. This hinges on whether China would like to play a leadership role in addressing global problems and whether other states or actors are willing to be led by China.

Those who welcome China's growth and its increasing involvement in world affairs try to engage it. Those who are cautious or are worried about its rise try to take measures to contain or restrain it. In practice, most countries do both, engaging while hedging, acting as rational players do in international political games. Inevitably, the outside world has to go some distance to accommodate this rising power, give it a seat or a bigger, better seat, a voice or a bigger voice in running world affairs. Is there a new world order? How new is it? These are the questions that will puzzle the minds of analysts for years to come.

In examining global collective action across a number of issues ranging from security to finance, and from environmental protection to global health, Todd Sandler offers two interesting observations. One is that reliance on the US alone as the engine of global economic growth is unstable. A more diversified engine of growth would be desirable, and the growing influence of the EU, China, India, Brazil and others may eventually provide this diversity. The other observation is a caution against over-generalization of analysis across issues; that is, there is a need to recognize the special circumstances that promote or inhibit global collection action.[6] In the light of these two observations, the rise of China and its growing demand for a greater say in global governance should be welcomed as they may provide greater diversity and greater stability in global development. But a caveat is that it may lead to a low level of global collective action. What this means is that other major states, eager to accommodate China and bring it to their collective fold, may inevitably have to lower their expectations of the standard of collective action.

The change from a mainly US-led global order to a diffuse one is likely to be gradual, unless unforeseen circumstances like wars or natural disasters intervene. It will take place over a long stretch of time, sometimes unnoticed by casual observers. And it will affect many issues at different rates, with the resultant outcome a complex, even a confused, one.

A likely scenario of the emerging world order is characterized by 'leadership deficit': fewer states will look to the US for global leadership, which has been weakened materially and morally by the financial crisis that began in the summer of 2007, and China is unable to replace it as the hegemon. China is best described as an emerging yet reactive power with little capability to offer any attractive normative social order to international society. A latent danger to global order is that there are at least two competing great powers with shifting coalitions of followers across various issue areas. A tough challenge facing world leaders is how to avoid 'lowest common denominator' international politics in which little or no effective global action can be taken when confronting a wide range of life- or wealth-threatening issues.

Appendices

Appendix A

CDOs and the US housing market: a perspective

Created by Wall Street in 1987, CDOs and securitization were tacitly endorsed when US regulators (e.g. the Federal Reserve) allowed in the 1980s and 1990s the breakdown of the traditional institutional barriers between deposit-taking commercial banks and investment banks. To encourage home ownership, the US government-sponsored Fannie Mae (Federal National Mortgage Association) and Freddie Mac (Federal Home Loan Mortgage Corporation), created in 1938 and 1970 respectively, also bought and securitized a large proportion of US mortgages.[1] China and Japan were among the large investors in the Fannie and Freddie outstanding debt.[2] Securitization allowed both the recycling of capital that enabled increased availability of credit and the devolution or dispersal of risk to other financial institutions by moving the loans off the balance sheets of the issuing banks. The success of Fannie Mae and Freddie Mac encouraged Wall Street investment banks to join the market. Believing that the prevailing housing boom was sustainable,[3] they had a greater yet perverted incentive to be more lax than ever before in granting and monitoring loans. They offered higher-risk, adjustable-rate mortgage loans (subprime mortgages) to the less creditworthy, in particular NINJA (no income, no job or assets), borrowers. Having passed their peak around September 2006, housing prices fell as soon as a glut of unsold homes came onto the market and low-income home-owning borrowers began to default at the end of 2006 once their mortgages were reset to much higher interest rates after the expiry of the initial 'teaser' period. This was followed by foreclosures on mortgages by the lenders, but the assets were worth less than the debts. The crisis first impaired the capital base of the highly leveraged financial institutions due to write-downs.[4] Consequently, they hoarded liquid assets and refused to lend to each other, tightening up credit supply and leading to unprecedented illiquidity in the interbank loan markets. Like a virus, the shockwaves of the crisis soon spread from the financial sector to the rest of the economy.

Appendix B

Appendix B Major carbon dioxide emitters (cumulative emissions, 1850–2007)

	Cumulative emissions (million tonnes)	Percentage of world total (%)	Emissions per person (tonnes) (rank)
United States	339,174.0	28.75	1,125.7 (3)
China	105,915.4	8.98	80.4 (89)
Russia	94,678.7	8.03	666.3 (10)
Germany	81,194.5	6.88	987.0 (6)
United Kingdom	68,763.4	5.83	1,127.2 (2)
Japan	45,629.1	3.87	357.1 (36)
France	32,666.6	2.77	527.4 (23)
India	28,824.4	2.44	25.6 (123)
Canada	25,716.0	2.18	779.8 (8)
Ukraine	25,431.0	2.16	546.8 (22)
Poland	22,664.5	1.92	594.5 (16)
Italy	19,269.2	1.63	324.5 (38)
South Africa	13,133.6	1.11	274.5 (47)
Australia	13,108.5	1.11	622.1 (15)
Mexico	12,242.8	1.04	116.3 (78)

Source: *Climate Analysis Indicators Tool (CAIT)*, Version 8.0 (Washington, DC: World Resources Institute, 2008), http://cait.wri.org (accessed 14 December 2010).

Note
Luxembourg is ranked first with 1,429.3 tonnes per head.

Appendix C

Appendix C Major carbon dioxide emitters (annual emissions in 2007)

	Annual emissions (million tonnes)	Percentage of world total (%)	Emissions per person (tonnes) (rank)
China	6,702.6	22.70	5.1 (66)
United States	5,826.7	19.73	19.3 (7)
Russia	1,626.3	5.51	11.4 (18)
India	1,410.4	4.78	1.3 (122)
Japan	1,270.1	4.30	9.9 (25)
Germany	817.2	2.77	9.9 (26)
Canada	583.9	1.98	17.7 (9)
United Kingdom	530.2	1.80	8.7 (34)
South Korea	517.1	1.75	10.7 (21)
Iran	512.1	1.73	7.2 (47)
Mexico	467.3	1.58	4.4 (73)
Italy	461.3	1.56	7.8 (43)
Australia	401.1	1.36	19.0 (8)
Indonesia	400.4	1.36	1.8 (107)
France	380.4	1.29	6.1 (56)
Brazil	373.7	1.27	2.0 (104)
Saudi Arabia	373.4	1.26	15.5 (11)
Spain	371.9	1.26	8.3 (37)
South Africa	352.6	1.19	7.4 (45)
Ukraine	321.4	1.09	6.9 (51)
Poland	313.2	1.06	8.2 (40)

Source: *Climate Analysis Indicators Tool (CAIT)*, Version 8.0 (Washington, DC: World Resources Institute, 2008), http://cait.wri.org (accessed 14 December 2010).

Notes

1 Qatar, United Arab Emirates and Bahrain are respectively ranked first, second and third with 48.8, 31.7 and 28.1 tonnes per head.
2 A tricky question arises as to which country should bear greater responsibility for cutting carbon dioxide emissions (and that of other greenhouse gases). If emissions per capita is a good indicator of which country should take the lead in addressing the looming problem of climate change, then tiny states such as Bahrain, Kuwait, Luxembourg, Qatar and the United Arab Emirates should do so. Also, the per capita emissions in Nauru (10.6 tonnes) and Palau (10.5 tonnes), two small island states in the South Pacific, are higher than those of China. Should they therefore contribute more to cut greenhouse gases than China? Nauru, a country with a tiny population of less than 10,000 people, depends very heavily on mining, a polluting industry, for its national income. It would seem unfair to require a small or a poor country to contribute more to cleaning up the environment. Do they have the capacity to do so? Also of interest is Australia. Australia is one of the world's largest emitters per capita of greenhouse gases, which include methane belched out by farm animals. Although some countries were not happy that it refused initially to ratify the Kyoto Protocol, few complain that the country is a large 'polluter' in the world. (On 3 December 2007 Kevin Rudd signed the instrument of ratification of the Kyoto Protocol in his first act after being sworn in as Prime Minister of Australia that morning.) Perhaps a balance should be struck between absolute amounts of emissions and emissions on a per capita basis when assessing the responsibility of polluting countries. On this score, the US should take a lead as it is a high emitter on both counts. The idea of apportioning responsibility is a complex one and will remain controversial – an interesting line of enquiry.

Notes

Introduction

1 Some of the books in this area have been reviewed by Gerald Chan, 'The rise of China: (how) does it matter?', *Global Society: Journal of Interdisciplinary International Relations*, Vol. 19, No. 3 (July 2005), pp. 307–16. Using 'China rise' as keywords to check available books in Amazon.com on 13 January 2011 produced 553 results.
2 Before the formation of the Group of Seven, global trade negotiations were steered by a 'quad' comprising the US, EU, Canada and Japan. Stephen Castle, 'Balance of power shifts to China at global trade talks', *New York Times*, 28 July 2008, www.nytimes.com/2008/07/28/business/worldbusiness/28iht-wto.3.14835752.html (accessed 29 July 2008).
3 The Group of 20 was set up in 1999 in the wake of the Asian financial crisis of 1997–98. Initially it was a forum for finance ministers and central bank governors to discuss key issues about the global economy. After the economic meltdown that started to spread across the globe in 2008, summit meetings of the heads of government or state of the grouping have been held in Washington in 2008, in London and Pittsburgh in 2009, and in Toronto and Seoul in 2010. G-20, 'What is the G-20', www.g20.org/about_what_is_g20.aspx (accessed 11 January 2011).
4 Gerald F. Seib, 'U.S. woes open door for China', *Wall Street Journal Online*, 23 December 2008, http://online.wsj.com/article/SB122999122677028455.html (accessed 26 December 2008).
5 The global trade talks ground to a halt in late July 2008 because of a standoff between the US on one side and India and China on the other over access to sensitive agricultural sectors of developing countries. Both India and China insisted that they should be allowed to raise tariffs on cotton, sugar and rice if there was a sudden increase in imports of 10 per cent. But the US wanted to set the threshold much higher at a 40 per cent surge. Alan Beattie and Frances Williams, 'Doha trade talks collapse', *Financial Times*, 29 July 2008, www.ft.com/cms/s/0/0638a320–5d8a-11dd-8129–000077b07658.html, Alan Beattie, 'Negotiators sift debris', *Financial Times*, 29 July 2008, www.ft.com/cms/s/0/dde1e23a-5da0–11dd-8129–000077b07658.html; John W. Miller, 'Global trade talks fail as new giants flex muscle', *Wall Street Journal Online*, 30 July 2008, http://online.wsj.com/article/SB121734618198593583.html (accessed 30 July 2008).
6 World Bank, 'GNI per capita, Atlas method (current US$)', http://data.worldbank.org/indicator/NY.GNP.PCAP.CD; 'GNI per capita, PPP (current international $)', http://data.worldbank.org/indicator/NY.GNP.PCAP.PP.CD (accessed 11 January 2011).
7 The G2 was first proposed by Zbigniew Brzezinski in his 'The Group of Two that could change the world', *Financial Times*, 13 January 2009, www.ft.com/cms/s/0/d99369b8-e178–11dd-afa0–0000779fd2ac.html; and 'Moving toward a reconciliation

of civilizations', *China Daily*, 15 January 2009, www.chinadaily.com.cn/opinion/2009-01/15/content_7399628.htm (all accessed 12 January 2011).
8 A commonsense understanding is that China aspires to recover its past greatness and to establish a well-recognized place in East Asia as well as in the world. Deborah Welch Larson and Alexei Shevchenko also argue that China is a status-seeking state in their 'Status seekers: Chinese and Russian responses to U.S. primacy', *International Security*, Vol. 34, No. 4 (Spring 2010), pp. 63–95. For an authoritative account of China's disagreement with the notion of a G2, see 'Wen: China disagrees to so-called G2', *China Daily*, 18 November 2009, www.chinadaily.com.cn/china/2009-11/18/content_8998039.htm (accessed 13 January 2011). Interestingly, Hillary Clinton also rejects the G2 concept. See her Inaugural Richard C. Holbrooke Lecture on a 'Broad vision of U.S.–China relations in the 21st century', delivered in Washington, DC, on 14 January 2011, www.state.gov/secretary/rm/2011/01/154653.htm (accessed 11 February 2011).
9 David C. Kang, *East Asia before the West: Five Centuries of Trade and Tribute* (New York, NY: Columbia University Press, 2010), pp. 17–24.
10 Hereafter, hegemony, in inverted commas, refers to the Chinese understanding of the notion.
11 Jonathan Joseph, *Hegemony: A Realist Analysis* (London: Routledge, 2002), p. 1.
12 G. John Ikenberry and Charles A. Kupchan, 'Socialization and hegemonic power', *International Organization*, Vol. 44, No. 3 (Summer 1990), pp. 283–315.
13 From the perspective of the English School of International Relations, Ian Clark analyses the hegemon as an institution in international order rather than treating it from the angle of power competition and primacy succession based on material power. In his words, hegemony 'should be associated not simply with the exercise of dominant power but with the creation of a distinctive, and acceptable, pattern of order'. See his 'China and the United States: a succession of hegemonies?', *International Affairs*, Vol. 87, No. 1 (2011), pp. 13–28 at p. 24.
14 Kang, *East Asia before the West*, pp. 17–24.
15 The two prime focuses are on whether China complies with global rules and norms and on China's behaviour in the realm of high politics with special reference to its bilateral relations and conflicts with the US.
16 Gerald Chan, *China's Compliance in Global Affairs: Trade, Arms Control, Environmental Protection, Human Rights* (Singapore: World Scientific, 2006); Ann E. Kent, *Beyond Compliance: China, International Organizations, and Global Security* (Stanford, CA: Stanford University Press, 2007).
17 Daniel W. Drezner, *All Politics is Global: Explaining International Regulatory Regimes* (Princeton, NJ: Princeton University Press, 2007).
18 The thesis is discussed and criticized by Daniel Deudney and G. John Ikenberry, 'The myth of the autocratic revival: why liberal democracy will prevail', *Foreign Affairs*, Vol. 88, No. 1 (2009), pp. 77–93.
19 Cited in David Scott, 'China and the EU: a strategic axis for the twenty-first century', *International Relations*, Vol. 21, No. 1 (2007), p. 35.
20 An aspiration that started shortly after it came to realize its national weakness in facing the demands of Western imperialism under the so-called gunboat diplomacy in the mid-nineteenth century under the Qing Dynasty. As said before, this aspiration still remains.
21 See Chan, *China's Compliance in Global Affairs*, especially Chapter 2.
22 See Wang Hongying, 'National image building and Chinese foreign policy', *China: An International Journal*, Vol. 1, No. 1 (March 2003), pp. 46–72.
23 Jia Qingguo, 'Economic development, political stability and international respect', *Journal of International Affairs*, Vol. 49, Issue 2 (Winter 1996), pp. 572–89.
24 Before the rise of the West as a result of the Renaissance and the Industrial Revolution, China at various times was the strongest power on earth. The current rise of

China should be interpreted, according to some observers, not as a new rise, but as a revival of China's former glory and power status.
25 In examining China's peacekeeping operations, Pang Zhongying argues that these activities help to achieve one of Beijing's foreign policy objectives of 'democratizing interstate relations'. See his 'China's changing attitude to UN peacekeeping', *International Peacekeeping*, Vol. 12, No. 1 (Spring 2005), pp. 87–104.
26 A slight exception is perhaps Rosemary Foot and Andrew Walter, *China, the United States, and Global Order* (Cambridge: Cambridge University Press, 2011). While Foot and Walter's book focuses on Sino-US relations and global order, our book has a wider global perspective, taking global governance as our guiding light and going beyond norm consistency and compliance.

1 Global governance: the building blocks

1 Oran R. Young, *Governance in World Affairs* (Ithaca, NY, and London: Cornell University Press, 1999), p. 1.
2 Anne Mette Kjær, *Governance* (Cambridge: Polity Press, 2004), back cover.
3 Commission on Global Governance, *Our Global Neighbourhood: The Report of the Commission on Global Governance* (Oxford: Oxford University Press, 1995).
4 Ibid., p. 2.
5 Ibid., p. 4.
6 Ibid., pp. xvi, 4.
7 Quoted in Thomas G. Weiss, 'Governance, good governance and global governance: conceptual and actual challenges', in Rorden Wilkinson (ed.), *The Global Governance Reader* (London: Routledge, 2005), pp. 69–70.
8 Kjær, *Governance*, pp. 1, 3.
9 Stephen Bell and Andrew Hindmoor, *Rethinking Governance: The Centrality of the State in Modern Society* (Cambridge: Cambridge University Press, 2009), p. 1.
10 John Gerard Ruggie, 'Foreword', in Thomas G. Weiss and Ramesh Thakur, *Global Governance and the UN: An Unfinished Journey* (Bloomington, IN: Indiana University Press, 2010), p. xv.
11 James N. Rosenau, 'Governance in a new global order', in David Held and Anthony McGrew (eds), *Governing Globalization: Power, Authority and Global Governance* (Cambridge: Polity Press, 2002), p. 72. Norms can be defined as 'collective expectations for the proper behavior of actors with a given identity'. Peter J. Katzenstein, 'Introduction: alternative perspectives on national security', in Peter J. Katzenstein (ed.), *The Culture of National Security: Norms and Identity in World Politics* (New York: Columbia University Press, 1996), p. 5.
12 Ruggie, 'Foreword', pp. xv–xix.
13 Weiss and Thakur, *Global Governance and the UN*, pp. 3–7
14 Väyrynen attaches much importance to the role of norms, compliance with them and their enforcement in global governance. He dismisses the definition of governance offered by the Commission on Global Governance as too broad, making it 'virtually meaningless both for theory construction and social action'. See Raimo Väyrynen, 'Norms, compliance and enforcement in global governance', in Raimo Väyrynen (ed.), *Globalization and Global Governance* (Lanham, MD: Rowman & Littlefield, 1999), p. 25.
15 Margaret P. Karns and Karen A. Mingst, *International Organizations: The Politics and Processes of Global Governance*, 2nd edn (Boulder, CO: Lynne Rienner, 2009), pp. 4–14.
16 Robert O. Keohane and Joseph S. Nye Jr., 'Introduction', in Joseph S. Nye Jr. and John D. Donahue (eds), *Governance in a Globalizing World* (Washington, DC: Brookings Institution Press, 2000), pp. 1–41.
17 James P. Muldoon Jr., *The Architecture of Global Governance: An Introduction to the Study of International Organizations* (Boulder, CO: Westview Press, 2004), pp. 4–9.

Notes 191

18 James N. Rosenau, 'Governance, order, and change in world politics', in James N. Rosenau and Ernst-Otto Czempiel (eds), *Governance without Government: Order and Change in World Politics* (Cambridge: Cambridge University Press, 1992), p. 4.
19 Michael Barnett and Kathryn Sikkink, 'From international relations to global society', in Christian Rues-Smit and Duncan Snidal (eds), *The Oxford Handbook of International Relations* (Oxford: Oxford University Press, 2008), p. 63.
20 Timothy J. Sinclair, 'Global governance', in Martin Griffiths (ed.), *Encyclopedia of International Relations and Global Politics* (Abingdon: Routledge, 2005), pp. 325–30.
21 This section draws on Barnett and Sikkink, 'From international relations to global society', pp. 62–83; Tanja Brühl and Volker Rittberger, 'From international to global governance: actors, collective decision-making, and the United Nations in the world of the twenty-first century', in Volker Rittberger (ed.), *Global Governance and the United Nations System* (Tokyo: United Nations University Press, 2001), pp. 1–47.
22 Inge Kaul and Pedro Conceição, 'Why revisit public finance today? What this book is about', in Inge Kaul and Pedro Conceição (eds), *The New Public Finance: Responding to Global Challenges* (Oxford: Oxford University Press for the United Nations Development Programme, 2006), p. 11.
23 Trans-sovereign problems are defined as problems that 'transcend state boundaries in ways over which states have little control and which cannot be solved by individual state actions alone'. Cited in Maryann Cusimano Love, 'Global problems, global solutions', in idem (ed.), *Beyond Sovereignty: Issues for a Global Agenda* (Belmont, CA: Wadsworth/Thomson Learning, 2003), p. 2.
24 Ibid., p. 9.
25 Ibid., pp. 13–18.
26 Ibid., pp. 35–7.
27 The number of IGOs reached its peak at 378 in 1985. See Table 1.1.
28 John Gerard Ruggie, 'Reconstituting the global public domain – issues, actors, and practices', *European Journal of International Relations*, Vol. 10, No. 4 (2004), p. 499.
29 These correspond to the approaches of globalists, traditionalists and transformationalists or of the schools of thought of the hyperglobalizers, the sceptics and the transformationalists. See David Held, Anthony McGrew, David Goldblatt and Jonathan Perraton, *Global Transformations: Politics, Economics and Culture* (Cambridge: Polity Press, 1999), pp. 2–10; Chamsy el-Ojeili and Patrick Hayden, *Critical Theories of Globalization* (Basingstoke: Palgrave Macmillan, 2006), pp. 14–16.
30 Susan Strange, *The Retreat of the State: The Diffusion of Power in the World Economy* (Cambridge: Cambridge University Press, 1996), p. 82.
31 For a discussion of divided opinion on this 'race to the bottom' argument, see Jan Aart Scholte, *Globalization: A Critical Introduction* (Basingstoke: Palgrave Macmillan, 2005), pp. 194–8.
32 Strange, *The Retreat of the State*, p. 4. See Kenichi Ohmae, *The End of the Nation State: The Rise of Regional Economics* (London: HarperCollins, 1996), and W. B. Wriston, *The Twilight of Sovereignty: How the Information Revolution is Transforming Our World* (New York: Charles Scribner's Son, 1992), for the most dramatic versions of the 'retreat' argument.
33 James N. Rosenau and Ernst-Otto Czempiel (eds), Governance without Government; *Order and Change in World Order* (Cambridge: Cambridge University Press, 1992); James N. Rosenau, 'Toward an ontology for global governance', in Martin Hewson and Timothy J. Sinclair (eds), *Approaches to Global Governance Theory* (Albany, NY: State University of New York Press, 1999), pp. 287–301.
34 Stephen D. Krasner, *Sovereignty: Organized Hypocrisy* (Princeton, NJ: Princeton University Press, 1999).

35 Kenneth N. Waltz, 'Globalization and governance', *PS: Political Science and Politics*, Vol. 32, No. 4 (1999), pp. 693–700; Robert Gilpin, *Global Political Economy: Understanding the International Economic Order* (Princeton, NJ: Princeton University Press, 2001), pp. 362–76; Robert Gilpin, 'A realist perspective on international governance', in Held and McGrew (eds), *Governing Globalization*, pp. 237–48.
36 Stephen Krasner, 'Realism, imperialism, and democracy', *Political Theory*, Vol. 20, No. 1 (February 1992), p. 39.
37 John J. Mearsheimer, 'The false promise of international institutions', *International Security*, Vol. 19, No. 3 (Winter 1994/95), p. 13.
38 Anne-Marie Slaughter, 'The real new world order', *Foreign Affairs*, Vol. 76, No. 5 (1997), pp. 183–197; Anne-Marie Slaughter, *A New World Order* (Princeton, NJ, and Oxford: Princeton University Press, 2004).
39 David Held and Anthony McGrew, 'Introduction', in Held and McGrew (eds), *Governing Globalization*, p. 10.
40 Georg Sorensen, *The Transformation of the State: Beyond the Myth of Retreat* (Basingstoke: Palgrave Macmillan, 2004), pp. 112–16.
41 Hendrik Spruyt, *The Sovereign State and Its Competitors* (Princeton, NJ: Princeton University Press, 1994), p. 3.
42 F. H. Hinsley, *Sovereignty* (Cambridge: Cambridge University Press, 1986), p. 26.
43 Sorensen, *The Transformation of the State*, pp. 103–106.
44 Ramesh Thakur, 'Humanitarian intervention', in Thomas G. Weiss and Sam Daws (eds), *The Oxford Handbook on the United Nations* (Oxford: Oxford University Press, 2007), pp. 387–403.
45 Boutros Boutros-Ghali, *An Agenda for Peace: Preventive Diplomacy, Peacemaking, and Peace-keeping* (New York: UN Document A/47/277-S/24111, 17 June 1992), para. 17, www.un.org/Docs/SG/agpeace.html (accessed 28 December 2010).
46 International Commission on Intervention and State Sovereignty, *The Responsibility to Protect* (Ottawa: International Development Research Centre, 2001), p. xi, www.iciss.ca/report-en.asp (accessed 28 December 2010).
47 Ramesh Thakur, *The United Nations, Peace and Security: From Collective Security to the Responsibility to Protect* (Cambridge: Cambridge University Press, 2006), p. 255.
48 Kofi Annan, 'Two concepts of sovereignty', *The Economist*, 18 September 1999; United Nations General Assembly, *2005 World Summit Outcome* (UN Document A/60/L/1, 15 September 2005), paras. 138–40, www.un.org/summit2005/documents.html (accessed 28 December 2010).
49 See David A. Lake, *Hierarchy in International Relations* (Ithaca, NY: Cornell University Press, 2009).
50 Volker Rittberger, Carmen Huckel, Lothar Rieth and Melanie Zimmer, 'Inclusive global institutions for a global political economy', in Volker Rittberger, Martin Nettesheim and Carmen Huckel (eds), *Authority in the Global Political Economy* (Basingstoke: Palgrave Macmillan, 2008), pp. 15–19.
51 See also Brühl and Rittberger, 'From international to global governance', pp. 34–5.
52 An inclusive institution is defined as 'an international institution that (1) provides a variety of actors with the possibility of membership and (2) endows them with certain rights in the policy-making process'. Rittberger *et al.*, 'Inclusive global institutions for a global political economy', p. 18.
53 GAVI Alliance, 'Innovative partnership', www.gavialliance.org/about/in_partnership/index.php (accessed 12 January 2011).
54 Inge Kaul, 'Providing (contested) global public goods', in Rittberger *et al.* (eds), *Authority in the Global Political Economy*, pp. 89–115.
55 Inge Kaul, Pedro Conceição, Katell Le Goulven and Ronald U. Mendoza, 'How to improve the provision of global public goods', in Inge Kaul, Pedro Conceição, Katell Le Goulven and Ronald U. Mendoza (eds), *Providing Global Public Goods: Managing Globalization* (New York: Oxford University Press, 2003), pp. 21–3.

56 Todd Sander, *Global Collective Action* (Cambridge: Cambridge University Press, 2004), Chapter 2.
57 Charles P. Kindleberger, *The World in Depression 1929–1939* (Harmondsworth: Penguin, 1973), especially Chapter 14.
58 This is discussed, in part, in Carla Norrlof, *America's Global Advantage: US Hegemony and International Cooperation* (Cambridge: Cambridge University Press, 2010), especially Chapter 3. The classical treatment of relative gains versus absolute gains is Joseph M. Grieco, 'Anarchy and the limits of cooperation: a realist critique of the newest liberal institutionalism', *International Organization*, Vol. 42, No. 3 (Summer 1988), pp. 485–507.
59 Kaul, 'Providing (contested) global public goods'.
60 Karns and Mingst, *International Organizations*, pp. 43–5.
61 Chris Brown and Kirsten Ainley, *Understanding International Relations*, 4th edn (Basingstoke: Palgrave Macmillan, 2009), p. 129.

2 Chinese perspectives on global governance

1 Li Keqiang, 'The world should not fear a growing China', *Financial Times*, 9 January 2011, www.ft.com/cms/s/0/e9063e6e-1a5d-11e0-b003-00144feab49a.html (accessed 10 January 2011). The piece was published when Li, Vice Premier, was visiting the United Kingdom.
2 Pang Zhongying, 'Zhongguo zai guoji tixi zhong de diwei yu zuoyong' (The status and impact of China in international system), *Xiandai guoji guanxi* (*Contemporary International Relations*), No. 4, 2006, pp. 17–22.
3 An international journal, *Global Governance: A Review for Multilateralism and International Organisations*, focusing on this subject, was launched in 1995. In addition, abundant articles and books have been published on this subject; to name but a few: James N. Rosenau, and Ernst-Otto Czempiel (eds) *Governance without Government: Order and Change in World Politics* (Cambridge: Cambridge University Press, 1992); Joseph A. Camilleri and Jim Falk, *The End of Sovereignty? The Politics of a Shrinking and Fragmenting World* (Aldershot: Edward Elgar, 1992); Richard A. Falk, *On Humane Governance: Toward a New Global Politics: The World Order Models Project Report of the Global Civilisation Initiative* (Cambridge: Polity Press in association with Blackwell Publishers, 1995).
4 For a detailed account of the evolution of the Chinese new security concept, see Pak K. Lee and Lai-Ha Chan, 'Non-traditional security threats in China: challenges of energy shortage and infectious diseases', in Joseph Y. S. Cheng (ed.), *Challenges and Policy Programmes of China's New Leadership* (Hong Kong: City University of Hong Kong Press, 2007), pp. 297–336.
5 Reinhard Drifte, *Japan's Security Relations with China since 1989: From Balancing to Bandwagoning?* (London and New York: RoutledgeCurzon, 2003), p. 36.
6 As Michael Yahuda notes, the new security concept 'had an anti-American edge' at least until 2002. Michael Yahuda, 'The evolving Asian order: the accommodation of rising Chinese power', in David Shambaugh (ed.), *Power Shift: China and Asia's New Dynamics* (Berkeley, CA: University of California Press, 2005), p. 356.
7 Foreign Ministry of the PRC, 'China's position paper on enhanced cooperation in the field of non-traditional security issues', www.fmprc.gov.cn/eng/wjb/zzjg/gjs/gjzzyhy/2612/2614/t15318.htm (accessed 3 April 2007).
8 Dan Xingwu, 'Zhongguo guoji guanxi xueke zhong de quanqiuhua yanjiu' (Globalization research in the discipline of International Relations in China), in Wang Yizhou and Yuan Zhengqing (eds) *Zhongguo guoji guanxi yanjiu (1995–2005)* (*International Relations Studies in China, 1995–2005*) (Beijing: Beijing daxue chubanshe, 2006), p. 475.
9 Cai Tuo, 'Global governance: the Chinese angle of view and practice', *Social Sciences in China*, Vol. 25, No. 2 (Summer 2004), p. 57.

10 Ibid.
11 For a more detailed discussion of the five changes, see the original Chinese version from Cai Tuo, 'Quanqiu zhili de Zhongguo shijiao yu shijian' (The Chinese view and practice of global governance), *Zhongguo shehui kexue* (*Social Sciences in China*), No. 1 (2004), pp. 94–106.
12 Cai, 'Global governance', p. 66.
13 Yu Zhengliang, Chen Yugang and Su Changhe, *21 shiji quanqiu zhengzhi fanshi* (*The Paradigms of Global Politics in the 21st Century*) (Shanghai: Fudan daxue chubanshe, 2005), pp. 237–52.
14 Yu Keping, *Minzhu yu tuoluo* (*Democracy and Top*) (Beijing: Beijing daxue chubanshe 2006), pp. 87–8. Yu refers to McGrew and cites the Chinese version of the following definition of global governance given in David Held, Anthony McGrew, David Goldblatt and Jonathan Perraton, *Global Transformations: Politics, Economics and Culture* (Cambridge: Polity Press, 1999), p. 50. By global governance is meant not only the formal institutions and organizations through which the rules and norms governing world order are (or are not) made and sustained – the institutions of state, intergovernmental cooperation and so on – but also all those organizations and pressure groups – from MNCs and transnational social movements to the plethora of non-governmental organizations – which pursue goals and objectives which have a bearing on transnational rule and authority systems. Clearly, the United Nations system, the World Trade Organization and the array of activities of national governments are among the central components of global governance, but they are by no means the only components. If social movements, non-governmental organizations, regional political associations and so on are excluded from the notion of global governance, its form and dynamics will not be properly understood.
15 Sun Kuanping and Teng Shihua, *Quanqiuhua yu quanqiu zhili* (*Globalization and Global Governance*) (Changsha: Hunan renmin chubanshe, 2003), pp. 41–50.
16 Yang Jiemian, *Dahezuo: bianhua zhong de shijie he Zhongguo guoji zhanlue* (*Grand Cooperation: The Changing World and China's Global Strategy*) (Tianjin: Tianjin renmin chubanshe, 2005), pp. 102–103.
17 Cai Tuo, 'Global governance', p. 59.
18 This view is shared by most Chinese scholars working on the subject of global governance and international order. To name but a few, Cai, 'Global governance'; Liu Jinyuan, 'Cong quanqiuhua kan quanqiu zhili' (To view global governance from the effect of globalization), *Tansuo yu zhengming* (*Exploration and Contestation*), No. 2 (2005), pp. 21–4; Yu Keping, *Quanqiuhua yu guojia zhuquan* (*Globalization and National Sovereignty*) (Beijing: Shehui kexue wenxian Chubanshe, 2004); Zhou Yanzhao and Xie Xiaojuan, 'Quanqiu zhili yu guoji zhuquan' (Global governance and national sovereignty), *Makesizhuyi yu xianshi* (*Marxism and Reality*) No. 3 (2003), pp. 65–9.
19 Wang Yizhou, 'Zhuquan fanwei zai sikao' (Rethinking the scope of sovereignty), *Ouzhou* (*Europe*), No. 6 (2000), pp. 4–11.
20 Yu Keping, 'Quanqiu zhili yinlun' (Introduction to global governance), *Makesizhuyi yu xianshi* (*Marxism and Reality*), No. 1 (2002), pp. 20–32; reprinted as 'Weishenme quanqiu zhili shi biyao de yu jinbi de?' (Why is global governance necessary and pressing?) in Pang Zhongying (ed.), *Quanqiuhua, fan quanqiuhua yu Zhongguo: lijie quanqiuhua de fuzaxing yu duoyangxing* (*Globalization, Anti-globalization and China: Understanding the Complexity and Diversity of Globalization*) (Shanghai: Shanghai renmin chubanshe, 2006), pp. 313–44; and as the preface to Sun Kuanping and Teng Shihua, *Quanqiuhua*, pp. 1–29.
21 Liu Jinyuan, 'Cong quanqiuhua kan quanqiu zhili' (To view global governance from the effect of globalization).
22 Wang Miao, 'Quanqiu zhili zhong de guoji zuzhi – yi shijie weisheng zuzhi duikang SARS wei anli' (International organizations and global governance: a study of the

World Health Organization in fighting SARS), *Jiaoxue yu yanjiu* (*Pedagogy and Research*), No. 9 (September 2003), pp. 36–41. See also Sun Hui and Yu Yu, 'Guoji zhengfu zuzhi yu quanqiu zhili' (Intergovernmental organizations and global governance), *Tongji daxue xuebao (shehui kexue ban)* (Tongji University Journal (Social Science Section)), Vol. 15, No. 5 (October 2004), pp. 48–53 and 73.

23 Tang Xianxing and Zhang Xiang, 'Quanqiuhua yu quanqiu zhili: yige "zhili shehui" de lailin?' (Globalization and global governance: the arrival of a 'governance society'?), *Shijie jingji yu zhengzhi* (*World Economy and Politics*), No. 1 (2001), pp. 26–30.

24 Bates Gill, *Rising Star: China's New Security Diplomacy* (Washington, DC: Brookings Institution Press, 2010), p. 109.

25 This contrasts with the unbundling of sovereignty advocated by Keohane and Krasner. See Robert O. Keohane, 'Sovereignty in international society', in David Held and Anthony McGrew (eds), *The Global Transformations Reader: An Introduction to the Globalisation Debate*, 2nd edn (Cambridge: Polity, 2003), pp. 147–61; Stephen D. Krasner, *Sovereignty: Organized Hypocrisy* (Princeton, NJ: Princeton University Press, 1999); and 'Sharing sovereignty: new institutions for collapsed and failing states', *International Security*, Vol. 29, No. 2 (2004), pp. 85–120.

26 Allen Carlson, 'Helping to keep the peace (albeit reluctantly): China's recent stance on sovereignty and multilateral intervention', *Pacific Affairs*, Vol. 77, No. 1 (Spring 2004), pp. 9–27; Allen Carlson, *Unifying China, Integrating with the World: Securing Chinese Sovereignty in the Reform Era* (Stanford, CA: Stanford University Press, 2005).

27 Gill, *Rising Star*, pp. 104–36.

28 Chu Shulong, 'China, Asia and issues of intervention and sovereignty', *Pugwash Occasional Papers*, Vol. 2, No. 1 (January 2001), www.pugwash.org/publication/op/opv2n1.htm (accessed 28 December 2010).

29 Su Changhe, 'Shijie zhengzhi de zhuanhuan yu Zhongguo waijiao yanjiu zhong de wenti' (The transformation of world politics and issues of Chinese foreign policy research), *Jiaoxue yu yanjiu* (*Pedagogy and Research*), No. 11 (2005), pp. 32–5.

30 Liu Dongguo, 'Quanqiu zhili zhong de guannian jianggou' (The construction of ideas in global governance), *Jiaoxue yu yanjiu* (*Pedagogy and Research*), No. 4 (2005), pp. 41–6.

31 Wang Yizhou, 'SARS yu fei chuantong anquan' (SARS and non-traditional security) in his webpage at www.iwep.org.cn/chinese/gerenzhuye/wangyizhou/index.htm (accessed 1 April 2007).

32 Wang Yizhou, 'Rethinking the scope of sovereignty' and 'China's diplomacy for the 21st century: balance among three demands', in his website at www.iwep.org.cn/chinese/gerenzhuye/wangyizhou/index.htm (accessed 1 April 2007).

33 Ramesh Thakur, *The United Nations, Peace and Security: From Collective Security to the Responsibility to Protect* (Cambridge: Cambridge University Press, 2006), pp. 268–9.

34 Ministry of Foreign Affairs of the PRC, 'Position paper of the People's Republic of China on the United Nations reforms' (7 June 2005), www.fmprc.gov.cn/eng/zxxx/t199318.htm (accessed 14 September 2007).

35 Wang Jun, 'Zhongguo de zhuquan wenti yanjiu' (Chinese research on sovereignty), in Wang Yizhou and Yuan Zhengqing (eds), *International Relations Studies in China, 1995–2005*, pp. 341–69. The notion and the Rwandan crisis are only slightly touched on by Wang Yizhou in his introduction to the edited volume (p. 28).

36 Sun Hui and Yu Yu, 'Guoji zhengfu zuzhi yu quanqiu zhili' (Intergovernmental organizations and global governance).

37 Zhang Yunling, 'China: whither the world order after Kosovo?', in Albrecht Schnabel and Ramesh Thakur (eds), *Kosovo and the Challenge of Humanitarian Intervention* (Tokyo: United Nations University Press, 2000), p. 117.

38 Ian Martin, 'International intervention in East Timor', in Jennifer M. Welsh (ed.), *Humanitarian Intervention and International Relations* (Oxford: Oxford University Press, 2003), pp. 142–62.
39 This is a question frequently posed by the constructivist approach which argues that states' preferences and interests are neither pre-given nor fixed. Instead, it gives prominence to the role of identities, beliefs, normative ideas and values as well as interactions among actors in the construction of preferences and interests. As a result, the preferences and interests of actors are more fluid and changing than rationalists (neo-realists) and liberal institutionalists would assume.
40 With expanding and deepening linkages between China and the rest of the world, Samuel Kim has argued, there has been a steady rise in global learning for post-Mao reformers. Kim has defined global learning as

> a two-way interactive linkage process, in which domestic reform and restructuring and an ongoing transformational process taking place in the world fueled by the so-called 'complex global interdependence and interpenetration' merge as cause and effect, constituting mutually essential parts of the same local–global process'.

See Samuel S. Kim, 'Thinking globally in post-Mao China', *Journal of Peace Research*, Vol. 27, No. 2 (1990), pp. 193–4.
41 Steve Chan, 'Chinese perspectives on world order', in T. V. Paul and John A. Hall (eds), *International Order and the Future of World Politics* (Cambridge: Cambridge University Press, 1999), p. 200.
42 Shogo Suzuki, 'China's perceptions of international society in the nineteenth century: learning more about power politics?', *Asian Perspective*, Vol. 28, No. 3 (2004), pp. 115–44; Robert Jackson, 'Sovereignty in world politics: a glance at the conceptual and historical landscape', *Political Studies*, Vol. 47, No. 3 (1999), pp. 431–56; Gerrit W. Gong, *The Standard of 'Civilization' in International Society* (Oxford: Clarendon Press, 1984).
43 The Treaty of Nanjing was signed on 29 August 1842 at the end of the Opium War of 1839–42. Regarded as the most important treaty settlement in the modern history of China, it demanded, among others, that five Chinese cities – Guangzhou, Fuzhou, Xiamen, Ningbo and Shanghai – be open to residence by British subjects for mercantile purposes and that the island of Hong Kong be possessed in perpetuity by Queen Victoria and her successors. Jonathan D. Spence, *The Search for Modern China* (New York: W. W. Norton, 1990), pp. 158–60. See also Suzuki, 'China's perceptions of international society in the nineteenth century.'
44 Rana Mitter, 'An uneasy engagement: Chinese ideas of global order and justice in historical perspective', in Rosemary Foot, John Gaddis and Andrew Hurrell (eds), *Order and Justice in International Relations* (Oxford: Oxford University Press, 2003), p. 221.
45 The five principles are mutual respect for territorial integrity and sovereignty, mutual non-aggression, non-interference in each other's internal affairs, equality and mutual benefit, and peaceful coexistence.
46 Samuel S. Kim, 'Sovereignty in the Chinese image of world order', in Ronald St J. Macdonald (ed.), *Essays in Honor of Wang Tieya* (Dordrecht: Martinus Nijhoff Publishers, 1993), pp. 425–45. The internal crisis was due to the military crackdown on the pro-democracy student movement in 1989 and the external one was the consequence of the demise of Communism in Eastern Europe and the former Soviet Union in the early 1990s.
47 Men Honghua, 'Zhongguo jueqi yu guoji zhixu' (The rise of China and international order), *Taipingyang xuebao* (*Pacific Journal*), No. 2 (2004), pp. 4–13. Reprinted in Qin Yaqing (ed.), *Zhongguo xuezhe kan shijie 1: guoji zhixu juan* (*World Politics – Views from China*, Vol. 1, *International Order*) (Hong Kong: Heping tushu youxian gongsi, 2006), pp. 305–25; Steve Chan, 'Chinese perspectives on world order'.

Notes 197

48 Cai Tuo, 'Global governance', p. 58.
49 Permanent Mission of the PRC to the United Nations Office at Geneva and Other International Organizations in Switzerland. 'Statement by Ambassador Shen Guofang, Deputy Permanent Representative of China to the UN, at the Second High-level Dialogue on Strengthening International Economic Cooperation for Development through Partnership, 20 September 2001', 19 April 2004, www.china-un.ch/eng/qtzz/wtojjwt/t85645.htm (accessed 30 September 2005).
50 'China urges strengthening of effective global governance', *People's Daily Online*, 3 October 2000 http://english.people.com.cn/english/200010/03/print20001003_51768.html (accessed 28 December 2010).
51 Jean Part Scholte, 'Civil society and democracy in global governance', in Rorden Wilkinson (ed.), *The Global Governance Reader* (Abingdon: Routledge, 2005), p. 330.
52 For studies about whether or not China would adopt a revisionist strategy, see Alastair Iain Johnston, 'Is China a status quo power?', *International Security*, Vol. 27, No. 4 (Spring 2003), pp. 5–56; and Jason W. Davidson, *The Origins of Revisionist and Status-quo States* (Basingstoke: Palgrave Macmillan, 2006), pp. 136–49.
53 Rosemary Foot, 'Chinese power and the idea of a responsible state', in Zhang Yongjin and Greg Austin (eds), *Power and Responsibility in Chinese Foreign Policy* (Canberra: Asia Pacific Press, 2001), pp. 21–47.
54 Mitter, 'An uneasy engagement', pp. 224–9.
55 Yong Deng, 'Reputation and the security dilemma: China reacts to the China threat theory', in Alastair Iain Johnston and Robert S. Ross (eds), *New Directions in the Study of China's Foreign Policy* (Stanford, CA: Stanford University Press, 2006), pp. 191–5.
56 Mitter, 'An uneasy engagement'.
57 Pang Zhongying, 'Zhongguo zai guoji tixi zhong de diwei yu zuoyong' (The status and impact of China in international system).
58 The term was coined by John Williamson, 'What Washington means by policy reform', in John Williamson (ed.), *Latin American Adjustment: How Much Has Changed* (Washington, DC: Institute of International Economics, 1990), pp. 7–20.
59 Caroline Thomas, 'Globalisation and development in the South', in John Ravenhill (ed.), *Global Political Economy* (Oxford: Oxford University Press, 2005), pp. 328–9 at p. 328. Or one can argue that the traditional concept of state sovereignty has been replaced by the notion of popular sovereignty or sovereignty of the people. Thomas G. Weiss, David P. Forsythe and Roger A. Coate, *The United Nations and Changing World Politics* (Boulder, CO: Westview Press, 2004), p. 274.
60 Weiss *et al.*, *The United Nations and Changing World Politics*, pp. 248–52. The authors say, '"good" governance consists of applying the liberal capitalist model … rather than the "bad" governance that had characterised the development models in vogue in the heyday of UNCTAD [United Nations Conference on Trade and Development] and NIEO [New International Economic Order]' (p. 274).
61 Since the end of the Cold War, the political conditionality of good governance has often been imposed on developing countries seeking financial assistance. For a comprehensive discussion, see B. C. Smith, *Good Governance and Development* (Basingstoke: Palgrave Macmillan, 2007).
62 Joshua Cooper Ramo, *The Beijing Consensus* (London: Foreign Policy Centre, 2004), http://fpc.org.uk/publications/123 (accessed on 28 December 2010).
63 After Ramo coined the term in 2004, Huang Ping and Cui Zhiyuan edited a book on the same topic in 2005. See Huang Ping and Cui Zhiyuan (eds), *Zhongguo yu quanqiuhua: Huashengdun gongshi haisi Beijing gongshi* (*China and Globalization: The Washington Consensus, or the Beijing Consensus*) (Beijing: Shehui kexue wenxian chubanshe, 2005). In addition, a conference entitled 'Zhongguo fazhan daolu guoji xueshu yantaohui' (International academic conference on the path of China's development) was held in Tianjin in 2005. Subsequently a book based on the discussions in the conference was published by the Social Sciences Academic Press in 2006.

During the conference, there was a debate on the 'Beijing Consensus' and 'China model'. Ironically, most Chinese scholars at the conference were reluctant or even refused to use the term 'Beijing Consensus'. They argued that consensus should be an 'ideal model' which can be promoted to other states. However, the China model is just a model which tells others about China's experience of development. Therefore, they preferred to use the term 'China model', rather than Beijing Consensus. For example, Arif Dirlik argued that 'consensus is a hegemonic term' which should be consensual in nature, such as Washington consensus. For him, 'Beijing consensus' is a notion, neither a concept nor an idea. He sternly criticized Ramo's explanation of 'Beijing Consensus' for being a sophistry and a 'sales gimmick'. See Arif Dirlik, '"Beijing gongshi": shui chengren shui mudi hezai ('Beijing Consensus': Who recognizes whom and to what end?)' in Yu Keping, Huang Ping, Xie Shuguang and Gao Jian (eds), *Zhongguo moshi yu 'Beijing gongshi': chaoyue 'Huashengdun gongshi'* (*China Model and the 'Beijing Consensus': Beyond the 'Washington Consensus'*) (Beijing: Shehui kexue wenxian chubanshe, 2006), pp. 99–120. An English version of this article can be found: *Globalisation and Autonomy Online Compendium*, www.globalautonomy.ca/global1/position.jsp?index=PP_Dirlik_BeijingConsensus.xml (accessed 28 December 2010).
64 Yu Keping, 'Zhongguo moshi: jingyan yu jianjie' (China model: experience and lessons), in Yu Keping et al., *China Model and the 'Beijing Consensus'*, pp. 11–20.
65 Randall Peerenboom, *China Modernises: Threat to the West or Model for the Rest?* (Oxford: Oxford University Press, 2007), pp. 4–10.
66 Zhang Youwen and Huang Renwei et al., *2005 Zhongguo guoji diwei baogao* (*China's International Status Report 2005*) (Beijing: Renmin chubanshe, 2005), pp. 32–3; Zhao Xiao, 'Zhongguo jingyan ji qi pushi yiyi – cong "Huashengdun" gongshi dao "Beijing gongshi"' (China's experience and its worldwide significance: from the 'Washington Consensus' to the 'Beijing Consensus'), *Wenhui bao* (Shanghai), 14 June 2004.
67 Yang Taoyuan, 'Zhongguo tisheng ruan shili: "Beijing gongshi" qudai "Huashengdun gongshi"' (China promotes soft power: replacing 'Washington Consensus' with "Beijing Consensus'), Xinhuanet, 13 June 2004, http://news.xinhuanet.com/newscenter/2004–06/13/content_1522884.htm (accessed 28 December 2010).
68 Chen Yugang, 'Shilun quanqiuhua beijing xia Zhongguo ruanshili di goujiang' (Discussing the construction of China's soft power against the background of globalization), *Guoji guancha* (*International Review*), No. 2 (2007), pp. 36–42, 59.
69 One way of envisaging global governance is to view it as a project that would lead to the emergence and spread of a pro-West, liberal world order. Matthew J. Hoffmann and Alice D. Ba, 'Introduction: coherence and contestation', in Alice D. Ba and Matthew J. Hoffmann (eds), *Contending Perspectives on Global Governance: Coherence, Contestation and World Order* (London and New York: Routledge, 2005), p. 4.
70 Naazneen Barma and Ely Ratner, 'China's illiberal challenge', *Democracy: A Journal of Idea*, No. 2 (Fall 2006), www.democracyjournal.org/article.php?ID=6485 (accessed 28 December 2010).
71 Drew Thompson, 'China's soft power in Africa: from the "Beijing Consensus" to health diplomacy', *China Brief*, Vol. 5, No. 21 (13 October 2005), http://jamestown.org/china_brief/article.php?articleid=2373140 (accessed 10 October 2007).
72 John Reed, 'China on track to win friends in oil-rich Angola', *Financial Times*, 4 March 2006.
73 Cited in Chris Alden, *China in Africa* (London and New York: Zed Books, 2007), pp. 68–9.
74 Andrew Higgins, 'Iran studies China model to craft economic map', *Wall Street Journal Online*, 18 May 2007, http://online.wsj.com/article/SB117944654831706926.html (accessed 28 December 2010).
75 Françoise Crouigneau and Richard Hiault, 'Wolfowitz slams China banks on Africa lending', *Financial Times*, 24 October 2006.

76 Michael M. Phillips, 'G-7 to warn China over costly loans to poor countries', *Wall Street Journal Online*, 15 September 2006, http://online.wsj.com/article/SB115826 807563263495.html (accessed 28 December 2010).
77 Cited in Extractive Industries Transparency Initiative, 'EITI factsheet', August 2005, www.eitransparency.org (accessed 19 September 2007); Lord Malloch-Brown, 'Africa: new partnerships and opportunities' (a speech delivered to the China Institute of International Studies, Beijing, 30 August 2007, www.uk.cn/bj/index.asp?menu_id=327&artid=2574 (accessed 20 September 2007); Bates Gill, Huang Chi-hao and J. Stephen Morrison, *China's Expanding Role in Africa: Implications for the United States* (Washington, DC: Center for Strategic and International Studies, 2007), pp. 19–20.
78 Seven of the ten most vulnerable states in the world in 2010 were in sub-Saharan Africa: Somalia, Chad, Sudan, Zimbabwe, Democratic Republic of Congo, Central African Republic and Guinea. 'The failed states index 2010', *Foreign Policy*, www.foreignpolicy.com/articles/2010/06/21/2010_failed_states_index_interactive_map_and_rankings (accessed 16 February 2011). Partly due to widespread human rights abuses in the failing states in the continent, Africans are in general more willing than their counterparts in Asia and Latin America to accept outside intervention (Thakur, *The United Nations, Peace and Security*, pp. 271–2). Article 4(h) of the Constitutive Act of the AU, adopted in Lomé, Togo in July 2000 and coming into force in May 2001, stipulates that the Union has the right to 'intervene in a Member State pursuant to a decision of the Assembly [of Heads of State and Government of the Union] in respect of grave circumstances; namely: war crimes, genocide and crimes against humanity'. The Constitutive Act of the AU is available at www.africa-union.org/root/AU/AboutAU/Constitutive_Act_en.htm (accessed 28 December 2010).
79 Joshua Kurlantzick, 'How China is changing global diplomacy: cultural revolution', *New Republic*, 27 June 2005, pp. 16–21; Bates Gill and Yanzhong Huang, 'Sources and limits of Chinese "soft power" ', *Survival*, Vol. 48, No. 2 (2006), pp. 17–36.
80 Hu Jintao, 'Build towards a harmonious world of lasting peace and common prosperity' (a speech delivered at the High-level Plenary Meeting of the United Nations 60th Session, New York, 15 September 2005), www.mfa.gov.cn/wjdt/zyjh/t213091.htm (accessed 17 January 2011); 'Zhonggong zhongyang guanyu jiaqiang dang de zhizheng nengli jianshe de jueding' (CCP Central Committee Decision on the Enhancement of the Party's Governance Capability), *Renmin ribao* (*People's Daily*), 27 September 2004, reprinted in *Zhongguo Gongchandang* (*The Chinese Communist Party*) (People's University of China), No. 11 (2004), pp. 4–13; Jiang Zhuqing, 'Hu calls for a harmonious world', *China Daily*, 16 September 2005; Tang Guanghong, 'Shijie duoyangxing yu Zhongguo waijiao xinlinian' (The diversity of the world and new ideas of China's diplomacy), *Guoji wenti yanjiu* (*Research on International Issues*), No. 5 (2005), pp. 22–7; Wang Yusheng and Yin Chengde, 'Guanyu "goujian hexie shijie" de jidian sikao' (Several thoughts on 'constructing a harmonious world'), *Guoji wenti yanjiu* (*Research on International Issues*), No. 4 (2006), pp. 1–4, 23.
81 Lu Xiaohong, ' "Hexie shijie": Zhongguo de quanqiu zhili lilun' (A 'harmonious world': China's global governance theory), *Waijiao pinglun* (*Foreign Affairs Review*), December 2006, pp. 63–8; Pang Zhongying, 'Guanyu Zhongguo de quanqiu zhili yanjiu' (On the research of global governance in China), in Pang Zhongying (ed.), *Zhongguo xuezhe kan shijie 8: quanqiu zhili juan* (*World Politics – Views from China, Vol. 8, Global Governance*) (Hong Kong: Heping tushu youxian gongsi, 2006), pp. xvii–xxx; Yu Keping, 'Hexie shijie yu quanqiu zhili' (A harmonious world and global governance), *Zhonggong Tianjin shiwei dangxiao xuebao* (*Journal of the CCP Tianjin Municipal Party School*), No. 2 (2007), pp. 5–10.
82 Hu Jintao, 'Build towards a harmonious world of lasting peace and common prosperity'.
83 Lu Xiaohong, 'Hexie shijie' (A 'harmonious world'); Yu Keping, 'Hexie shijie yu quanqiu zhili' (A harmonious world and global governance).

84 According to the hegemonic stability theory, a hegemon, such as the US in the post-Cold War era, should act as a conservative state to maintain the prevailing international order as this order is shaped and maintained according to its interests. Ironically, the US is now acting as a revolutionary state rather than a quintessential status quo power. One of the major missions for neo-conservatism is to transform the prevailing Westphalian international system into a self-proclaimed 'democratic system'. For a detailed account of hegemonic stability theory, see Robert Gilpin, *War and Change in World Politics* (Cambridge: Cambridge University Press, 1981); for an account of the neo-conservative mission, see Robert Jervis, 'The remaking of a unipolar world', *Washington Quarterly*, Vol. 29, No. 3 (Summer 2006), pp. 7–19.
85 Andrew Linklater, "The English School', in Scott Burchill and Andrew Linklater *et al. Theories of International Relations* (Basingstoke: Palgrave Macmillan, 2005), pp. 84–109.
86 Chen Zhimin, 'Soft balancing and reciprocal engagement: international structures and China's foreign policy choices', in David Zweig and Chen Zhimin (eds), *China's Reforms and International Political Economy* (London: Routledge, 2007), pp. 42–61.
87 Sebastian Mallaby, 'A palace for Sudan: China's no-strings aid undermines the West', *Washington Post*, 5 February 2007, www.washingtonpost.com/wp-dyn/content/article/2007/02/04/AR2007020401047.html (accessed 18 February 2011).
88 For example, both African and Chinese NGOs were excluded from the Forum on China–Africa Cooperation, dubbed as the China–Africa Summit, in November 2006. Alden, *China in Africa*, p. 2.

3 Peace and security

1 Quoted in Jiang Wenran, 'CCP celebrates 50 years of nuclear achievements', *China Brief*, The Jamestown Foundation, Vol. 5, Issue 23 (8 November 2005).
2 Quoted in Yoichi Funabashi, *The Peninsula Question: A Chronicle of the Second Korean Nuclear Crisis* (Washington, DC: Brookings Institution Press, 2007), p. 450.
3 Exceptions to this general rule may include countries such as New Zealand, a self-proclaimed nuclear-free country, and Japan, bound by its constitution, and Germany, because of its past in the Second World War.
4 Paul Kennedy, 'Global challenges at the beginning of the twenty-first century', in Paul Kennedy, Dirk Messner and Franz Nuscheler (eds), *Global Trends and Global Governance* (London: Pluto Press, 2002), p. 14.
5 There are of course other opinions, although they might be in the minority. For example, speaking in his BBC Reith Lecture entitled 'The African condition' in 1979, Ali Mazrui argued 'that violence had been necessary to end white rule on the [African] continent and that nuclear proliferation should be extended to African states'. See *Times Higher Education*, 28 May 2009, p. 35.
6 Robert Einhorn, 'China and non-proliferation', *National Interest*, Vol. 2, Issue 13 (2 April 2003), p. 1.
7 Other issues such as the suspected North Korea–Myanmar collaboration in nuclear weapons proliferation and the Iran nuclear ambition could have been incorporated into this chapter, but it would then have become too lengthy for the book's purpose.
8 Samuel S. Kim, 'China and the United Nations', in Elizabeth Economy and Michel Oksenberg (eds), *China Joins the World: Progress and Prospects* (New York: Council on Foreign Relations Press, 1999), pp. 66–7.
9 Shi Jiangtao, 'Beijing vows to play much bigger role on world stage', *South China Morning Post*, 25 October 2005. The net contributions for the year were US$36.5 million.
10 The West is defined broadly as consisting of the members of North Atlantic Treaty Organization (NATO) and European Union, and Australia, Japan and New Zealand, their close allies in the Asia-Pacific region. The West's ambivalent attitude towards UN

peace operations since the end of the Second World War is briefly studied by Alex J. Bellamy and Paul D. Williams, 'The West and contemporary peace operations', *Journal of Peace Research*, Vol. 46, No. 1 (January 2009), pp. 39–57. While Western countries account for the bulk of the peacekeeping budget, they contribute fewer personnel to the operations than developing states, especially after the fiascos in Somalia, Rwanda and Bosnia between 1993 and 1995. International Crisis Group, *China's Growing Role in UN Peacekeeping*, Asia Report No. 166 (Brussels: International Crisis Group, 2009), p. 8, www.crisisgroup.org/library/documents/asia/north_east_asia/166_chinas_growing_role_in_un_peacekeeping.pdf (accessed 14 September 2009).

11 'Hybrid missions' refer to those that 'work in tandem with UN forces or troops from other international organizations' while non-UN peace operations are those 'not authorized by the UN Security Council or operations wholly conducted by international organizations other than the UN'. Bellamy and Williams, 'The West and contemporary peace operations', pp. 46, 49.

12 Ibid., pp. 50–51.

13 Tang Yongsheng, 'Zhongguo dui Lianheguo weihe jizhi de canyu' (China's participation in the United Nations peacekeeping regime), in Wang Yizhou (ed.), *Mohe zhong de jiangou: Zhongguo yu guoji zuzhi guanxi de duo shijiao toushi (Construction in Contradiction: Multiple Perspectives on the Relations between China and International Organisations)* (Beijing: Zhongguo fazhan chubanshe, 2003), p. 71; Yin He, *China's Changing Policy on UN Peacekeeping Operations* (Stockholm: Institute for Security and Development Policy, 2007), p. 13, www.silkroadstudies.org/new/docs/Silkroadpapers/2007/YinHe0409073.pdf (accessed 10 September 2009).

14 UN Peacekeeping, 'Monthly summary of contributors of military and civilian police personnel', www.un.org/en/peacekeeping/contributors/ (accessed 19 December 2010); *United Nations Peacekeeping Fact Sheet*, March 2010, www.un.org/en/peacekeeping/documents/factsheet.pdf (accessed 19 December 2010). Throughout the decade of the 1990s China's contribution was 0.9 per cent; it rose to 1.5 per cent by the end of 2000. In the period 2001–2003, the assessment rate was 1.91 per cent. Tang Yongsheng, 'Zhongguo dui Lianheguo weihe jizhi de canyu' (China's participation in the United Nations peacekeeping regime), p. 73; International Crisis Group, *China's Growing Role in UN Peacekeeping*, p. 8.

15 Tang Yongsheng, 'Zhongguo dui Lianheguo weihe jizhi de canyu' (China's participation in the United Nations peacekeeping regime), p. 75; International Crisis Group, *China's Growing Role in UN Peacekeeping*, p. 7.

16 'UN mission's contributions by country', UN Department of Peacekeeping Operations, 31 July 2009, www.un.org/Depts/dpko/dpko/contributors/2009/july09_4.pdf (accessed 12 September 2009).

17 China created the so-called 'fifth voting style' in which it was present at, but did not participate in, the vote. Yin He, *China's Changing Policy on UN Peacekeeping Operations*, p. 20.

18 Because China did not vote, it did not, in effect, veto Security Council resolutions that established peacekeeping operations.

19 It began to vote in favour of various peacekeeping operations and to make financial contributions to the peacekeeping budget. But it did not dispatch any personnel to the operations until 1990. M. Taylor Fravel, 'China's attitude toward UN peacekeeping operations since 1989', *Asian Survey*, Vol. 36, No. 11 (November 1996), p. 1104; Pang Zhongying, 'China's changing attitude to UN peacekeeping', *International Peacekeeping*, Vol. 12, No. 1 (Spring 2005), pp. 89–90; Tang Yongsheng, 'Zhongguo dui Lianheguo weihe jizhi de canyu' (China's participation in the United Nations peacekeeping regime), pp. 70–71.

20 They include: establishment of operations before ceasefire; without the need to have consent of all parties to the conflict; the authorization to use force; and under

national (i.e. non-UN) command. Fravel, 'China's attitude toward U.N. peacekeeping operations since 1989', p. 1106.
21 Ibid., p. 1114.
22 Cited in ibid., p. 1113.
23 China reversed its decision on Guatemala eleven days later, after a promise from the Latin American country to stop championing UN membership for Taiwan. Paul Lewis, 'China lifts U.N. veto on Guatemala monitors', *New York Times*, 21 January 1997, www.nytimes.com/1997/01/21/world/china-lifts-un-veto-on-guatemala-monitors.html (accessed 15 September 2009).
24 Pang Zhongying also discusses China's concern over the unipolar world order, but his conclusion differs from ours. Pang Zhougying, 'China's changing attitude to UN peacekeeping', p. 90.
25 Fravel, 'China's attitude toward U.N. peacekeeping operations since 1989', p. 1115ff.; Pang Zhongying, 'China's changing attitude to UN peacekeeping', p. 100.
26 According to Yin He of the China Peacekeeping CIVPOL (Civilian Police) Training Centre, the year 1999 marked the beginning of a new era in China's participation in UNPKO. Yin He, *China's Changing Policy on UN Peacekeeping Operations*, p. 10.
27 Yin He, *China's Changing Policy on UN Peacekeeping Operations*, pp. 24–5n39. UNSAS was created for the purpose of rapid deployment of UN peacekeeping operations. It is 'based upon commitments by Member States to contribute specified resources within agreed response time for United Nations peacekeeping operations'. 'UN Standby Arrangements system description', Department of Peacekeeping Operation, 1 September 1999, www.un.org/Depts/dpko/dpko/rapid/body_sys.htm (accessed 14 September 2009). But according to Bates Gill and Chin-Hao Huang, China has submitted neither its planning data sheet nor formal commitment to contribute standby resources to the system. Bates Gill and Chin-Hao Huang, 'China's expanding peacekeeping role: its significance and the policy implications', *SIPRI Policy Brief*, February 2009, pp. 5–6, http://books.sipri.org/files/misc/SIPRIPB0902.pdf (accessed 13 September 2009).
28 'Report of the Panel on United Nations Peace Operations', August 2000, www.un.org/peace/reports/peace_operations (accessed 14 September 2009).
29 Stefan Stähle, 'China's shifting attitude towards United Nations peacekeeping operations', *The China Quarterly*, No. 195 (September 2008), p. 639.
30 Cited in Pang Zhongying, 'China's changing attitude to UN peacekeeping', p. 94.
31 International Crisis Group, *China's Growing Role in UN Peacekeeping*, p. 12n102.
32 Pang Zhongying, 'China's changing attitude to UN peacekeeping', pp. 95–6.
33 Yin He, *China's Changing Policy on UN Peacekeeping Operations*, pp. 44–5.
34 According to Pang Zhongying, the notion was coined by Zhu Rongji, the then Chinese Premier, who argued that China should not only play the role of a responsible economic actor but also be a responsible political player to promote international peace and justice. Pang Zhongying, 'China's changing attitude to UN peacekeeping', pp. 96–7.
35 See Chapter 5 for more discussion on humanitarian intervention.
36 Stähle, 'China's shifting attitude towards United Nations peacekeeping operations', pp. 653–4. See also International Crisis Group, *China's Growing Role in UN Peacekeeping*, pp. 14–15.
37 International Crisis Group, *China's Growing Role in UN Peacekeeping*, pp. 15–17. See also Pak K. Lee, Gerald Chan and Lai-Ha Chan, 'China in Darfur: humanitarian rule-taker or rule-maker?', *Review of International Studies*, first published online 1 March 2011, doi: 10.1017/SO260210511000040.
38 Zhao Lei, 'Zhongguo canyu Lianheguo weihe xingdong de leixing ji diyu fenxi' (China's participation in UN peacekeeping operations: an analysis of types and regions), *Dangdai Ya Tai (Contemporary Asia-Pacific)*, No. 2 (2009), p. 65.

39 Lewis, 'China lifts U.N. veto on Guatemala monitors'; Paul Lewis, 'Continuation of U.N. force in Macedonia faces a Chinese veto', *New York Times*, 25 February 1999, www.nytimes.com/1999/02/25/world/continuation-of-un-force-in-macedonia-faces-a-chinese-veto.html (accessed 15 September 2009); 'Security Council fails to extend mandate of United Nations Preventive Deployment Force in Former Yugoslav Republic of Macedonia', United Nations Press Release, SC/6648, 25 February 1999, www.un.org/News/Press/docs/1999/19990225.sc6648.html (accessed 15 September 2009); International Crisis Group, *China's Growing Role in UN Peacekeeping*, pp. 17–18.
40 China calls for partnerships between regional organizations and the Security Council in addressing international conflicts. International Crisis Group, *China's Glowing Role in UN Peacekeeping*, pp. 23–5.
41 Ibid., pp. 21–2.
42 The official website is: www.un.org/disarmament/WMD/Nuclear/NPT.shtml (accessed 26 January 2011).
43 The official website is: www.opbw.org (accessed 26 January 2011).
44 The official website is: www.opcw.org/chemical-weapons-convention (accessed 26 January 2011).
45 The official website is: www.ctbto.org (accessed 26 January 2011).
46 The official website is: www.nuclearsuppliersgroup.org/Leng/default.htm (accessed 20 December 2010).
47 The official website is: www.australiagroup.net/en/index.html (accessed 20 December 2010).
48 It succeeded the Coordinating Committee for Multilateral Export Controls (COCOM) which was dissolved in March 1994, www.wassenaar.org/introduction/origins.html (accessed 2 September 2009).
49 The official website is: www.mtcr.info (accessed 20 December 2010).
50 See 'List of subscribing states to the HCOC as of August 2010', www.bmeia.gv.at/fileadmin/user_upload/bmeia/media/2-Aussenpolitik_Zentrale/List_of_HCOC_Subscribing_States.pdf (accessed 20 December 2010). Austria hosts the secretariat of the regime, www.bmeia.gv.at/en/foreign-ministry/foreign-policy/disarmament.html (accessed 20 December 2010).
51 Gerald Chan, *China's Compliance in Global Affairs: Trade, Arms Control, Environmental Protection, Human Rights* (Singapore: World Scientific, 2006), pp. 115–16; Ann E. Kent, *Beyond Compliance: China, International Organizations, and Global Security* (Stanford, CA: Stanford University Press, 2007), pp. 69ff.; Evan S. Medeiros, *Reluctant Restraint: The Evolution of China's Non-proliferation Policies and Practices, 1980–2004* (Stanford, CA: Stanford University Press, 2007), p. 2; Michael D. Swaine and Alastair Iain Johnston, 'China and arms control institutions', in Economy and Oksenberg (eds), *China Joins the World*, pp. 101–104.
52 Although as a nuclear weapon state, China was not required by the NPT after joining it to submit its civilian nuclear activities to the safeguards of the IAEA. It began in September 1985 to accept voluntarily IAEA safeguards on two civilian nuclear reactors. Kent, *Beyond Compliance*, p. 79; Li Shaojun, 'Guoji he bu kuosan tizhi yu Zhongguo' (International nuclear non-proliferation regimes and China), in Wang Yizhou (ed.), *Mohe zhong de jiangou* (*Construction in Contradiction*), p. 62.
53 For a discussion of the compromises China made in the negotiation process of acceding to the CTBT and the resultant costs to China, see Kent, *Beyond Compliance*, pp. 80–83. The Chinese government submitted the treaty to the NPC for ratification in April 2000, but held back in light of the ratification defeat in the US Senate in November 1999. Ibid., p. 83.
54 Sean Lucas, 'China enters the Nuclear Suppliers Group: positive steps in the global campaign against nuclear weapons proliferation', NTI, November 2004, www.nti.org/e_research/e3_57a.html (accessed 20 December 2010).

55 Chan, *China's Compliance in Global Affairs*, p. 137; Wang Jun, 'Zhongguo yu duobian chukou kongzhi jizhi guanxi zhi yanbian ji yuanyin tanxi' (An analysis of the evolution of China's relations with multilateral export control mechanisms and reasons), *Liaoning daxue xuebao (zhexue shehui kexue ban)* (*Journal of Liaoning University (Philosophy and Social Sciences)*), Vol. 33, No. 2 (March 2005), pp. 76–81; Ian Anthony and Sibylle Bauer, 'Controls on security-related international transfers', in Stockholm International Peace Research Institute (SIPRI) (ed.), *SIPRI Yearbook 2009: Armaments, Disarmament and International Security* (Oxford: Oxford University Press, 2009), p. 465.
56 Anupam Srivastava, 'China's export controls: can Beijing's actions match its word?', *Arms Control Today*, Arms Control Association, Washington, DC, November 2005. See also US Defense Treaty Inspection Readiness Program, 'Missile technology control regime', http://dtirp.dtra.mil/TIC/synopses/mtcr.aspx (accessed 20 December 2010).
57 Shirley A. Kan, *China and Proliferation of Weapons of Mass Destruction and Missiles: Policy Issues* (Washington, DC: Congressional Research Service, 2009), p. 53, http://assets.opencrs.com/rpts/RL31555_20090727.pdf (accessed 4 September 2009).
58 Wang Jun, 'Zhongguo yu duobian chukou kongzhi jizhi guanxi zhi yanbian ji yuanyin tanxi' (An analysis of the evolution of China's relations with multilateral export control mechanisms and reasons); Mark Bromley and Noel Kelly, 'Appendix 7C. Transparency in arms transfers', in SIPRI (ed.), *SIPRI Yearbook 2009*, pp. 336–8.
59 Ding Yuanhong, 'He bu kuosan jizhi mianlin weiji de genyou suozai' (The origin of the crisis nuclear non-proliferation regimes are faced with), *Heping yu fazhan* (*Peace and Development*), No. 3 (2005), pp. 29–30; Hou Hongyu, 'Hekuosan genyuan tanxi' (An analysis of the reasons for nuclear proliferation), *Guoji luntan* (*International Forum*), Vol. 9, No. 3 (May 2007), pp. 1–6; Li Shaojun, 'Guoji he bu kuosan tizhi yu Zhongguo' (International nuclear non-proliferation regimes and China), pp. 52–5; Wang Jun, 'He bu kuosan tiaoyue de kunjing ji yingdui' (The predicament and response of the Nuclear Non-Proliferation Treaty), *Dangdai Ya Tai* (*Contemporary Asia-Pacific*), No. 3 (2009), pp. 110–18. In January 2010 India had an arsenal of 60–80 operational nuclear weapons; Pakistan possessed 70–90 nuclear weapons; and Israel was said to have about eighty. Whether North Korea has any operational nuclear weapons is open to dispute; it declared in June 2008 that it held a stock of separated plutonium of 30.8 kg. Shannon N. Kile, Vitaly Fedchenko, Bharath Gopalaswamy and Hans M. Kristensen, 'World nuclear forces', in SIPRI (ed.), *SIRPI Yearbook 2010*, pp. 334, 364–6.
60 Glenn Kessler, 'Questionable China–Pakistan deal draws little comment from U.S.', *Washington Post*, 20 May 2010, www.washingtonpost.com/wp-dyn/content/article/2010/05/19/AR2010051905471.html (accessed 25 May 2010).
61 For a detailed account of China's suspected proliferation of weapons of mass destruction and missiles to Pakistan, Iran and North Korea, see Khan, *China and Proliferation of Weapons of Mass Destruction and Missiles*, pp. 2–24.
62 'Nuclear disarmament II', 12 May 2005, www.china.org.cn/english/features/Nuclear/128498.htm (accessed 12 September 2009); Li Shaojun, 'Guoji he bu kuosan tizhi yu Zhongguo' (International nuclear non-proliferation regimes and China), p. 61.
63 China proposed in 1996 in the UN General Assembly that no outer space weapons system should be developed or deployed. Li Shaojun, 'Guoji he bu kuosan tizhi yu Zhongguo' (International nuclear non-proliferation regimes and China), p. 58.
64 The US announcement was made in December 2001 in http://georgewbush-whitehouse.archives.gov/news/releases/2001/12/20011213–2.html (accessed 26 August 2009). The abrogation took effect in June 2002.

65 China has insisted on the need for both the US and the USSR/Russia, in particular the former, to make progress in disarmament before other nuclear weapon states follow suit. Kent, *Beyond Compliance*, p. 101; Li Shaojun, 'Guoji he bu kuosan tizhi yu Zhongguo' (International nuclear non-proliferation regimes and China), pp. 53, 58.
66 Shannon N. Kile, 'Nuclear arms control and non-proliferation', in SIPRI (ed.), *SIPRI Yearbook 2007*, pp. 477–513, esp. 506–12; Medeiros, *Reluctant Restraint*, pp. 205–207.
67 Kile, 'Nuclear arms control and non-proliferation', in SIPRI (ed.), *SIPRI Yearbook 2008*, pp. 361–623.
68 Cole Harvey, 'CD breaks deadlock on work plan', *Arms Control Today*, June 2009, www.armscontrol.org/act/2009_6/CD (accessed 8 September 2009).
69 Alastair Iain Johnston, *Social States: China in International Institutions, 1980–2000* (Princeton, NJ: Princeton University Press, 2008), pp. 108, 115. For the number of nuclear tests, see Vitaly Fedchenko, 'Appendix 8B. Nuclear explosions, 1945–2009', in SIPRI (ed.), *SIPRI Yearbook 2010*, pp. 375–6.
70 Kan, *China and Proliferation of Weapons of Mass Destruction and Missiles*, p. 54.
71 Cited in ibid., p. 47. The *Yinhe* incident refers to a US claim that a Chinese container vessel, *Yinhe* ('galaxy'), delivered chemical weapons to Iran. After an 'intrusive' inspection in Saudi Arabia by a joint Saudi–US team, no weapons were found on the ship, but the US government refused to apologize for any wrongdoing because it claimed that it 'had acted in good faith on intelligence from a number of sources, all of which proved to be wrong'. Patrick E. Tyler, 'No chemical arms aboard China ship', *New York Times*, 6 September 1993, www.nytimes.com/1993/09/06/world/no-chemical-arms-aboard-china-ship.html (accessed 7 September 2009).
72 Medeiros, *Reluctant Restraint*, p. 92.
73 Charles L. Pritchard, *Failed Diplomacy: The Tragic Story of How North Korea Got the Bomb* (Washington, DC: Brookings Institution Press, 2007), p. 57.
74 The multilateral option was a response to many Republican complaints that the Agreed Framework, made between the US under the Clinton administration and North Korea, excluded South Korea from participation. The initial idea was to convene a P5 plus 5 multilateral meeting, comprising the five permanent members of the UNSC, plus Japan, North Korea and South Korea, Australia and the European Union. The Bush administration remained steadfast in its refusal to hold bilateral talks with North Korea until after the latter accepted unconditionally a 'complete, verifiable and irreversible disarmament' of its entire nuclear weapons programme. Pritchard, *Failed Diplomacy*, pp. 59–60; Gu Guoliang and Steven E. Miller, 'Arms control and the spread of weapons of mass destruction', in Richard Rosecrance and Gu Guoliang (eds), *Power and Restraint: A Shared Vision for the U.S.–China Relationship* (New York: PublicAffairs, 2009), p. 170; International Crisis Group, *North Korea: Getting Back to Talks*, Asia Report No. 169 (Brussels: International Crisis Group, 2009), p. 9, www.crisisgroup.org/library/documents/asia/north_korea/169_north_korea___getting_back_to_talks.pdf (accessed 17 September 2009); Andrew O'Neil, *Nuclear Proliferation in Northeast Asia: The Quest for Security* (Basingstoke: Palgrave Macmillan, 2007), p. 65.
75 Pritchard, *Failed Diplomacy*, pp. 59–60; Kim Jong-il told China's visiting Vice-Premier, Qian Qichen, in March 2003 that North Korea's nuclear programme 'was a strategic issue between the United States and North Korea'. Funabashi, *The Peninsula Question*, p. 263.
76 Cited in Pang Zhongying, *The Six-Party Process, Regional Security Mechanisms, and China–U.S. Cooperation: Toward a Regional Security Mechanism for a New Northeast Asia?* A CNAPS Visiting Fellow Working Paper (Washington, DC: Brookings Institution Press, 2009), pp. 9–10.
77 Pritchard, *Failed Diplomacy*, p. 62; Funabashi, *The Peninsula Question*, pp. 271–5.
78 Pritchard, *Failed Diplomacy*, pp. 64–5.

79 The initial plan excluded Russia. Powell changed his mind after a telephone conversation with Russian Foreign Minister Igor Ivanov. Pritchard, *Failed Diplomacy*, p. 85.
80 Funabashi, *The Peninsula Question*, pp. 283–4.
81 Pritchard, *Failed Diplomacy*, p. 85.
82 Funabashi, *The Peninsula Question*, p. 280. See also Pritchard, *Failed Diplomacy*, p. 85. China accepted the US request to host the Six-Party Talks partly because it wanted to increase American 'dependence' on it. Shi Yinhong, 'China and the North Korean nuclear issue: competing interests and persistent policy dilemmas', *Korea Journal of Defense Analysis*, Vol. 21, No. 1 (March 2009), p. 35. This is echoed by Funabashi, who argues that by hosting the multilateral talks China wanted to improve and stabilize its relations with the US. Funabashi, *The Peninsula Question*, p. 305.
83 'N. Korea hopes for direct talks with US', *Korea Times*, 27 July 2009, https://www.koreatimes.co.kr/www/news/nation/2009/07/113_49134.htm (accessed 19 September 2009); Associated Press, 'US prepared to meet with N Korea', CBS News, 16 September 2009, www.cbsnews.com/stories/2009/09/16/ap/cabstatepent/main5315508.shtml (accessed 19 September 2009). Eight days after North Korea test-fired a ballistic missile on 5 April 2009 in defiance of international warnings, the United Nations Security Council issued a president's statement condemning the missile launch. Pyongyang declared in response that it would permanently withdraw from the Six-Party Talks and revive its nuclear weapons programme. International Crisis Group, *North Korea*, p. 4.
84 The two incidents are studied in International Crisis Group, *China and Inter-Korean Clashes in the Yellow Sea*, Asia Report No. 200 (Brussels: International Crisis Group, 2011), www.crisisgroup.org/en/regions/asia/north-east-asia/north-korea/200-china-and-inter-korean-clashes-in-the-yellow-sea.aspx (accessed 17 February 2011).
85 The Joint Statement outlines the general principles for future talks aimed at the verifiable denuclearization of the Korean Peninsula in a peaceful manner. But the US and North Korea disagreed shortly after the agreement about the sequencing of the deal on dismantling North Korea's nuclear infrastructure. According to the Action Plan, there are two phases of action. During the sixty-day initial period, Pyongyang pledged to shut down and seal the 5-megawatt electric graphite-moderated research reactor, the reprocessing facility and the nuclear fuel fabrication plant at Yongbyon 'for the purpose of eventual abandonment', subject to monitoring and verification by the IAEA, and to provide a list of all its nuclear programmes. The other parties, in return, pledged to offer emergency energy assistance equivalent to half a million tonnes of heavy fuel oil. In the second phase, announced in October 2007, North Korea agreed to disable the nuclear facilities at the Yongbyon complex and to provide a 'complete and correct declaration' of all its nuclear programmes by the end of December 2007 in return for, among others, a US pledge to take steps to lift financial and commercial sanctions against North Korea. Subsequent negotiations were stalled by a disagreement between the US and North Korea over whether destructive measures should be used for the proposed disablement. Another bone of contention was that the US requested North Korea to fully disclose its nuclear weapons programme, including the number of warheads, the amount of weapon-grade fissile material and the alleged transfer of nuclear material, equipment or expertise to third parties, in particular Syria. North Korea missed the 31 December 2007 deadline for disabling all its nuclear facilities at Yongbyon and for giving a comprehensive declaration of its nuclear programmes. The US said in January 2008 that North Korea needed to disclose its undeclared uranium enrichment programme. Eventually North Korea delivered to China in June 2008 its formal declaration of its nuclear weapons programme, in which, however, it said little about suspected uranium enrichment activities and proliferation to Syria. Despite the problems with the declaration, the George W. Bush administration announced the lifting of the

sanctions against North Korea, including removing the country from the State Department's list of state sponsors of terrorism. In the face of mounting criticisms at home, the US government proposed in August 2008 sweeping and stringent verification and inspection mechanisms, which could cover military installations. North Korea, however, found them unacceptable, and hence suspended further disablement of its nuclear facilities. Both Kim Jong-il's suspected stroke in August 2008 and the impasse over verification blocked any progress in the Six-Party Talks, which did not resume after December 2008. Shannon N. Kile, 'Nuclear arms control and non-proliferation', in SIPRI (ed.), *SIPRI Yearbook 2008*, pp. 350–56, 399–401; Blaine Harden, 'All nuclear efforts disclosed, N. Korea says', *Washington Post*, 5 January 2008, www.washingtonpost.com/wp-dyn/content/article/2008/01/04/AR2008010403 710.html (accessed 18 September 2009); Stephan Haggard and Marcus Noland, 'North Korea in 2008: twilight of the God?', *Asian Survey*, Vol. 49, No. 1 (January/February 2009), pp. 103–105.

86 Funabashi, *The Peninsula Question*, pp. 301–302, 305.
87 China has a 'two-no' policy towards North Korea. The first no is that 'the US must absolutely not use military means to solve the North Korea [sic] nuclear problem'. The second is 'North Korea must not cross the nuclear threshold'. Shi Yinhong, 'China and the North Korean nuclear issue', p. 45n1.
88 Gilbert Rozman, *Strategic Thinking about the Korean Nuclear Crisis: Four Parties Caught between North Korea and the United States* (Basingstoke: Palgrave Macmillan, 2007), p. 104; Dingli Shen of Fudan University argues that both North Korea and Taiwan form the key elements of mutual hedging between China and US. As continued US arms sales to Taiwan represent a security threat to China, the latter needs to maintain North Korea's role as a buffer zone against the US. Dingli Shen, 'Cooperative denuclearisation toward North Korea', *Washington Quarterly*, Vol. 32, No. 4 (October 2009), pp. 179–80. According to Yoichi Funabashi, China's People's Liberation Army also views North Korea as 'an area that is "interlocked" with Taiwan'. Funabashi, *The Peninsula Question*, p. 291.
89 China dispatched Yang Shangkun and Qian Qichen to North Korea in April and July 1992 to explain China's intention to establish diplomatic relations with the South, but they met with a frosty reception from Kim Il-sung. Jiang Zemin was quoted as saying in November 1995 that he 'know[s] nothing of North Korea'. Kim Jong-il did not visit China in the 1990s. After his first unannounced visit to China with his father in 1983, he made his second visit in May 2000. Funabashi, *The Peninsula Question*, pp. 264–6, 268, 439–42.
90 Rozman, *Strategic Thinking about the Korean Nuclear Crisis*, p. 115.
91 Wu Bangguo was the chairman of the Standing Committee of the National People's Congress and a member of the Standing Committee of the CCP Politburo; Li Changchun was a member of the Standing Committee of the CCP Politburo; and Wang Jiarui was the head of the CCP International Liaison Department. Funabashi, *The Peninsula Question*, pp. 320–21.
92 Ibid., pp. 320–21.
93 Rozman, *Strategic Thinking about the Korean Nuclear Crisis*, pp. 115–16; Shi Yinhong, 'China and the North Korean nuclear issue', p. 37; China–North Korea bilateral trade has increased to US$2.8 billion in 2008 from US$1.5 billion in 2005. Evan Ramstad, 'North Korea says U.S. key to disarmament talks', *Wall Street Journal Online*, 6 October 2009, www.online.wsj.com/article/SB125473768056 064121.html (accessed 6 October 2009).
94 China refused to take part in any consultation among the five parties (China, Japan, Russia, South Korea and the US), and the US pointed out that that was the main weakness of the Six-Party Talks. Funabashi, *The Peninsula Question*, p. 285.
95 During Hu's visit to Pyongyang, Chinese new reports did not allude to the Joint Statement issued just a month before. Xing Zhigang and Jiang Zhuqing, 'President

Hu ends fruitful visit to Pyongyang', *China Daily*, 31 October 2005, www.chinadaily.com.cn/english/doc/2005-10/31/content_488922.htm (accessed 23 September 2009).
96 But the launch of the intercontinental Taepodong-2 failed. China did not veto the resolution after it was assured that Chapter VII would not be invoked. Ilsoo David Cho and Meredith Jung-En Woo, 'North Korea in 2006: the year of living dangerously', *Asian Survey*, Vol. 47, No. 1 (January/February 2007), pp. 68–70.
97 Shi Yinhong, 'China and the North Korean nuclear issue', pp. 38–40. According to Funabashi, the Bank of China was also involved. We shall return to this issue in Chapter 10 on transnational organized crime. See Kile, 'Nuclear arms control and non-proliferation', in SIPRI (ed.), *SIPRI Yearbook 2007*, p. 479, for a brief account of the financial sanction. The frozen assets in BDA worth US$24 billion was transferred in June 2007 to accounts controlled by North Korean entities in a Russian bank. Stephan Haggard and Marcus Noland, 'North Korea in 2007: shuffling in from the cold', *Asian Survey*, Vol. 48, No. 1 (January/February 2008), pp. 108–109.
98 O'Neil, *Nuclear Proliferation in Northeast Asia*, p. 73.
99 The estimated actual yield of the explosion (less than 1 kt) was much smaller than the pre-announced yield (4 kt). Vitaly Fedchenko and Ragnhild Ferm Hellgren, 'Appendix 12B. Nuclear explosions, 1945–2006', in SIPRI (ed.), *SIPRI Yearbook 2007*, pp. 552–3.
100 Shao Feng, 'Chao he wenti zouxiang ji Zhongguo de yingdui' (The development of the North Korean nuclear issue and China's response), *Ya Fei zongheng* (*Across Asia and Africa*), No. 1 (2007), p. 48.
101 Kile, 'Nuclear arms control and non-proliferation', in SIPRI (ed.), *SIPRI Yearbook 2007*, p. 483.
102 UN Department of Public Information, 'Security Council, acting unanimously, condemns in strongest terms Democratic People's Republic of Korea nuclear test, toughens sanctions', 12 June 2009, www.un.org/News/Press/docs/2009/sc9679.doc.htm (accessed 20 December 2010); Kile, 'Nuclear arms control and non-proliferation', in SIPRI (ed.), *SIPRI Yearbook 2010*, pp. 390–93.
103 Funabashi, *The Peninsula Question*, pp. 298–9.
104 Shao Feng, 'Chao he wenti zouxiang ji Zhongguo de yingdui' (The development of the North Korean nuclear issue and China's response), p. 48. Junichiro Koizumi, Japan's former Prime Minister, held a similar view. Funabashi, *The Peninsula Question*, p. 469.
105 Shi Yinhong, 'China and the North Korean nuclear issue', pp. 40–41.
106 United Nations Security Council Resolution 1718 (2006), 14 October 2006, p. 3, http://daccessdds.un.org/doc/UNDOC/GEN/N06/572/07/PDF/N0657207.pdf (accessed 23 September 2009); Kile, 'Nuclear arms control and non-proliferation', in SIPRI (ed.), *SIPRI Yearbook 2007*, p. 482.
107 During Xi's visit, China reportedly offered 5,000 tonnes of jet fuel and 100 million yuan in cash. In the following visit by Wang, China allegedly promised to provide economic aid to the tune of US$20–40 million. Jeong Jae Sung, 'North Korea reveals Chinese aid', *The Daily NK*, 6 February 2009, www.dailynk.com/english/read.php?cataId=nk00400&num=4524 (accessed 15 October 2009). See also Bonnie S. Glaser and Scott Snyder, 'Wang Jiarui's new year's visit to Pyongyang and China's new approach to North Korea', *China Brief*, Vol. 9, No. 4 (20 February 2009), pp. 4–6, www.jamestown.org/uploads/media/cb_009_4_03.pdf (accessed 22 October 2009).
108 For two accounts that hint that China wants to exploit North Korea's mineral resources in the bilateral cooperation deals, see Christian Oliver, 'China eyes N Korea's mineral wealth', *Financial Times*, 6 October 2009; 'China, North Korea and its nukes: smile, please', *The Economist*, 10–16 October 2009.
109 Choe Sang-hun, 'China aims to steady North Korea', *New York Times*, 7 October 2009, www.nytimes.com/2009/10/07/world/asia/07korea.html (accessed 7 October 2009); idem, 'Japan and S. Korea agree to joint stance on North', *New York Times*, 9 October 2009, www.nytimes.com/2009/10/10/world/asia/10korea.html (accessed 11 October 2009).

110 Dick K. Nanto, Mark E. Manyin and Kerry Dumbaugh, *China–North Korea Relations*, CRS Report for Congress No. R41043 (Washington, DC: Congressional Research Service, 2010), pp. 17–19, www.fas.org/sgp/crs/row/R41043.pdf (accessed 11 March 2010). For the sanctions against North Korea, see Security Council Committee established pursuant to resolution 1718 (2006), www.un.org/sc/committees/1718/index.shtml (accessed 30 March 2010).
111 John Pomfret, 'U.S. steps up pressure on China to rein in North Korea', *Washington Post*, 6 December 2010, www.washingtonpost.com/wp-dyn/content/article/2010/12/05/AR2010120503513.html (accessed 6 December 2010).
112 David E. Sanger, 'North Koreans unveil new plant for nuclear use', *New York Times*, 20 November 2010, www.nytimes.com/2010/11/21/world/asia/21intel.html (accessed 3 December 2010).
113 Kathrin Hille, 'WikiLeaks: China drags feet on N Korea', *Financial Times*, 29 November 2009, www.ft.com/cms/s/0/f3b2edda-fbc7-11df-b79a-00144feab49a.html#axzz17LZFkFjK (accessed 30 November 2010); Jeremy Page and Jay Solomon, 'China stood aside on Iran', *Wall Street Journal Online*, 29 November 2010, http://online.wsj.com/article/SB10001424052748704584804575644031813953758.html (accessed 1 December 2010); 'U.S. asked China to stop missile parts shipment to Iran', *Washington Post*, 29 November 2010, www.washingtonpost.com/wp-dyn/content/article/2010/11/28/AR2010112803909.html (accessed 6 December 2010); David E. Sanger, 'North Korea keeps the world guessing', *New York Times*, 29 November 2010, www.nytimes.com/2010/11/30/world/asia/30korea.html (accessed 1 December 2010).
114 Mark Landler and Martin Fackler, 'U.S. warning to China sends ripples to the Koreas', *New York Times*, 20 January 2011, www.nytimes.com/2011/01/21/world/asia/21diplo.html; 'Editorial: a newly cooperative China', *New York Times*, 21 January 2011, www.nytimes.com/2011/01/22/opinion/22sat1.html; 'US expresses satisfaction with Chinese concern over North Korea's uranium programme', *Korean Times*, 22 January 2011, www.koreatimes.co.kr/www/news/nation/2011/01/113_80133.html (all accessed 28 January 2011).
115 Obama said,

> China's extraordinary economic growth has lifted hundreds of millions of people out of poverty. And this is a tribute to the Chinese people. But it's also thanks to decades of stability in Asia made possible by America's forward presence in the region, by strong trade with America, and by an open international economic system championed by the United States of America.

> The White House, 'Press conference with President Obama and President Hu of the People's Republic of China, 19 January 2011, www.whitehouse.gov/the-press-office/2011/01/19/press-conference-president-obama-and-president-hu-peoples-republic-china (accessed 28 January 2011).

116 To be fair, China should not be blamed in particular for the absence of a multilateral security architecture in East Asia. Key actors in the region are at best ambivalent about it. O'Neil, *Nuclear Proliferation in Northeast Asia*, pp. 31–3.
117 Glaser and Snyder, 'Wang Jiarui's new year's visit to Pyongyang and China's new approach to North Korea'.
118 Kim Myong Chol, 'North Korea begins "plan C"', *Asia Times Online*, 14 October 2009, www.atimes.com/atimes/Korea/KJ14Dg01.html (accessed 17 October 2009). Based in Tokyo, Kim is an 'unofficial' spokesperson of North Korea and Kim Jong-il.
119 'N Korea "ready for nuclear talks"', BBC News, 18 September 2009, http://news.bbc.co.uk/1/hi/world/asia-pacific/8262223.stm (accessed 18 September 2009); Blaine Harden, 'N. Korea open to talk, Kim tells China', *Washington Post*, 19 September 2009, www.washingtonpost.com/wp-dyn/content/article/2009/09/18/AR2009091800481.html (accessed 19 September 2009).

120 Ramstad, 'North Korea says U.S. key to disarmament talks'; Xinhua, 'Wen's DPRK visit rich in content, weighty in outcome: Chinese FM', *People's Daily Online*, 7 October 2009, http://english.peopledaily.com.cn/90001/90776/90883/6777228.html (accessed 7 October 2009).
121 David Barboza, 'Chinese premier calls for dialogue between U.S. and North Korea', *New York Times*, 10 October 2009, www.nytimes.com/2009/10/11/world/asia/11korea.html (accessed 11 October 2009).
122 *Northeast Asia Peace and Security Network Daily Report* (Nautilus Institute), 11 December 2009; Choe Sang-Hun, 'U.S. envoy returns from talks with North Korea', *New York Times*, 11 December 2009, www.nytimes.com/2009/12/11/world/asia/11korea.html (accessed 11 December 2009).
123 Ian Johnson and Helen Cooper, 'China seeks talks to ease Korean tension', *New York Times*, 28 November 2010, www.nytimes.com/2010/11/29/world/asia/29korea.html (accessed 17 December 2010).
124 Remaining issues are: without participating in the PSI, how can China, in cooperation with other parties, deter North Korea from using nuclear weapons and proliferating fissile material to hot spots around the world? Given that North Korea's demand for a denuclearization of the Korean Peninsula is that there be no nuclear weapons in South Korea, can China use its leverage to ensure that South Korea and US military bases there do not hold or develop any nuclear weapons? More crucially, should the five parties (China, Japan, Russia, South Korea and the US) jointly consider giving up the non-proliferation strategy in view of the reality that North Korea is a new nuclear weapon state? The North requests that it be accepted as a permanent nuclear state and the hostility between the US and it be ended by signing a peace treaty and establishing formal diplomatic relations. In return, the North will behave responsibly, promising not to proliferate nuclear weapons elsewhere. See Kile, 'Nuclear arms control and non-proliferation', in SIPRI (ed.), *SIPRI Yearbook 2007*, p. 482; International Crisis Group, *North Korea*, pp. 17–19.

4 Finance and trade

1 *China, Inc.: How the Rise of the Next Superpower Challenges America and the World* (New York: Scribner, 2005), p. 1.
2 'Premier Wen Jiabao's interview with the *Financial Times*', Ministry of Foreign Affairs of the PRC, 2 February 2009, www.fmprc.gov.cn/eng/zxxx/t535971.htm (accessed 6 May 2010).
3 Hiroko Tabuchi, 'China replaced Japan in 2010 as No. 2 economy', *New York Times*, 13 February 2011, www.nytimes.com/2011/02/14/business/global/14yen.html (accessed 18 February 2011). China's merchandise trade in 2008 was $2,560.8 billion (7.88 per cent of the world total), after US's $3,456.9 billion (10.64 per cent) and Germany's $2,665.7 billion (8.2 per cent). World Trade Organization, *International Trade Statistics 2009* (Geneva: World Trade Organization, 2009), p. 12, www.wto.org/english/res_e/statis_e/its2009_e/its2009_e.pdf (accessed 6 May 2010). China has already overtaken Germany as the world's largest merchandise exporter, accounting for 9.6 per cent of world exports in 2009 'Trade to expand by 9.5 per cent in 2010 after a dismal 2009. WTO report', *WTO Press Release*, 26 March 2010, available at www.wto.org/english/news_e/pres10_e/pr598_e.htm (accessed 26 September 2010).
4 Keith Bradsher, 'Chinese economy grows to 4th largest in the world', *New York Times*, 25 January 2006, www.nytimes.com/2006/01/25/business/worldbusiness/25cnd-yuan.html (accessed 6 January 2011).
5 Albert Keidal, 'China's economic rise – fact and fiction', Carnegie Endowment for International Peace, Policy Brief No. 61, July 2008, www.carnegieendowment.org/files/pb61_keidel_final.pdf (accessed 6 May 2010).

Notes 211

6 'China's GDP rises 9.1 per cent in 2009, surpassing Japan', *People's Daily Online*, 2 July 2010, http://english.peopledaily.com.cn/90001/90778/90862/7050765.html; National Bureau of Statistics of China, 'National economy showed good momentum of development in 2010', 20 January 2011, www.stats.gov.cn/english/newsandcomingevents/t20110120_402699463.htm (accessed 18 February 2011).
7 *Taipei Times*, 1 November 2009, p. 11.
8 *The Business Herald*, Auckland, 5 March 2010, p. 16.
9 Jeremy Warner, 'Excitement, confusion and fear: the reaction to the Chinese phenomenon at the World Economic Forum in Davos', *Independent*, UK, 27 January 2006.
10 The amount grew to $87 billion in 2007 and $92.4 billion in 2008. 'China to draw US$50bn FDI, to be world's No. 1 recipient', *People's Daily*, 5 December 2002; Trevor Houser and Roy Levy, 'Energy security and China's UN diplomacy', *China Security*, Vol. 4, No. 3 (Summer 2008), p. 65; 'China's FDI up 23.6 per cent in 2008', www.chinaview.cn, 15 January 2009.
11 Houser and Levy, 'Energy security and China's UN diplomacy'.
12 Daniel H. Rosen, 'How much can China really diversify its reserves?', Peterson Institute of International Economics, Update Newsletter, 25 March 2010. In the third quarter of 2009, however, its overseas investments nearly tripled from a year earlier to $20.5 billion. See 'China says investment overseas up sharply', Associated Press, 27 October 2009. According to the 2009 issue of *China Statistical Yearbook* (p. 752), China's net overseas direct investment in 2007 was $26.51 billion; and that for 2008 was $55.91 billion.
13 An example is Arvind Subramanian, 'China is the key to unwinding global imbalances', *Financial Times*, 20 April 2010, www.piie.com/publications/opeds/oped.cfm?ResearchID=1550 (accessed 23 April 2010). The writer is senior fellow at the Peterson Institute for International Economics. Current account balance is the sum of net exports of goods and services, net factor income from abroad, and net current transfer payments. For the data on China's current account balance, see Table 4.3.
14 The Ministry of Foreign Affairs, PRC, www.fmprc.gov.cn/chn/pds/gjhdq/gjhdqzz/lhg_18/ (accessed 23 December 2010).
15 Margaret P. Karns and Karen A. Mingst, *International Organizations: The Politics and Processes of Global Governance* (Boulder, CO: Lynne Rienner, 2010), p. 405.
16 Hugh Williamson, Chris Giles and Krishna Guha, 'China to donate to World Bank's loan fund', *Financial Times*, 14 December 2007, www.ft.com/cms/s/0/0ec30f26-a9e9-11dc-aa8b-0000779fd2ac.html (accessed 18 February 2011).
17 Howard W. French, 'A challenge from within for the World Bank', *New York Times*, 25 January 2008, www.nytimes.com/2008/01/25/world/asia/25iht-letter26.4.9508142.html (accessed 18 February 2011).
18 Ibid.
19 UN University Report on Global Governance, 2 May 2001, www.sovereignty.net/center/unu-report.html (accessed 28 December 2010).
20 The Ministry of Foreign Affairs, PRC, www.fmprc.gov.cn/chn/pds/gjhdq/gjhdqzz/lhg_18/ (accessed 23 December 2010). For a full table of the subscriptions and voting power of the 186 member countries of the International Bank for Reconstruction and Development as of 1 November 2010, see http://siteresources.worldbank.org/BODINT/Resources/278027–1215524804501/IBRDCountryVotingTable.pdf (accessed 23 December 2010).
21 Alan Beattie, 'World Bank wins rise in capital', *Financial Times*, 25 April 2010, www.ft.com/cms/s/0/c8b8937e-5095–11df-bc86–00144feab49a.html (accessed 26 April 2010); Xin Zhiming, 'China gains more say in World Bank', *China Daily*, 27 April 2010, www.chinadaily.com.cn/business/2010–04/27/content_9778666.htm (accessed 27 April 2010); World Bank, 'World Bank reforms voting powers, gets $86 billion boost', Press Release No. 2010/363/EXT, 25 April 2010, http://web.worldbank.org/WBSITE/EXTERNAL/NEWS/0,,contentMDK:22556045~pagePK:34370~

piPK:34424~theSitePK:4607,00.html (accessed 27 April 2010). The voting powers of the member states of the IBRD before the reform are shown in http://siteresources.worldbank.org/BODINT/Resources/278027–1215524804501/IBRDCountryVotingTable.pdf (accessed 27 April 2010). The quote is from Xin Zhiming, 'China gains more say in World Bank'. The official name of the G24 is the Intergovernmental Group of Twenty-Four on International Monetary Affairs and Development, of which China is not a formal member but has been a 'special invitee' since 1981 (www.g24.org).
22 Former finance minister of Spain.
23 Rodrigo Rato, 'How the IMF can help promote a collaborative solution to global imbalances', 4 April 2006, www.imf.org/external/np/speeches/2006/040406.htm (accessed 18 February 2011); *Weekend Herald*, New Zealand, 22 April 2006, p. C6.
24 David Gow, 'Cheap Chinese good? Blame America', *Guardian*, 29 November 2007, www.guardian.co.uk/business/2007/nov/29/china (accessed 18 February 2011).
25 Keith Bradsher, 'Rich in reserves, Chinese central bank is short of capital', *New York Times*, 5 September 2008, www.nytimes.com/2008/09/05/business/worldbusiness/05iht-05yuan.15914016.html (accessed 18 February 2011).
26 'China's foreign exchange reserves top 2.8 trillion USD in 2010', *People's Daily Online*, 12 January 2011, http://english.peopledaily.com.cn/90001/90778/7258242.html (accessed 18 February 2011).
27 UN University Report on Global Governance, 2 May 2001.
28 Karns and Mingst, *International Organizations*, p. 394.
29 Fu Jing, 'Nation urges more say in global finance', *China Daily*, 16 March 2009, www.chinadaily.com.cn/china/2009-03/16/content_7580323.htm (accessed 17 March 2009); 'China looking stronger after G-20 summit', *The Strait Times*, Internet edn, 4 April 2009. But the changes have yet to come into effect. Bob Davis, 'Developing nations try to build long-term leverage at the IMF', *Wall Street Journal Online*, 27 April 2009, http://online.wsj.com/article/SB124070499662656469.html (accessed 29 April 2009).
30 'Communiqué, meeting of finance ministers and central banks governors, Gyeongju, Republic of Korea, October 23, 2010', para. 5, www.g20.org/documents/201010_communique_gyeongju.pdf (accessed 27 October 2010); Bob Davis and Evan Ramstad, 'G-20 presses on with plan to cool currency battles', *Wall Street Journal Online*, 25 October 2010, http://online.wsj.com/article/SB10001424052702303864404575571912336670770.html (accessed 25 October 2010). Currently five (the US, Japan, Germany, France and the United Kingdom) of the twenty-four directors are appointed while the rest are elected by member countries or groups of countries. Altogether, the five Western countries hold 38.32 per cent of the total votes. IMF, 'IMF executive directors and voting power', 23 November 2010, www.imf.org/external/np/sec/memdir/eds.htm (accessed 21 December 2010).
31 'IMF executive board approves major overhaul of quotas and governance', *International Monetary Fund Press Release*, No. 10/418, 5 November 2010, www.imf.org/external/np/sec/pr/2010/pr10418.htm (accessed 21 December 2010). For details about individual members' quotas and voting rights, see 'IMF members' quotas and voting power, and IMF Board of Governors', 10 December 2010, www.imf.org/external/np/sec/memdir/members.htm (accessed 21 December 2010).
32 'G20's greatest win?', *The New Zealand Herald*, 17 March 2009, p. B2; Shi Jianxun, 'What is meant by re-apportioning China's IMF voting rights to 3rd', *People's Daily Online*, 26 October 2010, http://english.peopledaily.com.cn/90001/90780/91421/7178000.html (accessed 17 December 2010). The IMF requires an 85 per cent vote to make major decisions. This in effect gives the US, which holds 16.74 per cent of votes, veto power.
33 British Prime Minister Gordon Brown, the host of the London G20 summit, said that China would lend $40 billion to the IMF. But the IMF responded that China never committed to that amount and made no reference to China in its statement. Davis, 'Developing nations try to build long-term leverage at the IMF'; 'G-20 reaffirms

IMF's central role in combating crisis', IMF Survey Online, 3 April 2009, www.imf. org/external/pubs/survey/so/2009/NEW040309A.htm (accessed 7 April 2009).
34 According to a Chinese estimate, as a result of China's $40 billion contribution to the IMF, its voting rights would increase from 3.807 per cent to 3.997 per cent. See Xinhua, 'China raises financial status at G20', *China Daily*, 4 April 2009, www.chinadaily.com.cn/china/2009–04/04/content_7649423.htm (accessed 30 April 2009).
35 Geoff Dyer, 'Hesitating to take on global leadership', *Financial Times*, 1 April 2009, www.ft.com/cms/s/0/bc06204e-1d95-11de-9eb3-00144feabdc0.html (accessed 15 August 2011); Jamil Anderlini and Charles Clover, 'China explores buying $50bn in IMF bonds', *Financial Times*, 5 June 2009, www.ft.com/cms/s/0/6fee1d66-51ec-11de-b986-00144feabdc0.html (accessed 15 August 2011); Andrew Batson, 'China willing to buy as much as $50 billion in IMF bonds', *Wall Street Journal Online*, 6 June 2009, http://online.wsj.com/article/SB124419697110288633.html (accessed 8 June 2009).
36 Daniel Flynn, 'France scales back G20 monetary ambitions', Reuters, 14 January 2011, http://uk.mobile.reuters.com/article/stocksNews/idUKLNE70D00520110114 (21 January 2011); David Gauthier-Villars, 'France proposes way to raise yuan', *Wall Street Journal Online*, 25 January 2011, http://online.wsj.com/article/SB10001424052748703555804576101590792737426.html (accessed 25 January 2011).
37 Sewell Chan, 'G-20 vows to avoid a currency war', *New York Times*, 23 October 2010, www.nytimes.com/2010/10/24/business/global/24g20.html (accessed 17 December 2010); Don Lee and Christi Parsons, 'Key G-20 allies oppose U.S. proposal on trade', *Los Angeles Times*, 24 October 2010, through LexisNexis.
38 Xinhua News Agency, 'China urges IMF reform to reflect position of members', 23 October 2010, www.china.org.cn/english/international/229336.htm (accessed 17 December 2010); 'Q&A with Hu Jintao', *Wall Street Journal Online*, 16 January 2011, http://online.wsj.com/article/SB10001424052748703551604576085514147521334.html (accessed 17 January 2011). Hu made the statement in response to a question about what he thought would be the US dollar's future role in the world.
39 Lesley Wroughton, 'Lagarde to give China senior IMF job: sources', Reuters, Canada, 6 July 2011, http://ca.reuters.com/article/topNews/idCATRE7655JM20110706 (accessed 11 July 2011); 'Zhu Min nominated as Deputy Managing Director of IMF', *People's Daily Online*, 13 July 2011, http://english.peopledaily.com.cn/90001/90777/90856/7438176.html (accessed 14 July 2011).
40 'White paper on peaceful development road published', 22 December 2005, www.china.org.cn/english/2005/Dec/152669.htm (accessed 23 December 2010).
41 *South China Morning Post*, Internet edn, 12 December 2005.
42 Ibid.; www.chinaview.cn, 18 December 2005.
43 Susan Schwab, 'Chinese voices that oppose reform grow louder', *Financial Times*, 10 December 2006, www.ft.com/cms/s/0/6e3b8036–88bc-11db-b485–0000779e2340.html (accessed 18 February 2011).
44 The green room, named after the colour of the walls in the WTO director-general's office in Geneva, is the forum where actual, important decisions are hashed out before being presented to other economies for ratification in a wider setting. See *South China Morning Post*, 20 December 2005.
45 *Huanqiu shibao* (*Global Times*), 14 December 2005.
46 David Lague and Donald Greenlees, 'China officials take low-key role at WTO talks in Hong Kong', *New York Times*, 15 December 2005, www.nytimes.com/2005/12/15/business/worldbusiness/15iht-deals.html (accessed 15 August 2011).
47 PriceWaterhouseCoopers, *China's Free Trade Agreements: Lowering Landed Costs and Gaining Competitive Advantage*, 2009, www.pwccustoms.com/webmedia/doc/633910492656405807_fta_lower_land_cost.pdf (accessed 23 December 2010).
48 Raphael Minder and Richard McGregor, 'Asian nations keep on sidelines of debates', *Financial Times*, 4 December 2005, http://www.ft.com/cms/s/0/9def7a08-64f5-11da-8cff-0000779e2340.html (accessed 12 July 2011).

49 Ibid.
50 Yu Yongding, 'Jueqi de Zhongguo yu qiguo jituan ershiguo jituan' (The rise of China and the G7 and G20), *Guoji jingji pinglun (International Economic Review)*, No. 5 (2004), pp. 9–12.
51 'What is the G-20', https://www.g20.org/about_what_is_g20.aspx (accessed 2 November 2009).
52 'G20 statement on global development issues', G20 Information Centre, University of Toronto, 16 October 2005, www.g20.utoronto.ca/2005/2005development.html (accessed 23 December 2010).
53 'Full text of G20 statement on reforming Bretton Woods institutions', G20 Information Centre, University of Toronto, 16 October 2005, www.g20.utoronto.ca/2005/2005bwi.html (accessed 23 December 2010).
54 Chan, 'G-20 vows to avoid a currency war'; Lee and Parsons, 'Key G-20 allies oppose U.S. proposal on trade'.
55 Chen Suquan, 'Ershiguo jituan zai quanqiu jinrong yu jingji zhili zhong de juese fenxi' (An analysis of the role of the G20 in the global financial and economic governance), *Shijie jingji yu zhengzhi luntan* (*World Economic and Politics Forum*), No. 4 (2009), pp. 1–7; Zhang Haibing, 'Ershiguo jituan Jizhihua de qushi ji yingxiang' (G20's institutionalization: trends and impacts), *Shijie jingji yanjiu* (*World Economy Study*), No. 9 (2010), pp. 8–12.
56 Ao Yunbo, 'Ershiguo jituan de jueqi yu Zhongguo waijiao duice' (The rise of the G20 and China's diplomatic policy), *Shehuizhuyi yanjiao* (*Socialism Studies*), No. 4 (2010), pp. 122–6.
57 'Time to decide who should steer world economy', Reuters, Internet edn, 26 September 2005.
58 For a succinct elaboration, see Bi Jianhai, 'An Asian monetary fund?', *New Zealand International Review*, Vol. 34, No. 6 (November/December 2009), pp. 8–11.
59 As of June 2008 China's holding of US Treasury securities amounted to $1,205 billion while China's foreign reserves at the same time were $1,808 billion. Wayne M. Morrison and Marc Labonte, *China's Holding of U.S. Securities: Implications for the U.S. Economy*, CRS Report for Congress RL34314 (Washington, DC: Congressional Research Service, 2009), p. 4, www.fas.org/sgp/crs/row/RL34314.pdf; 'China's foreign exchange reserves, 1977–2010', www.chinability.com/Reserves.htm (accessed 18 February 2011).
60 Daniel W. Drezner, 'Bad debts: assessing China's financial influence in great power politics', *International Security*, Vol. 34, No. 2 (Fall 2009), pp. 7–45.
61 Ibid., p. 20.
62 The other factors are decline in lending standards and 'innovations' of the US banking sector; and the Federal Reserve adopted a lax interest rate policy. They also contributed to an unprecedented credit expansion in the US. Markus K. Brunnermeier, 'Deciphering the liquidity and credit crunch 2007–2008', *Journal of Economic Perspectives*, Vol. 23, No. 1 (Winter 2009), pp. 77–100.
63 *China Statistical Yearbook 2009*, p. 724.
64 The following account of the cause of the global financial crisis draws on Randall Dodd, 'Subprime: tentacles of a crisis', *Finance & Development*, Vol. 44, No. 4 (December 2007), pp. 15–19; Randall Dodd and Paul Mills, 'Outbreak: U.S. subprime contagion', *Finance & Development*, Vol. 45, No. 2 (June 2008), pp. 14–18; Ricardo I. Caballero, Emmanuel Farhi and Pierre-Olivier Gourinchas, 'Financial crash, commodity prices, and global imbalances', *Brookings Papers on Economic Activity*, Fall 2008, pp. 1–55; Brunnermeier, 'Deciphering the liquidity and credit crunch 2007–2008'; Leonard Seabrooke, 'What do I get? The everyday politics of expectations and the subprime crisis', *New Political Economy*, Vol. 15, No. 1 (March 2010), pp. 51–70.

65 They were the least risky or senior tranche with the highest triple-A credit rating, the middle or mezzanine tranche with below-investment-grade credit rating, and the usually unrated lowest or equity tranche. It was erroneously assumed that as they were sold separately and had different levels of risk, the three tranches would not collapse simultaneously.
66 This process of transforming a relatively illiquid asset (e.g. bank loans) into securities that can be bought and sold to other interested parties is called 'securitization'.
67 Maurice Obstfeld and Kenneth Rogoff, 'Global imbalances and the financial crisis: products of common cause', November 2009, paper prepared for the Federal Reserve Bank of San Francisco Asia Economic Policy Conference, Santa Barbara, CA, 18–20 October 2009, http://elsa.berkeley.edu/~obstfeld/santabarbara.pdf (accessed 30 April 2010); Richard Portes, 'Global imbalances', in Mathias Dewatripont, Xavier Freixas and Richard Portes (eds), *Macroeconomic Stability and Financial Regulation: Key Issues for the G20* (London: Centre for Economic Policy Research, 2009), pp. 19–26, www.voxeu.org/reports/G20_ebook.pdf (accessed 28 April 2010); Krishna Guha, 'Paulson says crisis sown by imbalance', *Financial Times*, 1 January 2009, www.ft.com/cms/s/0/ff671f66-d838-11dd-bcc0-000077b07658.html (accessed 30 April 2010); Roger C. Altman, 'The great crash, 2008: a geopolitical setback for the West', *Foreign Affairs*, January/February 2009, pp. 2–14; Steven Dunaway, *Global Imbalances and the Financial Crisis*, Council on Foreign Relations Special Report No. 44 (Washington, DC: Council on Foreign Relations, 2009), www.cfr.org/publication/18690 (accessed 30 April 2010); Martin Wolf, *Fixing Global Finance: How to Curb Financial Crises in the 21st Century* (New Haven, CT, and London: Yale University Press, 2010), Chapter 8. Portes in particular argues that greed, flawed incentives and regulatory deficiencies happened in the past financial crises. What was new to the crisis of 2007–2009 was the macroeconomic environment. Many of the financial excesses were brought about by global macroeconomic imbalances. A counter-argument is provided by Karl Whelan, 'Global imbalances and the financial crisis', Committee on Economic and Monetary Affairs, European Parliament, 8 March 2010, www.europarl.europa.eu/document/activities/cont/201003/20100309ATT70296/20100309ATT70296EN.pdf (accessed 30 April 2010). Whelan posits that largely due to financial globalization, there would have been plenty of foreign funds entering the US financial market even if the US had not had any trade deficit at all. The fact that many European banks invested in subprime mortgage securities while the trade balance between the US and the EU remained even demonstrated that.
68 Obstfeld and Rogoff, 'Global imbalances and the financial crisis', pp. 15, 17.
69 Ben S. Bernanke, 'The global saving glut and the U.S. current account deficit', remarks by Governor Ben S. Bernanke at the Sandridge Lecture, Virginia Association of Economics, Richmond, VA, www.federalreserve.gov/boarddocs/speeches/2005/200503102 (accessed 1 May 2010).
70 This can in theory continue as long as the interest rates of buying US assets are higher than those paid to the holders of domestic government bonds.
71 Obstfeld and Rogoff, 'Global imbalances and the financial crisis', p. 37.
72 Morris Goldstein and Nicholas R. Lardy, *The Future of China's Exchange Policy* (Washington, DC: Peterson Institute for International Economics, 2009), pp. 24–6. From October 1997 to July 2005 China's nominal exchange rate against the US dollar was pegged at Rmb8.28. However, as soon as the dollar began to depreciate in February 2002, the renminbi depreciated on a real effective basis. According to the IMF, if the Chinese real effective exchange rate in 2000 is 100, the rate of the following years will be 104.30 (2001), 101.89 (2002), 95.21 (2003), 92.70 (2004), 92.49 (2005), 94.42 (2006) and 99.10 (2007). International Monetary Fund, *International Financial Statistics Yearbook 2008* (Washington, DC: International Monetary Fund, 2008), p. 219. See Goldstein and Lardy, *The Future of China's Exchange Policy*, p. 11, for an explanation of the real effective exchange rate.

73 Geoff Dyer, 'Brazil and India add to pressure on China', *Financial Times*, 21 April 2010, www.ft.com/cms/s/0/1d692fd2-4d1c-11df-baf3-00144feab49a.html (accessed 22 April 2010).
74 Yu Yongding, 'Global imbalances and China', *Australian Economic Review*, Vol. 40, No. 1 (2007), pp. 3–23 at p. 18.
75 Phillip L. Swagel, 'Yuan answers?', American Enterprise Institute for Public Policy Research, June 2005, www.aei.org/docLib/20050622_2118596Swagel_g.pdf (accessed 2 May 2010).
76 This is echoed by Yang Yao, 'Renminbi adjustment will not cure trade imbalance', *Financial Times*, 11 April 2010, www.ft.com/cms/s/0/76d54674-4596-11df-9e46-00144feab49a,dwp_uuid=9c33700c-4c86-11da-89df-0000779e2340.html (accessed 30 April 2010). The writer is the director of the China Centre for Economic Research at Peking University and the editor of *China Economic Quarterly*.
77 'Implementation plan for the recent priorities of the health care system reform (2009–2011)', www.china.org.cn/government/scio-press-conferences/2009-04/09/content_17575401.htm (accessed 8 May 2010).
78 'Announcement of the Ministers of Finance and Central Bank Governors of France, Germany, Japan, the United Kingdom, and the United States (Plaza Accord)', 22 September 1985, www.aei.org/docLib/20050622_2118596Swagel_g.pdf (accessed 2 May 2010).
79 The micro-factors Zhou suggests include

> problems with credit rating agencies, mark to market and fair value accounting rules, problems with financial institutions including lax lending standards, excessive leverage and deficient corporate governance, frivolous development of derivative products, chaos in the originate-to-distribute models of asset securitisation, and etc.

Zhou Xiaochuan, 'Address at the Global Think-Tank Summit', Beijing, 3 July 2009, www.pbc.gov.cn/english//detail.asp?col=6500&ID=183 (accessed 2 May 2010).
80 'China vice minister: yuan rise won't fix U.S. trade imbalance', *Wall Street Journal Online*, 5 January 2010, http://online.wsj.com/article/SB10001424052748704723104576062862747418524.html (accessed 6 January 2010). Processing trade (*jiagong maoyi*) refers to the importation of duty-free raw materials and parts and the subsequent exportation of finished goods.
81 After US Treasury Secretary Timothy Geithner paid a brief visit to Beijing on 8 April 2010, holding talks with Chinese Vice-Premier Wang Qishan, it was expected that Beijing would soon slightly appreciate the renminbi and allow it to move more freely on a day-to-day basis. However, this did not happen. Keith Bradsher, 'China seems set to loosen hold on its currency', *New York Times*, 8 April 2010, www.nytimes.com/2010/04/09/business/global/09yuan.html (accessed 3 May 2010); Simon Derrick, 'When will China change yuan policy?', *BBC News*, 8 April 2010, http://news.bbc.co.uk/1/hi/business/8609007.stm (accessed 6 May 2010).
82 Fran O'Sullivan, 'China ready to back NZ's UN bid', *Weekend Herald*, Auckland, 19 June 2010, p. A19.
83 Wayne M. Morrison and Marc Labonte, *China's Currency: An Analysis of the Economic Issues*, Congressional Research Service Report for Congress RS21625 (Washington, DC: Congressional Research Service, 2010), http://assets.opencrs.com/rpts/RS21625_20101001.pdf (accessed 25 December 2010).
84 Tim Webb, 'World gripped by "international currency war"', *Guardian*, 28 September 2010, www.guardian.co.uk/business/2010/sep/28/world-in-international-currency-war-warns-brazil (accessed 23 December 2010); Jonathan Wheatley and Peter Granham, 'Brazil in global "currency war" alert', *Financial Times*, 28 September 2010, through LexisNexis. Brazil's President Dilma Rousseff, who took office on 1 January 2011, was expected to discuss the value of the renmimbi during her visit to

Beijing in April 2011. John Lyons and Matthew Cowley, 'Brazil is poised to pressure Beijing on currency policy', *Wall Street Journal Online*, 4 January 2010, http://online.wsj.com/article/SB10001424052748704835504576060211379610444.html (accessed 5 January 2011).

85 Ralph Atkins, Quentin Peel, Peggy Hollinger and Alan Beattie, 'Rift lowers hopes for G20 breakthrough', *Financial Times*, 18 February 2011, www.ft.com/cms/s/582f27d2-3b75-11e0-9970-00144feabdc0.html; Xinhua, 'G20 members divided over imbalance indicators', www.china.org.cn/business/2011-02/19/content_21958571.htm; Ralph Atkins and Quentin Peel, 'G20 strikes compromise on global imbalances', *Financial Times*, 19 February 2011, www.ft.com/cms/s/0/1a12713e-3c56-11e0-b073-00144feabdc0.html; Ian Telley, Paul Hannon and Costas Paris, 'China agrees to international scrutiny of yuan policy', *Wall Street Journal Online*, 19 February 2011, http://online.wsj.com/article/SB1000142405274870340730457615441 3705164454.html (accessed 23 February 2011).

86 Zhou Xiaochuan, 'Reform the international monetary system', The People's Bank of China, 23 March 2009, www.pbc.gov.cn/english/detail.asp?col=6500&id=178 (accessed 5 May 2010); 'China goes to G20 summit with reform proposal', *China Daily*, 1 April 2009, www.chinadaily.com/china/2009-04/01/content_7640191.htm (accessed 2 April 2009). Zhou's proposal is regarded as impractical because at the time of making it, the total special drawing rights outstanding amounted to merely $32 billion, almost nothing compared to $11,000 billion of US Treasury bonds. 'Handle with care: the dollar as a reserve currency', *The Economist*, 28 March 2009, through LexisNexis. Some senior Chinese officials allegedly pointed out that the initiative was simply 'meant to mollify domestic critics of China's lacklustre investments in US equities'. Evans S. Medeiros, 'Is Beijing ready for global leadership?', *Current History*, September 2009, pp. 250–6 at p. 255.

87 When the South Korea Finance Minister, Yoon Jeung-hyun visited the IMF in April 2010, he advised Dominique Strauss-Kahn not to repeat the mishandling of the Asian financial crisis by Michel Camdessus, the former Managing Director. The Minister was quoted as saying that 'the IMF has had an image problem in Korea because of its actions taken during the Asian crisis, and ... [the IMF] should try to improve the image by more actively listening to the voices of emerging nations'. Cho Jin-seo, 'Finance minister admonishes IMF', *Korea Times*, 27 April 2010, through LexisNexis.

88 Alan Beattie, 'Change in voting may be more symbol than substance', *Financial Times*, 11 November 2010, through LexisNexis.

89 Sewell Chan, 'I.M.F. lends its support to charging bank fees', *New York Times*, 20 April 2010, www.nytimes.com/2010/04/21/business/global/21fund.html (accessed 4 May 2010).

90 Wang Xu, 'Groundwork laid to reform global financial systems', *China Daily*, 24 November 2008, www.chinadaily.com.cn/bizchina/2008-11/24/content_7232819.htm (accessed 25 November 2008); 'Asian leaders see growth driver', *Wall Street Journal Online*, 15 December 2008, http://online.wsj.com/article/SB122928619846704835.html (accessed 15 December 2008).

5 Human rights and humanitarian intervention

1 Permanent Mission of the People's Republic of China to the United Nations Office at Geneva and Other International Organizations in Switzerland, 'Statement by H.E. Ambassador SHA Zukang, head of the Chinese delegation, on item 9 at the 59th session of the Commission on Human Rights (1 April 2003, Geneva) ', 16 April 2004, http://big5.fmprc.gov.cn/gate/big5/www.china-un.ch/eng/rqrd/thsm/t85158.htm (accessed 4 December 2010).

2 Christian Tomuschat, *Human Rights: Between Idealism and Realism* (Oxford: Oxford University Press, 2008), pp. 25–68.

218 *Notes*

3 Bertrand G. Ramcharan, 'Norms and machinery', in Thomas G. Weiss and Sam Daws (eds), *The Oxford Handbook on the United Nations* (Oxford: Oxford University Press, 2007), pp. 441–2.
4 Eleanor Roosevelt, 'Adoption of the Declaration of Human Rights', 9 December 1948, www.udhr.org/history/ergeas48.htm (accessed 6 December 2010).
5 Richard Jolly, Louis Emmerij and Thomas G. Weiss, *UN Ideas that Changed the World* (Bloomington, IN: Indiana University Press, 2009), p. 56. It is claimed that the Western states, and the Soviet Union and its Eastern European allies, formed an 'unholy alliance'. Philip Alston, 'The Commission on Human Rights', in idem (ed.), *The United Nations and Human Rights: A Critical Appraisal* (Oxford: Clarendon Press, 1992), p. 141.
6 Julie A. Mertus, *The United Nations and Human Rights: A Guide for a New Era* (Abingdon: Routledge, 2005), pp. 54–5; Thomas G. Weiss and Ramesh Thakur, *Global Governance and the UN: An Unfinished Journey* (Bloomington, IN: Indiana University Press, 2010), p. 266.
7 UN General Assembly Resolution 41/128, 4 December 1986, www.un.org/documents/ga/res/41/a41r128.htm (accessed 7 December 2010).
8 Mertus, *The United Nations and Human Rights*, pp. 13–14. The eight countries were Denmark, Finland, the Federal Republic of Germany, Iceland, Israel, Japan, Sweden and the United Kingdom. Arjun Sengupta, 'On the theory and practice of the right to development', *Human Rights Quarterly*, Vol. 24, No. 4 (2002), p. 840, note 10.
9 Jolly *et al.*, *UN Ideas that Changed the World*, pp. 58–9. For a discussion of the debates about the validity of the right to development, see Sengupta, 'On the theory and practice of the right to development', pp. 857–76.
10 International Commission on Intervention and State Sovereignty, *The Responsibility to Protect*, 2001, p. xi, www.iciss.ca/report-en.asp (accessed 24 July 2007).
11 Kofi Annan, 'Two concepts of sovereignty', *The Economist*, 18 September 1999, through LexisNexis; United Nations General Assembly, 'World Summit outcome', United Nations Document A/60/L/1, 15 September 2005, para. 138–40, www.un.org/summit2005/documents.html (accessed 26 July 2007). With reservations from the US, China and Russia about the R2P report, it was agreed in the World Summit that forcible humanitarian intervention must have prior UNSC authorization. See Alex J. Bellamy and Nicholas J. Wheeler, 'Humanitarian intervention in world politics', in John Baylis, Steve Smith and Patricia Owens (eds), *The Globalization of World Politics: An Introduction to International Relations* (Oxford: Oxford University Press, 2008), pp. 537–8. The 2005 World Summit is discussed in detail in Alex J. Bellamy, *Responsibility to Protect: The Global Effort to End Mass Atrocities* (Cambridge: Polity Press, 2009), pp. 66–97.
12 The Sub-Commission was made up of twenty-six 'independent experts', and its annual meetings in August were attended by non-governmental and intergovernmental organizations and government representatives. Ann Kent, *China, the United Nations, and Human Rights: The Limits of Compliance* (Philadelphia, PA: University of Pennsylvania Press, 1999), pp. 54–5.
13 Initially ECOSOC Resolution 1235 was aimed at apartheid in South Africa and racial discrimination in Southern Rhodesia. But the coup in Greece in April 1967, resulting in the formation of the 'Regime of the Colonels' between 1967 and 1974, prompted the Commission to use the authority under the Resolution to investigate human rights situations beyond southern Africa. ECOSOC further established in Resolution 1503 a confidential procedure for considering complaints of, and monitoring, 'gross and reliably attested violations of human rights' in any countries, defying the opposition of Communist and developing countries. The path-breaking ECOSOC Resolution 1235 (1967) and Resolution 1503 (1970) are available at the University of Minnesota Human Rights Library, http://www1.umn.edu/humanrts/procedures/1235.html; http://www1.umn.edu/humanrts/procedures/1503.html (accessed 13 September 2010). See

Notes   219

also Joan Fitzpatrick, *Human Rights in Crisis: The International System for Protecting Rights during States of Emergency* (Philadelphia, PA: University of Pennsylvania Press, 1994), p. 118.
14 Mertus, *The United Nations and Human Rights*, p. 56; Weiss and Thakur, *Global Governance and the UN*, p. 268; Secretary-General's High-level Panel on Threats, Challenges and Change, *A More Secure World: Our Shared Responsibility* (New York: United Nations, 2004), para. 283, www.un.org/secureworld/ (accessed 29 September 2010).
15 The membership was distributed by geographical regions: fifteen from Africa, twelve from Asia, five from Eastern Europe, eleven from Latin America and the Caribbean and ten from Western Europe and other states.
16 Qiu Guirong, 'Lianheguo renquan lingyu gaige ji qi yingxiang' (Reform of the domain of human rights in the United Nations and its impact), *Xiandai guoji guanxi (Contemporary International Relations)*, No. 7 (2007), pp. 30–35; Wu Xiaoming, 'Cong Lianheguo renquan lishihui kan guoji renquan fa de fazhan' (Observing the development of international human rights law from the United Nations Human Rights Council), *Jingji yanjiu daokan (Economic Research Guide)*, No. 11 (2010), pp. 228–9. This is despite the fact that Qian Qichen, the former Chinese State Councillor and Foreign Minister, was a member of the High-level Panel.
17 Annan's report, *In Larger Freedom: Towards Development, Security and Human Rights for All*, is available at www.un.org/largerfreedom/ (accessed 29 September 2010).
18 The members of the dismantled HRC was elected by ECOSOC by simple majority, i.e. twenty-eight votes out of fifty-four.
19 Initially it was proposed that members be chosen by a two-thirds vote of the General Assembly. Jolly et al., *UN Ideas that Changed the World*, p. 63; Thomas G. Weiss, David P. Forsythe, Roger A. Coate and Kelly-Kate Pease, *The United Nations and Changing World Politics* (Boulder, CO: Westview Press, 2010), p. 201.
20 Libya was first elected to the body in May 2010. United Nations Human Rights Council, 'Membership of the Human Rights Council', http://www2.ohchr.org/english/bodies/hrcouncil/membership.htm; 'Human Rights Council elections', http://www2.ohchr.org/english/bodies/hrcouncil/elections.htm (accessed 13 September 2010). See also Weiss and Thakur, *Global Governance and the UN*, p. 270; Yvonne Terlingen, 'The Human Rights Council: a new era in UN human rights work?', *Ethics & International Affairs*, Vol. 21, No. 2 (Summer 2007), p. 172.
21 There was a reduction of six seats from the UNCHR to the UNHRC.
22 UN General Assembly Resolution 60/251, 3 April 2006, http://www2.ohchr.org/english/bodies/hrcouncil/docs/A.RES.60.251_En.pdf (accessed 29 September 2010). The High-level Panel called for creating a Human Rights Council which would be a Charter-based body on a par with the Security Council and ECOSOC. Secretary-General's High-level Panel on Threats, Challenges and Change, *A More Secure World*, para. 291. Due to the cumbersome procedures involved in any formal amendment of the UN Charter, it was later decided to establish the Council as a subsidiary body of the General Assembly. Weiss et al., *The United Nations and Changing World Politics*, p. 201. Yvonne Terlingen, however, argues that it was due to the opposition of 'some key developing countries'. Terlingen, 'The Human Rights Council', p. 170.
23 United Nations General Assembly Resolution 60/251, p. 3.
24 Margaret P. Karns and Karen A. Mingst, *International Organizations: The Politics and Processes of Global Governance* (Boulder, CO: Lynne Rienner, 2010), p. 460.
25 Patrizia Scannella and Peter Splinter, 'The United Nations Human Rights Council: a promise to be fulfilled', *Human Rights Law Review*, Vol. 7, No. 1 (2007), p. 64.
26 They are: Human Rights Committee, Committee on Economic, Social and Cultural Rights, Committee on the Elimination of Racial Discrimination, Committee on the Elimination of Discrimination Against Women, Committee Against Torture, Committee on the Rights of the Child, Committee on Migrant Workers, and Committee on the

Rights of Persons with Disabilities. Office of the High Commissioner for Human Rights, 'Human rights bodies', www.ohchr.org/EN/HRBodies/Pages/HumanRightsBodies.aspx (accessed 22 September 2010).
27 Office of the High Commissioner for Human Rights, 'Special procedures of the Human Rights Council', http://www2.ohchr.org/english/bodies/chr/special/index.htm (accessed 9 December 2010). Because the system of country mandates attracted much criticism during the discussion of the country reports on Belarus and Cuba in June 2007, the offices of special rapporteur for Belarus and Cuba were abolished. William French, 'UN rights body scraps Cuba, Belarus experts under new rules', Agence France Presse, 19 June 2007, through LexisNexis; Tomuschat, *Human Rights*, p. 149.
28 For details, see Mertus, *The United Nations and Human Rights*, pp. 8–43.
29 The 2004 data are from ibid., p. 15; the rest is from the Office of the High Commissioner for Human Rights, 'Funding and budget', www.ohchr.org/EN/AboutUs/Pages/FundingBudget.aspx (accessed 2 December 2010). It is said that the operation of the Office is hampered by the small regular budget. Karns and Mingst, *International Organizations*, p. 461.
30 The regional offices cover East Africa, Southern Africa, Central America, Latin America, Southeast Asia, the Middle East and the Pacific. In addition, there is a Regional Centre for Human Rights and Democracy for Central Asia. Office of the High Commissioner for Human Rights, 'OHCHR in the world: making human rights a reality on the ground', www.ohchr.org/EN/Countries/Pages/WorkInField.aspx (accessed 2 December 2010).
31 See the UNSC Resolution 232 (1966) and 418 (1977) respectively; Mertus, *The United Nations and Human Rights*, p. 123.
32 Mertus, *The United Nations and Human Rights*, pp. 123–4.
33 Kent, *China, the United Nations, and Human Rights*, p. 43.
34 The Republic of China was a UNCHR member in 1947–63. For details about China's membership of both the Commission on Human Rights and the Human Rights Council, see Office of the United Nations High Commissioner for Human Rights, 'Commission on Human Rights membership', http://www2.ohchr.org/english/bodies/chr/membership.htm, and United Nations Human Rights Council, 'Membership of the Human Rights Council', http://www2.ohchr.org/english/bodies/hrcouncil/membership.htm (accessed 13 September 2010).
35 The report is available at UN Human Rights Council, http://daccess-dds-ny.un.org/doc/UNDOC/GEN/G09/162/99/PDF/G0916299.pdf?OpenElement (accessed 23 September 2010).
36 Kent, *China, the United Nations, and Human Rights*, p. 55. As will be discussed below, China came under the spotlight when the Sub-Commission was in session in August 1989.
37 A list of the mandate-holders is available in the Office of the United Nations High Commissioner for Human Rights, 'Special Procedures of the Human Rights Council', http://www2.ohchr.org/english/bodies/chr/special/index.htm (accessed 28 September 2010).
38 The Office of United Nations High Commissioner for Human Rights, 'United Nations Special Procedures: facts and figures 2009', http://www2.ohchr.org/english/bodies/chr/special/docs/Facts_Figures2009.pdf (accessed 28 September 2010).
39 Katie Lee, 'China and the International Covenant on Civil and Political Rights: prospects and challenges', *Chinese Journal of International Law*, Vol. 6, No. 2 (2007), pp. 445–74.
40 Cited in Oliver Hoehne, 'Special procedures and the new Human Rights Council – a need for strategic positioning', *Essex Human Rights Review*, Vol. 4, No. 1 (2007), p. 8, http://projects.essex.ac.uk/ehrr/V4N1/Hoehne.pdf (accessed 29 September 2010).
41 Yang Jiechi, 'Hexie hezuo kaichuang guoji renquan shiye xin jumian' (Harmony and cooperation: to start a new phase of international human rights undertakings),

Renquan (*Human Rights*), No. 4 (2006), pp. 6–7. The author was a Vice-Minister of Foreign Affairs and the speech was delivered to the first meeting of the UNHRC in June 2006. Jiang Guoqing and Xiong Zhiqiang, 'Lianheguo Renquan Lishihui falu zhidu tanxi' (On the legal system of the United Nations Human Rights Council), *Waijiao pinglun* (*Foreign Affairs Review*), August 2006, pp. 21–8.

42 Ministry of Foreign Affairs, China, 'Statement by H.E. SHA Zukang, on behalf of the Like Minded Group, at the meeting between the president of the General Assembly and the Commission on Human Rights', 25 November 2005, www.fmprc.gov.cn/eng/wjb/zwjg/zwbd/t223170.htm (accessed 8 December 2010). The Like-Minded Group is composed of Algeria, Bangladesh, Belarus, Bhutan, China, Cuba, Egypt, India, Indonesia, Iran, Malaysia, Myanmar, Nepal, Pakistan, the Philippines, Sri Lanka, Sudan, Syria, Vietnam and Zimbabwe.

43 'Embassies represented at the Nobel Peace Prize ceremony on December 10', Norwegian Nobel Committee, 14 December 2010, http://nobelpeaceprize.org/en_GB/embassies-2010/ (accessed 1 January 2011).

44 Kent, *China, the United Nations, and Human Rights*, p. 50. Due to space limitations, only the country-specific resolutions and special procedures are discussed in this chapter.

45 Rosemary Foot, *Rights beyond Borders: The Global Community and the Struggle over Human Rights in China* (Oxford: Oxford University Press, 2000), pp. 118–20; Kent, *China, the United Nations, and Human Rights*, pp. 52, 56–60.

46 Embassy of the People's Republic of China in the United States, 'US won't rap China on human rights', 18 March 2005, www.china-embassy.org/eng/zt/zgrq/t188036.htm (accessed 1 October 2010).

47 China's move was unique in the sense that no other country resorted to a 'no action' motion to prevent debate on its own human rights conditions. Foot, *Rights beyond Borders*, pp. 178, 194.

48 From 1994 onwards, the Sub-Commission did not discuss country situations that were covered by the parent Commission. Ibid., pp. 121, 132, 175.

49 Ibid., p. 196.

50 Wang Dongrong, 'Lun Lianheguo Renquan Lishihui de zhidu chuangxin: bijiao de shijiao' (On the institutional innovations of the United Nations Human Rights Council: a comparative perspective), *Fazhi yu shehui* (*Legal System and Society*), No. 9 (2006), pp. 208–2009; Luo Yanhua, 'Lianheguo Renquan Lishihui de sheli ji qi beihou de douzheng' (The establishment of the United Nations Human Rights Council and the struggle behind it), *Renquan* (*Human Rights*), No. 3 (2006), pp. 54–7.

51 Interview in Geneva, November 2010.

52 'Agreement reached on UN rights council rules', Agence France Presse, 18 June 2007; William French, 'China blocks consensus on UN rights council rules', Agence France Presse, 18 June 2007; 'China defends holding up adoption of UNHRC's new working rules', The Press Trust of India, 20 June 2007, all through LexisNexis.

53 Qiu Guirong, 'Lianheguo renquan lingyu gaige ji qi yingxiang' (Reform of the domain of human rights in the United Nations and its impact), p. 32; 'UN human rights: China's proposal on country-specific resolutions make headway, says FM spokesman', Xinhua General News Service, 19 June 2007, through LexisNexis; French, 'UN rights body scraps Cuba, Belarus experts under new rules'.

54 One of the recommendations was to appoint Special Rapporteurs on the basis of equitable geographical distribution rather than of professional background. Foot, *Rights beyond Borders*, pp. 178–83, 188, 196, 205, 270.

55 Karns and Mingst, *International Organizations*, p. 469. The Special Rapporteur noted the 'continuing practice of torture in China', despite the fact that there was reduced use of it in urban areas. The Special Rapporteur, Manfred Nowak, also indicated that the Chinese Ministry of State Security obstructed his mission while the Ministry of Foreign Affairs was very helpful. Commission on Human Rights, 'Report of the

Special Rapporteur on torture and other cruel, inhuman or degrading treatment or punishment, Manfred Nowak, Mission to China', 30 March 2006, p. 2, http://daccess-dds-ny.un.org/doc/UNDOC/GEN/G06/117/50/PDF/G0611750.pdf; 'An interview with Manfred Nowak, UN Special Rapporteur on Torture', *Dialogue* (The Duihua Foundation), Winter 2006, www.duihua.org/hrjournal/20071007_interview_un-sr.pdf (accessed 6 December 2010).

56 'China supports creating new UN council despite deficiencies', Xinhua General News Service, 15 March 2006, through LexisNexis; Jiang Guoqing and Xiong Zhiqiang, 'Lianheguo Renquan Lishihui falu zhidu tanxi' (On the legal system of the United Nations Human Rights Council); Luo Yanhua, 'Lianheguo Renquan Lishihui de sheli ji qi beihou de douzheng' (The establishment of the United Nations Human Rights Council and the struggle behind it).

57 Scannella and Splinter, 'The United Nations Human Rights Council', p. 45. Terlingen warns that it is imperative to 'preserve and strengthen the system of Special Rapportuers and to defeat attempts by some members to weaken their independence'. Terlingen, 'The Human Rights Council', p. 177.

58 Weiss *et al.*, *The United Nations and Changing World Politics*, pp. 202–203.

59 There were debates as to whether the new Council had paid undue attention to the Palestine issue. Nico Schrijver, 'The UN Human Rights Council: a new "society of the committed" or just old wine in new bottles?', *Leiden Journal of International Law*, Vol. 20 (2007), p. 820.

60 Human Rights Council, '4th Special session of the Human Rights Council on the human rights situation in Darfur, Geneva, 12–13 December 2006', http://www2.ohchr.org/english/bodies/hrcouncil/specialsession/4/index.htm (accessed 4 October 2010). But the group was refused entry into Sudan. Schrijver, 'The UN Human Rights Council', p. 820.

61 In the replaced HRC, they had twenty-seven seats or just 51 per cent of the votes.

62 Human Rights Council, 'Human rights situations that require the Council attention: progress report of the Special Rapporteur on the situation of human rights in Myanmar, Tomás Ojea Quintana', 10 March 2010, para. 121, http://www2.ohchr.org/english/bodies/hrcouncil/docs/13session/A-HRC-13-48.pdf (accessed 16 December 2010); Colum Lynch, 'China campaign against Burma war crimes inquiry', *Washington Post*, 26 October 2010, www.washingtonpost.com/wp-dyn/content/article/2010/10/25/AR2010102505462.html (accessed 16 December 2010).

63 Ministry of Foreign Affairs, China, 'Statement by H.E. SHA Zukang, on behalf of the Like Minded Group, at the meeting between the president of the General Assembly and the Commission on Human Rights'; Terlingen, 'The Human Rights Council', p. 171.

64 Kofi Annan, *In Larger Freedom*, Addendum 1, para. 4.

65 Terlingen, 'The Human Rights Council', p. 176. There were four special sessions in 2006, one in 2007, three in 2008, four in 2009 and one in January 2010. Human Rights Council, http://www2.ohchr.org/english/bodies/hrcouncil/specialsession (accessed 4 October 2010).

66 Xiao Wei, 'Fazhan, renquan yu minzhu' (Development, human rights and democracy), *Zhonggong zhongyang dangxiao xuebao* (*Journal of the Party School of the Central Committee of the Chinese Communist Party*), Vol. 14, No. 2 (2010), pp. 57–61.

67 United Nations General Assembly Resolution 60/251, p. 2; Schrijver, 'The UN Human Rights Council', p. 817.

68 Foot, *Rights beyond Borders*, p. 271.

69 Tomuschat, *Human Rights*, pp. 57–60.

70 See Human Rights Council, A/HRC/4/L.16, 28 March 2007, http://daccess-dds-ny.un.org/doc/UNDOC/LTD/G07/122/46/PDF/G0712246.pdf (accessed 8 December 2010).

71 Weiss *et al.*, *The United Nations and Changing World Politics*, p. 214.

72 Karns and Mingst, *International Organizations*, p. 476.

73 UNDP, *Human Development Report 2009*, p. 172, http://hdr.undp.org/en/media/HDR_2009_EN_Complete.pdf (accessed 19 October 2010).
74 This section draws on Pak K. Lee, Gerald Chan and Lai-Ha Chan, 'China in Darfur: humanitarian rule-taker or rule-maker?', *Review of International Studies* (2011).
75 David Chang, 'Taiwan watches Kosovo's independence', *China Post*, 18 February 2008, www.chinapost.com.tw/taiwan/2008/02/18/143322/Taiwan-watches.htm; 'ICJ, Kosovo and Taiwan's future', *Taiwan News Online*, 3 August 2010, www.etaiwannews.com/etn/news_content.php?id=1330828&lang=eng_news&cate_rss=news_Editorial (accessed 10 August 2010).
76 In defending his country's stance on Darfur, Liu Guijin, China's special representative on the Darfur issue, said, 'It is not China's Darfur, it is first Sudan's Darfur and then Africa's Darfur'. Cited in Mure Dickie, 'China defends its stance on Darfur', *Financial Times*, 28 July 2007, through Factiva.
77 'Chinese President puts forward four-point principle on solving Darfur issue', Xinhua News Agency, 3 February 2007, through Factiva; Xinhua, 'Chinese President wraps up Africa tour', *China Daily*, 11 February 2007, www.chinadaily.com.cn/china/2007-02/11/content_806503.htm (accessed 19 June 2010).
78 Bellamy, *Responsibility to Protect*, p. 153.
79 Sudan made it be known in April 2007 that '[t]he force will be hybrid only in that the UN will provide the funding' and that the UN 'could provide technicians and office worker *but no combat troops*'. Gérard Prunier, *Darfur: A 21st Century Genocide* (Ithaca, NY: Cornell University Press, 2008), p. 182 (emphasis original).

6 Environmental protection

1 Tobias Rapp, Christian Schwägerl and Gerald Traufetter, 'The Copenhagen protocol: how China and India sabotaged the UN climate summit', *Spiegel Online*, 5 May 2010, www.spiegel.de/international/world/0,1518,692861,00.html (accessed 16 May 2010).
2 Ibid. He Yafei was then a Vice-Minister of Foreign Affairs. US President Barack Obama, German Chancellor Angela Merkel, British Prime Minister Gordon Brown, French President Nicolas Sarkozy and Indian Prime Minister Manmohan Singh gathered in the Arne Jacobsen conference room in Bella Centre in Copenhagen on the night of 17 December 2009 in a bid to hammer out the details of the global climate change agreement. The meeting was dubbed the 'mini-summit of the 25'. China's Premier Wen Jiabao did not attend; instead he sent He Yafei to represent China. According to the *Spiegel* and China's Xinhua accounts, Wen felt offended by not being invited to the crucial meeting. For the Chinese account, see 'Endeavors to build global hope: Chinese permier's 60 hours in Copenhagen', Xinhua News Agency, 25 December 2009, http://news.xinhaunet.com/english/2009-12/25/content_12701355.htm (accessed 6 January 2010).
3 For a judicious account, see Liu Jianguo and Jared Diamond, 'China's environment in a globalizing world: how China and the rest of the world affect each other', *Nature*, Vol. 435 (30 June 2005), pp. 1179–86; *Development and Change*, Vol. 37, No. 1 (January 2006), special issue on 'China's limits to growth: greening state and society'; Neil Carter and Arthur P. J. Mol (eds), *Environmental Governance in China* (London and New York: Routledge, 2007); Elizabeth Economy, *The River Turns Black: The Environmental Challenge to China's Future*, 2nd edn (Ithaca, NY: Cornell University Press, 2010).
4 A recent study of an aspect of this interface is Katherine Morton, *International Aid and China's Environment: Taming the Yellow Dragon* (London and New York: Routledge, 2005). This book looks into how international aid helps to build China's capacity to deal with environmental problems, arguing that apart from legal compliance, capacity building is an important aspect of environmental improvement.

224 Notes

5 The US Environmental Protection Agency estimates that on certain days almost 25 per cent of the particulate matter clogging the skies above Los Angeles can be traced to China. See Jim Yardley, 'China's next big boom could be the foul air', *New York Times*, 30 October 2005, www.nytimes.com/2005/10/30/weekinreview/30yardley.html; Keith Bradsher and David Barboza, 'Pollution from Chinese coal casts a global shadow', *New York Times*, 11 June 2006, www.nytimes.com/2006/06/11/business/worldbusiness/11chinacoal.html (accessed 19 February 2011).

6 An environmental official in New Zealand pointed out in 2006 that the local carbon dioxide levels were at an all-time high and China was implicated for causing the problem through the consumption of coal and petrol. See Matthew Torbit, 'NZ carbon dioxide surge blamed on Chinese boom', *Dominion Post*, Wellington, 1 June 2006.

7 Benjamin Robertson, 'Caught in the ebb', *South China Morning Post*, 19 October 2006; Evelyn Goh, 'China in the Mekong River Basin: the regional security implications of resource development on the Lancang Jiang', in Mely Caballero-Anthony, Ralf Emmers and Amitav Acharya (eds), *Non-Traditional Security in Asia: Dilemmas in Securitization* (Aldershot: Ashgate, 2006), pp. 225–46.

8 According to the Netherlands Environmental Assessment Agency, China led the world in carbon dioxide emissions in 2006 by producing 6,200 tonnes of the gas. The US churned out 5,800 tonnes. The rise was due to the country's dependence on coal as its major energy source as well as its rising cement output. John Vidal and David Adam, 'China overtakes US as world's biggest CO_2 emitter', *Guardian*, 19 June 2007, www.guardian.co.uk/environment/2007/jun/19/china.usnews; Elizabeth Rosenthal, 'China increases lead as biggest carbon dioxide emitter', *New York Times*, 14 June 2008, www.nytimes.com/2008/06/14/world/asia/14china.html (accessed 19 February 2011).

9 Yang Dongping, 'Shizi lukou de Zhongguo huanjing baohu' (China's environmental protection at a crossroads), in Liang Congjie (ed.), *2005 nian: Zhongguo de huanjing weiji yu tuwei* (*2005: Crisis and Breakthrough of China's Environment*) (Beijing: Shehui kexue wenxian chubanshe, 2006), p. 18.

10 SEPA was upgraded to a ministry called the Ministry of Environmental Protection in March 2008. Cary Huang, 'State Council shake-up plan unveiled', *South China Morning Post*, 12 March 2008.

11 The calculation is done based on sources derived from the website of the Ministry of Foreign Affairs of the PRC, accessed over the years from 2006 to 2010.

12 Gerald Chan, *China's Compliance in Global Affairs: Trade, Arms Control, Environmental Protection, Human Rights* (Singapore: World Scientific, 2006), pp. 148–9; China's white paper is entitled *Environmental Protection in China (1996–2005)* (Beijing: Information Office, State Council, 2006). A complete list of international environmental treaties that China has signed or ratified can be found at www.zhb.gov.cn/eic/651615674891763712/20031017/1042166.shtml (accessed 21 June 2006). See also Ministry of Environmental Protection of the PRC, http://gjs.mep.gov.cn (accessed 19 December 2010).

13 According to the US Energy Department, China has joined a global partnership to build FutureGen, a $1 billion project billed as the world's cleanest coal-burning power plant. See 'China joins FutureGen; signs efficiency and renewable energy protocol with US', Green Car Congress, 16 December 2006, www.greencarcongress.com (accessed 8 May 2007).

14 As of late 2006 China and Australia have entered into eleven projects worth $4 million to improve safety at China's coal mines, to cut greenhouse gas emissions, and to develop alternative sources of energy. Australia funded half the project costs. See 'Australian pact to study coal projects', *South China Morning Post*, 18 October 2006.

15 Embassy of Brazil in London, 'International Biofuels Forum', 1 March 2007, www.brazil.org.uk/press/pressreleases_files/20070301.html (accessed 19 February 2011).

Notes 225

16 Hu Jintao and George W. Bush established the US–China Strategic Economic Dialogue in September 2006. In the third such dialogue held in Beijing in December 2007, the two countries reached an agreement on collaboration on energy and the environment for ten years. In the fourth dialogue, in Annapolis, Maryland, in June 2008 they agreed to set up joint research laboratories for developing renewable energy and other energy-saving technologies. Geoff Dyer, 'China warms to green alliance with US', *Financial Times*, 15 June 2008, www.ft.com/intl/cms/s/0/1b7ea2e0-3af6-11dd-b1a1-0000779fd2ac.html (accessed 15 August 2011).
17 Daniel C. Esty and Maria H. Ivanova, 'Globalization and environmental protection: a global governance perspective', *ICFAI Journal of Environmental Law*, Vol. 4, No. 4 (October 2005), pp. 41–66.
18 According to Seyom Brown, the UN Environment Programme, 'despite the vigorous leadership of its first Secretary General Maurice Strong, was provided with few carrots (financial resources) and no punitive sticks whatsoever with which to induce adherence to its resolutions'. See Seyom Brown, *International Relations in a Changing Global System: Toward a Theory of World Polity* (Boulder, CO: Westview Press, 1992), p. 95.
19 China's official status is a non-Annex I party to the Convention. China's State Development Planning Commission submitted in December 2004 its first 'Initial national communication on climate change'. See 'China', on the United Nations Framework Convention on Climate Change website, http://maindb.unfccc.int/public/country.pl?country=CN (accessed 18 April 2007).
20 John M. Broder, 'Global climate change talks begin in Cancún', *New York Times*, 29 November 2010, www.nytimes.com/2010/11/30/science/earth/30cancun.html (accessed 7 December 2010).
21 'Gov't seen as opposing Kyoto extension at next week's climate talks in Mexico', *Daily Yomiuri*, 29 November 2010; John M. Broder, 'China and U.S. narrow gap in climate talks', *New York Times*, 7 December 2010, www.nytimes.com/2010/12/08/science/earth/08climate.html (accessed 7 December 2010); Shi Jiangtao, 'China bid to break climate deadlock; Beijing may act with world on warming', *South China Morning Post*, 8 December 2010; Fiona Harvey, 'Developing world steps up push to renew Kyoto', *Financial Times*, 9 December 2010, www.ft.com/cms/s/0/e6b6bb64-03d5-11e0-8c3f-00144feabdc0.html (accessed 19 February 2011).
22 John M. Broder, 'Climate talks end with modest deal on emissions', *New York Times*, 11 December 2010, www.nytimes.com/2010/12/12/science/earth/12climate.html (accessed 12 December 2010).
23 SEPA has got tough with even four of the six biggest power groups in China, ordering the halt of all new projects in, for example, Tangshan in the northern Hebei province, to force them to take immediate action to meet environment standards. Shi Jiangtao, 'Beijing gets tough with penalties for polluters', *South China Morning Post*, 11 January 2007.
24 The figures and statistics in this paragraph are taken from *Environmental Protection in China (1996–2005)*.
25 'China hit by rising air pollution', *BBC News*, 3 August 2006, http://news.bbc.co.uk/1/hi/world/asia-pacific/5241844.stm (accessed 20 April 2007); Cheung Chi-fai and Shi Jiangtao, '7b yuan bill put on mainland emissions', *South China Morning Post*, 31 August 2006; 'Cap-and-trade system urged to curb sulphur dioxide emissions', Gov.cn (Chinese Government's Official Web Portal), 14 September 2006, www.gov.cn/english/2006–09/14/content_388553.htm (accessed 21 August 2007); 'China fails to achieve pollution control goal in 2006', Gov.cn, 12 February 2007, www.gov.cn/english/2007–02/12/content_525059.htm (accessed 21 August 2007). In the first half of 2007 the emissions were 12.63 million tonnes, down 0.88 per cent from the same period of the previous year. Sun Xiaohua, 'Emission cuts miss green goal', *China Daily*, 22 August 2007, www.chinadaily.com.cn/olympics/2007–08/22/content_6036098.htm (accessed 19 February 2011).

26 David Dollar, *Lessons from China for Africa*, Policy Research Working Paper 4531 (Washington, DC: China/Mongolia Department, East Asia and Pacific Region, World Bank, 2008), p. 19, http://www-wds.worldbank.org/external/default/WDS-ContentServer/IW3P/IB/2008/02/25/000158349_20080225161200/Rendered/PDF/wps4531.pdf (accessed 28 June 2008); Blacksmith Institute, 'World's worst polluted places 2007', www.blacksmithinstitute.org/ten.php (accessed 30 June 2008). The two Chinese cities were Lifeng in Shanxi province and Tianying in Anhui province.
27 Shi Jiangtao, '500b-yuan loss from sulfur cloud', *South China Morning Post*, 4 August 2006.
28 'Third of China "hit by acid rain"', BBC News, 27 August 2006, http://news.bbc.co.uk/1/hi/world/asia-pacific/5290236.stm (accessed 15 August 2011).
29 'Pollution costs China 511.8b yuan in 2004', Gov.cn, 7 September 2006, www.gov.cn/english/2006-09/07/content_381756.htm (assessed 21 August 2007); Jane Spencer, 'Why Beijing is trying to tally the hidden costs of pollution as China's economy booms', *Wall Street Journal*, 2 October 2006.
30 Kenneth Lieberthal, *Governing China: From Revolution through Reform* (New York and London: W. W. Norton, 2004), p. 282; 'China's environment: a great wall of waste', *The Economist*, 21–27 August 2004.
31 'China says environment spending falls short', Reuters, 29 March 2005, www.three-gorgesprobe.org (accessed 16 June 2006).
32 'Premier pledges green performance assessment amidst dust-filled skies', *China Development Brief*, 24 April 2006, www.chinadevelopmentbrief.com/node/559 (accessed 3 May 2006). Premier Wen Jiabao stunned the nation by admitting that the government failed to meet its environmental targets in the Tenth Five-Year Plan – a rare admission by a PRC head of government.
33 Mao Rubai, 'Time to break free from extensive growth mode', *China Daily*, 25 July 2006, reprinted at http://english.peopledaily.com.cn/200607/25/eng20060725_286357.html (accessed 15 August 2011).
34 *Shengtai guanli yu baohu* (*Ecological Management and Protection*) (Fuyin baokan jiliao (Reprints of Materials from Books and Journals), published by China Renda Social Sciences Information Centre, Renmin University of China), No. 3, 2003, p. 25.
35 'Premier pledges green performance assessment amidst dust-filled skies'.
36 Francesco Sisci, 'Is China headed for a social "red alert"?', *Asia Times Online*, 20 October 2005, www.atimes.com/atimes/China_Business/GJ20Cb01.html (accessed 23 April 2007).
37 'China's pristine rise to "power"? Implications for Asia's political and ecological footprint', Singapore Institute of International Affairs, www.siiaonline.org, June 2006.
38 Tracy Quek, 'Chinese fuming over pollution', *Straits Times*, 6 July 2007; Jonathan Watts, 'China blames growing social unrest on anger over pollution', *Guardian*, 6 July 2007 www.guardian.co.uk/environment/2007/jul/06/china.pollution (accessed 19 February 2011).
39 '"Text protest" blocks China plant', BBC News, 30 May 2007, http://news.bbc.co.uk/1/hi/world/asia-pacific/6704359.stm; Edward Cody, 'Text messages giving voice to Chinese', *Washington Post*, 28 June 2007, www.washingtonpost.com/wp-dyn/content/article/2007/06/27/AR2007062702962.html (accessed 19 February 2011).
40 'China to install 3 more regional environment centers', Xinhua, 5 May 2006, http://china-environmental-news.blogspot.com/2006/05/china-to-install-3-more-regional.html (accessed 19 February 2011).
41 Shi Jiangtao, 'Green watchdog extends its reach', *South China Morning Post*, 2 August 2006.
42 That its status was raised to a full ministerial level in March 2008 indicates the central leadership's increased resolve to tackle the environmental problems. However, it is open to dispute as to whether the new ministry has the authority to enforce compliance.

43 'Follow the chopsticks', *New York Times*, editorial, 25 March 2006, www.nytimes.com/2006/03/25/opinion/25sat2.html (accessed 19 February 2011); Keith Bradsher, 'China aims taxes at cars and the rich', *International Herald Tribune*, 22 March 2006, www.iht.com/articles/2006/03/22/business/tax.php (accessed 10 August 2008).
44 Nathan Nankivell, 'China's pollution and the threat to domestic and regional stability', *China Brief*, Vol. 5, No. 22 (25 October 2005), http://jamestown.org/china_brief/article.php?articleid=2373143 (accessed 11 August 2008).
45 'Toxic leak threat to Chinese city', BBC News, 23 November 2005, http://news.bbc.co.uk/2/hi/asia-pacific/4462760.stm; 'China apologises for river spill', BBC News, 26 November 2005, http://news.bbc.co.uk/2/hi/asia-pacific/4474284.stm; 'China's environment chief quits', BBC News, 2 December 2005, http://news.bbc.co.uk/2/hi/asia-pacific/4491562.stm; 'New spills hit Chinese rivers', BBC News, 9 January 2006, http://news.bbc.co.uk/2/hi/asia-pacific/4595168.stm (accessed 17 April 2007).
46 'China tackles pollution – top official steps up campaign to enforce environmental rules', *Asian Wall Street Journal*, 13 March 2006.
47 It is reported that Anhui province is likely to achieve the target cut of 20 per cent, according to www.cnanhui.org, 14 December 2010 (accessed 19 December 2010). Other reports are yet to appear.
48 'Environmental pollution major problem in China's development', *Beijing Review*, 14 March 2006, www.bjreview.com.cn/EN/06-10-e/lianghui-06/3-14/3-14-7.htm; 'China in 2010', *Beijing Review*, www.bjreview.com.cn/EN/06-15-e/bus-1.htm (accessed 19 April 2007).
49 Decision No. 39 made by the State Council to increase environmental protection, 3 December 2005. See Report on the State of the Environment in China 2005, State Environmental Protection Administration, in particular p. 5, http://english.mep.gov.cn/down_load/Documents/200710/P020071023479859455977.pdf (accessed 22 February 2011).
50 Li Jing, 'Fight hard and long to save environment, Wen tells nation', *China Daily*, 6 March 2010, www.chinadaily.com.cn/china/2010npc/2010-03/06/content_9546849.htm (accessed 14 December 2010).
51 Stephen Howes, 'China's energy intensity target: on-track or off?', East Asia Forum, 31 March 2010, www.eastasiaforum.org/2010/03/31/chinas-energy-intensity-target-on-track-or-off/ (accessed 14 December 2010). This prompts debate over how reliable are China's energy statistics and how accurately the international community can gauge China's progress towards the targets it announced. See below for more discussion.
52 Shi Jiangtao, 'Energy target slips from Beijing's grasp', *South China Morning Post*, 20 September 2010.
53 Information in this section is largely taken from Chan, *China's Compliance in Global Affairs*, pp. 158–62, with some modifications and updates.
54 See, for example, Han Shasha, 'Lun huanjing guihua zhong de gongzhong canyu' (On public participation in environmental planning), *Huanjing daobao (Environmental Herald)*, Nanjing, No. 3 (2001), pp. 13–14.
55 For a graphical presentation of the growth of these NGOs, see Yang Guobin, 'Environmental NGOs and institutional dynamics in China', *China Quarterly*, No. 181 (March 2005), p. 51, Figures 2 and 3.
56 See *Zhongguo tongji nianjian 2009 (China Statistical Yearbook 2009)* (Beijing: Zhongguo tongji chubanshe, 2010), Tables 22–34, p. 437. Zhuang Ailing, founder of Shanghai-based Non-Profit Organization Development Centre, estimated that China had approximately 700,000 to 800,000 NGOs. See *Shanghai Daily*, 23 August 2004, p. 12.
57 Although the China Environment and Development International Cooperation Committee, formed in April 1992, was billed as an NGO, it is largely a government-sponsored organization.

58 *Far Eastern Economic Review*, 10 April 2003, p. 30.
59 Yang Dongping, 'Shizi lukou de Zhongguo huanjing baohu' (China's environmental protection at a crossroads), in Liang Congjie *et al.* (eds), *2005 nian*, pp. 21–23, 28. The figure of more than 1,000 green NGOs in China is also confirmed by China's white paper entitled *Environmental Protection in China (1996–2005)*. Estimates outside China point to a number of around 2,000. See Liu and Diamond, 'China's environment in a globalizing world', p. 1186; and Elizabeth Economy, 'China's environment movement', Testimony before the Congressional–Executive Commission on China Roundtable on 'Environmental NGOs in China: encouraging action and addressing public grievances', Washington, DC, 7 February 2005, www.cecc.gov/pages/roundtables/020705/index.php (accessed 29 August 2007).
60 Obviously, these are registered NGOs in China. Jennifer Turner of the Woodrow Wilson International Center for Scholars, Washington, DC, is of the opinion that there are 2,000 unregistered ones. See 'China's NGOs: independent actors or government puppets', China Environment Forum, Woodrow Wilson International Center for Scholars, Washington, DC, 15 May 2006, www.wilsoncenter.org (accessed 20 June 2006). According to the All-China Environmental Federation, only about 200 of these 2,768 green groups have no official background. See Shi Jiangtao, 'Ease control of NGOs, experts urge Beijing', *South China Morning Post*, 30 October 2006.
61 Li Fangchao, 'NGOs in difficulty, survey shows', *China Daily*, 24 April 2006, reprinted at http://www.china.org.cn/english/MATERIAL/166602.htm (accessed 15 August 2011).
62 Ibid.
63 In the first major UN conference on the environment held in Stockholm in 1972, Chinese government officials were there to introduce themselves and to learn from the experience of others. In the second major UN conference on the environment held in Rio de Janeiro in 1992, Chinese officials were embarrassed by the fact that there was no NGO representation from China. It was only in Johannesburg in 2002 that Chinese green NGOs made their debut.
64 Liao Xiaoyi in *Luse jizhe shalong* (*Green Journalist Saloon*) (Beijing: Zhongguo huanjing kexue chubanshe, 2005), p. 136.
65 Vivien Pik-Kwan Chan, 'Mainland NGOs join world stage at summit', *South China Morning Post*, 16 August 2002. See also 'Mainland NGOs to attend Johannesburg Development Summit', *China News Digest*, 23 August 2002, www.cnd.org/CND-Global/CND-Global.02-08-22.html (accessed 29 August 2007).
66 Yu Nan, 'NGOs to voice their views louder,' *China Daily*, 26 August 2002, through LexisNexis.
67 Liao Xiaoyi in *Green Journalist Saloon*, p. 137.
68 Elizabeth Economy, 'Environmental enforcement in China', in Kristen A. Day (ed.), *China's Environment and the Challenge of Sustainable Development* (Armonk, NY, and London: M. E. Sharpe, 2005), p. 113.
69 Robin Kwong, 'Victory is a rare pleasure for China's Erin Brockovich', *South China Morning Post*, 23 July 2006.
70 'China rising', *Eugene Weekly*, Vol. 26, No. 9 (1 March 2007), www.eugeneweekly.com (accessed 19 December 2010).
71 Wang Canfa, 'Chinese environmental law enforcement: current deficiencies and suggested reforms', *Vermont Journal of Environmental Law*, Vol. 8, No. 2 (Spring 2007), pp. 159–93.
72 Liang was the founder of Friends of Nature. He was the grandson of Liang Qichao (1873–1929), an influential turn-of-the-century scholar who hoped to reform China's moribund imperial system along democratic lines. Liang was also a member of the Chinese People's Political Consultative Committee. See Todd Lappin, 'Can green mix with red? Environmentalism in China', *The Nation*, 14 February 1994. Liang died on 28 October 2010, aged seventy-eight.

73 See the website of SEE, http://see.sina.com.cn/.
74 'NGOs unite to protect environment', *China Daily*, 10 November 2005, www.chinadaily.com.cn/english/doc/2005-11/10/content_493311.htm (accessed 19 February 2011).
75 Fu Tao, 'Zhongguo minjian huanjing zuzhi de fazhan' (Development of NGOs in China), in Liang Congjie *et al.* (eds), *2005 nian* (*2005*), p. 244.
76 All-China Environment Federation website, www.acef.com.cn.
77 Ru Jiang's testimony before the Congressional–Executive Commission on China Roundtable on 'Environmental NGOs in China: encouraging action and addressing public grievances', Washington, DC, 7 February 2005, www.cecc.gov/pages/roundtables/020705/index.php (accessed 29 August 2007).
78 Wu Fengshi, 'New partners or old brothers? GONGOs in transnational environmental advocacy in China', *China Environment Series* 5, 2002, www.wilsoncenter.org/topics/pubs/ACF3C9.pdf (accessed 20 April 2007).
79 See Yang Guobin, 'Global environmentalism hits China', *YaleGlobal Online*, 4 February 2004, http://yaleglobal.yale.edu/acticle.print?id=3250 (accessed 6 February 2004).
80 Bruce Tremayne and Penny de Waal, 'Business opportunities for foreign firms related to China's environment', *China Quarterly*, No. 156 (December 1998), p. 1030.
81 www.gefchina.org.cn (accessed 21 June 2006).
82 Simon Kuznets, Nobel laureate in economic science in 1971, argued that economic inequality rises as the process of economic development proceeds until a turning point. Thereafter, economic inequality falls and remains stable as per capita income rises. The inverted U-shaped relationship that he portrayed havs since been called the Kuznets Curve.
83 Zmarak Shalizi, 'Energy and emissions: local and global efforts of the giants' rise', in L. Alan Winters and Shahid Yusuf (eds), *Dancing with Giants: China, India, and the Global Economy* (Washington, DC: World Bank, 2007), p. 144. There is no conclusive evidence to show that the EKC hypothesis holds true. Environmental economists are of the view that it holds true for some pollutants such as sulphur dioxide, but not for carbon dioxide and municipal waste or for the global environment at large. Roger Perman, Yue Ma, James McGilvray and Michael Common, *Natural Resources and Environmental Economics* (Harlow, Essex: Pearson Education, 2003), pp. 36–40.
84 For the purpose of this chapter about the environment, an externality is said to occur (1) when an agent does harm to the environment and no compensation is made by the agent to the affected parties or (2) when an agent contributes to the cleaning of the environment and receives no payment from the beneficiaries. The provision of public goods refers to all spillover activities that address environmental deterioration. The goods are therefore undersupplied by the market.
85 Perman *et al.*, *Natural Resources and Environmental Economics*, pp. 126–7 and 134.
86 Lieberthal, *Governing China*, pp. 281–6; Pan Yue, 'China's green debt', Project Syndicate, November 2006, www.project-syndicate.org/commentary/pan1 (accessed 23 April 2007).
87 Shi Jiangtao, 'Conservation comes first, Hu warns local officials', *South China Morning Post*, 27 December 2006.
88 Rong Jiaojiao, 'Central gov't seeks strengthened authority to improve efficiency', Xinhua, 14 March 2007, http://news.xinhuanet.com/english/2007-03/14/content_5847475.htm (accessed 19 February 2011); Stephen Chen, 'Shanxi city shut polluting factories', *South China Morning Post*, 8 March 2007.
89 Shi Jiangtao, 'Heavy industrial polluters to be refused bank loans', *South China Morning Post*, 6 July 2007; 'Green credit: to fight pollution, China takes the capitalist route', *International Herald Tribune*, 30 July 2007, www.iht.com/articles/2007/07/30/business/pollute.php (accessed 29 August 2007); Stephen Chen, 'Top creditors still in the dark about green regulations', *South China Morning Post*, 31 July 2007.

230 *Notes*

90 Pu Ping, 'Huanjing wenti: Zhongguo guoji zhanlue de xin keti' (Environment: a new issue in China's international strategy), *Jiaoxue yu yanjiu* (*Pedagogy and Study*), No. 4 (2006), pp. 18–24.
91 Jim Yardley, 'China says rich countries should take lead on global warming', *New York Times*, 7 February 2007, www.nytimes.com/2007/02/07/world/asia/07china.html (accessed 15 August 2011); Sebastian Moffett and Shai Oster, 'China signs on to tackle global-warming issues', *Wall Street Journal Online*, 12 April 2007, http://online.wsj.com/article/SB117629147324066237.html (accessed 20 April 2007); 'Emission cuts but no caps, review suggests', *South China Morning Post*, 17 April 2007; 'Beijing admits climate change will be harmful', *South China Morning Post*, 23 April 2007.
92 Joseph Kahn and Jim Yardley, 'As China roars, pollution reaches deadly extremes', New York Times, 26 August 2007, http://www.nytimes.com/2007/08/26/world/asca/26china.html (accessed 4 July 2011).
93 In 2003, China's per capita emissions of carbon dioxide were 3.2 tonnes while the world average was 3.7 tonnes and the US's was 20 tonnes. 'China about to become top carbon emitter', *Financial Times*, 19 April 2007, www.ft.com/cms/s/d5289ae4-ee25-11db-8584-000b5df10621.html (accessed 15 August 2011).
94 However, Fatih Birol of the International Energy Agency (IEA) is concerned that the surge in China's greenhouse gas emissions, if unchecked, could offset reductions in emissions from Europe, the US and Japan. Shai Oster, 'China seems poised to pass U.S. as top greenhouse-gas emitter', *Wall Street Journal Online*, 24 April 2007, http://online.wsj.com/article/SB117735208071379218.html (accessed 24 April 2007). Whether there should be mandatory emission reduction targets for China is a controversial issue with much implication for China's foreign relations. One commentary in Canada asked sarcastically why Canada, a small-population country, should make sacrifices to lower greenhouse gas emissions if China could expand emissions. It said,

> Canada produces 160 million tonnes a year of the world's eight billion tonnes of carbon dioxide emissions. Were Canada to eliminate all of its GHG [greenhouse gas] emissions, China's increases would replace them – every last ounce – in 18 months. Were Canada to eliminate 10 percent of its emissions, China's increases would replace them all in 60 days. As noble as self-sacrifice can occasionally be, it must have – somewhere – a rational purpose.

Neil Reynolds, 'As China spews pell-mell, why bother with Kyoto?', *The Globe and Mail*, 21 February 2007.
95 The World Resources Institute shows that the share of China's CO_2 emissions in the world total rose from 18.85 per cent in 2004 to 22.70 per cent in 2007. A similar, though less spectacular, growth pattern emerged in India (from 4.42 per cent to 4.78 per cent) and Mexico (from 1.49 per cent to 1.58 per cent). See Appendices B and C for the source of the data.
96 'China about to become top carbon emitter'. That is why the *New York Times* criticizes in an editorial the US and China for forming an 'alliance of denial', 'using each other's inaction as an excuse to do nothing'. See 'Warming and global security', *New York Times*, 20 April 2007, www.nytimes.com/2007/04/20/opinion/20fri2.html (accessed 19 February 2011).
97 The four large developing countries are Brazil, India, Mexico and South Africa. Sheryl Gay Stolberg, 'A deal on emission cuts, but not on timing', *International Herald Tribune*, 9 July 2008, www.iht.com/articles/2008/07/09/asia/summit.php (accessed 10 August 2008); Ng Tze-wei, 'China's voice loud and clear in new "G5" bloc', *South China Morning Post*, 10 July 2008.
98 The West wished to push forward a collective agreement to reduce global greenhouse gas emissions by 50 per cent by 2050. Andrew C. Revkin and John M. Broder, 'U.N.

climate talks "take note" of accord backed by U.S.', *New York Times*, 19 December 2009, www.nytimes.com/2009/12/20/science/earth/20climate.html (accessed 19 February 2011); Rapp *et al.*, 'The Copenhagen protocol'. In response to the question from journalists why the '80 per cent by 2050' pledge was not in the final document, Lars-Erik Liljelund of Sweden said, 'China don't like numbers'. 'Climate change after Copenhagen: China's thing about numbers', *The Economist*, 30 December 2009.

99 Juliet Eilperin and Anthony Faiola, 'Climate deal falls short of key goals', *Washington Post*, 19 December 2009, www.washingtonpost.com/wp-dyn/content/article/2009/12/18/AR2009121800637.html (accessed 19 February 2011). See also United Nations Framework Convention on Climate Change, 'Copenhagen Accord', 18 December 2009, paras. 4 and 5, http://unfccc.int/resource/docs/2009/cop15/eng/l07.pdf (accessed 10 December 2010).

100 Joanna Lewis, 'Environmental challenges: from the local to the global', in Joseph Fewsmith (ed.), *China Today, China Tomorrow: Domestic Politics, Economy, and Society* (Lanham, MD: Rowman & Littlefield, 2010), p. 272.

101 Edward Wong and Jonathan Ansfield, 'China insists that its steps on climate be voluntary', *New York Times*, 30 January 2010, www.nytimes.com/2010/01/30/world/asia/30china.html; John M. Broder, 'Countries submit emission goals', *New York Times*, 1 February 2010, www.nytimes.com/2010/02/02/science/earth/02copenhagen.html (accessed 19 February 2011).

102 Shi Jiangtao, 'Calm front as China and US bury hatchet over climate discord', *South China Morning Post*, 9 December 2010.

103 Broder, 'China and U.S. narrow gap in climate talks'; Urmi A. Goswami, 'Ramesh's ICA proposal gets support from BASIC countries', *Economic Times* (India), 8 December 2010 http://economictimes.indiatimes.com/news/economy/foreign-trade/Rameshs-ICA-proposal-gets-support-from-BASIC-countries/articleshow/7063637.cms (accessed 13 December 2010).

104 Broder, 'Climate talks end with modest deal on emissions'.

105 Fiona Harvey *et al.* 'Rich nations step up pressure on Beijing', *Financial Times*, 15 December 2009 through LexisNexis; Shai Oster, 'China acts to raise profile on climate change', *Wall Street Journal Online*, 7 May 2010, http://online.wsj.com/article/SB10001424052748704292004575229862516272730.html (accessed 10 May 2010).

106 India's Minister of Environment, Jairam Ramesh said, '[The Chinese] know the world's radar is on them'. He continued, 'If transparency becomes the stumbling block, China doesn't want to be blamed. If China is the only party holding out, they will come on board'. Broder, 'China and U.S. narrow gap in climate talks'; Suzanne Goldenberg, 'China on path to redemption in Cancun', *Guardian*, 7 December 2010, www.guardian.co.uk/environment/2010/dec/07/cancun-climate-change-summit-china. For the US stance, see Darryl Fears, 'Cancun climate-change summit hinges on U.S.–China transparency issues', *Washington Post*, 10 December 2010, www.washingtonpost.com/wp-dyn/content/article/2010/12/09/AR2010120906553.html (accessed 19 February 2011).

107 Shi, 'Calm front as China and US bury hatchet over climate discord'.

108 Robert Falkner, 'International sources of environmental policy change in China: the case of genetically modified food', *Pacific Review*, Vol. 19, No. 4 (December 2006), pp. 473–94.

109 *Environmental Protection in China (1996–2005)*.

110 The pilot programme is to cover Qinghai, Tibet, Ningxia, Shanxi, Liaoning, Inner Mongolia and Hebei. Eventually, it would be extended to all provinces and regions. Sun Xiaohua, 'New program will take climate fight to provinces', *China Daily*, 18 April 2007, www.china.org.cn/english/environment/207639.htm (accessed 19 February 2011).

111 Robert W. Mead and Victor Brajer quantify the health benefits of the air and water cleanup activities to Beijing in their 'Environmental cleanup and health gains from Beijing's Green Olympics', *China Quarterly*, No. 194 (June 2008), pp. 275–93. A caveat is in order, however. According to a report edited by Dai Qing, a prominent Chinese critic of the country's environmental problem, the hosting of the Beijing Games does not promote water conservation. Instead, it worsens Beijing and its neighbouring provinces' water crisis by pumping water from diminishing reserves of groundwater and diverting water from them. A huge supply of water is needed for sports venues and such 'prestige projects' as musical fountains in Beijing. Shai Oster, 'Water crisis exacerbated by Games, report says', *Wall Street Journal Online*, 27 June 2008, http://online.wsj.com/article/SB121450746799308037.html (accessed 30 June 2008). The full text of the report entitled *Beijing's Water Crisis 1949–2008 Olympics* (Toronto: Probe International Beijing Group, June 2008) is available at www.probeinternational.org/catalog/pdfs/BeijingWaterCrisis1949–2008.pdf (accessed 30 June 2008).

112 'Air quality could affect games', CNN.com, 7 August 2007, www.cnn.com/video/#/video/international/2007/08/07/intv.cdb.ioc.pres.jacques.rogge.cnn (accessed 22 August 2007).

113 Stephen Chen, 'Race is on to clean waterways by Olympic Games deadline', *South China Morning Post*, 11 May 2007; Richard McGregor, 'Beijing claims success for clean air drive', *Financial Times*, 21 August 2007, www.ft.com/cms/s/0/0e483652-4ff3-11dc-a6b0-0000779fd2ac.html (accessed 16 August 2011).

114 Depending on the last digit of their number plates, motor vehicles could only be on the streets on either odd or even days. Mure Dickie, 'China cracks down on cars for Olympics', *Financial Times*, 21 June 2008, through LexisNexis; Mei Fong, 'China maps out new route to cleaner air', *Wall Street Journal Online*, 21 June 2008, http://online.wsj.com/article/SB121396559276791697.html (accessed 23 June 2008).

115 For example, motorists were not allowed to drive their vehicles with plates ending in 9 on 9 or 19 August, while other cars whose last number on the plates is odd (1, 3, 5 or 7) could.

116 Shai Oster, 'Beijing considers new curbs as pollution threatens Games', *Wall Street Journal Online*, 29 July 2008, http://online.wsj.com/article/SB121729514547791995.html (accessed 30 July 2008); Guo Shipeng, 'China unveils emergency pollution plans for Games', *Reuters News*, 30 July 2008, www.reuters.com/article/GCA-Olympics/idUSPEK17203320080731 (accessed 31 July 2008); Jim Yardley, 'China adds rules to cut pollution', *International Herald Tribune*, 31 July 2008, www.iht.com/articles/2008/07/31/asia/beijing.php (accessed 1 August 2008).

117 Shai Oster, 'China sees vast pollution', *Wall Street Journal Online*, 10 February 2010, http://online.wsj.com/article/SB30001424052748704182004575054811793594150.html (accessed 10 February 2010); idem, 'Pollution levels in China resume rise', ibid., 4 June 2010, http://online.wsj.com/article/SB30001424052748704025304575284301693028326.html (accessed 4 June 2010).

118 While prospering from outsourcing, multinational corporations are a contributor to China's growing environmental hazards by demanding ever-lower prices for Chinese products. Manufacturers in China, in turn, dump industrial waste into rivers to keep the production cost low. Jane Spencer, 'Ravaged rivers: China pays steep price as textile exports boom', *Wall Street Journal Online*, 22 August 2007, http://online.wsj.com/article/SB118580938555882301.html (accessed 22 August 2007).

119 Neil T. Carter and Arthur P. J. Mol, 'Domestic and transnational dynamics of a future hegemon', *Environmental Politics*, Vol. 15, No. 2 (April 2006), p. 341.

120 Elizabeth Economy, 'Environmental governance: the emerging economic dimension', *Environmental Politics*, Vol. 15, No. 2 (April 2006), pp. 171–89.

121 James D. Seymour, 'China's environment: a bibliographic essay', In Day (ed.); *China's Environment and the Challenges of Sustainable Development*, p. 262.

7 Public health

1. Cited in Richard Ingham, 'China, India should open wallets for AIDS war: Global Fund', Agence France Presse, 23 July 2010, www.google.com/hostednews/afp/article/ALeqM5iBt5r4f1MU-1eyT9VNbDdedZA23Q (accessed 8 January 2011); emphasis added.
2. This definition draws on the discussion of global governance in Chapter 1 and Adrian Kay and Owain Williams, 'Introduction: the international political economy of global health governance', in Adrian Kay and Owain David Williams (eds), *Global Health Governance: Crisis, Institutions and Political Economy* (Basingstoke: Palgrave Macmillan, 2009), pp. 1–3.
3. A detailed account of China's participation in global health governance is Lai-Ha Chan, *China Engages Global Health Governance: Responsible Stakeholder or System-Transformer?* (New York: Palgrave Macmillan, 2011).
4. Yuanli Liu, 'China's public healthcare system: facing the challenges', *Bulletin of the World Health Organization*, Vol. 82, No. 7 (July 2004), pp. 532–8.
5. In the *World Health Report 2000 – Health Systems: Improving Performance*, published by the World Health Organization in 2000, China's healthcare system was rated poorly. Not long ago still an admired model for developing countries, it was, however, ranked 188th on the dimension of fairness of financial contribution, leading China to become one of the most unfair countries in the world. See The World Health Organization, *The World Health Report 2000 – Health Systems: Improving Performance*, www.who.int/whr/2000/en/. The Statistical Annex is available at www.who.int/whr/2000/en/whr00_annex_en.pdf (accessed 11 January 2011).
6. *Zhongguo tongji nianjian (China Statistical Yearbook)*, 2001, in the chapter on culture, sports and public health.
7. Joan Kaufman, 'Policy case study: public health', in William A. Joseph (ed.), *Politics in China: An Introduction* (New York: Oxford University Press, 2010), p. 291.
8. Liu Yating, 'Kanbing nan, nan zai nali? Kanbing gui, gui zai hechu? (Getting health care is hard, why is it hard? Seeing a doctor is expensive, why is it expensive?), *Zhongguo Shangye (Business China)*, No. 3 (2008), pp. 36–8.
9. The survey was conducted by *China Youth Daily (Zhongguo qingnian bao)* in August 2005 with 733 people aged 30 or above in the country. See Tang Yonglin, 'Yiliao gaige: jiucheng gongzhong bumanyi' (Health-care reform: 90 per cent of the population were not satisfied), Yi gai wang (Health-care reform net), 23 August 2005, http://yigai.org/NewsInfo.aspx?id=1 (accessed 23 February 2011).
10. Quoted in World Health Organization, *Access and Human Rights Issues*, 2008 www.who.int/medicines_technologies/human_rights/en/ (accessed 4 February 2008).
11. It was defined by Mary Robinson, then UN High Commissioner for Human Rights, in 2002. Cited in Kelley Lee, 'Understandings of global health governance: the contested landscape', in Kay and Williams (eds), *Global Health Governance*, p. 37.
12. Alan Collins (ed.), *Contemporary Security Studies* (Oxford: Oxford University Press, 2007); Peter Hough, *Understanding Global Security* (Abingdon: Routledge, 2008); Michael E. Smith, *International Security: Politics, Policy, Prospects* (Basingstoke: Palgrave Macmillan, 2010); Paul D. Williams (ed.), *Security Studies: An Introduction* (Abingdon: Routledge, 2008).
13. Chan, *China Engages Global Health Governance*, pp. 127–30. For the Resolution 1308 (2000), see http://daccess-dds-ny.un.org/doc/UNDOC/GEN/N00/536/02/PDF/N0053602.pdf (accessed 6 January 2010). The security and human rights perspectives of global health governance are briefly discussed in Lee, 'Understandings of global health governance', pp. 35–7.
14. Yuan Ye and Jiang Guocheng, 'China unveils action plan for universal access to basic health care', Chinaview.cn, 7 April 2009, http://news.xinhuanet.com/english/2009-04/07/content_11141889.htm (accessed 3 January 2011).

15 'Ministers taken to task over healthcare reforms', *People's Daily Online*, 25 December 2010, http://english.peopledaily.com.cn/90001/90776/90882/7242174.html (accessed 3 January 2011).
16 Gao Zhan, director of Haoyisheng (literally meaning good doctor), a company that trains rural doctors in China, was quoted as saying, 'Purchasing equipment is quick and easy. Education and training is not a simple issue that can be directly solved by money'. The 'skill gap' has slowed down the implementation of the said healthcare reforms. Jane Lanhee Lee and Lucy Hornby, 'China's healthcare plans bump against rural skills gap', Reuters, 1 December 2010, www.reuters.com/article/idUS-TRE6B00X320101201 (accessed 5 January 2011).
17 For example, the proportion of spending on preventive care in the government's recurrent health budget dropped from 23 per cent in 1978 to 18 per cent in 1994. See Hu Shanlian and Jiang Minghe, 'The People's Republic of China', in Douglas H. Brooks and Myo Thant (eds), *Social Sector Issues in Transitional Economics of Asia* (Hong Kong: Oxford University Press, 1998), p. 192.
18 A total of 842,525 people had schistosomiasis (also known as snail fever) in China in 2004 and an estimated 30 million are at risk. See '2005 nian Zhongguo weisheng tongji zhaiyao' (2005 China's Public Health Statistic Summary), Ministry of Health, People's Republic of China, www.moh.gov.cn (accessed on 1 March 2006); and Jim Yardley, 'A deadly fever, once defeated, lurks in a Chinese lake', *New York Times*, 22 February 2005, www.nytimes.com/2005/02/22/international/asia/22snail.html (accessed 25 February 2011).
19 An unofficial English summary of the 'Ministry of Health Report on China's Healthcare System and Reform', *China AIDS Survey*, www.casy.org/Chindoc/MOH_report_0805.htm (accessed 12 January 2006).
20 Cited in Alan Schnur, 'The role of the WHO in combating SARS, focusing on the efforts in China', in Arthur Kleinman and James L. Watson (eds), *SARS in China: Prelude to Pandemic?* (Stanford, CA: Stanford University Press, 2006), p. 39.
21 Ibid., p. 40.
22 Cited in Tony Saich, *Providing Public Goods in Transitional China* (New York: Palgrave Macmillan, 2008), p. 120.
23 *Implementing the New Cooperative Medical Schemes in Rapidly Changing China: Issues and Options* (Beijing: WHO in China, 2004), p. 13.
24 'Medical reform "basically unsuccessful"', *China Daily*, 30 July 2005; www.chinadaily.com.cn/english/doc/2005-07/30/content_464795.htm (accessed 3 January 2011).
25 For a more detailed account of how China has tried to improve its disease surveillance and reporting system, see Lai-Ha Chan, 'Oscillating between Mao and Deng? The domestic–global nexus of China's public health reform', in Lai-Ha Chan, Gerald Chan and Fung Kwan (eds), *China at 60: Global-Local Interactions* (Singapore: World Scientific, 2011), pp. 255–81.
26 Inge Kaul, Isabelle Grunberg and Marc A. Stern (eds), *Global Public Goods: International Cooperation in the 21st Century* (New York and Oxford: Oxford University Press, 1999); and Richard Smith, 'Global health governance and global public goods', in Kent Buse, Wolfgang Hein and Nick Drager (eds), *Making Sense of Global Health Governance: A Policy Perspective* (Basingstoke: Palgrave Macmillan, 2009), pp. 122–36.
27 For a succinct analysis of China's increasing participation in multilateral health governance, see Lai-Ha Chan, Pak K. Lee and Gerald Chan, 'China engages global health governance: processes and dilemmas', *Global Public Health*, Vol. 4, No. 1 (2009), pp. 1–30; and Yanzhong Huang, 'Pursuing health as foreign policy: the case of China', *Indiana Journal of Global Legal Studies*, Vol. 17, No. 1 (2010), pp. 105–46.
28 Simon Shen, 'Borrowing the Hong Kong identity for Chinese diplomacy: implications of Margaret Chan's World Health Organization election campaign', *Pacific Affairs*, Vol. 81, No. 3 (Fall 2008), pp. 363, 370–71; Chan, *China Engages Global Health Governance*, pp. 118–21.

Notes 235

29 World Health Organization, 'Revision process of the International Health Regulations (IHR) ', www.who.int/ihr/revisionprocess/revision/en/ (accessed 10 January 2010). For more detailed discussions of the revision, see David P. Fidler, 'From International Sanitary Conventions to global health security: the new International Health Regulations', *Chinese Journal of International Law*, Vol. 4, No. 2 (2005), pp. 325–92; Simon Rushton, 'Global governance capacities in health: WHO and infectious diseases', in Kay and Williams (eds), *Global Health Governance*, pp. 60–80; Mark W. Zacher and Tania J. Keefe, *The Politics of Global Health Governance: United by Contagion* (New York: Palgrave Macmillan, 2008), pp. 31–43, 64–74.

30 A public health emergency of international concern is defined as an extraordinary event that (a) may constitute a public health risk to other member states through the international spread of disease and (b) may require a coordinated international response. Public health risk refers to a likelihood of an event that may affect adversely the health of human populations, with an emphasis on one which may spread internationally or may present a serious and direct danger. *Fifty-eighth World Health Assembly Resolution WHA58.3: Revision of the International Health Regulations* (Geneva: World Health Organization, 2005), www.who.int/csr/ihr/WHA58-en.pdf (accessed 8 January 2011).

31 China's response to its domestic HIV/AIDS crisis is discussed in Chan, *China Engages Global Health Governance*, pp. 67–93.

32 World Health Organization, *International Health Regulations (2005)* (Geneva: World Health Organization, 2008), p. 62; Chinalawinfo Company, 'Frontier Health and Quarantine Law of the People's Republic of China', www.lawinfochina.com/law/display.asp?id=1171 (accessed 11 January 2011).

33 India has had a ban on imports of milk and milk products from China since September 2008. 'India extends ban on import of milk, milk products from China', *Deccan Herald*, 4 January 2011, www.deccanherald.com/content/126185/india-extends-ban-import-milk.html (accessed 11 January 2011).

34 Jane Macartney and Sophie Yu, 'Chinese milk powder contaminated with melamine sickens 1,253 babies', *The Times*, 16 September 2008, www.timesonline.co.uk/tol/news/world/asia/article4758549.ece (accessed 10 January 2011); 'Embassy officials slow to call toxic alert', *New Zealand Herald*, 21 September 2008, through LexisNexis.

35 However, according to the IHR 2005 decision instrument (Annex 2), the food crisis should have constituted an event of potential international public health concern because there was a serious health impact, the event was unusual or unexpected and there was risk of international spread.

36 'Contamination known weeks before milk recall – officials', *New Zealand Herald*, 14 September 2008, through LexisNexis; Edward Wong, 'Milk scandal pushes China to set limits on melamine', *New York Times*, 9 October 2008, www.nytimes.com/2008/10/09/world/asia/09milk.html (accessed 10 January 2011).

37 Concerned about their commercial interests, developed countries in the nineteenth and twentieth centuries were strongly opposed to 'excessive measures'. The ISR (1926) stipulated that 'measures laid out in this chapter constitute a maximum'. Zacher and Keefe, *The Politics of Global Health Governance*, pp. 35, 37.

38 Lai-Ha Chan, Lucy Chen and Jin Xu, 'China's engagement with global health diplomacy: was SARS a watershed?', *PLoS Medicine*, Vol. 7, Issue 4 (April 2010), pp. 1–6; Zacher and Keefe, *The Politics of Global Health Governance*, pp. 70–71.

39 WHO, *International Health Regulations (2005)*, p. 62.

40 Rushton, 'Global governance capacities in health', p. 72.

41 For a detailed analysis of Taiwan's return to the WHO, see Joanne Jaw-ling Chang, 'Woguo canyu shijie weisheng zuzhi zhi celüe yanbian yu meiguo jiaose fenxi: 1997–2009' (The changing strategy of Taiwan's participation in the World Health Organisation and the role of the United States, 1997–2009), *Oumei yanjiu (EuroAmerica)*, Taipei, Vol. 41, No. 2 (June 2010), pp. 431–517.

42 Zacher and Keefe, *The Politics of Global Health Governance*, pp. 35–7.
43 See Chan, *China Engages Global Health Governance*, pp. 95–122, for a detailed account of China's 'strategic health diplomacy'.
44 Li Anshan, 'Zhongguo yuanwai yiliaodui de lishi, guimo ji qi yingxiang' (The history, scope and effect of China's medical aid), *Waijiao pinglun* (*Foreign Affairs Review*), No. 1 (2009), pp. 25–45.
45 Ministry of Foreign Affairs of the PRC, *China's African Policy*, January 2006, www.fmprc.gov.cn/eng/zxxx/t230615.htm (accessed 14 January 2010).
46 Shen, 'Borrowing the Hong Kong identity for Chinese diplomacy', p. 364; Deborah Brautigam, *The Dragon's Gift: The Real Story of China in Africa* (Oxford: Oxford University Press, 2009), p. 173.
47 Discussions with a global public health specialist in Hong Kong, Hong Kong, 11 November 2010.
48 Chan, *China Engages Global Health Governance*, p. 120; Shen, 'Borrowing the Hong Kong identity for Chinese diplomacy', pp. 374–5.
49 *Coordinates 2002, Charting Progress against AIDS, TB and Malaria* (Geneva: World Health Organization, UNAIDS and UNICEF, 2002), p. 23.
50 World Health Organization, UNAIDS, and UNICEF, *Towards Universal Access: Scaling up Priority HIV/AIDS Interventions in the Health Sector: Progress Report 2009* (Geneva: WHO, September 2009), p. 4; www.who.int/hiv/pub/2009progressreport/en/index.html (accessed 15 January 2011).
51 World Health Organization, *Globalisation and Access to Drugs: Perspectives on the WTO/TRIPS Agreement*, January 1999; www.who.int/medicines/areas/policy/whodap-98-9rev.pdf (accessed 4 February 2008).
52 See Tony Barnett and Alan Whiteside, *AIDS in the Twenty-First Century: Disease and Globalization* (Basingstoke: Palgrave Macmillan, 2002); Daniel W. Drezner, *All Politics is Global: Explaining International Regulatory Regimes* (Princeton, NJ, and Oxford: Princeton University Press, 2007), especially Chapter 7; Anton A. van Niekerk and Loretta M. Kopelman (eds), *Ethics & AIDS in Africa: The Challenge to Our Thinking* (Walnut Creek, CA: Left Coast Press, 2005); Nana K. Poku, *AIDS in Africa: How the Poor are Dying* (Cambridge: Polity Press, 2005); and Nana K. Poku, Alan Whiteside and Bjorg Sandkjaer (eds), *AIDS and Governance* (Aldershot: Ashgate, 2007).
53 For a detailed study of China's position on the 2001 Doha Declaration on TRIPS and China's failure to help African countries to contain and control their HIV/AIDS crisis, see Chan, *China Engages Global Health Governance*, pp. 95–122.
54 GlaxoSmithKline, 'Drug research and collaborations in China', www.gsk-china.com/english/html/research-development/collaborations-in-china.html (accessed 11 January 2011).
55 Shanghai Clinical Research Centre website: www.scrcnet.org/PCRU_en.asp (accessed 11 January 2011).
56 BGI, 'Overview', www.genomics.cn/en/bgi.php?id=158 (accessed 11 January 2011).
57 World Intellectual Property Organization, *The International Patents System Yearly Review: Developments and Performance in 2009* (Geneva: WIPO, 2009), pp. 14–15.
58 Chinese patent filings includes utility-model and invention patents, but there are no utility-model patents in the US. Steve Lohr, 'When innovation, too, is made in China', *New York Times*, 1 January 2011, www.nytimes.com/2011/01/02/business/02unboxed.html; Raja Murthy, 'China on patents overdrive', *Asia Times Online*, 7 January 2011, www.atimes.com/atimes/China_Business/MA07Cb01.html (all accessed 8 January 2011).
59 'Goal 6: Combat HIV/AIDS, Malaria and Other Diseases', www.un.org/millenniumgoals/aids.shtml (accessed 9 January 2011); and United Nations, *The Millennium Development Goals Report 2010* (New York: UN, 2010), pp. 40–51; www.un.org/millenniumgoals/pdf/MDG%20Report%202010%20En%20r15%20-low%20res%20 20100615%20-.pdf (accessed 11 January 2011).

Notes   237

60 United Nations, *The Millennium Development Goals Report 2010*, p. 45.
61 Laurie Garrett and El'Haum Alavian, 'Global health governance in a G-20 world', *Global Health Governance*, Vol. 4, No. 1 (Fall 2010), pp. 2–3.
62 Ibid., pp. 6–7.
63 Jennifer Kates, Kim Boortz, Eric Lief, Carlos Avila, and Benjamin Gobet, *Financing the Response to AIDS in Low- and Middle-Income Countries: International Assistance from the G8, European Commission and Other Donor Governments in 2009* (Menlo Park, CA: Kaiser Family Foundation and UNAIDS, July 2010), p. 12.
64 Ibid.
65 In addition to the members of G8 and the EU, the G20 comprises Argentina, Australia, Brazil, China, India, Indonesia, Mexico, Saudi Arabia, South Africa, South Korea and Turkey.
66 Garrett and Alavian, 'Global health governance in a G-20 world', p. 5.
67 'The G20 and development: a new era (updated)', October 2010, www.reliefweb.int/rw/RWFiles2010.nsf/FilesByRWDocUnidFilename/MMAH-8A846A-full_report.pdf/$File/full_report.pdf (accessed 10 January 2011).
68 Garrett and Alavian, 'Global health governance in a G-20 world', p. 5.
69 Institute for Health Metrics and Evaluation, *Financing Global Health 2009: Tracking Development Assistance for Health* (Seattle, WA: Institute for Health Metrics and Evaluation, 2009), p. 50, Figure 32, www.healthmetricsandevaluation.org/print/reports/2009/financing/financing_global_health_report_full_IHME_0709.pdf (accessed 9 January 2011).
70 Keith Bradsher, 'Chinese foreign currency reserves swell by record amount', *New York Times*, 11 January 2011, www.nytimes.com/2011/01/12/business/global/12yuan.html (accessed 18 January 2011). See also Chapter 4 above for the growth of China's economic clout.
71 Ingham, 'China, India should open wallets for AIDS war'.
72 China's pledges and contributions are $30 million for 2003–13. The annual pledges and contributions in 2008, 2009 and 2010 were $2 million. The Global Fund to Fight HIV/AIDS, Tuberculosis and Malaria, 'Pledges and contributions', www.theglobalfund.org/en/pledges/?lang=en (accessed 9 January 2011). See also Ingham, 'China, India should open wallets for AIDS war'; Jack C. Chow, 'China's billion-dollar aid appetite', *Foreign Policy*, 21 July 2010.
73 The Global Fund to Fight AIDS, Tuberculosis and Malaria, 'Global Fund Third Voluntary Replenishment 2011–2013 Pledges for 2011–2013 at 5 October 2010', www.theglobalfund.org/documents/replenishment/newyork/Replenishment_NewYorkMeeting_Pledges_en.pdf; Communications Department, Global Fund to Fight AIDS, Tuberculosis and Malaria, 'The Global Fund's Voluntary Replenishment round brings hope, but not plenty', *Africa Health*, November 2010, pp. 26–7, www.africa-health.com/articles/november_2010/Global%20Fund.pdf (accessed 13 January 2011).
74 The Global Fund to Fight AIDS, Tuberculosis and Malaria, *Resource Scenarios 2011–2013: Funding the Global Fight against HIV/AIDS, Tuberculosis and Malaria* (Geneva: The Global Fund to Fight AIDS, Tuberculosis and Malaria, March 2010), p. 5, www.theglobalfund.org/documents/replenishment/2010/Resource_Scenarios_en.pdf (accessed 10 January 2011).
75 The Global Fund to Fight HIV, Tuberculosis and Malaria, 'Press releases: donors commit US$11.7 billion to the Global Fund for three years', 5 October 2010, www.theglobalfund.org/en/pressreleases/?pr=pr_101005c (accessed 10 January 2011).
76 Communications Department, Global Fund to Fight AIDS, Tuberculosis and Malaria, 'The Global Fund's voluntary replenishment round brings hope, but not plenty'.
77 World Health Organization, 'Voluntary contributions by fund and by donor for the financial period 2008–2009', Sixty-Third World Health Assembly, A63/INF.COC./4, 29 April 2010, http://apps.who.int/gb/ebwha/pdf_files/WHA63/A63_ID4-en.pdf (accessed 11 January 2011).

238 *Notes*

78 Javed Siddiqi, *World Health and World Politics: The World Health Organization and the UN System* (London: Hurst, 1995), p. 216.
79 For an analysis of how China's rational utilitarian calculations have helped the country to receive external resources to halt its HIV/AIDS disease, see Chan, *China Engages Global Health Governance*, pp. 125–7.
80 Samuel S. Kim, 'International organizations in Chinese foreign policy', *Annals of the American Academy of Political and Social Science*, Vol. 519 (1992), pp. 140–57; idem, 'China's international organization behaviour', in Thomas W. Robinson and David Shambaugh (eds), *Chinese Foreign Policy: Theory and Practice* (Oxford: Clarendon Press, 1994), pp. 401–34. The saying is quoted from an official from the Ministry of Health of the PRC during a Workshop on South–South Health Cooperation, organized by the Institute of Global Health at Peking University, Beijing, China, on 12–23 July 2010.
81 Zhang Baijia, 'Gaibian ziji yingxiang shijie: 20 shiji zhongguo waijiao siansuo chuyi' (Transform itself, influence the world: an outline of Chinese diplomacy in the 20th century), *Zhongguo shehui kexue* (*Social Sciences in China*), No. 1 (2002), pp. 4–19.

8 Food safety

1 The quote is an excerpt of Li Keqiang's speech to a State Council meeting in Beijing on 19 April 2010. See 'Vice premier orders efforts to improve food safety', *China Daily*, 20 April 2010, http://www2.chinadaily.com.cn/china/2010–04/20/content_9749703.htm (accessed 2 October 2010). Li, the executive Vice-Premier, is concurrently the head of the State Council Food Safety Commission, established in February 2010.
2 'Trade to expand by 9.5% in 2010 after a dismal 2009, WTO Report', *WTO Press Release*, 26 March 2010, www.wto.org/english/news_e/pres10_e/pr598_e.htm (accessed 26 September 2010).
3 World Trade Organization, *International Trade Statistics 2009*, Table II.20, www.wto.org/english/res_e/statis_e/its2009_e/its09_merch_trade_product_e.htm (accessed 2 October 2010).
4 'All merchandise – country quarterly update', United States International Trade Commission, http://dataweb.usitc.gov/scripts/trade_shift/trade_by_ctry_mv.asp (26 September 2010).
5 Linden J. Ellis and Jennifer L. Turner, *Sowing the Seeds: Opportunities for U.S.–China Cooperation on Food Safety* (Washington, DC: Woodrow Wilson International Center for Scholars, September 2008), p. 3, www.wilsoncenter.org/topics/pubs/CEF_food_safety_text.pdf (accessed 2 January 2011).
6 The total value of global food exports in 2000 was $432 billion; it grew to $1,114 billion in 2008, according to WTO's *International Trade Statistics 2009*. The 2000 figure is available at WTO statistical database's Time Series on International Trade. In observing the rapid growth in trade in processed food, Peter Oosterveer argues that '[g]lobalization in all stages of the food supply chain will continue to become a more important trait in the daily lives of producers and consumers'. Peter Oosterveer, *Global Governance of Food Production and Consumption: Issues and Challenges* (Cheltenham: Edward Elgar, 2007), p. 5.
7 Melamine-tainted dairy products, believed to be leftovers from the 2008 recall, reappeared in various provinces in China in 2009 and 2010. Michael Wines, 'Tainted dairy products seized in western China', *New York Times*, 9 July 2010, www.nytimes.com/2010/07/10/world/asia/10china.html (accessed 4 October 2010).
8 Globalized food supply chains pose a greater risk and expose more people over wider geographical regions to contaminated food or pathogens than in the past. Oosterveer, *Global Governance of Food Production and Consumption*, pp. 7–8.

9 See e.g. Dan Carney, 'With Chinese tires, it's buyer beware', msnbc.com, 24 September 2009, www.msnbc.msn.com/id/32899266/ns/business-autos/ (accessed 11 October 2010); 'Beware the cheap Chinese products', http://hubpages.com/hub/Beware-of-cheap-chinese-products (accessed 4 October 2010).
10 Minxin Pei, '"Made in China" Label won't survive without rule of law', *Global Viewpoint*, Carnegie Endowment for International Peace, 16 June 2007, http://carnegieendowment.org/publications/index.cfm?fa=view&id=19466 (accessed 8 October 2010).
11 Ellis and Turner, *Sowing the Seeds*, p. 23, www.wilsoncenter.org/topics/pubs/CEF_food_safety_text.pdf (accessed 2 January 2011).
12 Ibid., p. 23.
13 European Commission, *The Rapid Alert System for Food and Feed (RASFF) Annual Report 2009* (Luxembourg: Publications Office of the European Union, 2010), p. 66, http://ec.europa.eu/food/food/rapidalert/docs/report2009_en.pdf (accessed 2 October 2010).
14 Ellis and Turner, *Sowing the Seeds*, p. 23.
15 However, bringing their own food went against the Beijing municipality's safety protocol which forbids uncertified food from entering the Olympic village. As a result, the US athletes cooked and dined on their imported food at a local university instead. See Ellis and Turner, *Sowing the Seeds*, pp. 8–9.
16 Yang Xiao and Li Bin, 'Shipin anquan wenti dui Zhongguo guojia xingxiang de yingxiang' (The impact of food safety on China's national image), *Xiandai guoji guanxi (Contemporary International Relations)*, No. 6 (2010), pp. 42–6.
17 Steven R. Weisman, 'Food safety joins issues at U.S.–China talks', *New York Times*, 23 May 2007, www.nytimes.com/2007/05/23/business/worldbusiness/23trade.html (accessed 16 August 2011).
18 David Barboza, 'China blocks some imports of U.S. chicken and pork', *New York Times*, 15 July 2007, www.nytimes.com/2007/07/15/business/worldbusiness/15china.html (accessed 16 August 2011).
19 Wayne M. Morrison, *Health and Safety Concerns over US Imports of Chinese Products: An Overview* (Washington, DC: Congressional Research Service, 13 January 2009), p. 3, http://assets.opencrs.com/rpts/RS22713_20090113.pdf (accessed 10 October 2010).
20 Barboza, 'China blocks some imports of U.S. chicken and pork'.
21 David Barboza, 'Food-safety crackdown in China', *New York Times*, 28 June 2007, www.nytimes.com/2007/06/28/business/worldbusiness/28food.html (accessed 2 October 2010).
22 Adam Jones, 'China seizes shipment of Evian water', *Financial Times*, 30 May 2007, www.ft.com/cms/s/0/c0d886d2-0ed0-11dc-b444-000b5df10621.html (accessed 16 August 2011).
23 Liu Xiaoxing, 'Women hai neng chi shenmen? shipin hangye mianlin chengxin weiji' (What can we eat? Food industry faces faith crisis), *Huanjing jingji zazhi (Environmental Economy)*, No. 20 (August 2005), pp. 20–22.
24 Ibid.; Zhang Jiawei 'Food safety tops people's concerns in survey', *China Daily*, 30 June 2010, www.chinadaily.com.cn/china/2010-06/30/content_10042303.htm (accessed 16 August 2011); and 'Chinese worry most about earthquake risks, food safety', *People's Daily Online*, 20 October 2010; http://english.peopledaily.com.cn/90001/90782/7171413.html (accessed 24 October 2010).
25 Ellis and Turner, *Sowing the Seeds*, p. 16.
26 Morrison, *Health and Safety Concerns over US Imports of Chinese Products*, p. 4; and George Reynolds, 'China expects to close half of smaller processors', Foodnavigator-usa.com, 12 July 2007, www.foodnavigator-usa.com/Legislation/China-expects-to-close-half-of-smaller-processors (accessed 10 October 2010).
27 Chris Buckley, 'China finds 15 percent of foods fail quality check', *Reuters News*, 17 August 2007, www.bdnews24.com/details.php?id=72157&cid=4 (accessed 10 October 2010).

28 World Bank, 'Dramatic decline in global poverty, but progress uneven', http://web.worldbank.org/WBSITE/EXTERNAL/TOPICS/EXTPOVERTY/0,,contentMDK:20195240~pagePK:148956~piPK:216618~theSitePK:336992,00.html (accessed 27 December 2010).
29 Ellis and Turner, *Sowing the Seeds*, p. 45.
30 AQSIQ, 'Guojia zhijianzongju fabu "guanyu jinyibu jiaqiang shipinshengchan jiagong xiaozuofang jianguan gongzuo de yijian" tuchu sanxiang jianguan zhidu quebao shipin zhiliang anquan', AQSIQ promulgates 'Opinion Concerning Further Strengthening the Monitoring of Small-Scale Food Production and Processing Workshops', 10 July 2007, www.aqsiq.gov.cn/zjxw/zjxw/zjftpxw/200707/t20070711_33419.htm (accessed 27 September 2010); 'Full text: China's food quality and safety', Chinese Government's Official Web Portal, 17 August 2007, www.gov.cn/english/2007–08/17/content_720346.htm (accessed 27 September 2010). Similar data can be found in Tam Waikeung and Dali L. Yang, 'Food safety and the development of regulatory institutions in China', in Dali L. Yang (ed.), *Discontented Miracle: Growth, Conflict, and Institutional Adaptations in China* (Singapore: World Scientific, 2007), pp. 182–4; and Ellis and Turner, *Sowing the Seeds*, p. 48.
31 Ellis and Turner, *Sowing the Seeds*, p. 26; Tam and Yang, 'Food safety and the development of regulatory institutions in China', pp. 182–4; Steve Suppan, *U.S.–China Agreement on Food Safety: Terms and Enforcement Capacity* (Minneapolis, MN: Institute for Agriculture and Trade Policy, May 2008), p. 7, www.iatp.org/iatp/publications.cfm?accountID=451&refID=102837 (accessed 11 October 2010).
32 AQSIQ, 'Guojia zhijianzongju fabu "guanyu jinyibu jiaqiang shipinshengchan jiagong xiaozuofang jianguan gongzuo de yijian" tuchu sanxiang jianguan zhidu quebao shipin zhiliang anquan' (AQSIQ promulgates 'Opinion Concerning Further Strengthening the Monitoring of Small-Scale Food Production and Processing Workshops').
33 Kerry Beach, 'World markets: examining China's food safety complexities', AIB Update, March/April 2008, pp. 10–13, https://www.aibonline.org/newsletter/Magazine/Mar_Apr2008/8China.pdf (accessed 27 September 2010).
34 'Full text: China's food quality and wafety'.
35 Ellis and Turner, *Sowing the Seeds*, p. 17.
36 Barboza, 'Food-Safety crackdown in China'.
37 There was a saying prevalent in China in the early 1990s; it was 'Yaoxiang dang xianzhang, jiuyao ban yaochang' (To be a county magistrate, you must run drug factories). Peng Liu, 'From decentralised developmental state towards authoritarian regulatory state: a case study on drug safety regulation in China', *China: An International Journal*, Vol. 8, No. 1 (March 2010), pp. 118, 120.
38 Peng Liu, 'Tracing and periodizing China's food safety regulation: a study on China's food safety regime change', *Regulation & Governance*, Vol. 4, No. 2 (June 2010), pp. 247–9.
39 On local levels more agencies are involved in food safety control. The Food Safety Commission in Guangdong, for instance, is composed of representatives of eighteen departments. Yan Haina, 'Woguo shipin anquan jianguan tizhi gaige – jiyu zhengti zhengfu lilun de fenxi' (The reform of China's food safety monitoring system: an analysis based on the theory of holistic government), *Xueshu yanjiu* (*Academic Research*), No. 5 (2010), p. 45, note 1.
40 It is argued that the authority of the MoH has been weakened as a result of the power to regulate the food processing industry being transferred to AQSIQ. Li Bai, Chenglin Ma, Shunlong Gong and Yinsheng Yang, 'Food safety assurance system in China', *Food Control*, Vol. 18, No. 5 (May 2007), pp. 480–84.
41 Ellis and Turner, *Sowing the Seeds*, p. 43; Liu, 'Tracing and periodizing China's food safety regulation', pp. 253–4; Yan Haina, 'Woguo shipin anquan jianguan tizhi gaige' (The reform of China's food safety monitoring system), pp. 45–6.

42 Liu, 'From decentralised developmental state towards authoritarian regulatory state', p. 122.
43 Ibid., p. 130.
44 David Barboza, 'A Chinese reformer betrays his cause, and pays', *New York Times*, 13 July 2007, www.nytimes.com/2007/07/13/business/worldbusiness/13corrupt.html (accessed 24 October 2010).
45 Liu, 'From decentralised developmental state towards authoritarian regulatory state', p. 130.
46 Its website is www.panchina.org (accessed 3 October 2010). See also Ellis and Turner, *Sowing the Seeds*, p. 27.
47 Gabriel Ascher, 'Fight the bootlegs: consumer rights in China', eChinacities.com, 11 May 2010, www.echinacities.com/expat-corner/fight-the-bootlegs-consumer-rights-in-china.html (accessed 3 October 2010). See also Ellis and Turner, *Sowing the Seeds*, p. 27.
48 Ellis and Turner, *Sowing the Seeds*, pp. 40–42.
49 Wines, 'Tainted dairy products seized in western China'; 'Father who lost child to melamine-tainted milk gets a year of hard labour', AsiaNews.it, 7 July 2010, www.asianews.it/news-en/Father-who-lost-child-to-melamine-tainted-milk-gets-a-year-of-hard-labour-18872.html (accessed 11 October 2010).
50 Andrew Jacobs, 'China sentences activist in milk scandal to prison', *New York Times*, 10 November 2010, www.nytimes.com/2010/11/11/world/asia/11beijing.html (accessed 24 December 2010); Verna Yu and Priscilla Jiao, 'Outrage as tainted milk "hero" goes to jail', *South China Morning Post*, 11 November 2010, through LexisNexis.
51 The verdict even came under criticism from Hong Kong deputies to the National People's Congress and Hong Kong delegates to the Chinese People's Political Consultative Conference. 'China: milk scandal protester reported free', *New York Times*, 28 December 2010, www.nytimes.com/2010/12/29/world/asia/web-briefs-Chinabrf.html; 'Melamine activist "thanks" government for support', *Global Times*, 29 December 2010, http://china.globaltimes.cn/society/2010–12/606541.html; 'Official warns against interference', *Global Times*, 30 December 2010, http://china.globaltimes.cn/society/2010–12/607081.html (all accessed 30 December 2010).
52 Ellis and Turner, *Sowing the Seeds*, pp. 28–30.
53 'Sanwei fuzhongli he shiwuwei buzhan zucheng shipin anquan weiyuanhui' (Three Vice-Premiers and fifteen ministers to form the Food Safety Commission), *Zhongguo shipin xuebao* (*Journal of China's Food*), No. 1 (2010), p. 160. Details of the eighteen members of the Commission are at http://big5.gov.cn/gate/big5/www.gov.cn/xxgk/pub/govpublic/mrlm/201002/t20100210_56388.html (accessed 10 October 2010).
54 'China to overhaul diary supervision before festivals', *People's Daily Online*, 24 December 2010, http://english.peopledaily.com.cn/90001/90776/90882/7242183.html (accessed 25 December 2010).
55 The official website is: www.codexalimentarius.net/web/index_en.jsp (accessed 26 January 2011).
56 Member states may adopt higher standards if these are applied without any unjustifiable discrimination against any countries and wholly based on scientific evidence. Oosterveer, *Global Governance of Food Production and Consumption*, p. 73; Ellis and Turner, *Sowing the Seeds*, pp. 36–7. The official website of the SPS Agreement is: www.wto.org/english/tratop_e/sps_e/spsagr_e.htm (accessed 26 January 2011).
57 The Chinese white paper on food quality and safety, published in 2007, indicates all of these standards for food safety control. See 'Full text: China's food quality and safety'.
58 World Health Organization, *International Food Safety Authorities Network (INFOSAN)*, October 2007, www.who.int/foodsafety/fs_management/infosan_1007_en.pdf (accessed 22 December 2010).

59 World Health Organization, 'INFOSAN Information Note No. 4/2007 – IRH (2005)', 10 May 2007, www.who.int/foodsafety/fs_management/No_04_IHR_May07_en.pdf (accessed 22 December 2010).
60 World Health Organization, 'Expert meeting to review toxicological aspects of melamine and cyanuric acid, 1–4 December 2008', www.who.int/foodsafety/fs_management/infosan_events/en/index4.html (accessed 22 December 2010).
61 In an interview conducted by one of the authors of this book on 19 November 2010 in Geneva.
62 Jacobs, 'China sentences activist in milk scandal to prison'.
63 David Barboza, 'China admits new tainted-milk case is older', *New York Times*, 6 January 2010, www.nytimes.com/2010/01/07/world/asia/07milk.html (accessed 10 October 2010). The Food Safety Act (*Shipin anquanfa shishi tiaoli*) is at www.gov.cn/zwgk/2009–07/24/content_1373609.htm (accessed 10 October 2010).
64 'ppm' denotes parts-per-million. One part per million (ppm) denotes one part per 1,000,000 parts, one part in 10^6, and a value of 1×10^{-6}. This is equivalent to one drop of water diluted into 50 litres.
65 Chen Chunlai, Yang Jun and Christopher Findlay, 'Measuring the effect of food safety standards on China's agricultural exports', *Review of World Economics*, Vol. 144, No. 1 (2008), p. 86.
66 Suppan, *U.S.–China Agreement on Food Safety*, p. 9.
67 Ellis and Turner, *Sowing the Seeds*, p. 4.
68 Suppan, *U.S.–China Agreement on Food Safety*, p. 7.
69 Alicia Mundy, 'China never investigated tainted heparin, says probe', *Wall Street Journal Online*, 22 July 2010, http://online.wsj.com/article/SB10001424052748703954804575381540372921432.html (accessed 9 October 2010); 'China may be the source of tainted heparin', Associated Press, 5 March 2008, www.msnbc.msn.com/id/23485723/ (accessed 9 October 2010).
70 But China's SFDA countered that a very thorough investigation was done in accordance with an agreement signed with the US FDA in 2007. But there was no report on the results of the Chinese investigation. Mundy, 'China never investigated tainted heparin, says Probe'.
71 James T. Areddy, 'Amid Chinese food scares FDA has limited scope', *Wall Street Journal Online*, 15 August 2010, http://blogs.wsj.com/chinarealtime/2010/08/15/amid-chinese-food-scares-fda-has-limited-scope/ (accessed 9 October 2010).
72 Information is obtained from the website of the Delegation of the European Union to China, http://ec.europa.eu/delegations/china/eu_china/food_safety_and_consumer_protection/food_safety/index_en.htm (accessed 22 December 2010).
73 'EU–China Food Safety Workshop, 4 November 2009', www.euchinawto.org/index.php?option=com_content&task=view&id=350&Itemid=36 (accessed 2 January 2011).
74 'Opening remarks by the Secretary General of ASEAN at the China–ASEAN Ministerial Meeting on Quality Supervision Inspection and Quarantine, Nanning, China, 28–29 October 2007', www.aseansec.org/21019.htm; '2nd ASEAN-China ministerial meeting deepens cooperation on quality supervision, inspection and quarantine', Xinhuanet.com, http://news.xinhuanet.com/english2010/china/2010–10/25/c_13574635.htm (both accessed 23 December 2010).
75 'Food safety better, but still huge issue', *People's Daily Online*, 13 June 2010; http://english.peopledaily.com.cn/90001/90776/90882/7024738.html (accessed 25 October 2010).
76 Ellis and Turner, *Sowing the Seeds*, p. 52.
77 Oosterveer, *Global Governance of Food Production and Consumption*, p. 18.

9 Energy security

1. Robert B. Zoellick, 'Whither China: from membership to responsibility?', Remarks to National Committee on U.S.–China Relations, 21 September 2005, www.ncuscr.org/files/2005Gala_RobertZoellick_Whither_China1.pdf (accessed 15 December 2009). Zoellick was then Deputy Secretary of State, United States.
2. The benchmark price is West Texas Intermediate (WTI) light sweet future contract 1 price, traded on the New York Merchandise Exchange (NYMEX). The daily closing price data are available at http://tonto.eia.doe.gov/dnav/pet/hist/LeafHandler.ashx?n=PET&s=RCLC1&f=D (accessed 25 December 2010).
3. In a form known as 'dollar carry trade', investors borrow heavily in US dollars at low interest rates and use the money to buy assets that yield higher returns such as oil and other commodities. Aline van Duyn, 'Why dollar carry trade faces hidden dangers', *Financial Times*, 7 November 2009.
4. Since 2007, Christophe de Margerie, chief executive of France's Total, has argued that world oil production will not exceed the threshold of 100 million barrels per day because many oil-rich countries do not allow international oil companies to explore their reserves. Russell Gold and Ann Davis, 'Oil officials see limit looming on production', *Wall Street Journal*, 19 November 2009, reprinted in http://royaldutchshellplc.com/2007/11/19/the-wall-street-journal-oil-officials-see-limit-looming-on-production (accessed 7 November 2009); Carola Hoyos, 'Burning ambition', *Financial Times*, 4 November 2009 through LexisNexis.
5. In 2009 the US accounted for 21.7 per cent of the world's total oil consumption while the shares of China, Japan and India were respectively 10.4 per cent, 5.1 per cent and 3.8 per cent. In the same year China's net crude oil imports were 198.8 million tonnes, behind the US (440.6 million tonnes). BP, *BP Statistical Review of World Energy June 2010* (London: BP, 2010), pp. 12, 21.
6. International Energy Agency, *World Energy Outlook 2010* (Paris: International Energy Agency/OECD, 2010), pp. 48, 85.
7. Alexander Kwiatkowski, 'Oil price swings to worsen as spare OPEC capacity shrinks: energy markets', Bloomberg, 28 June 2010, www.bloomberg.com/news/2010-06-27/oil-price-swings-to-worsen-as-spare-opec-capacity-shrinks-energy-markets.html. See also Yee Kai Pin, 'Oil to exceed $100 in 2011 as OPEC spare capacity shrinks, Goldman says', Bloomberg, 14 December 2010, www.bloomberg.com/news/2010-12-14/oil-to-exceed-100-by-second-half-of-2011-as-demand-recovers-goldman-says.html (all accessed 29 December 2010).
8. Jan H. Kalicki and David L. Goldwyn, 'Introduction: the need to integrate energy and foreign policy', in idem (eds), *Energy and Security: Toward a New Foreign Policy Strategy* (Washington, DC: Woodrow Wilson Center Press, 2005), pp. 2–3; Amy Myers Jaffe and Ronald Soligo, *Militarization of Energy: Geopolitical Threats to the Global Energy System*, a working paper in the series of The Global Energy Market: Comprehensive Strategies to Meet Geopolitical and Financial Risks, Energy Forum of James A. Baker III Institute for Public Policy, Rice University, United States, May 2008, p. 7, www.rice.edu/energy/publications/WorkingPapers/IEEJMilitarization.pdf (accessed 1 November 2009); Michael Klare, *Rising Powers, Shrinking Planet: How Scarce Energy Is Creating a New World Order* (Oxford: Oneworld Publications, 2008), Chapter 2; Edward L. Morse and Amy Myers Jaffe, 'OPEC in confrontation with globalization', in Kalicki and Goldwyn (eds), *Energy and Security*, pp. 77–81.
9. International Energy Agency, *World Energy Outlook 2009*, p. 84.
10. Morse and Jaffe, 'OPEC in confrontation with globalization', p. 79; Robert Pirog, *The Role of National Oil Companies in the International Oil Market*, CRS Report for Congress RL34137 (Washington, DC: Congressional Research Service, 2007), www.fas.org/sgp/crs/misc/RL34137.pdf (accessed 3 November 2009).

244 *Notes*

11 Daniel Yergin, 'Energy security in the 1990s', *Foreign Affairs*, Vol. 67, No. 1 (Fall 1988), pp. 110–32, at p. 111.
12 Adrienne Héritier, 'Introduction', in idem (ed), *Common Goods: Reinventing European and International Governance* (Lanham, MD: Rowman & Littlefield, 2002), p. 2.
13 The European Commission argues that 'Well-functioning world markets are the best way of ensuring safe and affordable energy supplies'. European Commission, 'An external policy to serve Europe's energy interests', Paper from Commission/SG/HR for the European Council S160/06, 2006, p. 2, http://ec.europa.eu/dgs/energy_transport/international/doc/paper_solana_sg_energy_en.pdf (accessed 8 July 2009).
14 Five of the 'seven sisters' were American firms, namely Standard Oil of New Jersey, now called Exxon; Standard Oil of California, now known as Chevron; Gulf, now part of Chevron; Mobil; and Texaco. The others were British Petroleum and the Anglo-Dutch firm, Royal Dutch Shell. Joan E. Spero and Jeffrey A. Hart, *The Politics of International Economic Relations* (Boston, MA: Wadsworth, 2010), p. 373.
15 John Mitchell with Koji Morita, Norman Selley and Jonathan Stern, *The New Economy of Oil: Impacts on Business, Geopolitics and Society* (London: Royal Institute of International Affairs and Earthscan Publications, 2001), pp. 179–80.
16 Between 1973 and 1983 OPEC's share of the world oil market fell from 63 per cent to more or less 30 per cent. Spero and Hart, *The Politics of International Economic Relations*, p. 356.
17 Ibid., pp. 289–95; Daniel Yergin, *The Prize: The Epic Quest for Oil, Money and Power* (New York: Simon & Schuster, 1993), pp. 721–6.
18 The first two versions of the Brent futures contract, launched in November 1983 and October 1985, however, failed. The IPE introduced a third and successful version in June 1988. Paul Horsnell and Robert Mabro, *Oil Markets and Prices: The Brent Market and the Formation of World Oil Prices* (Oxford: Oxford University Press for the Oxford Institute for Energy Studies, 1993), pp. 46–50, 73–82.
19 Saudi Arabia decided in September 1985 to abandon the OPEC-administered price system in order to arrest a reduction in its production and exports. In view of its production declining from eleven million barrels per day in 1980 to 3–3.5 million barrels per day in 1985 and the concomitant fall in oil income from $113 billion in 1981 to just $28 billion in 1985, it introduced a short-lived pricing measure known as netback pricing for its oil exports whereby its oil was paid on the basis of the market prices of the refined petroleum products (e.g. gasoline and heating oil) minus the refining and transportation costs involved. Initially aimed at assuring refiners which bought Saudi oil of a profit and at regaining Saudi Arabia's market share, this pricing experiment was disgraced because of the price collapse afterwards. With a guarantee of a profit margin, refiners increased oil purchases from Saudi Arabia and netback pricing became prevalent in other oil-producing countries. In the first half of 1986, oil prices fell to $12 per barrel; in contrast, the prices were over $40 in 1980–81 as a consequence of the Iranian Revolution. Netback pricing was replaced by market-related pricing formulaes, first implemented by Mexico in March 1986. Horsnell and Mabro, *Oil Markets and Prices*, pp. 79–81, 291–2; Edward L. Morse, 'After the fall: the politics of oil', *Foreign Affairs*, Vol. 64 (Spring 1986), pp. 792–811; Yergin, *The Prize*, pp. 748–50.
20 Horsnell and Mabro, *Oil Markets and Prices*, pp. 313–20.
21 Toby Shelley, *Oil: Politics, Poverty and the Planet* (London: Zed Books, 2005), pp. 95–100.
22 Joel Dreyfuss and Philip Mattera, 'BNOC fades out', *Fortune*, 15 April 1985, http://money.cnn.com/magazines/fortune/fortune_archive/1985/04/15/65828/index.htm (accessed 26 November 2009); Yergin, *The Prize*, p. 746.
23 Mitchell *et al.*, *The New Economy of Oil*, p. 181.
24 Coby van der Linde, *Energy in a Changing World*, Clingendael Energy Papers No. 11 (The Hague: Clingendael International Energy Programme, Netherlands Insti-

tute of International Relations Clingendael, 2005), www.clingendael.nl/publications/2006/20060308_ciep_paper_vanderlinde.pdf (accessed 3 July 2009). See also Richard Youngs, *Energy Security: Europe's New Foreign Policy Challenge* (Abingdon: Routledge, 2009), pp. 6–10.
25 Kalicki and Goldwyn, 'Introduction', p. 9.
26 Daniel Yergin's testimony before the US House of Representatives Committee on Foreign Affairs hearing on 'Foreign policy and national security implications of oil dependence', 22 March 2007, www.cera.com/aspx/cda/public1/news/articles/newsArticleDetails.aspx?CID=8689 (accessed 10 July 2007). Cited in Peter C. Evans and Erica S. Downs, *Untangling China's Quest for Oil through State-Backed Financial Deals*, Brookings Institution Policy Brief No. 154 (Washington, DC: Brookings Institution, May 2006), p. 5, www.brookings.edu/comm/policybriefs/pb154.pdf (accessed 30 June 2009).
27 Klare, *Rising Powers, Shrinking Planet*. Neo-mercantilism argues that national power is derived from productive capability and that productive capability in turn flows from economic growth. National interests are understood as 'maximizing a country's power in relations to its competitors' and 'reducing the vulnerabilities that accompany the integration into the global economy'. Unlike classical mercantilism, followers of the new school are more concerned about industrial capacity to generate wealth and secure access to vital scarce raw resources and finance than accumulation of specie. Cited in Charles E. Ziegler, 'Neomercantilism and energy interdependence: Russian strategies in East Asia', *Asian Security*, Vol. 6, No. 1 (2010), p. 78. See also Jonathan Kirshner, 'The political economy of realism', in Ethan B. Kapstein and Michael Mastanduno (eds), *Unipolar Politics: Realism and State Strategies after the Cold War* (New York, NY: Columbia University Press, 1999), pp. 70–71.
28 Jaffe and Soligo, *Militarization of Energy*, p. 45.
29 Robert Gilpin with the assistance of Jean M. Gilpin, *The Political Economy of International Relations* (Princeton, NJ: Princeton University Press, 1987), pp. 31–4; Daniel Yergin and Joseph Stanislaw, *The Commanding Heights: The Battle between Government and the Marketplace That Is Remaking the Modern World* (New York: Simon & Schuster, 1998), p. 12.
30 Andreas Goldthau, 'Energy diplomacy in trade and investment of oil and gas', in Andreas Goldthau and Jan Martin Witte (eds), *Global Energy Governance: The New Rules of the Game* (Berlin and Washington, DC: Global Public Policy Institute/Brookings Institution Press, 2010), p. 28.
31 Ibid., pp. 25–47.
32 Morse and Jaffe, 'OPEC in confrontation with globalization', p. 87.
33 Flynt Leverett, 'The geopolitics of oil and America's international standing', testimony to the Committee on Energy and Natural Resources, United States Senate, 10 January 2007, p. 3, www.newamerica.net/files/070110leverett_testimony.pdf (accessed 29 November 2009). See also idem, 'Resource mercantilism and the militarization of resource management: rising Asia and the future of American primacy in the Persian Gulf', in Daniel Moran and James A. Russell (eds), *Energy Security and Global Politics: The Militarization of Resource Management* (Abingdon: Routledge, 2009), pp. 211–42.
34 Erica S. Downs, 'The fact and fiction of Sino-African energy relations', *China Security*, Vol. 3, No. 3 (2007), pp. 42–68; Wenran Jiang, 'Fuelling the dragon: China's rise and its energy and resources extraction in Africa', *China Quarterly*, No. 199 (September 2009), pp. 585–609.
35 This section draws on, with updates in appropriate places, Pak K. Lee, 'China's quest for oil security: oil (wars) in the pipeline?', *Pacific Review*, Vol. 18, No. 2 (2005), pp. 265–301; Pak K. Lee and Lai-Ha Chan, 'Non-traditional security threats in China: challenges of energy shortage and infectious diseases', in Joseph Y. S.

Cheng (ed.), *Challenges and Policy Programmes of China's New Leadership* (Hong Kong: City University of Hong Kong Press, 2007), pp. 297–336; and Pak K. Lee, 'The power politics of China's search for energy security: from pre-Daqing to post-Daqing', in Chan Lai-Ha, Gerald Chan and Kwan Fung (eds), *China at 60: Global–Local Interactions* (Singapore: World Scientific Publications, 2011), pp. 229–54.

36 The Yukos decision angered the Kremlin for two reasons. It threatened to end state-owned Transneft's monopoly over Russian oil pipelines and the oil contracts with the Chinese were not approved by the state. Marshall Goldman, *Oilopoly: Putin, Power and the Rise of the New Russia* (Oxford: Oneworld Publications, 2008), pp. 111, 115.

37 The Japanese were lobbying for a rival pipeline to the Pacific port of Nakhodka, near Vladivostok by promising to give $7 billion's worth low-interest loans to Russia. Lee, 'China's quest for oil security', p. 277.

38 Due to protests by environmentalists, Transneft decided in July 2006 to construct the tanker port in Kozmino rather than Perevoznaya. Rafael Kandiyoti, *Pipelines: Flowing Oil and Crude Politics* (London and New York: I. B. Tauris, 2008), pp. 217–18.

39 Russian domestic politics also played a role here. The emergence of *siloviki*, officials with links to the security apparatus, in Putin's presidency, of which an exemplary figure is Igor Sechin, contributed to the derailing of Russian–Japanese cooperation. Bobo Lo, *Axis of Convenience: Moscow, Beijing, and the New Geopolitics* (London: Chatham House, 2008), pp. 145–6. German Gref, a close aide to Putin, said in September 2005 that 'ceding' the Kuril Islands to Japan was 'inadmissible'. Cited in Kandiyoti, *Pipelines*, p. 223.

40 The construction of the Daqing-bound Chinese pipeline started in May 2009. Eric Watkins, 'China to begin construction of 992-km ESPO "extension"', *Oil & Gas Journal Online*, 5 May 2009, www.ogj.com/articles/article_display.cfm?ARTICLE_ID=361235&p=7 (accessed 13 May 2008).

41 Referring to the construction of the branch line, Sergei Shmatko, Russian Energy Minister, said in October 2008, 'There is no way. It cannot be put into operation next year'. He added that while there was political will, an agreement on the pipeline would depend on commercial terms. Eric Watkins, 'China to get no ESPO spur before 2009', *Oil & Gas Journal Online*, 23 October 2008, www.ogj.com/articles/article_display.cfm?ARTICLE_ID=343444&p=7 (accessed 28 October 2008). Russia and China signed in April 2009 an intergovernmental agreement to build a pipeline from Skovorodino to Mohe county, Heilongjiang province. Russia began to conduct test runs in the pipeline in November 2010. 'Russia, China sign oil deal, start new pipeline branch', RIA Novosti, 21 April 2009, http://en.rian.ru/business/20090421/121220680.html (accessed 16 August 2009); 'Launch of ESPO shipments heralds new era for Russia–China energy relations', *BMI Emerging Europe Oil and Gas Insights*, 1 December 2010, through LexisNexis.

42 'Wen, Putin seal long-awaited deal on pipeline link to Siberian oil', *South China Morning Post*, 29 October 2008; Eric Watkins, 'Russia, China agree on ESPO pipeline spur', *Oil & Gas Journal Online*, 29 October 2008, www.ogj.com/articles/article_display.cfm?ARTICLE_ID=343905&p=7 (accessed 30 October 2008).

43 Rosneft is an oil-producing corporation while Transneft is a pipeline operator. While the $10 billion loan was supposedly used by Transneft to construct the China-bound spur, the building cost of the line was only $280 million. So China indirectly financed the construction of the ESPO pipeline. Eric Watkins, 'Russians initially tag ESPO spur at $280 million', *Oil & Gas Journal Online*, 27 February 2009, www.ogj.com/articles/article_display.cfm?ARTICLE_ID=354771&p=7 (accessed 28 February 2008); 'Launch of ESPO shipments heralds new era for Russia–China energy relations'; 'Rosneft and CNPC to build US$5 billion oil refinery in Tianjin city', *Russia Briefing*, 23 September 2010, http://russia-briefing.com/news/rosneft-and-cnpc-to-build-us5-billion-oil-refinery-in-tianjin-city.html (accessed 29 December 2010).

Notes 247

44 'ESPO oil price cut not discussed at Russia, China talks', *Platts Commodity News*, 21 September 2010, through Factiva; Eric Watkins, 'Russia, China to keep to agreement over ESPO oil price', *Oil & Gas Journal*, 24 September 2010, www.ogj.com/index/article-display.articles.oil-gas-journal.transportation-2.pipelines.2010.09.russia_-china_to_keep.html (accessed 28 September 2010); Yu Bin, 'China–Russia relations: Peace Mission 2010 and Medvedev's visit to China', *Comparative Connections*, October 2010, http://csis.org/files/publication/1003qchina_russia.pdf (accessed 28 January 2011).
45 *China's African Policy* (Beijing: Ministry of Foreign Affairs of the PRC, January 2006), www.fmprc.gov.cn/eng/zxxx/t230615.htm (accessed 15 February 2010).
46 'Africa tour highlights relations', *China Daily*, 12 February 2007 through LexisNexis.
47 Joshua Eisenman and Joshua Kurlantzick, 'China's Africa strategy', *Current History*, May 2006, pp. 219–24. The Sovereign Wealth Fund Institute gives the CADFund a rating of 4 in transparency. The minimum score is 1 and the maximum 10. But the Institute points out that only those which receive 8 or above have adequate transparency. Sovereign Wealth Fund Institute, 'China–Africa Development Fund', www.swfinstitute.org/fund/cad.php (accessed 28 December 2010).
48 William Wallis and Geoff Dyer, 'Financing: lending rattles the traditional donors', *Financial Times*, 23 January 2008, www.ft.com/cms/s/0/56b70b80-c897-11dc-94a6-0000779fd2ac.html (accessed 15 August 2011).
49 The reported economic assistance includes government-sponsored investment, concessional loans, grants, debt cancellation and in-kind aid. Thomas Lum, *China's Assistance and Government-Sponsored Investment Activities in Africa, Latin America, and Southeast Asia*, CRS Report for Congress R40940 (Washington, DC: Congressional Research Service, 25 November 2009), p. 7, www.fas.org/sgp/crs/row/R40940.pdf (accessed 11 March 2010).
50 China's official development aid is composed of external assistance expenditure by the Ministry of Finance and concessional loans from China's Eximbank. Since the OECD treats debt relief as aid, so China's outlays on debt relief are added. Deborah Brautigam, *The Dragon's Gift: The Real Story of China in Africa* (Oxford: Oxford University Press, 2009), pp. 168–72.
51 Scott Baldauf, 'China, eager for oil, expands investment in Nigeria and Guinea', *Christian Science Monitor*, 30 October 2009, www.csmonitor.com/World/Africa/2009/1030/p06s04-woaf.html (accessed 28 December 2010).
52 The aid covers construction of the road and railway system, electric power plants, housing and medical care. Ricardo Soares de Oliveira, 'Making sense of Chinese oil investment in Africa', in Chris Alden, Daniel Large and Ricardo Soares de Oliveira (eds), *China Returns to Africa: A Rising Power and a Continent Embrace* (London: Hurst, 2008), pp. 83–109; Henry Lee and Dan Shalmon, 'Searching for oil: China's oil strategies in Africa', in Robert I. Rotberg (ed.), *China into Africa: Trade, Aid, and Influence* (Washington, DC: Brookings Institution Press, 2008), pp. 109–36; Lai-Ha Chan, *China Engages Global Health Governance: Responsible Stakeholder or System-Transformer* (New York: Palgrave Macmillan, 2011), pp. 105–106.
53 Lee and Shalmon, 'Searching for oil'.
54 Soares de Oliveira, 'Making sense of Chinese oil investment in Africa'. See also Goldthau, 'Energy diplomacy in trade and investment of oil and gas', especially pp. 34–5.
55 Matthew Green, 'Energy: Beijing learns to tread warily', *Financial Times*, 23 January 2008, www.ft.com/cms/s/0/5152546a-c897-11dc-94a6-0000779fd2ac.html (accessed 15 August 2011).
56 The following draws on Leverett, 'Resource mercantilism and the militarization of resource management'.
57 While a global market for oil is already in place, the one for gas is just in the making. Andreas Goldthau and Jan Martin Witte, 'Back to the future or forward to

the past? Strengthening markets and rules for effective global energy governance', *International Affairs*, Vol. 85, No. 2 (2009), pp. 373–90.
58 South Korea was not a member of the International Energy Agency, an energy organization of major industrial countries, until 2001. According to the US Energy Information Administration, as of April 2007, the Korea National Oil Corporation's strategic stockpiles had 76 million barrels of oil, amounting to approximately thirty-four days of net imports. Energy Information Administration, US Department of Energy, 'South Korea', June 2007, www.eia.doe.gov/emeu/cabs/South_Korea/Oil.html (accessed 25 May 2009); Keiichi Yokobori, 'Japan', in Kalicki and Goldwyn (eds), *Energy and Security*, pp. 305–28.
59 China took the lead in December 2006, holding in Beijing the first energy ministers' meeting of the five largest energy-consuming countries – the United States, China, Japan, South Korea and India. The second meeting was held in Aomori, Japan, in June 2008, www.enecho.meti.go.jp/topics/080607c.pdf (accessed 4 July 2009). The third meeting was supposed to be hosted by South Korea, but no report on the meeting has been found. At the second East Asian Summit in January 2007 in Cebu, the Philippines, the Cebu Declaration on East Asian Energy Security (www.aseansec.org/19319.htm; accessed 4 July 2009) was signed by the ten ASEAN states, Australia, China, India, Japan, New Zealand and South Korea. In August of the same year, the first annual EAS energy ministers' meetings were held in Singapore, www.aseansec.org/20848.htm; www.aseansec.org/21853.htm (accessed 4 July 2009).
60 If Chinese NOCs ship home the equity oil they produce abroad, they will buy less from international markets, leaving more oil for other consumer countries to purchase. Downs, 'The fact and fiction of Sino-African energy relations'.
61 Shoichi Itoh, 'Sino-Russian energy relations: the dilemma of strategic partnership and mutual distrust', in Hiroshi Kimura (ed.), *Russia's Shift toward Asia* (Tokyo: Sasakawa Peace Foundation, 2007), p. 71; Lee, 'China's quest for oil security', p. 279. According to Bo Kang, 'the family' and the St Petersburg faction, two powerful anti-China factional groups in Russia, lobbied Duma deputies to oppose the CNPC's bid. Another less well-known setback was the CNPC's acquisition of Stimul, a Russian energy company, in 2003–2004. Bo Kang, *China's International Petroleum Policy* (Santa Barbara, CA: Praeger Security International, 2010), pp. 104–108.
62 A Chinese analysis of this event from a statist perspective is Wu Xiaopeng, 'Zhonghaiyou binggou an de guoji jingjixue fenxi' (A political-economy analysis of CNOOC's merger and acquisition), *Guoji guanxi xueyuan xuebao* (*Journal of the University of International Relations*), No. 2 (2006), pp. 28–33.
63 House Resolution 344, US House of Representatives, 30 June 2005, www.govtrack.us/congress/billtext.xpd?bill=hr109-344 (accessed 25 May 2009).
64 Klare, *Rising Powers, Shrinking Planet*, pp. 1–8, at pp. 6, 7. This mistrust of the global market is likely being fuelled further since the Anglo-Australian mining corporation, Rio Tinto, scrapped in June 2009 a deal worth $19.5 billion with state-owned Aluminium Corporation of China (Chinalco). The deal, announced in February 2009 when commodity market prices were quite low, would have boosted Chinalco's stake in Rio Tinto to about 18 per cent from 9 per cent. It was alleged that China intended to make use of the deal to strengthen its sway over the pricing of iron ore. But the initial agreement met opposition in Australia. Barnaby Joyce, an Australian Senator, said, 'It is great for the Australian people that this deal falls over and we do not have the complications of the Communist People's Republic of China's government owning the wealth of Australia in the ground in Australia'. Cited in 'Rio Tinto scraps China firm deal', *BBC News*, 5 June 2009, http://news.bbc.co.uk/2/hi/business/8084350.stm (accessed 8 June 2009). But western governments have grounds for being leery about acquisitions from China. First, China does not allow reciprocal acquisitions of its energy companies by foreign companies. Second, China's state-owned banks offered loans on highly preferential terms to

Notes   249

Chinalco to finance its deal with Rio Tinto. Four large banks provided loans at an interest rate next to zero without any timeline for repayment. 'Chinese firms' foreign investments: Sino-Trojan horse', *The Economist*, 30 May–5 June 2009; Shujie Yao, 'China will learn from failed Chinalco–Rio deal', *Financial Times*, 7 June 2009, www.ft.com/cms/s/0/6334ed04-538e-11de-be08-00144feabdc0.html (accessed 15 August 2011).

65 It is argued that it is not in the interests of China to enhance the power of Russia as an oil exporter. Linda Jakobson and Zha Daojiong, 'China and the worldwide search for oil security', *Asia-Pacific Review*, Vol. 13, No. 2 (2006), pp. 60–73.

66 Itoh, 'Sino-Russian energy cooperation', p. 73; idem, 'Russia's energy diplomacy toward the Asia-Pacific: is Moscow's ambition dashed?', in Shinichiro Tabata (ed.), *Energy and Environment in Slavic Eurasia: Toward the Establishment of the Network of Environmental Studies in the Pan-Okhotsk Region* (Sapporo: Slavic Research Centre, Hokkaido University, 2008), p. 52, http://src-h.slav.hokudai.ac.jp/coe21/publish/no19_ses/contents.html (accessed 4 July 2009).

67 That explains why China extends the tentacles of its energy diplomacy to Latin America, in particular Venezuela and Brazil. Together they hold about 7.1 per cent of the world's total oil reserves, slightly less than the Russian share. Latin American countries in 2007 provided China with more than ten million tonnes of oil, accounting for 6.3 per cent of China's oil imports that year. The Editorial Board of China Commerce Yearbook (ed.), *China Commerce Yearbook 2008* (Beijing: China Commerce Publishing House, 2008), p. 176.

68 Bo Kang, *China's International Petroleum Policy*, pp. 129–30; discussions with an oil expert, Beijing, July 2009. The specialist pointed out that Jiang Zemin was sanguine about the Sino-Russian pipeline, believing that he had close relations with Russian leaders as he talked to them in Russian. China changed tack after Hu Jintao assumed the leadership of the CCP.

69 For a study about the importance of overland pipeline, see Sun Jing, 'Zhongguo shiyou anquan de lulu guandao zhanlue tanxi' (An analysis of China's overland oil pipeline security strategy), *Shehuizhuyi yanjiu* (*Socialism Studies*), No. 4 (2010), pp. 117–21.

70 Wu Lei and Shen Qinyu, 'Will China go to war over oil?', *Far Eastern Economic Review*, April 2006, pp. 38–40.

71 For a discussion of Russian preferences, see Lo, *Axis of Convenience*, p. 138.

72 Downs, 'The fact and fiction of Sino-African energy relations'.

73 Jakobson and Zha, 'China and the worldwide search for oil security'.

74 Wilfred L. Kohl, 'Consumer country energy cooperation: the International Energy Agency and the global energy order', in Goldthau and Witte (eds), *Global Energy Governance*, p. 217.

75 Carola Hoyos, 'Energy watchdog wants Beijing as member', *Financial Times*, 31 March 2010, through LexisNexis.

76 See also Kohl, 'Consumer country energy cooperation', pp. 218–19.

77 China is a dialogue country of the IEA. According to Hillary Clinton, the US government would support Chinese and Indian membership, which would require revision of the International Energy Programme that created IEA. Shai Oster, 'U.S. asks China to join global energy group', *Wall Street Journal Online*, 21 May 2008, http://online.wsj.com/article/SB121127520932506675.html (accessed 22 May 2005); Nick Snow, 'Clinton: energy security a major US foreign policy element', *Oil & Gas Journal Online*, 26 January 2009, www.ogj.com/articles/article_display.cfm?ARTICLE_ID=351434&p=7 (accessed 27 January 2009). Without delving into details, three Chinese scholars have argued that joining the IEA should be a priority of China's energy diplomacy in the future. Tao Ye, Xie Huifeng and Liu Chunjiang, 'Goujian quanqiu hezuo beijing xia de Zhongguo nengyuan waijiao fanglue' (Constructing the general plan for China's energy diplomacy against the backdrop of global cooperation), *Zhongguo nengyuan* (*China's Energy*), July 2007, pp. 27–9.

78 Krishna Guha, 'US calls for clarity from China on oil stocks', *Financial Times*, 16 June 2008, www.ft.com/cms/s/0/0ff43f1a-3bdd-11dd-9cb2-0000779fd2ac.html (accessed 15 August 2011).
79 'Crude oil reserve base likely in Gansu', *China Daily*, 12 March 2009, www.chinadaily.com.cn/bizchina/2009–03/12/content_7570809.html; 'China to build third phase strategic oil reserves', Xinhua News Agency, 25 September 2009, www.xinhuanet.com/english/2009–09/25/content_12111691.htm (accessed 30 December 2010); 'Factbox – China's strategic oil reserve plan', Reuters, http://in.reuters.com/article/idINIndia-45061520091230; Xina Xie, 'Strategic petroleum reserve in China', *Energy Tribune*, 8 July 2010, www.energytribune.com/articles.cfm/4596/Strategic-Petroleum-Reserve-in-China; Dan Strumpf, 'China may throw wrench into oil market', *Wall Street Journal Online*, 30 December 2010, http://online.wsj.com/article/SB10001424052970203525404576049381578825182.html (all accessed 30 December 2010).
80 Email communications with Daojiong Zha, Peking University, June 2009; discussions in the Central Party School, Beijing, July 2009; Leverett, 'Resource mercantilism and militarization of resource management'.
81 Gao Xiaohui, 'Time not yet ripe for China's IEA membership: analyst', *Global Times*, 1 April 2010, http://business.globaltimes.cn/comment/2010–04/518029.html (accessed 29 December 2010). Dong Xiucheng of China University of Petroleum was quoted as saying that '[d]espite the visible benefits, the ensuing storage and energy-efficiency obligations as an IEA member would present much pressure for China as a developing nation' and 'the relationship between China and [OPEC] also needs to be traded off before making the decisions over IEA membership.'
82 Joint Oil Data Initiative, 'Participation assessment', www.jodidata.org/database/data-quality-assessment.aspx (accessed 23 February 2011).
83 Matthew Saltmarsh, 'France seeks more open commodity markets among G-20', *New York Times*, 19 January 2011, www.nytimes.com/2011/01/20/business/global/20commod.html (accessed 23 February 2011).
84 A Brookings Institution study of the Unocal affair, however, argues that what should have really concerned US policy-makers was rather the subordinated loans at below-market or even zero interest rate CNOOC received from its wholly state-owned parent company. It contends that China's NOCs are at an advantage in their quest for overseas energy assets because of the 'soft budget constraint' of China's state-owned enterprises or banks. Evans and Downs, *Untangling China's Quest for Oil through State-Backed Financial Deals*. See also Michal Meidan, 'Perception and misperceptions of energy supply security in Europe and the "China factor"', in Antonio Marquina (ed.), *Energy Security: Visions from Asia and Europe* (Basingstoke: Palgrave Macmillan, 2008), p. 40.
85 Erica S. Downs, 'Business interest groups in Chinese politics: the case of the oil companies', in Cheng Li (ed.), *China's Changing Political Landscape: Prospects for Democracy* (Washington, DC: Brookings Institution Press, 2008), pp. 122, 134. Wu Yi, the former Vice-Premier, was the deputy general manager and party secretary of Yanshan Petroleum Corporation in 1983–88. Kong, *China's International Petroleum Policy*, p. 166.
86 In partnership with BP, China's CNPC was awarded a twenty-year technical service contract to boost production from Rumaila in Iraq, one of the biggest oilfields in the country, in 2009. However, it is not a production-sharing contract and the terms were not generous. BP and the CNPC are not entitled to any oil extracted. Instead, they would be paid for each barrel produced above the minimum production level (1.7 million barrels per day). Before that, they would have to lend the Iraqi treasury $500 million as a soft loan and to invest at least $300 million to raise production to the minimum level within five to seven years. They were granted the contract only after they agreed to reduce the remuneration rate from $4 per barrel to $2 per barrel.

'Oil companies reject Iraq's terms', *BBC News*, 30 June 2009, http://news.bbc.co.uk/1/hi/8125731.stm (accessed 14 January 2011); Gina Chon, 'Oil companies reject Iraq's contract terms', *Wall Street Journal Online*, 1 July 2009, http://online.wsj.com/article/SB124635835306572521.html (accessed 17 January 2011); Ben Lando, Kate Dourian and Takeo Kumagai, 'Iraq finalizes BP/CNPC contract on Rumaila', *Platts Oilgram News*, 4 November 2009, through LexisNexis; 'China nurtures Mideast oil relations', *Petroleum Economist*, December 2009, through LexisNexis.

87 This section draws on Friedemann Müller, *Energy Security: Demands Imposed on German and European Foreign Policy by a Changed Configuration in the World Energy Market*, SWP Research Paper 2 (Berlin: Stiftung Wissenschaft und Politik, 2007), pp. 12–18.

88 J. Stephen Morrison, 'China in Africa: implications for U.S. policy', testimony before the US Senate Committee on Foreign Relations Subcommittee on African Affairs, 4 June 2008, p. 7, http://csis.org/files/media/csis/congress/ts080604morrison.pdf (accessed 6 December 2009). See also Goldthau, 'Energy diplomacy in trade and investment of oil and gas', p. 38.

89 Downs, 'The fact and fiction of Sino-African energy relations'; Øystein Tunsjø, 'Hedging against oil dependency: new perspectives on China's energy security policy', *International Relations*, Vol. 24 (2010), p. 34. This is echoed by Daniel Rosen and Trevor Houser, *China Energy: A Guide for the Perplexed* (Washington, DC: Center for Strategic and International Studies and Peterson Institute for Internatonal Economics, 2007), p. 33.

90 The FACTS Global Energy report was cited by the Energy Information Administration, 'China', November 2010, www.eia.doe.gov/cabs/China/pdf.pdf (accessed 28 December 2010), and Paula Dittrick, 'Chinese oil companies invest heavily abroad', *Oil & Gas Journal*, 8 February 2010, pp. 20–23. Bo Kang echoes that 'Chinese NOCs shipped back home only a little more than one-third of their overseas equity production and sold the remaining two-thirds to the international market'. Kang, *China's International Petroleum Policy*, p. 94.

91 So it is argued that Chinese NOCs and the state do not form a 'monolithic bloc', directed by the central government. Jiang, 'Fuelling the dragon', p. 603; Morrison, 'China in Africa', p. 5. According to the IEA, China's NOCs are 'majority-owned by the government', but 'not government-run'. Julie Jiang and Jonathan Sinton, *Overseas Investments by Chinese National Oil Companies: Assessing the Drivers and Impacts*, International Energy Agency Information Paper February 2011 (Paris: IEA/OECD, 2011), p. 7, www.iea.org/papers/2011/overseas_china.pdf (accessed 22 February 2011).

92 The Russian state-owned oil company Rosneft in 2008 pressed for a rise in the price of the oil it sold to China's CNPC by threatening that it would not extend the contract as soon as it expired in 2010 if there was no price revision. Igor Danchenko, Erica Downs and Fiona Hill, *One Step Forward, Two Steps Back? The Realities of a Rising China and Implications for Russia's Energy Ambitions*, Brookings Institution Foreign Policy Paper Series No. 22 (Washington, DC: Brookings Institution, August 2010), p. 12, www.brookings.edu/papers/2010/08_china_russia_energy_downs_hill.aspx (accessed 22 January 2011).

93 Ibid., p. 2.

94 For more detailed discussions of the issue, see Pak K. Lee, Gerald Chan and Lai-Ha Chan, 'China in Darfur: humanitarian ruler-taker or rule-maker?', *Review of International Studies* (2011).

95 Sameera Anand, 'China's CNOOC and Sinopec pay $1.3 billion for Angola oil', *BusinessWeek*, 20 July 2009, www.businessweek.com/globalbiz/content/jul2009/gb20090720_097528.htm; Dittrick, 'Chinese oil companies invest heavily abroad'; 'China's oil and mineral deals in Africa', *China Mining*, 25 October 2010, www.chinamining.org/News/2010-10-25/1287988822d40053.html (all accessed 28 December 2010).

96 Amy Myers Jaffe and Kenneth B. Medlock III, 'China and northeast Asia', in Kalicki and Goldwyn (eds.), *Energy and Security*, p. 284. Nationalization is more likely to take place when oil prices are high and in countries when and where institutional constraints on executive power are weak. See Sergei M. Guriev, Anton Kolotilin and Konstantin Sonin, 'Determinants of nationalization in the oil sector: a theory and evidence from panel data', *Journal of Law, Economics, and Organization*, first published online 23 June 2009, doi: 10.1093/jleo/ewp011 (accessed 25 February 2011).

97 Keun-Wook Paik et al., *Trends in Asian NOC Investment Abroad*. Chatham House Working Background Paper, March 2007, www.chathamhouse.org.uk/files/6427_r0307anoc.pdf; Peter S. Goodman, 'CNOOC announces $2.3B Nigeria investment', *Washington Post*, 9 January 2006, www.washingtonpost.com/wp-dyn/content/article/2006/01/09/AR2006010901524.html; 'Being eaten by the dragon', *The Economist*, 13–19 November 2010, www.economist.com/node/17460954. But Robert Weiner of George Washington University counters that Chinese and Indian oil companies behave like their Western counterparts in overseas investment. Catherine Ngai, 'China, India not overpaying for oil, expert says', Market Watch, 22 October 2010, www.marketwatch.com/story/story/print?guid=C56EFFC4-DE0B-11DF-951A-002128049AD6 (all accessed 28 December 2010).

98 Sun Xuefeng and Wang Haibin, 'Zhongguo huoqu quanqiu shiyou ziyuan de zhanlue xuanze' (China's strategic options at tapping the world's crude oil resources), *Dangdai Ya Tai* (*Contemporary Asia-Pacific*), No. 1 (2010), p. 67.

99 Kang, *China's Interantional Petroleum Policy*, pp. 150–51.

100 While three existing international institutions – IEA, World Trade Organization and OECD – can have a role to play in regulating state-financed energy deals, the global rules of the game are hard to establish simply because China is not a member of two of them. Evans and Downs, *Untangling China's Quest for Oil through State-Backed Financial Deals*.

10 Transnational organized crime

1 Cited in Richard Weitz, 'Operation Somalia: China's first expeditionary force?', *China Security*, Vol. 5, No. 1 (Winter 2009), p. 37.
2 United Nations Office on Drugs and Crime, 'United Nations Convention against Transnational Organized Crime', 15 November 2000, Article 2(a), www.unodc.org/pdf/crime/a_res_55/res5525e.pdf (accessed 14 May 2010).
3 Frank G. Madsen, *Transnational Organized Crime* (Abingdon: Routledge, 2009), pp. 7–11.
4 Louise I. Shelley, 'Transnational organized crime: an imminent threat to the nation-state?', *Journal of International Affairs*, Vol. 48, No. 2 (Winter 1995), p. 464.
5 See also Adam Edwards and Peter Gill, 'Introduction', in idem (eds), *Transnational Organised Crime: Perspectives on Global Security* (Abingdon: Routledge, 2003), p. 3.
6 Shelley, 'Transnational organized crime', pp. 463–89, especially 481–5.
7 China ratified it in August 2003. Margaret K. Lewis, 'China's implementation of the United Nations Convention against Transnational Organized Crime', *Asian Criminology*, Vol. 2 (2007), pp. 179–96.
8 James Sheptycki, 'Global law enforcement as a protection racket: some sceptical notes on transnational organised crime as an object of global governance', in Edwards and Gill (eds), *Transnational Organised Crime*, pp. 42–58, esp. 45–50; Phil Williams and Gregory Baudin-O'Hayon, 'Global governance, organized crime and money laundering', in David Held and Anthony McGrew (eds), *Governing Globalization: Power, Authority and Global Governance* (Cambridge: Polity Press, 2002), pp. 127–44, especially p. 132.

Notes 253

9 Typical examples are drug trafficking, money laundering, cyber-attack and terrorism. Michael E. Smith, *International Security: Politics, Policy, Prospects* (Basingstoke: Palgrave Macmillan, 2010), pp. 192–3. How money laundering is defined as a problem that requires international action is discussed in Rainer Hülsse, 'Creating demand for global governance: the making of a global money-laundering problem', *Global Society*, Vol. 21, No. 2 (April 2007), pp. 155–78.

10 Adam Edwards and Peter Gill have argued that the US has long been the principal source of the approach to combating global organized crime. Edwards and Gill, 'Introduction', p. 3.

11 David Scott Mathieson, 'Money laundering', in Martin Griffiths (ed.), *Encyclopedia of International Relations and Global Politics* (Abingdon: Routledge, 2005), pp. 541–4; Financial Action Task Force, 'Money laundering FAQ', www.fatf-gafi.org/document/29/0,3343,en_32250379_32235720_33659613_1_1_1_1,00.html (accessed 4 March 2010).

12 Mathieson, 'Money laundering'; Bonnie Buchanan, 'Money laundering – a global obstacle', *Research in International Business and Finance*, Vol. 18, No. 1 (April 2004), pp. 115–27.

13 Hülsse, 'Creating demand for global governance', p. 166; Beth Simmons, 'International efforts against money laundering', in Dinah Shelton (ed.), *Commitment and Compliance: The Role of Non-Binding Norms in the International Legal System* (Oxford: Oxford University Press, 2000), pp. 244–63.

14 Bank for International Settlements, 'Basel Committee: Prevention of criminal use of the banking system for the purpose of money-laundering', December 1988, www.bis.org/publ/bcbsc137.htm (accessed 13 May 2010). The G10 refers to Belgium, Canada, France, Germany, Italy, Japan, the Netherlands, Sweden, the UK and the US. It was later joined by Switzerland.

15 Financial Action Task Force, 'History of the FATF', www.fatf-gafi.org/document/63/0,3343,en_32250379_32236836_34432255_1_1_1_1,00.html (accessed 4 March 2010).

16 After the 11 September 2001 terrorist attacks on the US, terrorist financing was added to the remit of FATF. Financial Action Task Force, 'History of the FATF', www.fatf-gafi.org/document/63/0,3343,en_32250379_32236836_34432255_1_1_1_1,00.html (accessed 4 March 2010).

17 Simmons, 'International efforts against money laundering'.

18 Financial Action Task Force, 'High-risk and non-cooperative jurisdictions', www.fatf-gafi.org/pages/0,3417,en_32250379_32236992_1_1_1_1_1,00.html (accessed 24 February 2011).

19 Todd Sandler, *Global Collective Action* (Cambridge: Cambridge University Press, 2004), pp. 160–61.

20 Nicole Schulte-Kulkmann, 'The architecture of anti-money laundering regulation in the People's Republic of China – shortfalls and requirements for reform', *European Journal of Crime, Criminal Law and Criminal Justice*, Vol. 14, No. 4 (2006), pp. 408–409.

21 The move was followed by the ratification of the UNTOC, the UN Convention against Corruption (UNCAC) and the International Convention for the Suppression of the Financing of Terrorism in September 2003, October 2005 and February 2006 respectively. Schulte-Kulkmann, 'The architecture of anti-money laundering regulation in the People's Republic of China', p. 413. The following discussion on the legal and institutional development of anti-money laundering in China draws on Gong Lingfei and Li Ting, 'Shi xi woguo fanxiqian xianzhuang ji duice' (An analysis of the current situation of China's anti-money laundering and countermeasures), *Jinrong yu jingji (Finance and Economy)*, No. 2 (2005), pp. 69–70; Ling Tao, 'Dangqian woguo fanxiqian gongzuo mianli de xingshi yu renwu' (The situation and

task China's anti-money laundering work is faced with), *Jinrong zongheng* (*Exploring Finance*), No. 3 (2005), pp. 3–6; Schulte-Kulkmann, 'The architecture of anti-money laundering regulation in the People's Republic of China', pp. 424–32. Ling Tao was the head of the People's Bank of China's Anti-Money Laundering Bureau.

22 United States Department of State, Bureau for International Narcotics and Law Enforcement Affairs, *International Narcotics Control Strategy Report*, Volume II: *Money Laundering and Financial Crimes* (Washington, DC: US Department of State, March 2010), p. 80, www.state.gov/documents/organization/137429.pdf (accessed 13 May 2010).

23 They are: the Regulation for Anti-Money Laundering by Financial Institutions, Administrative Measure for the Reporting of Large-Value and Suspicious Renminbi Payment Transactions, and Administrative Measure for the Reporting by Financial Institutions of Large-Value and Suspicious Foreign Exchange Transactions. In short, they are known as 'One Regulation, Two Measures' (*yige guiding liange banfa*).

24 Financial Action Task Force, 'FATF membership policy', 29 February 2008, www.fatf-gafi.org/dataoecd/25/48/41112798.pdf (accessed 8 May 2010).

25 Zhang Lu, 'Zhongguo jiaru FATF de lichen ji weilai fanxiqian he fankong rongzi mianlin de tiaozhan' (The course of China's admission to FATF and the future challenges of anti-money laundering and combating of the financing of terrorism), *Zhongguo jinrong* (*China Finance*), No. 15 (2007), pp. 50–52; Schulte-Kulkmann, 'The architecture of anti-money laundering regulation in the People's Republic of China', p. 436. China reactivated its APG membership in 2009. United States Department of State, *International Narcotics Control Strategy Report*, Volume II, p. 84.

26 The other four were China Banking Regulatory Commission (CBRC), China Securities Regulatory Commission (CSRC), China Insurance Regulatory Commission (CIRC) and State Administration of Foreign Exchange (SAFE).

27 The Joint Ministerial Conference was initially formed in May 2002 by the State Council. It was led by the Minister of Public Security and comprised representatives of sixteen ministries and commissions. The chairmanship passed to the PBC's President in May 2003.

28 Ling Tao, 'Dangqian woguo fanxiqian gongzuo mianli de xingshi yu renwu' (The situation and task China's anti-money laundering work is faced with); 'FATF welcomes China as an observer', Financial Action Task Force, www.fatf-gafi.org/LongAbstract/0,3425,en_32250379_32236869_34423128_70342_33632055_1_1,00.html (accessed 6 March 2010).

29 Zhang Lu, 'Zhongguo jiaru FATF de lichen' (The course of China's admission to FATF).

30 'China adopts anti-money laundering law', *China Daily*, 31 October 2006, www.chinadaily.com.cn/china/2006-10/31/content_721316.htm (accessed 28 March 2010). The Law is available at the website of the National Bureau of Corruption Prevention of China (*Guojia yufang fubai ju*) at www.nbcp.gov.cn/article/English/LawsRegulations/200903/20090300002187.shtml (accessed 28 March 2010).

31 Financial Action Task Force, 'First mutual evaluation of China', www.fatf-gafi.org/infobycountry/0,3380,en_32250379_32235720_1_70342_4338384_1_1,00.html (accessed 6 March 2010).

32 Wang Yanzhi, 'Zhongguo fanxiqian guoji hezuo jinru le yige xin de lishi fazhan shiqi' (China's international cooperation on anti-money laundering enters into a new period in its historical development), *Zhongguo jinrong* (*China Finance*), No. 15 (2007), pp. 48–50. The writer was the deputy head of PBC's Anti-Money Laundering Bureau.

33 Rich Carew and Max Colchester, 'China is admitted into anti-laundering group', *Wall Street Journal Online*, 2 July 2007, http://online.wsj.com/article/SB118332485691554540.html (accessed 3 July 2007).

Notes 255

34 In 2004 a total of fifty cases of money laundering, involving 570 million yuan and $447 million were uncovered. Three years later eighty-nine cases of money laundering, involving 28.8 billion yuan, were unearthed. Lang Sheng, 'Jinrong jigou fanxiqian yingdang zhuyi de jige wenti' (Several issues to which financial institutions ought to pay attention in combating money laundering), *Zhongguo jinrong* (*China Finance*), No. 24 (2007), pp. 34–6; United States Department of State, *International Narcotics Control Strategy Report*, Volume II, p. 83. Lang Sheng was the Director of the Department of Criminal Law in the Legislative Affairs Commission of the Standing Committee of the NPC. The reasons why money laundering is scarcely prosecuted in China are discussed in He Ping, 'Is money laundering a true problem in China?', *International Journal of Offender Therapy and Comparative Criminology*, Vol. 50, No. 1 (February 2006), pp. 101–16.
35 Financial Action Task Force, 'Summary of the first mutual evaluation report on anti-money laundering and combating the financing of terrorism, People's Republic of China', 29 June 2007, www.fatf-gafi.org/dataoecd/24/45/39148209.pdf (accessed 8 May 2010); Zhang Lu, 'Zhongguo jiaru FATF de lichen' (The course of China's admission to FATF).
36 United States Department of State, *International Narcotics Control Strategy Report*, Volume II, p. 84.
37 Previously only drug trafficking, organized crime, terrorist crime and smuggling constituted the predicate crimes. 'China adopts anti-money laundering law'; Schulte-Kulkmann, 'The architecture of anti-money laundering regulation in the People's Republic of China', pp. 414–15.
38 Recommendation 1 of FATF's 40 Recommendations, www.fatf-gafi.org/dataoecd/7/40/34849567.PDF (accessed 28 March 2010).
39 Peng Wei, Du Zhengyi and Chen Fan, 'Lun guoji gongyue yu woguo xiqianzui de lifa wanshan' (International conventions and improvement of China's legislation on money laundering crime), *Wuhan jinrong* (*Wuhan Finance*), No. 10 (2009), pp. 33–5.
40 According to Article 1 of UNTOC, serious crime refers to 'conduct constituting an offence punishable by a maximum deprivation of liberty of at least four years or a more serious penalty'. United Nations Office on Drugs and Crime, 'United Nations Convention against Transnational Organized Crime', 15 November 2000, www.unodc.org/pdf/crime/a_res_55/res5525e.pdf (accessed 14 May 2010).
41 United Nations Office on Drugs and Crime, 'United Nations Convention against Corruption', 31 October 2003, Chapter III, Articles 15–25, www.unodc.org/pdf/crime/convention_corruption/signing/Convention-e.pdf (accessed 14 May 2010).
42 National Bureau of Corruption Prevention of China, 'Anti-Money Laundering Law of the People's Republic of China', 30 March 2009, Article 2, www.nbcp.gov.cn/article/English/LawsRegulations/200903/20090300002187.shtml (accessed 15 May 2010).
43 While Hong Kong, Macao and Taiwan are members of the Egmont Group, China is not. A group of FIUs established in Egmont Arenberg Palace in Brussels in 1995 an informal intergovernmental group, now called the Egmont Group of FIUs, to promote international cooperation among the FIUs. Egmont Group, 'List of Members – Asia', www.egmontgroup.org/about/list-of-members/by-region/asia; Egmont Group, 'About', www.egmontgroup.org/about (accessed 24 February 2011).
44 The Supreme People's Court extended the applicability of laws concerning money laundering to non-banking/financial activities in a judicial interpretation in November 2009, but the interpretation has yet to be codified into law. United States Department of State, *International Narcotics Control Strategy Report*, Volume II, pp. 80–81.
45 Ibid., p. 81.
46 Ibid., p. 82.

47 The 2007 anti-money laundering report revealed that the Chinese authorities uncovered in 2006 a total of 47,867 cases of incomplete records of customer identity and 744 anonymous accounts. Chen Feifei, 'Tigao fanxiqian jianguan youxiaoxing de chuangxin anpai' (Innovative arrangements for raising the effectiveness of anti-money laundering supervision), *Zhejiang jinrong* (*Zhejiang Finance*), No. 9 (2009), pp. 22–3.
48 Michael Philips, 'Anti-laundering law's limitations', *Financial Times*, 15 March 2006, through LexisNexis; Lang Sheng, 'Jinrong jigou fanxiqian yingdang zhuyi de jige wenti' (Several issues to which financial institutions ought to pay attention in combating money laundering), *Zhongguo jinrong* (*China Finance*), No. 24 (2007), pp. 34–6. Lang Sheng was the Director of the Department of Criminal Law in the Legislative Affairs Commission of the Standing Committee of the NPC.
49 Chinese corrupt bureaucrats tend to launder 'black money' via bogus companies, companies operated by their relatives or 'underground banks' (*dixia qianzhuang*). Because of the high demand for funds from local non-state enterprises, which do not often receive preferential loans from state-owned commercial banks, underground banks provide a conduit for illicit money to enter legal business. It was reported in 2004 that the Chinese underground banks were involved in money laundering worth 200 billion yuan per annum. As noted in Chapter 4 above, the Caribbean Cayman Islands are one of the major destinations of China's overseas direct investment. The Cayman Islands were on the list of NCCTs in 2000. Schulte-Kulkmann, 'The architecture of anti-money laundering regulation in the People's Republic of China', pp. 408–39, esp. pp. 411–12; Williams and Baudin-O'Hayon, 'Global governance, organized crime and money laundering', p. 138.
50 Lewis, 'China's implementation of the United Nations Convention against Transnational Organized Crime', p. 187.
51 In its own words, the FATF 'does not have a tightly defined constitution or an unlimited life span'. Financial Action Task Force, 'About the FATF', www.fatf-gafi.org/pages/0,3417,en_32250379_32236836_1_1_1_1_1,00.html (accessed 8 May 2010). Schulte-Kulkmann, 'The architecture of anti-money laundering regulation in the People's Republic of China', p. 437.
52 The term is used by Williams and Baudin-O'Hayon in their 'Global governance, organized crime and money laundering', p. 140.
53 Yoichi Funabashi, *The Peninsula Question: A Chronicle of the Second Korean Nuclear Crisis* (Washington, DC: Brookings Institution Press, 2007), pp. 410–19.
54 'U.S. moves to formally shut out Macau bank for money laundering', *Wall Street Journal Online*, 14 March 2007, http://online.wsj.com/article/SB117388592108136881.html (accessed 20 March 2007). Subsequently China expressed 'deep regret' over the US decision, although it was unclear why it felt upset. 'China voices regret over decision to sever U.S. ties to Macau bank', *Wall Street Journal Online*, 16 March 2007, http://online.wsj.com/article/SB117396061716838087.html (accessed 20 March 2007).
55 Donald Greenlees, 'U.S. and Macao begin transferring funds to Pyongyang', *New York Times*, 14 June 2007, www.nytimes.com/2007/06/14/world/asia/14iht-korea.3.6141109.html (accessed 24 February 2011); Jay Solomon, 'North Korea transfer raises hope', *Wall Street Journal Online*, 15 June 2007, http://online.wsj.com/article/SB118182806343935322.html (accessed 16 June 2007).
56 Funabashi, *The Peninsula Question*, pp. 414–15.
57 David L. Asher, 'The North Korean criminal state, its ties to organized crime, and the possibility of WMD proliferation', Nautilus Institute Policy Forum Online 05–92A, 15 November 2005, www.nautilus.org/fora/security/0592Asher.html (accessed 17 May 2010); International Crisis Group, *China and North Korea: Comrades Forever?*, Asia Report No. 112 (Brussels: International Crisis Group, February 2006), p. 23, www.crisisgroup.org/library/documents/asia/north_korea/112_china_

and_north_Korea_comrades_forever.pdf (accessed 18 March 2009). Stanley Au, whose family has owned the bank for decades, was a member of the Chinese People's Political Consultative Committee.
58 'Isolating proliferators and sponsors of terror: the use of sanctions and the international financial system to change regime behaviour', House of Representatives, 18 April 2007, p. 74, http://foreignaffairs.house.gov/110/34715.pdf (accessed 15 May 2010). *Sha ji xia hou* ('to kill the chicken to frighten the monkey') is a Chinese saying, which means that to punish someone is a warning to others.
59 Funabashi, *The Peninsula Question*, p. 415.
60 Alastair Iain Johnston, *Social States: China in International Institutions, 1980–2000* (Princeton, NJ: Princeton University Press, 2008).
61 Martin N. Murphy, *Small Boats, Weak States, Dirty Money: Piracy and Maritime Terrorism in the Modern World* (London: Hurst, 2009), pp. 7–8.
62 United Nations Convention on the Law of the Sea, 10 December 1982, www.un.org/Depts/los/convention_agreements/texts/unclos/closindx.htm (accessed 3 July 2010).
63 Bruce A. Elleman, Andrew Forbes and David Rosenberg, 'Introduction', in idem (eds), *Piracy and Maritime Crime: Historical and Modern Case Studies*, Naval War College Newport Papers 35 (Newport, RI: Naval War College Press, 2010), pp. 8–10, www.usnwc.edu/Publications/Naval-War-College-Press/Newport-Papers/Documents/35.aspx (accessed 5 July 2010).
64 Murphy, *Small Boats, Weak States, Dirty Money*, pp. 14–16.
65 Ibid., p. 17.
66 Ibid., pp. 17–21.
67 Cases included the *Petro Ranger* (April 1998), *Tenyu* (September 1998) and *Alondra Rainbow* (October 1999). They were hijacked in Southeast Asia with cargo and crew offloaded before they were recovered. Adam J. Young, *Contemporary Maritime Piracy in Southeast Asia: History, Causes and Remedies* (Singapore: Institute of Southeast Asian Studies, 2007), p. 76. The case of the *Alondra Rainbow* is discussed in detail in Jayant Abhyandkar, 'Piracy, armed robbery and terrorism at sea: a global and regional outlook', in Graham Gerard Ong-Webb (ed.), *Piracy, Maritime Terrorism and Securing the Malacca Straits* (Singapore: Institute of Southeast Asian Studies, 2006), pp. 4–6.
68 International Maritime Organization, *Reports on Acts of Piracy and Armed Robbery against Ships Annual Report – 2009*, 29 March 2010, www.imo.org/includes/blastDataOnly.asp/data_id%3D28158/152.pdf (accessed 5 July 2010).
69 ICC International Maritime Bureau, '2009 worldwide piracy figures surpass 400', 14 January 2010, www.icc-ccs.org/news/385–2009-worldwide-piracy-figures-surpass-400 (accessed 24 February 2011); ICC International Maritime Bureau, *Piracy and Armed Robbery against Ships Annual Report 1 January–31 December 2009* (London: ICC International Maritime Bureau, 2010), pp. 5–6. The data on Southeast Asian pirate attacks in 1999 are from Ian Storey, 'Maritime security in Southeast Asia: two cheers for regional cooperation', in Daljit Singh (ed.), *Southeast Asian Affairs 2009* (Singapore: Institute of Southeast Asian Studies, 2009), p. 39. While Storey includes South China Sea, Cambodia and Vietnam into Southeast Asia, the IMB does not. The IMB notion of Southeast Asia is used throughout this chapter.
70 Spencer Swartz, 'Pirate attacks raise risks for oil tankers', *Wall Street Journal Online*, 4 January 2010, http://online.wsj.com/article/SB126239313390413141.html (accessed 9 January 2010).
71 David Rosenberg, 'The political economy of piracy in the South China Sea', in Elleman *et al.* (eds), *Piracy and Maritime Crime*, p. 83.
72 The economic costs of piracy include ransom payments, the recruitment of negotiators and lawyers, increased maritime insurance premiums and the cost of diverting vessels to avoid the Horn of Africa, which turn adds additional shipping days and

fuel costs to shipping companies. Lauren Ploch et al., *Piracy off the Horn of Africa*, Congressional Research Service Report for Congress R40528 (Washington, DC: Congressional Research Service, 2009), pp. 12, 14–16, www.fas.org/sgp/crs/row/R40528.pdf (accessed 24 February 2011). The US-based One Earth Future Foundation estimates that maritime piracy costs the global economy between $7 billion and $12 billion a year. More alarming, however, is, that the average ransom paid to Somali pirates rose from a mere $150,000 in 2005 to $3.4 million in 2009 and to $5.4 million in 2010. Anna Bowden et al., *The Economic Costs of Maritime Piracy* (One Earth Future Foundation Working Paper, December 2010), http://oneearthfuture.org/images/imagefiles/Cost%20of%20Piracy%20Final%20Report.pdf (accessed 24 January 2010); Robert Wright, 'Sharp rise in pirate ransom costs,' *Financial Times*, 16 January 2010, www.ft.com/cms/s/0/658138a6-219b-11e0-9e3b-00144feab49a.html (accessed 22 January 2010).

73 See e.g. Martin N. Murphy, *Contemporary Piracy and Maritime Terrorism: The Threat to International Security*, Adelphi Paper 388 (Abingdon: Routledge for the International Institute for Strategic Studies, 2007).

74 Wang Lirong, 'Guoji haidao wenti yu Zhongguo hai shang tongtao anquan' (International piracy and the security of China's sea lanes), *Dangdai Ya Tai* (*Contemporary Asia-Pacific*), No. 6 (2009), p. 127.

75 UN Security Council Resolutions 1846 and 1851 are available at www.un.org/News/Press/docs/2008/sc9514.doc.htm and www.un.org/News/Press/docs/2008/sc9541.doc.htm (accessed 14 July 2010).

76 'Saudi tanker "freed off Somalia"', *BBC News*, 9 January 2009, http://news.bbc.co.uk/1/hi/world/africa/7820311.stm (accessed 15 July 2010); Paul French and Sam Chambers, *Oil on Water: Tankers, Pirates and the Rise of China* (London: Zed Books, 2010), pp. 92–3.

77 The details are available at www.manw.nato.int/page_operation_ocean_shield.aspx; and www.aco.nato.int/page208433730.aspx (accessed 15 July 2010).

78 See European Union Council Secretariat, 'EU naval operation against piracy (EUNAVFOR Somalia – Operation ATALANTA)', July 2010, www.consilium.europa.eu/uedocs/cms_data/docs/missionPress/files/100713%20Factsheet%20EU%20NAVFOR%20Somalia%20-%20version%2020_EN.pdf (accessed 14 July 2010).

79 The details are available at US Department of State, 'Contact Group on Piracy off the Coast of Somalia', www.state.gov/t/pm/ppa/piracy/contactgroup/index.htm (accessed 15 July 2010). See also Ploch et al., *Piracy off the Horn of Africa*, p. i.

80 NATO Allied Command Operations, 'Operation Ocean Shield', www.aco.nato.int/page208433730.aspx (accessed 15 July 2010); Ploch et al., *Piracy off the Horn of Africa*, p. 20; US Navy, 'New counter-piracy task force established', 8 January 2009 www.navy.mil/search/display.asp?story_id=41687 (accessed 15 July 2010).

81 The official name is the Code of Conduct Concerning the Suppression of Piracy and Armed Robbery against Ships in the Western Indian Ocean and the Gulf of Aden. While India, Indonesia, Japan, the Philippines and Singapore, among others, were observers at the meeting, China was not present. For details, see www.fco.gov.uk/resources/en/pdf/pdf9/piracy-djibouti-meeting (accessed 16 July 2010). For Japan's contributions, see Ploch et al., *Piracy off the Horn of Africa*, p. 22.

82 'Somali pirates release Chinese fishing vessel', China.org.cn, 9 February 2009, www.china.org.cn/international/2009-02/09/content_17246761.htm (accessed 16 July 2010). A report said that the Somali pirates had asked for $1.7 million. Minnie Chan, 'Talks, payments used to free piracy victims', *South China Morning Post*, 22 October 2009, through LexisNexis (unless stated otherwise).

83 Anne Barrowclough, 'Chinese crew used beer bottles to fight off pirates', *The Times*, 20 December 2008, www.timesonline.co.uk/tol/news/world/africa/article5368675.ece (accessed 16 July 2010).

84 The ship was released in December 2009 after the payment of a ransom of $3.5 million – $4 million. Greg Torode and Kristine Kwok, "Ransom for Chinese ship "raising the bar"', *South China Morning Post*, 29 December 2009; Greg Torode, 'China to lead anti-piracy patrols', *South China Morning Post*, 28 January 2010.

85 Andrew Jacobs, 'China warns pirates who commandeered ship', *New York Times*, 22 October 2009, www.nytimes.com/2009/10/22/world/africa/22pirates.html (accessed 16 July 2010); Greg Torode, 'Beijing seeks lead role in piracy fight', *South China Morning Post*, 10 November 2009; Greg Torode, 'China to lead anti-piracy patrols', *South China Morning Post*, 28 January 2010; 'Navies agree on "set areas"' for Somali patrols', *People's Daily Online*, 30 January 2010, http://english.people.com.cn/90001/90776/90883/6883223.html (accessed 2 February 2010).

86 Greg Torode, 'Beijing hosts naval powers in anti-piracy talks', *South China Morning Post*, 5 November 2009.

87 Greg Torode, 'Regional rivals wary of China's role in Somalia', *South China Morning Post*, 24 April 2010.

88 Greg Torode, 'Navy offers to escort UN food aid', *South China Morning Post*, 5 March 2010, via LexisNexis; Minnie Chan and Greg Torode, 'PLA likely to send more ships for UN food aid escorts', *South China Morning Post*, 13 March 2010.

89 Stephen Chen and Greg Torode, 'PLA given nod to lead anti-piracy operations', *South China Morning Post*, 22 September 2010.

90 Cited in 'Cash and carry: China's navy off Somalia', *The Economist*, 31 October 2009 through LexisNexis.

91 Cited in Weitz, 'Operation Somalia', p. 37.

92 Torode, 'Regional rivals wary of China's role in Somalia',

93 Although the vessel is owned by a Singaporean company, it was chartered and operated by Shanghai Dingheng Shipping, a private Chinese firm. Greg Torode and Keith Wallis, '19 sailors languish in Somali pirate lair held for 3 month – and no sign of release', *South China Morning Post*, 26 September 2010.

94 Rosenberg, 'The political economy of piracy in the South China Sea', p. 80.

95 US Energy Information Administration, 'World oil transit chokepoints: Malacca', January 2008, www.eia.doe.gov/cabs/World_Oil_Transit_Chokepoints/Malacca.html (accessed 30 July 2010); Joshua H. Ho, 'The security of sea lanes in Southeast Asia', *Asian Survey*, Vol. 46, No. 4 (July/August 2006), p. 560.

96 As discussed in detail below, there has since 2004 been a reversal of trends. The piracy rate in the straits in 2005 was only 0.019 per cent. John F. Bradford, 'Shifting the tides against piracy in Southeast Asian waters', *Asian Survey*, Vol. 48, No. 3 (May/June 2008), p. 474; Rosenberg, 'The political economy of piracy in the South China Sea', p. 83. Joshua Ho also argues that only between 0.04 per cent and 0.11 per cent of the ships going through the straits were attacked by pirates in 2000–2005. Ho, 'The security of sea lanes in Southeast Asia', pp. 561–2. This is echoed by the studies cited in Murphy, *Small Boats, Weak States, Dirty Money*, p. 81.

97 China has allegedly elevated the South China Sea to the level of 'core interests' on a par with Taiwan, Tibet and Xinjiang. Kristine Kwok, 'South China Sea becomes Beijing's latest "core interest"', *South China Morning Post*, 7 July 2010; Jian Junbo, 'China takes new tack in maritime diplomacy', *Asia Times Online*, 14 July 2010, www.atimes.com/atimes/China/LG14Ad01.html (accessed 14 July 2010).

98 Murphy, *Small Boats, Weak States, Dirty Money*, p. 82; Rosenberg, 'The political economy of piracy in the South China Sea', pp. 89–91.

99 Murphy, *Small Boats, Weak States, Dirty Money*, pp. 72, 82; Rosenberg, 'The political economy of piracy in the South China Sea', p. 85.

100 Sudha Ramachandran, 'Divisions over terror threat in Malacca Straits', *Asia Times Online*, 16 June 2004, www.atimes.com/atimes/Southeast_Asia/FF16Ae01.html (accessed 9 July 2010); Murphy, *Small Boats, Weak States, Dirty Money*, p. 83.

260 *Notes*

101 Cited in Rosenberg, 'The political economy of piracy in the South China Sea', p. 86.
102 Bradford, 'Shifting the tide against piracy in Southeast Asian waters', p. 479.
103 Ho, 'The security of sea lanes in Southeast Asia', pp. 571–2; Murphy, *Small Boats, Weak States, Dirty Money*, p. 86; Rosenberg, 'The political economy of piracy in the South China Sea', p. 87.
104 Bradford, 'Shifting the tide against piracy in Southeast Asian waters', p. 482; Catherine Zara Raymond, 'Piracy and armed robbery in the Malacca Strait: a problem solved?', in Elleman *et al.* (eds), *Piracy and Maritime Crime*, pp. 114–16; Storey, 'Maritime security in Southeast Asia', p. 42.
105 China participated in the first meeting in Jakarta in September 2005, the first time it took part in a maritime security conference on the Strait of Malacca and Singapore. China was invited to the February 2006 meeting in Alameda, California, but did not show up. Rosenberg, 'The political economy of piracy in the South China Sea', p. 88; Wang Lirong, 'Guoji haidao wenti yu Zhongguo hai shang tongtao anquan' (International piracy and the security of China's sea lanes), p. 129.
106 Cited in Raymond, 'Piracy and armed robbery in the Malacca Strait', p. 118.
107 SUA was adopted in March 1988 and entered into force in March 1992, www.imo.org/Conventions/mainframe.asp?topic_id=259&doc_id=686 (accessed 4 July 2010); Raymond, 'Piracy and armed robbery in the Malacca Strait', p. 116; Rosenberg, 'The political economy of piracy in the South China Sea', pp. 88–9.
108 Young, *Contemporary Maritime Piracy in Southeast Asia*, pp. 9, 80–82.
109 Bradford, 'Shifting the tide against piracy in Southeast Asian waters', pp. 488–9.
110 Ho, 'The security of sea lanes in Southeast Asia', pp. 570–71.
111 Bradford, 'Shifting the tide against piracy in Southeast Asian waters', pp. 483–4; Storey, 'Maritime security in Southeast Asia', p. 43.
112 Mark J. Valencia, 'The politics of anti-piracy and anti-terrorism responses in Southeast Asia', in Ong-Webb, *Piracy, Maritime Terrorism and Securing the Malacca Straits*, p. 94; Wang Lirong, 'Guoji haidao wenti yu Zhongguo hai shang tongtao anquan' (International piracy and the security of China's sea lanes), pp. 127–8.
113 While drawing on the IMB's statistical data, Zhang Jiadong does not present the figures about China and the South China Sea available in the IMB's annual reports. See his 'Shijie haidao huodong zhuangkuang yu guoji fan haidao jizhi jianshe' (The state of affairs of world piracy and the building of international anti-piracy regimes), *Xiandai guoji guanxi* (*Contemporary International Relations*), No. 1 (2009), pp. 30–35. Wang Lirong makes use of the IMO annual reports to work out a table of pirate attacks in 'Southeast Asia'. But the IMO does not have such a regional category; instead it refers to the Far East, which is principally composed of the Strait of Malacca and the South China Sea. Compare International Maritime Organization, *Reports on Acts of Piracy and Armed Robbery against Ships Annual Report*, 2006 and 2007, www.imo.org/includes/blastDataOnly.asp/data_id%3D22585/115.pdf www.imo.org/includes/blastDataOnly.asp/data_id%3D18566/98.pdf (accessed 14 July 2010) and Wang Lirong, 'Guoji haidao wenti yu Zhongguo hai shang tongtao anquan' (International piracy and the security of China's sea lanes), p. 125 (Table 2). An exception is Ji Guoxing's paper written in English: Ji Guoxing, *Asian Pacific SLOC Security: The China Factor*, Royal Australian Navy Sea Power Centre Working Paper No. 10 (Canberra: Royal Australian Navy Sea Power Centre, 2002), p. 15, www.navy.gov.au/w/images/Working_Paper_10.pdf (accessed 14 July 2010).
114 See Storey, 'Maritime security in Southeast Asia', pp. 46–52, for an account of the South China Sea dispute between China on the one hand and the Philippines and Vietnam on the other.
115 Storey, 'Maritime security in Southeast Asia', p. 39; International Maritime Bureau, *Piracy and Armed Robbery against Ships Annual Report 1 January – 31 December 2009*, p. 5.

Conclusion

1 See e.g. Michael D. Swaine, 'Perceptions of an assertive China', *China Leadership Monitor*, No. 32 (Spring 2010), http://carnegieendowment.org/files/CLM32MS1.pdf; idem, 'China's assertive behavior, part one: on "core interests"', *China Leadership Monitor*, No. 34 (Fall 2010), http://carnegieendowment.org/files/Swaine_CLM_34_1114101.pdf; June Teufel Dreyer, 'Grimm foreign policy?', *The Diplomat*, 12 February 2011, http://the-diplomat.com/2011/02/12/grimm-foreign-policy/ (accessed 24 February 2011). This is also the starting point of David Shambaugh, 'Coping with a conflicted China', *The Washington Quarterly*, Vol. 34, No. 1 (Winter 2011), pp. 7–27.
2 Cited in David Pilling, 'Keeping its distance', *Financial Times*, 11 February 2010, through LexisNexis; emphasis added.
3 Shambaugh, 'Coping with a conflicted China', pp. 13, 17–20.
4 Wu Jianmin, 'What international responsibilities should China take?', *People's Daily Online*, 16 February 2011, www.english.peopledaily.com.cn/90001/90780/91342/7290103.html (accessed 22 February 2011).
5 Wang Jisi, 'China's search for a grand strategy', *Foreign Affairs*, Vol. 90, No. 2 (March/April 2011), p. 77
6 Todd Sandler, *Global Collective Action* (Cambridge: Cambridge University Press, 2004), p. 269.

Appendix A

1 For the role of the US government in encouraging tenants to become homeowners and the political purposes behind it, see Niall Ferguson, *The Ascent of Money: A Financial History of the World* (London: Penguin Books, 2009), pp. 242–54, 268–69. Government-sponsored entities in 2003 held 43 per cent of the mortgages. Ibid., p. 274.
2 Leonard Seabrooke, 'What do I get? The everyday politics of expectations and the subrime crisis', *New Political Economy*, Vol. 15, No. 1 (March 2010), p. 62.
3 As said by Brunnermeier, the US had not experienced any nationwide decline in housing prices since the Second World War. Markus K. Brunnermeier, 'Deciphering the liquidity and credit crunch 2007–2008', *Journal of Economic Perspectives*, Vol. 23, No. 1 (Winter 2009), p. 81.
4 As of May 2008 the write-downs by banks amounted to at least $318 billion. Ferguson, *The Ascent of Money*, p. 274. Outside the US, Northern Rock, the Royal Bank of Scotland and the Halifax Bank of Scotland, all in the UK, and IKB of Germany were the major victims of the crisis.

Index

Page numbers in *italics* denote tables, those in **bold** denote figures.

Administration of Quality Supervision, Inspection and Quarantine, China (AQSIQ) 129–31, 133, 138–9
advanced executive multilateralism 18–19
Africa 17, 34–6, 61–2, 87, 90, 106, 112, 117–24, 147, 149–50, 155–6, 177–8; China–Africa Development Fund (CADFund) 149; *China's African Policy* 118, 149
African Union (AU) 46, 90
Agreement on Trade-Related Intellectual Property Rights (TRIPS) 119, 121
Ainley, Kirsten 21
Albania 2
Algeria 45, 117, 155
All-China Environment Federation 100, 102
Alxa SEE Ecology Association 101
An Agenda for Peace (1992) 17
Angola 2, 35, *147*, 149, 156
Annan, Kofi 18, 45, 81, 83, 88
anti-imperialism 31, 43, 174; see also imperialism
anti-money laundering (AML) 161–5
Argentina 69
arms control and disarmament 3–4, 47, 175; Anti-Ballistic Missile Systems (ABM Treaty) 50; anti-satellite (ASAT) missile by China 51; Committee on Disarmament (CD) 50–1; Fissile Material Cut-off Treaty (FMCT) 50–1; Prevention of an Arms Race in Outer Space (PAROS) 50–1; UN Register of Conventional Arms (UNROCA) 49
Asian Development Bank 128
Asian financial crisis 34, 46, 64, 70, 73, 76, 142

Association of Southeast Asian Nations (ASEAN) 68–70, 90, 94, 138 9, 150, 172; ASEAN Plus Three 150, 172; ASEAN Regional Forum (ARF) 24
Australia 1, 68–9, 95, 123, 155
autocratic revival 4
avian flu (H5N1) 114, 116

Bahrain 169
Bangladesh 106, 172
Bank of China 164–5
baquan 霸權 (coercive dominance) 2; see also hegemony
Barma, Naazneen 35
Barnett, Michael 12
BASIC countries (Brazil, South Africa, India and China) 96, 105–6
Beijing Consensus 33, 37; see also China model
Beijing Olympics 87, 101, 107, 116, 128, 136
Belarus 152, 162
Bernanke, Ben 73
Bill and Melinda Gates Foundation 19
Bo'ao Forum of Asia 30
Bosworth, Stephen 57
Boutros-Ghali, Boutros 17
Brazil 1, 69–70, 74–5, 77, 95–6, 105, 121, 179, *180–2*, 184
Bretton Woods system 12, 19, 61, 67, 69, 77–8, 175
BRIC countries 65, 180–2; see also Brazil; Russia; India; China
Brown, Chris 21
Burma see Myanmar
Bush, George W. 51–2, 57, 64, 74, 152–3

buyao dangtou 不要當頭 (not seeking leadership) 23

Cai, Tuo 25–7, 32
Cambodia 175
Canada 17, 42, 81, 93, 96, 100, *123*, 154–5
Cancún Summit on Climate Change (2010) 96, 105–6; Cancún Agreement 96, 106
Carlson, Allen 28
Carlsson, Ingvar 9
Carter, Neil 108
Central Asia 73, 93, 147, 152
Centre for Legal Assistance to Pollution Victims in Beijing 101
Chan, Gerald 3–4
Chan, Margaret 1, 114–15, 118, 179; *see also* World Health Organization (WHO)
Chechnya 87
Chile 68
China; and global economic order 61–71; Cultural Revolution 94, 175; current account balances *72*; economic growth 5, 36, 59–61, 141; economic reform 62, 113, 175; environmental damage 74; exchange rate 76; exports and imports *60*; finance and trade 59–72; Five-Year Plan 97, 99; foreign exchange reserves *60*, 67, 71, 75–6, 176; global financial imbalances 71–7; global policy 5; great power status 3, 6, 39, 179, 183–4; gross domestic product (GDP) 2, *60*, 73, 97, 99, 103, 124; high savings ratio 59; international image 6, 100, 106; international respect 6; National People's Congress 96, 113, 133, 161; national security 41; peace and security 40–58; People's Liberation Army (PLA) 170; *Position Paper on the UN Reforms (2005)* 29, 47; responsibility 2–4, 5–6, 61–2, 121, 123–4, 175–7, 183; responsible great power 4–5, 38, 46, 51, 92; responsible stakeholder 164; rise of 1–2, 5–6, 92, 158, 174, 184; share of UN regular budget 42; stance on national sovereignty 27–33, 35, 37–8, 41, 44–6, 52, 78–9, 90, 116–17, 170, 173, 179, 183; state building 27; state-centric approach to global governance 19, 37, 178; State Council 67, 96, 114, 130, 133, 139
China Development Bank 148–9
China Environmental Culture Promotion Association 101
China model 4, 34–6; new paradigm for developing countries 35; *see also* Beijing Consensus
China National Offshore Oil Corporation (CNOOC) 147, 151, 154, 156
China National Petroleum Corporation (CNPC) 147–9, 151, 154, 156
China Petroleum and Chemical Corporation (Sinopec) 147, 149, 154
China threat 23, 33
China University of Political Science and Law 25, 63, 101
Chinese Academy of Social Sciences 30, 69, 74
Chinese Communist Party (CCP) 32, 54, 106, 174; Central Bureau of Translation 26; Central Committee 35–6; International Liaison Department 56; legitimation crises 32, 86; Politburo 35, 86, 104, 154; Propaganda Department 56
Chinese Ministry of Foreign Affairs 25
Chinese Realist school 183; *see also* Yan, Xuetong
Chu, Shulong 28
civil society 14, 16, 19, 26–7, 36, 38, 89, 119, 129, 132; China's scepticism 32
Clark, Helen 116
climate change 13, 21, 177
Clinton, Bill 50, 57
CNN effect 13
Cold War 19, 80, 84, 112, 159, 175, 183; Cold War mentality 32
collective actions 11, 19–21, 25, 41, 52–3, 55, 57–8, 174, 178, 184
Commission on Global Governance 9; *see also* Carlsson, Ingvar and Ramphal, Shridath
'common but differentiated responsibility' 95, 104, 177
Convention against Torture and Other Cruel, Inhuman or Degrading Treatment or Punishment (CAT) 81; China's participation *82*
Convention on the Elimination of All Forms of Discrimination against Women (CEDAW) 81; China's participation *82*
Convention on the Prevention and Punishment of the Crime of Genocide; China's participation *82*
Convention on the Rights of the Child (CRC) 81; China's participation *82*

Convention of the Rights of Persons with Disabilities (CRPD) 81; China's participation 82
Copenhagen Summit on Climate Change (2009) 94, 96, 104–6
Costa Rica 84
Côte d'Ivoire 43

da tong 大同 (universal community) 31
Dai, Bingguo 57
Darfur 43, 46, 85, 87–8, 90, 179, 181; see also Sudan
Declaration on the Right to Development 80
Democratic Republic of the Congo (DRC) 43, 46
Deng, Xiaoping 23, 40, 78, 113, 117
developing world 18, 27–8, 76, 87, 89

East China University of Political Science and Law 26
East Timor 17, 31, 81, 90
Eastern Europe 12, 17, 34, 83, 159
Economy, Elizabeth 42, 108
El Salvador 2
energy security 2, 4, 7, 141–57, 182; China's neo-mercantilism 146–55; China's top five crude oil supplying countries 147; crude oil consumption **142**; global energy governance 143–6; international oil companies (IOCs) 143–4, 148, 150–1; liberalism and neo-mercantilism 144–6, 156; national oil companies (NOCs) 143, 147, 149–51, 154–7; oil crisis 141; political weapon 157, 144–5; 'resource mercantilism' 157; 'resource nationalism' 152; 'self-reliance' 157; strategic petroleum reserves (SPRs) 153
English School; pluralist concepts 33, 37; solidarist values 32–3, 37
environmental governance in China 93, 96–104; compensation 101; global impact on 106–8; government-organized NGOs (GONGOS) 101–2; green GDP 97; impact on global environmental governance 104–6; local governments and 102–4; minban feiqiye danwei (民辦非企業單位; private non-enterprise units) 99; Ministry of Environmental Protection (MEP) 93, 107–8; NGOs 93–4, 97, 99–102, 108; non-states actors 99–102; petitions and protests 97–9; shehui tuanti (社會團體; social organizations) 99; Songhua benzene spill 98, 104; State Environmental Protection Administration (SEPA) 93, 97–8, 100, 103–4; see also environmental protection
environmental protection 2–4, 7, 92 109, 176, 181; 'environmental Kuznets curve' (EKC) 102–3; greenhouse gases emission 95–6, 99, 105, 179; historical responsibility 92, 177; industrialization in developed countries 92
Environmental Protection in China (1996–2005) 97
European Commission 95
European Union (EU) 1, 4, 17, 69, 84, 94, 105, 121–2, 127, 137–9, 159–60, 169–70, 184; see also European Commission
executive multilateralism 18–19
Extractive Industries Transparency Initiative 36
extraterritoriality 31

Falkner, Robert 106
Ferrero-Waldner, Benita 4–5
Financial Action Task Force on Money Laundering (FATF) 160–4, 178
financial stability 61, 64, 67, 73, 173; China and global financial imbalances 71–7; see also International Monetary Fund (IMF)
Five Principles of Peaceful Coexistence 32
food safety 4, 7, 125–40, 182–3; Agreement on the Application of Sanitary and Phytosanitary Measures (SPS Agreement) 134, 182; Codex Alimentarius Commission 134–5, 182; Food and Drug Administration (US) 128, 137–8; International Food Safety Authorities Network (INFOSAN) 134, 136; Rapid Alert System for Food and Feed (RASFF) (EU) 127; US Consumer Product Safety Commission 137; World Organization for Animal Health 134
food safety in China, China's Food Quality and Safety 130; China's foodstuff exports and imports 125; global concern on 127–9; civil society and 132; destinations of China's food exports **126**; disjointed production system 129–31; flaws in China's governance 129–33; Food Safety Law 131, 136; fragmented and corrupt regulatory system 131; measures to improve 133–9; melamine-tainted milk scandal 116, 126, 134, 136; Ministry of Agriculture 131, 133; Ministry of Health (MoH) 131, 133; multilateral cooperation 133, 136, 138; State Food and Drug

Administration (SFDA) 131, 133, 136; State Pharmaceutical Administration (SPA) 131
Foot, Rosemary 32, 87
foreign direct investment; China 59, 108, 158, 164; *see also* overseas direct investment (ODI)
France 42–3, 59, 63, 67, 75, 80, *120*, *123*, 128, 154
Fravel, Taylor 44
free-riding 7, 20–1, 42, 57, 69, 93, 103, 123–4, 174, 176–7, 183
Friends of Nature 94, 99–100
Fudan University 28

Gao, Qiang 115
Georgia 89
Germany 42–3, 59, 63, 70, 119–*20*, *123*, 125-**6**
Gill, Bates 28
Gilpin, Robert 15
GlaxoSmithKline (GSK) 119
Global Alliance for Vaccines and Immunization (GAVI) 19
global economy; 59; China's integration 61, 70; decision-making and norm-setting 89; global economic order 61; new international economic order (NIEO)
global environmental governance 92–6; agenda setting 94; Asian Pacific Partnership 95; domestic impact on 104–8; Global Environment Facility (GEF) 94, 102; International Biofuels Forum 95; international environmental law 95; rule compliance 94–5; rule negotiation 94; *see also* environmental protection
global financial crisis 2007–9, 59, 63, 73, 176; *see also* financial stability
Global Fund to Fight AIDS, Tuberculosis and Malaria 114, 121–4
global governance 5–6, 8, 15, 174, 183–4; Western perspectives 8–12; China's participation *180–2*; Chinese perspectives 23–39; China's role 21; definition 9–11, 21–2, 25; history 10; the growth of 12–19; *see also* executive multilateralism; advanced executive multilateralism; governance
global health governance and China 114–17, 177; containing disease 115–17; controlling disease 117–21; curing disease 118–21; International Health Regulations (IHR) 115–17, 124, 134, 136;

International Sanitary Bureau 117; International Sanitary Regulations (ISR) 115; patent cooperation treaty applications *120*; 'public health emergencies of international concern' (PHEIC) 115
global order 4–5, 7–8, 174; *see also* international order; world order
global social justice 3
Globe-spanning networks 16–17
Global Village of Beijing 99
globalization 6, 8–9, 14, 28–9, 110–12, 175; two processes 12–13
good governance 34, 38, 89
governance 8–9, 15–16; effectiveness 12; from government to governance 12; governance without government 12, 15; retreat school of 14–15, 17; state-centric argument 14–15, 17 (*see also* China); state transformation view 14, 16–17
government 10, 12; *see also* governance
governmental policy networks; *see also* globe-spanning networks
Great Depression 20, 71, 75
Group of 24 63
Group of 77 106
Group of Eight (G8) 1, 64, 110, 121–3; *see also* Group of Twenty
Group of One 78
Group of Seven (G7) 36, 61, 69–70, 77, 160
Group of Twenty (G20) 1–2, 61, 67, 69–70, 73, 75, 77, 95, 110–11, 122–3, 154, 179; China and 121–4; *see also* Group of Eight
Group of Two (G2) 2
Guatemala 44, 46
guoji zhixu 國際秩序 (international order) 28
guojia gongtong zhili 國家共同治理 (state co-governance) 26

H5N1 *see* avian flu
Haiti 46
'harmonious world' (*hexie shijie*; 和諧世界) 33, 36–7
Hatoyama, Yukio 57
He, Yafei 92
health governance in China 111–12; 'barefoot' doctors 117; cooperative medical scheme (CMS) 114; institutional weaknesses 113–14; medical reform 113; Ministry of Health 111, 113, 115; public health system 111
Hegemony/hegemon 2, 6, 15, 20–1, 25, 32, 37, 46, 51, 105, 108, 165, 183; *see also* baquan

Index

hierarchical system 31
Hinsley, F.H. 17
Hong Kong 59, 68, 93, 114–16, **126**, 173
Howes, Stephen 99
Hu, Jintao 36, 54, 56–7, 64, 67, 77, 90, 104, 106, 149
Hui, Liangyu 133
Human Immunodeficiency Virus/Acquired Immune Deficiency Syndrome (HIV/AIDS) 112, 114–15, 118–19, 121–4, 159, 177; antiretrovirals (ARVs) 118–19
human rights 3–4, 7, 29–30, 35–7, 45, 62, 79–91, 93, 106, 112, 176, 179, *181*, 183; China's engagement with global regimes 85–9; China's participation in major instruments *82*; China's passive contribution 91; China's violation of 86; civil and political rights 79, 86, 89, 176; collective rights of peoples 79; double standard 83; economic, social and cultural rights 79, 89; evolution of 80–1; institutional developments at the UN 81–5; ratification of treaties 85; right to development 88–9; universalism 79
humanitarian crisis; 17, 29, 90–1; ethnic cleansing 85; genocide 85; crime against humanity 85, 88; war crimes 88
humanitarian intervention 7, 17, 29–30, 44, 79, 81, 85, 91, *181*, 183; China and 89–90, 179; *see also* responsibility to protect (R2P)
humanitarianism 29

Ikenberry, John 2
imperialism 117; *see also* anti-imperialism
India 1–2, 49–50, 69–70, 74, 77, 84, 95–6, 105–6, 119, 141–**2**, 143, 152, 156, 169–70, 172, 177, 179, *180*–*2*, 184
Indonesia 2, 31, 69, 84, 100, **126**, *147*, 155, 171–3
infectious diseases 93, 110, 114, 177
intellectual property rights 30
interdependence 12, 15, 80
international anarchy 12, 18, 109
International Atomic Energy Agency (IAEA) 47, 53; China's accession 48
International Bill of Human Rights 80
International Congress on AIDS in Asia and the Pacific 114
International Commission on Intervention and State Sovereignty (ICISS) 17, 29, 81, 90; *see also* responsibility to protect (R2P); *Responsibility to Protect, The (2001)*
International Convention for the Protection of All Persons from Enforced Disappearance (CPED) 81; China's participation *82*
International Convention on the Elimination of All Forms of Racial Discrimination (ICERD) 80–1; China's participation *82*
International Convention on the Protection of the Rights of All Migrant Workers and Members of their Families (ICRMW) 81; China's participation *82*
International Court of Justice (ICJ) 90
International Covenant on Civil and Political Rights (ICCPR) 80; China's participation *82*, 85
International Covenant on Economic, Social and Cultural Rights (ICESCR) 80; China's participation *82*
International Covenant on the Suppression and Punishment of the Crime of Apartheid (ICSPCA) 81; China's participation *82*
International Criminal Court (ICC); 88; Rome Statute 88
International Energy Agency (IEA) 141, 143, 145, 150, 152–4, 178
international institutions 4, 9, 14–15, 21; decision-making 32; *see also* international organizations
International Maritime Organization (IMO) 165
International Monetary Fund (IMF) 34–6, 61, 68–9, 77, 149, 160–1, 179; China and 64–7; reform of power structure 64; special drawing rights (SDR) 67, 76; statistics *72*, *76*; voting rights 64
international norms and rules 4–5, 11–12, 21, 30, 38–9, 58, 78, 90–2, 102; China's compliance with 33; *see also* soft law
International Olympics Committee (IOC) 107
international order 35, 39; *see also* global order; world order
international organizations; business organizations 4, 107; call for reform 3; civil society 4; intergovernmental organizations (IGOs) 11, *14*, 17, 19, 30, 38; *see also* international institutions; non-governmental organizations (NGOs) 11, *14*, 19, 26
International Petroleum Exchange (IPE) 145
international political economy 20
international regimes 4, 11–12

international relations; democratization of 6, 32–3, 39; moving towards global governance 12
international society 78, 81, 184
inter-state relations 16, 18
intervention 15, 17, 27–30, 36, 44, 46, 85, 90, 179; interventionism 29, 79; non-intervention 16–18, 29, 32–3, 35–8, 44, 81; *see also* humanitarian intervention
Iran 36, 49–51, 56, 89, 147, 155
Iraq; 85, 155; Iraq War 58
Israel 49, 87
Italy 42–3, 59, 70, *123*

Japan 1, 33, 42–3, 52–4, 63–4, 67, 69, 73, 77, 93–6, 105, *120–3*, **126**, 134, 137, 141, 148, 150, 153, 156, 169, 172–3, 175; Japanese yen 75
Jiang, Yaoping 75
Jiang, Zemin 54
Jin, Yongjian 42
Johnston, Alastair Iain 51

Kang, Sok-ju 57
Karns, Margaret 11
Kazakhstan 147, 156, 162
Kazatchkine, Michel 110, 122
Kennedy, Paul 40
Kent, Ann 3
Kenya 168–9
Keohane, Robert 11
Kim, Gye-gwan 57
Kim, Jong-il 52, 54–5, 57–8
Kim, Jong-nam 55
Kim, Samuel S. 41, 78, 123
Kindleberger, Charles 20
Kjær, Anne Mette 10
Koizumi, Junichiro 172
Korean Peninsula; denuclearization 53–5, 58; Korean War 43; *see also* North Korea; South Korea; Six-Party Talks
Kosovo 17, 30, 46, 81, 90
Krasner, Stephen 15
Kupchan, Charles 2
Kyoto Protocol 30, 95–6, 177
Kyrgyzstan 162

Lamy, Pascal 1
Laos 93
Latin America 34, 59, 87, 147
Latvia 152
Lebanon 88
Lee, Katie 85
Lee, Myung-bak 57, 122

Li, Changchun 54
Li, Keqiang 23, 125, 133
Liang, Congjie 101
liberal democracy 32, 36–7
Liberia 43
Libya 83
Like-minded Group (LMG) 86, 89
Lin, Justin Yifu 62
Lithuania 152
Liu, Dongguo 29
Liu, Jinyuan 27
Liu, Xiaobo 86, 106
Liu, Yunshan 56
low politics 10, 118
Lu, Xiaohong 37
Luxembourg 123, 177

Macao 55, 116, 164
Macedonia 44, 46
McGrew, Anthony 26
Malaysia 100, **126**, 156, 171–3
Mantega, Guido 75
Mao, Zedong 117, 175; Mao era 131
market failure 20
Mearsheimer, John 15
Mengniu 116
Mexico 46, 69, 96, 105, 144, 154
Middle East 2, 73, 147, 154, 156, 178
Mingst, Karen 11
Mol, Arthur 108
Moody's Investors Service 11
multilateralism 3, 5, 30, 37–8, 58, 78, 110, 172, 183
multinational corporations (MNCs) 11, 14, 19, 26
multipolar world 4
Myanmar 1, 87–8, 93

Namibia 123
Nanjing University 27
national sovereignty *see* sovereignty
nation-state *see* role of state
NATO bombing of Chinese embassy in Belgrade 30–1, 51
neo-realism 20
Netherlands *120*, 123, **126**
new security concept 24–5, 31
New Zealand 68, 75, 93, 116
Nigeria 36, 123, 149, 156
Nobel Peace Prize 86, 106; *see also* Liu, Xiaobo
non-aligned developing countries 48
non-aligned states (G21) 51
non-intervention; 17–18, 29, 32–3, 36, 38,

non-intervention *continued*
  44, 81; *see also* intervention; non-interference 47, 183
non-state actors 10–18, 27, 29–30, 37–8, 174
non-traditional security threats 11, 18
North Atlantic Treaty Organization (NATO) 17, 31, 46, 81, 169, 178; *see also* humanitarian intervention; NATO bombing of Chinese embassy in Belgrade
North Korea 40–1, 49–50, 52–8, 88, 106, 164–5, 175, 178, 183; Banco Delta Asia (BDA) 55; bilateral and multilateral talks 57; China's aid and economic cooperation 56; 'military-first' politics (*sŏngun chŏngch'i*) 55; missile test-fire 55; nuclear tests 55–6; nuclear weapon crisis 1, 52; withdrawal from NPT 52; *see also* Korean Peninsula; Six-Party Talks
Northeast Asia 41, 54, 58, 150, 175
Norway 107, 123, 144, 177
nuclear proliferation; 40, 47; China and 48; China Nuclear Energy Industry Corporation (CNEIC) 49; no first use 50–2; non-proliferation 47, 52, 58, 165, 175; 'nuclear domino' theory 54; Nuclear Suppliers Group (NSG) 47, 49; Proliferation Security Initiative (PSI) 50–2, 55–6; superpowers' monopoly 48; Treaty on the Non-Proliferation of Nuclear Weapons (NPT) 47–9, 53; uranium 49–50, 57; Zangger Committee 48–9
nuclear weapons 40–1, 47
Nye, Joseph 11

Obama, Barack 57, 78
Obasanjo, Olusegun 36
Oman 147
Organization for Economic Co-operation and Development (OECD) 145, 149, 152–3, 160
Organization of Arab Petroleum Exporting Countries 144
Organization of Petroleum Exporting Countries (OPEC) 142–5, 154
Our Global Neighbourhood (1995) 9
overseas direct investment (ODI); China 59, 61, 158; *see also* foreign direct investment

Pakistan 49–51, 68, 87
Palestine 87–8
Pan, Yue 102–3

Paulson, Henry 153
peace and security 2, 7, 13, 20, 40–58, 175, 179, *180*; common security 25; human security 18, 38; non-traditional 4, 7, 16, 110, 112; security dilemma 13, 19, 154, 157; traditional 4, 7, 29; *see also* new security concept
peacebuilding 85
peacekeeping 85; *see also* United Nations Peacekeeping Operations (UNPKO)
Peerenboom, Randall 35
Peking University 183
People's Bank of China (PBC) 67, 75, 104, 161
Philippines 100, 171, 173
Plato 10
post-Westphalian system 10
poverty 13, 129
Powell, Colin 53
PriceWaterhouseCoopers 68
Pritchard, Charles 52
private governance 11
public goods 7–11, 13, 21, 61, 90, 93, 105, 109, 114, 116, 124, 136, 174–9, 183; definitions 19–20; *see also* collective actions
public health 4, 7, 20, 110–24, 177, *181*; changing norms 112; rights 112
public-private partnerships 13, 101

quanqiu gongzhi 全球共治 (global co-governance) 26
quanqiu zhili 全球治理 (global governance) 24
quanqiu zhuyi 全球主義 (globalism) 25

Ramo, Joshua Cooper 34–5
Ramphal, Shridath 9
Ratner, Ely 35
Rato, Rodrigo 64
Reagan, Ronald 145
realpolitik 31–3, 38
regionalism 55
Renmin University of China 28–9, 55
renminbi (Chinese yuan) 59, 61, 64, 67, 73–5, *76*, 176
Republic of China *see* Taiwan
Research and Technical Health Institute 19
responsibility to protect (R2P) 18, 29–30, 38, 47, 79, 81, 90; *see also* humanitarian intervention; *Responsibility to Protect, The (2001)*
Responsibility to Protect, The (2001) 17, 81
revisionist power 32

Rittberger, Volker 18
Roosevelt, Eleanor 80
Rosenau, James 10, 12
Ruggie, John Gerard 10, 13
Russia 2, 31, 46, 49–50, 52, 54, 69–70, 72–3, 76, 85, 96, 98, *123*, **126**, 146–9, 151–2, 154–6, 162, 164, 169–70, 179; Sino-Russian energy pipeline 148, 155, *180–2*
Rwanda 17, 44, 81

Sandler, Todd 184
Sanlu Group 116
Sarkozy, Nicholas 92
Saudi Arabia 69, *72*, 145–7, 154
Scotland 121
Second World War 27
self-determination 35
self-help 109
Serbia 90
Severe acute respiratory syndrome (SARS) 28, 110–11, 113–15, 177
Sha, Zukang 1, 79, 115; see also United Nations Department of Economic and Social Affairs
Shanghai Cooperation Organization (SCO) 30
Shanghai Institute of International Studies 27
Shanghai International Studies University 28
Shi, Yinhong 55
shijie zhixu 世界秩序 (world order) 28
Sikkink, Kathryn 12
Singapore 139, 170–3
Six-Party Talks 41, 52–3, 55–6, 58, 175; Berlin talks 56–7; see also North Korea
social learning theory 31
'socialist modernization with Chinese characteristics' 34
soft law 11; see also international norms
soft power 35–7, 39
Somalia 17, 81, 85, 90, *167*–70, 173; Horn of Africa 168–70, 173, 178
Sorensen, Georg 17
South Africa 51, 69, 77, 85, 94–6, 100, 169
South China Sea 173
South Korea; 52–4, 57–8, 69–70, *72*–3, 75, 77, 93–5, *120*, 122, **126**, 150, 169, 172, 175; *Cheonan* 53; Yeonpyeong Island 53
Southeast Asia 17, 34, 147, 167–8, 170–3
Southern Rhodesia 85

sovereignty 13–14, 21, 29–30, 33–5, 37–8, 44, 46, 52, 79, 90, 108, 166, 179, 183; as responsibility 17, 28; view from Chinese scholars 28–31; equality 47, 80; sovereign state 12, 15–16, 27–8, 30–1, 37, 44, 48, 90, 139
Soviet Union 12, 34, 40, 47, 80, 144, 159, 174; Sino-Soviet rift 48
Spain 51, 123
spread of communicable diseases 13
Srebrenica 17, 81
Sri Lanka 51, 88, 172
state, role of 9, 12, 14, 16–18, 20; diminished role in global governance 27–8
state-building 44
status quo powers 7, 32
Strait of Malacca 152, 168, 170–1, 173
Strange, Susan 15
Strauss-Kahn, Dominique 67
Su, Changhe 28
Sub-Saharan Africa 43, 46, 147–9, 155
Sudan 1, 43, 46, 83–5, 90, *147*, 149–50, 155–6, 168, 179; see also Darfur
Sun, Hui 30
Sun, Kuanping 26
Sweden 51, 94, 119–*20*, 123
swine flu Influenza A(H1N1) 114, 116
Switzerland 51, *120*
Syria 51

Taiwan 27–8, 30, 41, 44, 46, 49–51, 54, 90, 116–17, 152, 162, 170
Tajikistan 162
Tang, Xianxing 28
taoguang yanghui 韜光養晦 (hiding one's capacities and biding one's time) 23
technological revolution 13
Teng, Shihua 26
territorial integrity 32, 36–7, 44, 90
terrorism 46, 150, 159, 162, 164–8, 171–2; terrorists groups 13
Thailand 89, 93, 121
Thakur, Ramesh 11
Thatcher, Margaret 145
Third World 3, 14, 18, 24, 34–6, 38, 70, 104–5, 111, *123*, 176; development 24, 34
Tiananmen killings 33, 86
Tibet 28, 30, 41, 87
trade and finance 2–4, 7, *180*
trade imbalance 13, 176
transgovernmetal relations 16
transnational organized crime (TOC) 4, 7, 13, 158–73, 178, *182*; importance of

270 Index

transnational organized crime *continued*
cooperation 157–60; international criminal law 158; money laundering 160–5, 178; piracy 165–73, 178, 183; UN definition 158
trans-sovereign problems 13, 21, 174, 183
Tsinghua University 28, 183
Tunisia 123
Turkey 69

Ukraine 89, 152
UNITAID 19
United Kingdom; 1, 20, 42–3, 59, 63, 80, 100, *120*, *123*, 144–5; Pound Sterling 67
United Nations (UN) 19, 28, 33, 58, 69, 79, 90, 94, 106, 112, 114, 123, 159, 169; regular budget *42*
United Nations Charter; 18, 44, 80–1; Chapter VII 47, 85
United Nations Children's Fund (UNICEF) 19
United Nations Commission on Human Rights (UNCHR) 79–81, 83–8, 91, 176; China as a member 85; country-specific resolutions (*guobie ti'an*) 86; Sub-Commission on Prevention of Discrimination and Protection of Minorities 81, 86–7; Special Procedures 84–8, 176, 181; *see also* UN Human Rights Council
United Nations Conference on Human Environment, Stockholm 94
United Nations Conference on the Environment and Development 95
United Nations Convention against Illicit Traffic in Narcotic Drugs and Psychotropic Substances (Vienna Convention) 159
United Nations Convention against Transnational Organized Crime (UNTOC) 158–9, 163
United Nations Convention on the Law of the Sea (UNCLOS) 165–6; exclusive economic zone (EEZ) 166, 171
United Nations Department of Economic and Social Affairs 1; *see also* Sha, Zukang
United Nations Development Programme (UNDP) 9, 107; China's Human Development Index 89; *Human Development Report (HDR)* 89
United Nations Economic and Social Council (ECOSOC) 19, 80, 83
United Nations Environment Programme (UNEP) 95

United Nations Food and Agriculture Organization (FAO) 134
United Nations Framework Convention on Climate Change (UNFCCC) 30, 105, 179
United Nations General Assembly 18, 46, 80–3, 87, 121, 158
United Nations Global Compact 13, 19
United Nations Human Rights Council (UNHRC); 79, 85–6, 89, 91, 176; China as a member 85; independent investigators 84; membership 83; universal periodic review (UPR) 83, 86–7
United Nations Millennium Development Goals (MDGs) 89, 111, 122; China and 121–4
United Nations Office of the High Commissioner for Human Rights (OHCHR) 83–4
United Nations Peacekeeping Operations (UNPKO) 41–2, 44, 58, 175, 179; Brahimi Report 45; China's participation 42–7; UN Special Committee on Peacekeeping Operations 44
United Nations Security Council 17, 29–31, 45, 47, 55–6, 79, 81, 85–6, 90, 109, 112, 163, 168, 175, 179; China's abstention 44; five permanent members 41; veto power 32, 46
United Nations Special Rapporteurs' annual reports 87–8
United Nations University 62, 78
United Nations World Summit (2005) 18, 81, 83
United States 1–2, 4–5, 20, 30–3, 37–8, 40, 42–4, 46–7, 50–4, 56, 59, 61, 64, 69–70, *72*, 74, 76–8, 80, 84–5, 87–9, 93–6, 105–6, 119–*20*, 123, **126**, 130, 132, 137, 141–*2*, 145–6, 150–2, 154–6, 160, 165, 169–78, 184; *see also* China; competition with the US; Consumer Product Safety Commission **137**; Department of State 163; economic stimulus package 74; Federal Reserve 73; Food and Drug Administration (FDA) 127–8, 137–8; hegemony 3, 6, 25, 39, 46; National Security Council 49; Sino-US relations 54; Sino-US trade relations 70–1; terrorist attack of 11 September 2001 73; Treasury 34, 55, 164; Treasury bonds 72, 74; US–China Strategic Economic Dialogue 128, 153; US dollar 61, 67, 71, 75, 143; White House 34; World Bank voting power 63; *Yinhe* Incident 51

Index 271

Universal Declaration of Human Rights (UDHR) 79–80
Uruguay 84

Väyrynen, Raimo 11
Venezuela 154
Vienna Declaration and Programme of Action 84
Vietnam 93, 173

Waltz, Kenneth 15
Wang, Canfa 101
Wang, Hai 132
Wang, Jisi 183
Wang, Jiarui 54, 56–7
Wang, Miao 28
Wang, Qishan 133
Wang, Yizhou 25, 27, 29
Washington Consensus 33–5, 37, 62
weapons of mass destruction (WMD); 40–1, 51; Australia Group (AG) 48–9; Biological and Toxin Weapons Convention (BTWC) 47, 49; Chemical Weapons Convention (CWC) 47–9; Comprehensive Nuclear-Test-Ban Treaty (CTBT) 47–8, 50; The Hague Code of Conduct against Ballistic Missile Proliferation (HCOC) 48; Missile Technology Control Regime (MTCR) 48–9; Wassenaar Arrangement 48–9; *see also* nuclear proliferation; Nuclear Suppliers Group (NSG)
Weiss, Thomas 11
Wen, Jiabao 56–7, 99
Wolfowitz, Paul 36
World Bank 19, 34–6, 61, 67–9, 76, 161, 179; China and 62–4, 97, 107; 'Equator Principles' 36; International Bank for Reconstruction and Development (IBRD) 63; International Development Association 62; voting power 63
World Commission on Dams 19
World Conference on Sustainable Development 94
World Food Programme 170
world government 11
World Health Organization (WHO) 1, 19, 28, 112–16, 118–19, 123–4, 128, 134, 136, 177, 179; 'One China' principle 117; World Health Assembly 117; *see also* Chan, Margaret; global health governance and China
World Intellectual Property Organization (WIPO) 119
World Ministerial Conference on Organized Transnational Crime, Naples 159
world order; in China's imperial era 31; and a rising China 174; just world order 31–2, 39; new world order 183; post-Cold War 44; Westphalian 31–3; *see also* global order; international order
World Organization for Animal Health 134
World Summit on Sustainable Development, Johannesburg 100
World Trade Organization (WTO) 19, 30, 119, 154; China and 67–9, 107, 125, 134; China's entry 28, 61, 77, 121, 126, 139, 176; Dispute Settlement Mechanism 67; Doha round negotiation 1, 68; law and regulations 68; new grouping of core members 1; tariffs 68–9; voting 67
Wu, Bangguo 54
Wu, Yi 114, 128, 133

Xi, Jinping 56, 75
Xinjiang 41
Xue, Zhenhua 98, 105

Yan, Fang 63
Yan, Xuetong 183
Yang, Jiemian 27
Yeltsin, Boris 148
Yemen 147
Yu, Keping 25–7, 37
Yu, Myung-hwan 56
Yu, Yongding 69, 74
Yu, Yu 30
Yu, Zhengliang 25
Yugoslavia 30–1, 43
yuan *see* renminbi

Zeng, Qinghong 154
Zhang, Xiang 28
Zhang, Yunling 30
Zhao, Lianhai 133
Zheng, Xiaoyu 132
Zhou, Xiaochuan 75–6
Zhou, Yongkang 154
Zhu, Min 67
Zimbabwe 83, 88
Zoellick, Robert 62, 141

Taylor & Francis
eBooks
FOR LIBRARIES

ORDER YOUR FREE 30 DAY INSTITUTIONAL TRIAL TODAY!

Over 23,000 eBook titles in the Humanities, Social Sciences, STM and Law from some of the world's leading imprints.

Choose from a range of subject packages or create your own!

Benefits for you
- Free MARC records
- COUNTER-compliant usage statistics
- Flexible purchase and pricing options

Benefits for your user
- Off-site, anytime access via Athens or referring URL
- Print or copy pages or chapters
- Full content search
- Bookmark, highlight and annotate text
- Access to thousands of pages of quality research at the click of a button

For more information, pricing enquiries or to order a free trial, contact your local online sales team.

UK and Rest of World: **online.sales@tandf.co.uk**
US, Canada and Latin America:
e-reference@taylorandfrancis.com

www.ebooksubscriptions.com

A flexible and dynamic resource for teaching, learning and research.